War, Trade and the State

War, Trade and the State

Anglo-Dutch Conflict
1652–89

Edited by David Ormrod
and Gijs Rommelse

THE BOYDELL PRESS

First published 2020
The Boydell Press, Woodbridge

ISBN 978 1 78327 324 9

The Boydell Press is an imprint of Boydell & Brewer Ltd
PO Box 9, Woodbridge, Suffolk IP12 3DF, UK
and of Boydell & Brewer Inc.
668 Mt Hope Avenue, Rochester, NY 14620–2731, USA
website: www.boydellandbrewer.com

A CIP catalogue record for this book is available
from the British Library

The publisher has no responsibility for the continued existence or accuracy of
URLs for external or third-party internet websites referred to in this book, and
does not guarantee that any content on such websites is, or will remain, accurate or
appropriate

Contents

Contents

Illustrations

Figures

Maps

Part Pages

Tables

The editors, contributors and publisher are grateful to all the institutions
and persons listed for permission to reproduce the materials in which they
hold copyright. Every effort has been made to trace the copyright holders;
apologies are offered for any omission, and the publisher will be pleased to
add any necessary acknowledgement in subsequent editions.

Contributors

Richard J. Blakemore is a Lecturer in the History of the Atlantic World at the University of Reading; before coming to Reading he studied at the universities of Aberystwyth and Cambridge, and held research posts at the universities of Exeter and Oxford. He has published articles dealing with navigational culture, Atlantic piracy, British trade to West Africa, and seafarers' income and economic agency. With Elaine Murphy, he is the author of *The British Civil Wars at Sea, 1638–1653* (Boydell Press, 2018), and he is currently finishing a monograph entitled *Empires below Deck: Two Seafarers and Their Worlds in the Seventeenth Century*.

Pepijn Brandon is Assistant Professor at the Vrije Universiteit, Amsterdam and Senior Researcher at the International Institute of Social History. He obtained his PhD at the University of Amsterdam in 2013. He is the author of *War, Capital, and the Dutch State (1588–1795)* (Brill, 2015; paperback Haymarket Books, 2017), and has co-edited special issues on war and economic development and on maritime labour in *Business History*, the *Financial History Review* and the *International Review of Social History*. He has held visiting fellowships at the Huntington Library, the University of Pittsburgh and Harvard University, and will be the 2020 Erasmus Lecturer on the History and Civilization of the Netherlands and Flanders at Harvard.

Ann Coats gained her Sussex DPhil in 2000 for *'The Economy of the Navy and Portsmouth: A Discourse between the Civilian Naval Administration of Portsmouth Dockyard and the Surrounding Communities, 1650 to 1800'*. She is Senior Lecturer at the University of Portsmouth. Publications include 'From "Floating Tombs" to Foundations. The Contribution of Convicts to Naval Dockyards and Ordnance Sites', *Age of Sail*, 2 (London, 2003); 'Bermuda Naval Base: Management, Artisans and Their Enslaved Workers, 1795–1797', *Mariner's Mirror*, 95(2) (2009), 149–78; *The Naval Mutinies of 1797: Unity and Perseverance* (Woodbridge, 2011, co-authored); and 'English Naval Administration under Charles I – Top-Down and Bottom-Up – Tracing Continuities', in R. Riley (ed.), *Pepys and Chips (Transactions of the Naval Dockyards Society*, Portsmouth, 2012).

Remmelt Daalder studied history at the University of Amsterdam. He worked as a curator at the Historisch Museum Rotterdam from 1977 to 1990. Before retirement in 2014 he was Senior Curator of paintings, drawings and prints at the Netherlands Maritime Museum in Amsterdam. His books and articles cover areas such as Dutch history, industrial archaeology and maritime art, including a study of drawings made by sailors and travelling artists (*Tekenen op Zee*, 2000). Daalder's PhD thesis, *Van de Velde & Son: Marine Painters, 1640–1707*, was published in 2016 (Primavera Press, two editions, English and Dutch). He will contribute chapters on early modern naval history and the cultural impact of the maritime sector to the *Nieuwe Maritieme Geschiedenis van Nederland*, 4 vols, to be published in 2019 and subsequent years.

Roger Downing, following a career in industrial research, is active as an independent researcher specialising in the area of Anglo-Dutch relations and the rivalry between the two countries during the period of their seventeenth-century sea wars. Collaboration with Gijs Rommelse on aspects of the latter has resulted in a monograph entitled *A Fearful Gentleman. Sir George Downing in The Hague* (Verloren, 2011), as well as a series of articles dealing with the treatment in England of Dutch prisoners of war taken in the three conflicts, and their repatriation.

Elizabeth Edwards completed her PhD at University College London and is an Honorary Senior Research Fellow at the University of Kent, where she taught early modern European history and Kentish regional history. Since retirement she has been involved in an eclectic mix of projects in European and Kentish history, and is currently co-editing and contributing to works on migration and maritime Kent. However, her primary research interest remains the internal politics, international relations, and cultural history of the Dutch Republic in the later seventeenth century. In addition to writing on the Amsterdam ruling class, including most recently, 'Amsterdam and the Ambassadors of Louis XIV 1674–85', in T. Claydon and C.-E. Levillain (eds), *Louis XIV outside in* (2015), she has written several articles on the politics and career of the grand pensionary, Gaspar Fagel (1672–88).

John B. Hattendorf is special advisor at the U.S. Naval War College's John B. Hattendorf Center for Maritime Historical Research and Ernest J. King Professor Emeritus of Maritime History. From 1986 to 2003 he was Chairman of the Naval War College's Advanced Research Department, Chairman of the Maritime History Department, and from 2003 to 2016 Director of the Naval War College Museum. As a naval officer from 1964 to 1973, he saw combat action while serving in destroyers during the Vietnam War. He holds an Oxford DPhil (1979) and an Oxford DLitt (2016). His numerous awards include the Anderson Medal for Lifetime Achievement (Society of Nautical Research), the U.S. Navy's Distinguished Civilian Service Medal and Superior Civilian Service Medal, the American Library Association's Dartmouth Medal, and the Caird Medal of the National Maritime Museum, Greenwich. He is the author, co-author, editor, or co-editor of more than fifty books; his most recent is *Charles XII: Warrior-King* (2018).

Martine van Ittersum is Senior Lecturer in History at the University of Dundee. She is the author of *Profit and Principle: Hugo Grotius, Natural Rights Theories and the Rise of Dutch Power in the East Indies, 1595–1615* (Brill, 2006). She has published widely on the history of international law and on the theory and practice of Western imperialism and colonialism in the early modern period. Her most recent publications include 'Empire by Treaty? The Role of Written Documents in European Overseas Expansion, 1500–1800', in A. Clulow and T. Mostert (eds), *The Dutch and English East India Companies: Diplomacy, Trade and Violence in Early Modern Asia* (Amsterdam University Press, 2018); 'Global Constitutionalism in the Early Modern Period: The Role of Empires, Treaties and Natural Law', in *Handbook on Global Constitutionalism* (Edward Elgar Publishing, 2017); and 'Hugo Grotius (1583–1645): The Making of a Founding Father of International Law', in *Handbook of the Theory of International Law* (Oxford University Press, 2016).

Jaap Jacobs (PhD Leiden, 1999) is affiliated with the University of St Andrews. His research focuses on Dutch and early American history, specifically the Dutch in the Americas. He has taught at the universities of Leiden, Amsterdam, Cornell, Pennsylvania, Harvard, and St Andrews. His publications include *The Colony of New Netherland: A Dutch Settlement in Seventeenth-Century America* (Cornell University Press, 2009); *The Worlds of the Seventeenth-Century Hudson Valley* (co-edited with L.H. Roper) (SUNY Press, 2014); 'Sweet Resoundings: Friendship Poetry by Petrus Stuyvesant and Johan Farret on Curaçao, 1639–45' (with Joanne van der Woude), *William and Mary Quarterly*, 3rd ser., no. 3, July 2018; and '"Act with the Cunning of a Fox": The Political Dimensions of the Struggle for Hegemony over New Netherland, 1647–1653', *Journal of Early American History*, 8 (2018). He is currently working on a biography of Petrus Stuyvesant.

Alan Lemmers directed the catalogue project of the Dutch Navy Model Collection (1700–1885) at the Rijksmuseum in Amsterdam from 1985 to 1995. In 1996 he obtained his PhD at Leiden University with a thesis on the same collection. He subsequently joined the historical research department of the Royal Netherlands Navy, which in 2005 merged with the Netherlands Institute of Military History of the Dutch Ministry of Defence in The Hague. In books, articles, exhibitions and documentaries Lemmers has covered a wide variety of topics, such as eighteenth-century and post-1945 naval architecture, naval technology and naval bases, hydrography, the Dutch Submarine Service, the Dutch Marine Corps, piracy in the East Indies, the American Revolution and Dutch-Japanese relations.

Erik Odegard studied at Leiden University where he defended his dissertation in January 2018. This focused on the career-paths of Dutch colonial governors in the seventeenth century. He was awarded the first research fellowship of the Dutch National Archives on a project on the VOC archives. He is currently a Lecturer at Erasmus University, Rotterdam, and a researcher at the Mauritshuis museum in The Hague. In 2018, he was awarded the Dr. Ernst Crone fellowship at the National Maritime Museum of the Netherlands, Amsterdam, on a project focused on the preparation of the first Dutch voyage to Asia in 1595–97. His research focuses on Dutch maritime and colonial history, with articles on such topics as the VOC shipyard in Cochin, the use of VOC warships during the Second Anglo-Dutch War, bankruptcy, and the principal-agent problem in colonial governance.

David Ormrod was educated at the London School of Economics and Christ's College, Cambridge, and is Professor Emeritus of Economic & Cultural History at the University of Kent, and a Fellow of the Academy of Social Sciences. He is the author of *The Rise of Commercial Empires: England and the Netherlands in the Age of Mercantilism, 1650–1770* (Cambridge University Press, 2003), and numerous other publications in the fields of commercial and agrarian history. He has also written on the history of art markets, including *Art Markets in Europe, 1400–1800* (Ashgate, 1998, co-edited with Michael North), and has worked with museum curators and art historians whilst guest curator at the Museum of London and Visiting Fellow at the Institute of Historical Research, University of London.

Gijs Rommelse is an Honorary Visiting Fellow at the University of Leicester. His thesis research at Leiden University resulted in the publication of *The Second Anglo-Dutch War (1665–1667). International Raison d'État, Mercantilism and Maritime Strife* (Verloren, 2006). Subsequent books include *A Fearful Gentleman. Sir George Downing in The Hague* (co-authored with Roger Downing, Verloren, 2011) and *The Dutch in the Early Modern World. A History of a Global Power* (Cambridge University Press, 2019). He is co-editor of *Ideology and Foreign Policy in Early Modern Europe (1650–1750)* (Ashgate, 2011) and *Ideologies of Western Naval Power, c. 1500–1815* (Routledge, 2019).

Paul Seaward is British Academy/Wolfson Research Professor at the History of Parliament, having been its director from 2001 to 2017. Previously he was a clerk in the House of Commons. His publications include *The Cavalier Parliament and the Reconstruction of the Old Regime, 1661–1667* (Cambridge, 1989), an edition of *Behemoth* for the Clarendon edition of the works of Thomas Hobbes (2009), and a selection from the *History of the Rebellion and the Life of Edward Hyde, Earl of Clarendon*, for Oxford World's Classics (2010). He is, with Martin Dzelzainis, joint general editor of an Oxford edition of the works of Clarendon. He is currently working on a history of Parliament as an institution and will one day get back to a biography of Clarendon.

Nuala Zahedieh was educated at the London School of Economics and is currently Professor of Economic and Social History at the University of Edinburgh where she has taught since 1990. Her research focuses on the British Atlantic economy in the period of slavery and she is currently working on the history of early English Jamaica. Publications include *The Capital and Colonies. London and the Atlantic Economy, 1660–1700* (Cambridge, 2010), and contributions to *The Cambridge Economic History of Modern Britain, I, 1700–1870*, ed. R. Floud, J. Humphries and P. Johnson (Cambridge, 2014), and *The Oxford History of the British Empire, I, The Origins of Empire. British Overseas Enterprise to the Close of the Seventeenth Century*, ed. N. Canny (Oxford, 1998).

Preface

The essays which follow sprang from two conferences, Dutch and British, arranged to commemorate the 350th anniversary of the Dutch raid on the Medway of June 1667. The first was arranged jointly in Amsterdam by the Dutch historical association, *De Vrienden van De Witt*, and the British Naval Dockyards Society. The second conference, one week later, took place at the Historic Dockyard, Chatham, arranged by the University of Kent at Medway.

The 1667 raid is conventionally seen in Dutch historiography as a great victory marking the high water mark of Dutch naval power.[1] For many, the exploits of the De Witt brothers and Admiral De Ruyter compare with those of Nelson at Trafalgar, as Remmelt Daalder explains below. In Britain, on the other hand, the episode is remembered, if at all, as an embarrassment for Charles II and his circle rather than a moment of national humiliation. Nevertheless, the initiative for commemoration sprang as much from the British as the Dutch, through a shared passion for naval and maritime history. For the former, it is fair to say that enthusiasm for local history and heritage compensated for the lack of any sense of national pride, or indeed shame. As they gazed across the Medway towards Upnor Castle, participants attending the Chatham conference were acutely conscious of the benefits of doing 'history where it happened'. The position of the dockyard defences, the narrowness of the fairway, and the long winding course of the river beyond added new dimensions of understanding: the enterprise was indeed *een tocht*, a hazardous amphibious expedition rather than *een strijd* or a conventional battle.[2]

Leaving aside differences embedded in language and popular preconceptions, one of our challenges was to select and reshape a series of varied conference contributions within a wider perspective, that of Anglo-Dutch conflict running from the outbreak of war in 1652 to its resolution in 1689. Our starting point, set out by Gijs Rommelse and Roger Downing, is to emphasise the European context as distinct from the traditional bilateral treatment of the three Anglo-Dutch Wars. Our aim has been to produce not

---

[1] See, for example, www.facebook.com/pg/vriendenvandewitt/community/?ref= page_internal, 25 April 2017, 'De grootste Nederlandse maritieme overwinning ooit'.

[2] Medway Council's commemorative programme contains a Dutch-language summary alongside the English text which highlights the problem. The English, then and now, speak of an attack or a raid. The Dutch on the other hand use the words *slag* or *strijd*, viz. a battle, although their forebears preferred the more accurate term *tocht* – an expedition – which was also used to describe William's invasion of 1688, the culmination of three decades of Anglo-Dutch conflict.

another survey of the course of these wars but rather to explore the broader dimensions of conflict, of which war and armed struggle were only one, albeit the most significant, aspect. This, we felt, would avoid the familiar and somewhat reductionist debate about the character of the wars as primarily economic, ideological, or political in origin. Paul Seaward's essay provides a critical review of this historiography. By focusing on the *interconnections* between war, trade and nature of the state, we accept that all these aspects were present in different degrees and at different times, and aim to assemble a group of selected essays which range beyond the factors underlying the outbreak of war.

From this standpoint, elaborated in the Introduction, we can recognise that the entire period from 1652 to 1674 was one of low-intensity conflict between the Dutch Republic and England, punctuated by warfare. The former included state-sponsored privateering and raiding, aggressive diplomacy, pamphlet-eering, protectionist legislation, navigation laws, and claims-making over forts and disputed areas of settlement in the Americas and Asia. As Martine van Ittersum and Jaap Jacobs explain, Dutch and English overseas expansion was accompanied by a seemingly never-ending quest for legitimacy, involving the creation of long paper trails. Diplomatic correspondence and treaties between Europeans and with indigenous peoples may be read as plausible alternatives to conquest and war.

Interspersed with these confrontations were outbreaks of naval warfare conducted by heavily-armed standing navies in place of armed merchant vessels. John Hattendorf considers the strategic and tactical aspects of this critical change. As Richard Blakemore and Pepijn Brandon go on to argue, it amounted to nothing less than a 'naval revolution' spanning the 1650s and 1660s, following the Commonwealth's programme for massive naval expansion.[3] Its significance for state formation can hardly be over-estimated. Improved protection for seaborne trade in home and distant waters accel-erated the drive to imperial expansion, which in turn led to greater interstate rivalry. Above all, this new high-tech, capital-intensive, type of warfare required sustained investment by the state with appropriate fiscal provision. Historians are increasingly describing the maritime powers as 'fiscal-naval states', involving a series of revisions to the original formulation of the British fiscal-military state by John Brewer in 1988.[4]

---

[3] See also X. Duran and P. O'Brien, 'Total factor productivity for the Royal Navy from victory at Texel (1653) to triumph at Trafalgar (1805)', in *Shipping and economic growth, 1350–1850*, ed. R. Unger (Leiden, 2011), pp. 279–311; P. Brandon, *War, capital and the Dutch state (1588–1795)* (Leiden, 2015).

[4] A. Graham and P. Walsh (eds), *The British fiscal-military states, 1660–c.1783* (London and New York, 2016); J. Hoppit, *Britain's political economies, 1660–1800* (Cambridge, 2017); M. 't Hart, *The Dutch wars of independence, 1570–1680* (New York, 2014); Brandon, *War, capital and the Dutch state*.

In both countries, the main challenges of the naval revolution were administrative and fiscal, and both resorted to a combination of private contractors operating alongside state initiative. At mid-century, as Ann Coats and Alan Lemmers point out, 'Dutch financial and political institutions were better placed than the English to support their navies, dockyards and defence'. The advantages of representative federal government for revenue raising in the Netherlands contrast markedly with political discontinuity and financial disorder in England from 1649 to 1689, and it was precisely the failures of the Second Anglo-Dutch War which stimulated essential administrative and fiscal reform in England, well before the 'Glorious Revolution'.[5] For the Dutch however, facing the growing threat of French expansionism, the need to protect the Republic's land frontiers was added to the costs of naval rearmament which called for renewed reliance on princely military power and prestige. Elizabeth Edwards considers the realignment of Dutch politics in this light. Expectations about the future role of the Prince of Orange gave rise to political division between and within the two countries, and were in some degree a cause of the Second Anglo-Dutch War. Yet at the same time, of course, the Orangist movement provided a resolution to four decades of Anglo-Dutch conflict.

Although the naval revolution raised the costs of securing maritime supremacy, these were reduced by the outsourcing of armed confrontation in Asia and the Atlantic to the companies, privateers and colonial militias, but at the expense of effective metropolitan control. Nuala Zahedieh shows how the Second Anglo-Dutch War in particular highlighted England's problems in organising military action across the Atlantic, and the unsatisfactory results of reliance on local resources. Settlement rather than conquest came to form the basis of imperial ambitions. Neither state sent naval warships to Asia, and as Erik Odegard reminds us, the VOC directors famously followed the directive laid down by the Governor-General of the East Indies in 1614 that 'trade in Asia should be conducted and maintained under the protection and with the aid of your own weapons ... wielded with the profits gained from trade'. Low-intensity conflict remained the norm in Asia, where both companies preferred solutions that would not interfere with the course of trade. And so written reports of confrontations in Asia and the Americas often ended up in London and Amsterdam, and contributed to discussions about the validity of claims-making overseas and the business of concluding peace treaties.

The 'colonial prelude' to the approach of the Second Anglo-Dutch War in Africa and the West Indies is well known to historians, and revisionist perspectives on the value of Dutch transatlantic trade have progressed during the past two decades, along with recognition of trans-imperial mercantile and

---

[5] P. O'Brien, 'The formation of states and transitions to modern economies: England, Europe and Asia compared', in *The Cambridge History of Capitalism*, eds L. Neal and J.G. Williamson (2 vols, Cambridge, 2014), I, p. 366.

cultural connections. Unfortunately, the Asian dimension of the three wars has been seriously neglected. One of the aims of these essays is to arrive at a better balance between the course of events in the North Sea/Baltic area and the Atlantic World and Asia during the period 1652–74. The subdivisions of the book reflect this aim, in its second and third sections. The last section on public history arises from the commemorative origins of the two conferences referred to earlier.

In the final section of the book, we emphasise how 'public history' and memory studies have risen to prominence during the past twenty years or so. The volume aims to address this in David Ormrod's review of earlier Anglo-Dutch commemorations as well as the Medway raid itself, starting with events designed to celebrate Anglo-Dutch friendship at the time when Britain joined the EEC (1973) and concluding with British doubts about the benefits of federalism in the year of Brexit.

Acknowledgements

This book springs from two historical conferences, held in Amsterdam and Medway in the summer of 2017, both at the occasion of the 350th anniversary of the 1667 Raid on the Medway, or the *Tocht naar Chatham*, as it is known in Dutch. The conference in Amsterdam was organised by the *Nederlandse Vereniging Vrienden van De Witt* and the Naval Dockyards Society, together with the Royal Netherlands Navy which provided a wonderful conference setting at the *Marine Etablissement Amsterdam*, and *Het Scheepvaartmuseum*, while generous support was provided by the Dr. Ernst Crone Fellowship, the *Samenwerkende Maritieme Fondsen*, and the Society of Nautical Research. Jolien Bogaards, Ann Coats, Jan van Dam, Christian Melsen and Jan Spoelstra were pivotal in the organisation. The conference at Medway was organised by the University of Kent at Medway with generous support from the Historic Dockyard, Chatham, the Royal Historical Society, the Kent Archaeological Society, and the Humanities Faculty of the University of Kent. Professor Nick Grief, Elizabeth Edwards and Richard Holdsworth worked hard to ensure its success; and Richard's reflections on the 2017 commemorative events were invaluable in helping to shape Chapter 13.

The publication of this book was facilitated with the generous sponsorship of the *Vrienden van De Witt* and the Wardens of the Rochester Bridge Trust, for which we are very grateful. Finally, we would like to thank Peter Sowden, at Boydell Press, for guiding this book project to fruition.

I

Introduction

This etching of the Dutch ship of state was made on the occasion of the Peace of Breda of 1667. The artists responsible were François Schillemans and Jan Zoet. Source: Rijksmuseum (Amsterdam), RP-P-OB-78.632.

1

Introduction: Anglo-Dutch conflict in the North Sea and beyond

David Ormrod and Gijs Rommelse

It was about fifty years ago [the 1920s] that the social sciences made the discovery that human life was subject to fluctuations and swings of periodic movements, which carry on in endless succession. Such movements, harmonious or discordant, bring to mind the vibrating chords or sounding-boards of schoolday physics. G.H. Bousquet, for instance wrote in 1923: 'The different aspects of social movement [have] an undulating rhythmic profile, not one that is invariable ... but one marked by periods when intensity increases or diminishes.' [And] the combination of movements ... forms the *conjuncture* or rather the *conjunctures*. For there may be different conjunctural rhythms affecting the economy, political life, demography and indeed collective attitudes ...

(F. Braudel, *Civilization and capitalism, 15th–18th century*, vol. III, *The perspective of the world*, 1979 (English translation 1984), p. 71)

When we planned the two conferences on which this book is based, we expected that the United Kingdom would remain in the European Union, with some adjustments. Historians, it turns out, are no better than economists in anticipating the likely course of events.[1] Whatever the final outcome, the 'leave' result produced by the referendum, it now appears, forms part of a wider series of symptoms of a deep malaise afflicting European societies, including the resurgence of nationalism, xenophobia and rejection of multiculturalism, alongside growing demands for protectionism in some quarters. Growing disparities of wealth and income since the 1980s, widespread

---

[1] The Conservative MP Kenneth Clarke commented (11 January 2018), 'We are in the middle of historic events on Europe and absolutely nobody knows what their precise nature is or where we are going. All the political normalities of this country have collapsed in the past two or three years.' Politics Home, https://www.politicshome.com/news/uk/political-parties/conservative-party/house/house-magazine/91960/ken-clarke-i-am-very-glad-i. For a balanced summary of economic and cultural explanations of the Brexit vote, Anglo-centric versus international, and rational versus irrational explanations, see K. O'Rourke, *A short history of Brexit. From Brentry to Backstop* (London, 2019).

corporate tax evasion and the imposition of austerity programmes following in the wake of the financial crisis of 2008 have helped trigger these discontents. The root causes of that crisis, in turn, can be seen to lie in the deregulation of financial markets across the western world which began in 1971, when the United States of America withdrew dollar convertibility and effectively ended the Bretton Woods system.[2] Most commentators agree that globalisation has been seriously mismanaged over the past forty years, but disagreement reigns amongst those promoting policy prescriptions for its reform, as well as those who envisage a new post-capitalist world rising from the ashes of financial catastrophe. Some, indeed, have argued that we are moving into an era of 'disorganised capitalism', a form of systemic chaos, where regulation by national governments is no longer possible.[3]

Capitalism, globalisation and 'Atlanticisation'

Economists and policy makers are apt to forget that our globalised capitalist world has emerged not over the past fifty years, or even the past two centuries, but over at least five centuries. For the first three hundred years or so, Europe developed a form of merchant capitalism, originating in the city states of the Mediterranean, before moving northwards to the Low Countries and England.[4] Here, following a long war of independence from Spain (1568–1648) and a brief civil war and republican experiment in England ending in

[2] T. Piketty, *Capital in the twenty-first century* (Cambridge, Mass., 2014), introduction and chapters 9 and 10; J.E. Stiglitz, *The price of inequality. How today's divided society endangers our future* (New York, 2012), pp. ix–xxxv and 275–6; Y. Cassis, 'The rise of global finance, 1850–2000', in *Global economic history*, eds T. Roy and G. Riello (London, 2019), pp. 240–4.

[3] J. Frieden and R. Rogowski, 'Modern capitalism: enthusiasts, opponents, and reformers', in *The Cambridge History of Capitalism*, vol. II, *The spread of capitalism from 1848 to the present*, eds L. Neal and J.G. Williamson (Cambridge, 2014), pp. 422–3; G. Arrighi, *The long twentieth century. Money, power and the origin of our times* (London and New York, 1994), pp. 2–3.

[4] Since the financial crisis of 2008, a 'new' history of capitalism has emerged in the United States which tends to identify the concept with the emergence of market structures and the existence of secure private property rights. The recent *Cambridge History of Capitalism* follows this pattern which *inter alia* enables contributors to interrogate the possible 'capitalist' character of Babylonia or the ancient world (see above, vol. I, L. Neal, 'Introduction', pp. 2–7). For a useful critique, see J. Levy, 'Capital as process and the history of capitalism', *Business History Review*, 91 (2017), 483–510. The present essay takes a relatively orthodox approach which recognises the centrality of capital to capitalism, involving processes in which 'agents and institutions are … doing the ongoing work of capitalizing different legal forms of wealth and property'; seen in this light, investment in commerce – the accumulation of merchant capital – provides an authentic indicator of historical origins (Levy, 'Capital as process', pp. 487–9). See also D. Ormrod, 'Agrarian capitalism and

1660, these two maritime nations built up formidable commercial empires which linked newly-established American colonial markets with those of Eurasia. *Raison d'état*, mercantilist strategies, naval warfare and protection of trade supported an aggressive, outward-facing North Sea economy, which Charles Wilson described as forming, after 1689, a 'Protestant Capitalist International'.[5] British mercantilist strategies were intensified during the long eighteenth century wars against France, and remained in place until the free trade movement of the 1840s prepared the ground for a relatively brief period of 'hard', but incomplete and very uneven globalisation from 1870 to 1900. The protectionist backlash of the interwar years, it seems, was not an exogenous shock induced by the Great War, but arose from the inherently unequal distributional effects of globalisation.[6]

It would be a mistake, then, to view globalisation as a recent historical development, dependent primarily on the possibilities for trade liberalisation and increasing market integration. Rather than tracing a linear path through time, globalisation has followed cyclical patterns, long waves comprising a variety of movements including trade flows, capital movements, migration, information exchange, and cultural interaction. It was Fernand Braudel who, in his magisterial volumes on *Civilization and Capitalism*, explained the dimensions of time and space in terms of the 'rhythms of the conjuncture'. Formed from innumerable events and crises, the conjuncture followed a slowly undulating trend, the *tendance seculaire*, marked by alternating periods of expansion (phase A) and contraction (phase B). Since the 1520s, they have ranged from 80 to 150 years in length (Figure 1.1 below).[7] Giovanni Arrighi extended Braudel's analysis by distinguishing four long cycles of capitalist accumulation which overlap these rhythms. From the Italian city states of the late medieval period, principally Genoa, leadership passed to the newly independent Dutch Republic during a 'long' seventeenth century, then to Britain, before passing to the USA after 1945.[8] During the course of each

---

merchant capitalism. Tawney, Dobb, Brenner and beyond', in *Landlords and tenants in Britain, 1440–1660*, ed. J. Whittle (Woodbridge, 2013), pp. 200–15.

[5] In his paper on 'The Anglo-Dutch establishment in 18th-century England', given to an Anglo-Netherlands symposium in July 1974 (published in *The Anglo-Dutch contribution to the civilization of early modern society*, ed. A.G. Dickens (London, 1976), pp. 11–32.

[6] K. O'Rourke and J. Williamson, *Globalization and history. The evolution of a nineteenth-century Atlantic economy* (Cambridge, Mass., 1999), pp. 286–7.

[7] The length of a cycle as described by economists and social scientists can vary, unlike the frequency of a transverse wave in the physical sciences. J.S. Goldstein, *Long cycles. Prosperity and war in the modern age* (New Haven, 1988), p. 6; see also Braudel, *Civilization and capitalism, 15th–18th century*, vol. III, pp. 71–8.

[8] In the final volume of his trilogy, Arrighi predicted an 'eventual equalization of power between the conquering west and the conquered non-west' – a closure, perhaps, of the Great Divergence, led by China. *Adam Smith in Beijing. Lineages of the twenty-first century* (London, 2007), p. 2 and epilogue.

cycle, Arrighi saw the expansion of capital giving way to a closing phase of financial expansion (f), which in turn provided part of the capital needs of the emerging successor.

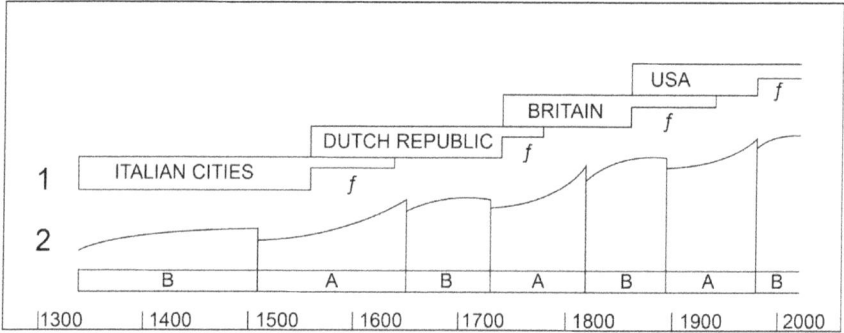

Figure 1.1 The rhythms of the conjuncture: Arrighi's four systemic cycles of accumulation (1), 'Genoese' or Italian, Dutch, British and USA, and the A/B phases of the Braudellian secular trend, (2). In Arrighi's model, periods of financialisation are represented by a narrow band (f); in the Braudellian scheme, following Goldstein, phase-B movements are indicated by declining rate of growth tending towards stagnation, while phase-A movements are shown as characterised by increasing growth rates.

The 'Anglo-Dutch moment' from 1652 to 1689 came at the end of two great political struggles, the Dutch wars of independence and the English revolution, and in several respects involved the resolution of long-standing contradictions between princely power and the desire for representative, efficient and stable government. Although the truce with Spain from 1609 to 1621 and the peace policy of James I reduced impediments to trade for both countries, civil war almost broke out in the Netherlands in 1617–18. It was during these years too that Anglo-Dutch trade disputes intensified, chiefly over the composition of England's premier export trade, woollen textiles, driven principally to the Low Countries. When the truce expired in 1621, Spanish trade embargoes and raiding ushered in a period of stagnation for Dutch trade, especially in the Baltic grain trade – the 'mother of all trades' – which fell to disastrous levels from 1622 to 1630.[9] Revival of Dutch trade in general came only after the peace of 1648. England also experienced economic crisis during the early 1620s, when overseas cloth markets were disrupted by the Thirty Years' War, and commercial crises coincided with harvest failure. But throughout the 1630s, English merchants took

---

[9] A.E. Christensen, *Dutch trade to the Baltic about 1600* (Copenhagen and The Hague, 1941), appendix C, diagram XIV.

advantage of their neutral status and the disruption of Dutch trade in the Mediterranean, and by the end of that decade they had achieved undisputed mastery of these trades.[10] The position was substantially reversed during the British civil wars of the 1640s when the Dutch were able to consolidate their political gains and from 1649 to 1651 to recapture Baltic and Mediterranean markets previously lost to the English.[11] Holland above all wanted a permanent peace, and seized the opportunity for regime change offered by the death of William II in 1650. A year later, the future of republicanism in England and Scotland seemed equally secure after Cromwell's victory at Worcester.

Many historians have regarded these events as forming part of a larger European 'general crisis', a conjunctural movement, which Eric Hobsbawm initially saw as the last phase of the transition from feudalism to capitalism. After much debate, a majority of participants persuaded themselves that the phenomenon represented a crisis in relations between society and the state – a crisis of absolutism – rather than a removal of obstacles to capitalist growth. In fact no real consensus was achieved, and economic perspectives were brought back into the equation through a separate but related debate about the *agrarian* origins of capitalist development led by Robert Brenner. Again, this proved inconclusive, but refocused attention on lord–peasant relations in shaping different paths to agrarian development in Europe. Unfortunately, Brenner employed an either/or logic which left little room for commercialisation, overseas trade, and market-induced growth; and with the exception of Niels Steensgaard, his critics failed to suggest or develop a more complete agenda.[12]

More recently, the rise of global history has provided a new and expanded context for these earlier insights: one which helps to explain why the Netherlands, and to a lesser extent England, were hardly affected by the downswing, the B-phase, of the world economy.[13] In an exhaustive analysis of the rebellions and disorders which spread across seventeenth-century Eurasia, including Ming China, Japan and Mughal India, Geoffrey Parker argues convincingly that climate change and extreme weather conditions acted as the prime-mover. The little ice age caused multiple harvest failures

---

[10] J.I. Israel, *Dutch primacy in world trade, 1585–1740* (Oxford, 1989), pp. 149–56; *idem, The Dutch Republic. Its rise, greatness and fall* (Oxford, 1995), p. 713.

[11] D. Ormrod, *The rise of commercial empires. England and the Netherlands in the age of mercantilism, 1650–1770* (Cambridge, 2003), p. 34.

[12] Brenner went on to provide an authoritative account in his *Merchants and revolution. Commercial change, political conflict and London's overseas traders, 1550–1653* (Cambridge, 1993). N. Steensgaard, 'The seventeenth-century crisis', in *The general crisis of the seventeenth century*, eds G. Parker and L.M. Smith (London and New York, 1978), pp. 32–56.

[13] S. Ogilvie, 'Germany and the seventeenth century general crisis', in *General crisis*, eds Parker and Smith, p. 59

and food shortage, producing 'episodes of distress' and demographic collapse, and also intensified popular resistance amongst those left with no means of support.[14] Critics have called for greater clarity in distinguishing between the cumulative effects of climate change and the short-term effects of climate variability, and emphasise that random outbreaks of disease, especially smallpox, contributed to different demographic outcomes across the globe.[15]

Nevertheless, one thing is abundantly clear: that England and the Netherlands remained largely immune from the worst of these catastrophes, with relatively well-fed populations and well-organised systems of food distribution which greatly enhanced resistance to disease and the chances of recovery.[16] Regular grain imports from the Baltic fed the cities and permitted the early development of dairy farming in the Republic, which, together with a flourishing fishing industry, contributed to a high-protein diet.[17] In England, it is generally agreed that the years from 1570 to 1640 saw a great leap forward in commercial farming and regional speciali-sation, as the 'partial elimination' of the smaller peasantry proceeded.[18] The economic structure of both countries was strikingly different in 1500: England was self-sufficient in food production and an exporter of primary products, while the Low Countries were dominated by export industries and food imports.[19] From the 1670s to 1750, however, Britain became a major grain-exporting country under the stimulus of export bounties. Her overseas shipments came to exceed the volume of Baltic surpluses from

---

[14] G. Parker, *Global crisis. War, climate change and catastrophe in the seventeenth century* (New Haven and London, 2013), chapter 17; Parker and Smith (eds), *General crisis*, pp. 4–6.

[15] J. de Vries, 'The crisis of the seventeenth century. The Little Ice Age and the mystery of the "Great Divergence"', *Journal of Interdisciplinary History*, 44:3 (2014), 372.

[16] C. Muldrew, *Food, energy and the creation of industriousness. Work and material culture in agrarian England, 1550–1780* (Cambridge, 2011), pp. 321–2 and chapter 3; I. Schöffer, 'Did Holland's Golden Age coincide with a period of crisis?', in Parker and Smith, *General crisis*, pp. 87–107; J. Walter and R. Schofield, 'Famine, disease and crisis mortality in early modern society', in *Famine, disease and the social order in early modern society*, eds J. Walter and R. Schofield (Cambridge, 1989), pp. 41–57.

[17] J. de Vries, *The Dutch rural economy in the Golden Age, 1500–1700* (New Haven and London, 1974), chapter 7; but see J. Bieleman, 'Dutch agriculture in the Golden Age, 1570–1660', in *The Dutch economy in the Golden Age. Nine studies*, eds K. Davids and L. Noordegraaf (Amsterdam, 1993), pp. 159–61.

[18] C.G.A. Clay, *Economic expansion and social change. England 1500–1700*, vol. I, *People, land and towns* (Cambridge, 1984), p. 116; A. Everitt, 'The marketing of agricultural produce', in *The agrarian history of England & Wales*, vol. IV, *1500–1640*, ed. J. Thirsk (Cambridge, 1967), pp. 466–592. It would be incorrect to view this as defining the onset of 'agrarian capitalism', following Brenner and Wood; this becomes a defining characteristic in the post-civil war decades: see Ormrod, 'Agrarian capitalism', pp. 208–11.

[19] J.L. van Zanden, *The long road to the Industrial Revolution. The European economy in a global perspective, 1000–1800* (Leiden, 2009), p. 99.

c. 1710 to 1750, the bulk of which were sent to Holland. As Jan Luiten van Zanden emphasises, the two countries came to form complementary parts of a single integrated North Sea region, linked by coastal shipping, inland waterways and improved river navigation.[20] From the turning of the conjuncture around mid-century – the onset of the B-phase – food prices in both countries began a slow decline, which released purchasing power for non-essential items and ushered in a long period of import-led growth, signs of which were already emerging in the 1630s. Both tendencies underlay uniquely high levels of per capita income in the Netherlands, with England catching up during the following century.[21]

It was during the long downswing after 1650 that the so-called 'Little Divergence' between the economies of northern and southern Europe began to accelerate, a movement which some have regarded as laying the foundations for what Kenneth Pomeranz described as a greater or 'Great Divergence' between Europe and Asia which had become apparent by 1800. The former began much earlier – quite how much earlier is disputed – but rising real wages show the market towns of the Low Countries leading from the early sixteenth century, followed by London half a century later. The Little Divergence, during the post-1650 phase, involved not only a permanent geographical shift away from the Mediterranean, but also increased concentration of capital and competition within the North Sea zone itself. Stagnant and falling prices intensified the struggle for all markets, old and new, and increased demands were directed to the state from mercantile interests for naval and other forms of protection.

The struggle for commercial hegemony between England and the United Provinces became increasingly acute after 1609, when Spain was no longer the common enemy. In the decades before 1640, the value of Dutch overseas trade was at least double that of England. The latter's smaller volume of trade was concentrated overwhelmingly in Europe which was then the destination for almost 90 per cent of her exports and the origin of 83 per cent of her imports. At this stage, Dutch progress in the Atlantic and Asian trades far outpaced that of England. The Dutch conquest of Brazil in the 1630s established effective control of the world sugar trade, whilst expansion in Java and Ambon secured a near-monopoly of the trade in fine spices. In 1636, almost one-third of the value of Dutch import business came from transatlantic trade, although the Baltic and northern European trades remained as the predominant elements, accounting for half the country's imports. Although English long-distance trade was insignificant in the 1630s, London merchants

---

[20] *Ibid.*, p. 100; D. Ormrod, 'Institutions and the environment. Shipping movements in the North Sea/Baltic Zone, 1650–1800', in *Shipping and economic growth, 1350–1850*, ed. R.W. Unger (Leiden, 2011), pp. 135–7.

[21] S. Broadberry, B. Campbell, A. Klein, M. Overton and B. van Leeuwen (eds), *British economic growth, 1270–1870* (Cambridge, 2015), chapter 10.

Table 1.1 Origin of imports reaching London and the United Provinces:
1620s, 1630s and 1660s

	London 1622		London 1634		United Provinces 1636		London 1660s	
	value (£'000)	%	value (£'000)	%	value (£'000)	%	value (£'000)	%
Atlantic	13.5	0.9	96.5	5.3	1,666.7	31.3	421.0	12.0
Asia	82.7	5.5	205.7	11.3	761.9	14.3	409.0	11.7
Northern Europe	937.1	62.4	722.8	39.7	2,609.5	49.0	1,553.0	44.4
Southern Europe	469.5	31.2	795.6	43.7	285.7	5.4	1,085.0	31.0
TOTAL	**1,502.9**		**1,820.7**		**5,323.8**		**3,495.0**	

Sources: Victor Enthoven, 'An assessment of Dutch transatlantic commerce, 1585–1817', in Johannes Postma and Victor Enthoven (eds), *Riches from Dutch Atlantic commerce* (Leiden, 2003), table 14.13, p. 437; J. Jonker and K. Sluyterman, *At home on the world markets* (Utrecht, 2000), p. 62; A.M. Millard, 'The import trade of London, 1600–1640' (unpublished PhD thesis, University of London, 1956), table II; R. Davis, 'English foreign trade, 1660–1700', *Economic History Review* 7 (1954), 150–66. 1660s figure based on an average of 1663 & 1669.

succeeded in expanding their share of imports from Southern Europe, mainly wines, groceries and silk, paid for by increased exports of lighter textiles (Table 1.1).

By the 1650s and 1660s England had begun, quite self-consciously, to catch up with the Dutch in a process often described as constituting a 'commercial revolution'. This involved not only increased investment in long-distance trade, shipping and ancillary services, but the development of a re-export or entrepot system along Dutch lines, shaped less by competitive advantage than by legal compulsion and coercion. Peace with Spain in 1648 promised the Dutch a new era of commercial expansion, and nowhere was this more threatening to the English than in the Baltic, following new concessions granted to the Dutch in 1651 by Denmark in relation to the Sound toll. The first Navigation Act of that year came largely as a response to Dutch recovery in the Baltic and Mediterranean trades, promoted by the London import merchants associated with the Eastland and Levant companies, supported by prominent West India traders. The aim was straightforward: to exclude the Dutch and other foreign merchants from the carrying trade, with sanctions backed by naval force. Not until Downing's new act of 1660 did the emphasis shift significantly from intra-European trade to transatlantic trade, with the requirement that all goods going to and from the colonies should be carried in English-owned or colonial ships, organised by English merchants. The 'enumeration' of plantation goods, such as tobacco, sugar and cotton, required that these commodities should be exported to European markets through English ports, a provision that also applied to selected European commodities. Two years later, the colonists were required to buy all the European goods they needed in England, and carry them in English or colonial vessels.

The navigation system introduced a new and ambitious model for conducting trade in the new political environment of the interregnum, and one which was explicitly designed to challenge Dutch commercial hegemony. The privileges enjoyed by the great trading companies, distributed at the Crown's pleasure, would be replaced with an overarching *national monopoly*, open to all English subjects and authorised by Parliament. The new model, in its essentials, remained in place for almost two centuries and, in short, laid the foundations for the British imperial state. English commentators became increasingly clear that the exploitation of the American colonies held the key to national prosperity, and the logic of the Navigation Acts was later endorsed by Adam Smith. Modern historians have largely agreed, and some have credited 'Atlanticisation' as the prime-mover behind the Great Divergence. In the Netherlands, on the other hand, greater weight was traditionally given to the impact of Dutch enterprise in East Asia, with an eye on the dazzling early successes of the VOC. But just as some revisionist writers have tended to balance the costs of the British Atlantic project against uncertain returns, so there has been a strong tendency to regard the contribution of the Dutch Atlantic in a much more favourable light than in the past, including an upward revision of trade values (Table 1.1).[22] This has been matched by recognition of the Atlantic world as a trans-imperial space in the seventeenth and eighteenth centuries, prefiguring the acceleration of globalisation in the nineteenth and twentieth centuries.[23]

The debate over the contribution of the Americas to European economic development will doubtless continue, but the geopolitical significance of the

---

[22] Victor Enthoven, 'An assessment of Dutch transatlantic commerce, 1585–1817', in *Riches from Atlantic commerce. Dutch transatlantic trade and shipping, 1585–1817*, eds J. Postma and V. Enthoven (Leiden, 2003), pp. 385–445; a more pessimistic but not entirely convincing view is taken by P. Emmer, 'The Dutch and the Atlantic challenge, 1600–1800', in *A deus ex machina revisited. Atlantic colonial trade and European economic development*, eds P.C. Emmer, O. Pétré-Grenouilleau and J. V. Roitman (Leiden, 2006), p. 158.

[23] G. Oostindie, 'Modernity and the demise of the Dutch Atlantic, 1650–1914', in *The Caribbean and the Atlantic world economy. Circuits of trade, money and knowledge, 1650–1914*, eds A. Leonard and D. Pretel (Basingstoke, 2015), p. 108; C. Antunes, 'Cross-cultural business cooperation in the Dutch trading world, 1580–1776. A view from Amsterdam's notarial contracts', in *Religion and trade. Cross-cultural exchanges in world history, 1000–1900*, eds F. Trivellato, L. Halevi and C. Antunes (Oxford, 2014), pp. 150–68.

Dutch-Spanish-English struggle for colonial trade is fairly clear. The plan to create a Dutch Atlantic empire mounted by the WIC was shaped as much by political as economic objectives, involving plunder and economic warfare against Spain and Portugal after the expiry of the 1621 truce. Its greatest coup came in the 1630s with the conquest of large parts of Brazil and the development of sugar plantations, together with the supply of slaves to the English and French plantations after the capture of Portugal's West African trading stations from 1633 to 1642. All of this was achieved at enormous human cost and loss of life, and the 'Grand Design' ended in grand failure with the surrender of New Holland in 1654. Prolonged guerrilla warfare and the accompanying devastation of many plantations produced insurmountable financial losses for the WIC. Cromwell's more modest design on Jamaica proved long-lasting. Nevertheless, the Dutch maintained a dominating role in the Atlantic from 1620 to 1670, operating through transnational networks of interest. By 1650, much of the inter-colonial carrying trade of New England, Virginia and the English West Indies appeared to have fallen into Dutch hands, as did the slave trade.

In London, increased Dutch involvement in shipping transatlantic cargoes with those English colonies still under Royalist control in the late 1640s was regarded as a growing threat by the city's 'new merchants', the pioneers of colonial trade. Even more serious was Dutch competition in the nearby North Sea and Baltic trades, and significantly, the First Anglo-Dutch War was fought largely in home waters. But the issue of colonial and transatlantic shipping assumed increasing importance during the 1650s, with the extension of sugar cultivation in Barbados, the taking of Jamaica in 1655, and the growth of colonial population.[24] The Second Anglo-Dutch War actually began as a global conflict, sparked off by the African raids of 1663–64, followed by operations in New Netherland and the West Indies, prior to the great set-piece battles in the North Sea of 1665–66. The revised post-Restoration navigation code was clearly global in scope, and insofar as it formed the core of English mercantilist ideology, its objectives fitted closely the new economic environment of falling prices, demographic slowdown, and limited opportunities for growth. Lower food prices released purchasing power for tropical goods, produced largely through coercion and increased slave trafficking, under favourable terms of trade. Modest increases in consumption for addictive commodities such as tobacco and sugar served to reduce prices still further, and expand the margins of cultivation. As the seventeenth-century English economy became increasingly import-led, the dynamic element in commercial expansion passed from the manufacturer to the merchant, and from the provinces to London.[25] Without a corresponding increase in export possibilities, London

---

[24] N. Zahedieh, *The capital and the colonies. London and the Atlantic economy, 1660–1700* (Cambridge, 2010), pp. 27–31.

[25] F.J. Fisher, 'London as an "engine of economic growth"', in *London and the English economy, 1500–1700*, eds P.J. Corfield and N.B. Harte (London, 1990), pp. 190–1.

merchant importers would need to find additional ways of making payment, and this was largely achieved through re-exporting.

Re-export growth and the navigation code both, in effect, involved novel forms of import substitution in which English colonies were substituted for alternative sources of supply and colonial shipping replaced that of foreigners, especially the Dutch. From the early 1670s, however, Parliament expressed growing concern with the balance of trade as the tide of imports increased, and demands for the protection of home industry and agriculture intensified. Steep tariff increases were introduced in the 1690s to help finance the war with France, with a rationale which went far beyond fiscal necessity. They became part of a piecemeal policy of import substitution which matured over a longer period, covering the linen, paper, silk, cotton, ceramics and glass industries, as well as several luxury trades. Industrial protectionism and the navigation code thus became the twin pillars of British mercantilism, in an approach which satisfied manufacturing interests as well as merchant pressure groups. The permanent granting of subsidies on grain exports in 1689 helped to bring landlords and farmers on board, as the Anglo-Dutch moment reached its completion. In these respects, the commercial revolution hastened Britain's progress down the long road to the industrial revolution.[26]

In a superficial sense, England was following the Republic's lead in developing a re-export system of its own, as part of a process which Charles Wilson famously described as 'England's apprenticeship' to the Netherlands. But the differences were more marked than the similarities during the early stages of the commercial revolution. In the Dutch Republic, a large group of processing industries had developed dependent on the staplemarket and imported primary products – the *verkeersindustrieën* (traffic industries) which overshadowed the rest of its industrial sector. These included brewing, malting and distilling, sawmilling, sugar refining, tobacco processing, salt refining, and white lead manufacture, located predominantly around Rotterdam and Schiedam where ample supplies of British coal were available. Zaandam became a centre for milling industries.[27] On the opposite side of the North Sea, the amount of processing prior to re-export remained relatively small, a situation which was encouraged by the English fiscal system of increasingly high import duties and payment of drawback (of duty) on re-export. The contrast between Dutch free trade and English protectionism continued to widen during the eighteenth century, and the introduction of

---

[26] Ormrod, *Commercial empires*, pp. 309–10.
[27] C. Visser, *Verkeersindustrieën te Rotterdam in de tweede helft der achttiende eeuw* (Rotterdam, 1927), pp. 9–15. The dyeing and bleaching industries of Leiden and Haarlem might also be included, based as they were on the import of semi-finished products. Visser stressed the special place of the traffic industries in the history of early capitalist organisation, involving linkages between staplemarket wholesalers and expanding external markets (*ibid.*, chapter 8).

the warehousing system in 1700, with Crown supervision, only served to increase the rate at which re-exports were diverted from the home market. English merchants continued to supply the Dutch entrepot with re-exports of Asian and colonial goods up to the 1730s and beyond, hence Matthew Decker's slightly exaggerated complaint of 1744 that 'high duties prevent our country's being an universal storehouse'.[28] High tariffs and protectionism indeed formed the defining characteristics of British mercantilism when measured against the 'incidental mercantilism' of the Netherlands, expressed mainly in the monopoly privileges of the great overseas trading companies. The difference arose less from ideology, since both nations were powerfully inclined towards mercantile interests, than geography. Holland's situation commanded the enormous transit trade along the Maas and Rhine into the heart of Europe, and low duties and river tolls were essential to preserve this, while Britain's island situation relieved her from the costs of defending a land frontier and reduced the problems of policing a protected entrepot.[29]

When the upward trend of the European economy resumed in the 1730s and 1740s and the population of the American mainland colonies began to grow significantly, the pace of commercial growth quickened, led increasingly by exports. Merchants began to experience the stimulus of colonial export markets which provided a 'quantum leap' for British manufacturers.[30] Atlanticisation, however, should not be viewed as a 'deus ex machina' or a windfall, for two reasons. First, intra-European trade remained much more important in value than Atlantic trade for England and the Netherlands up to c. 1750. Second, it was largely from its own material resources that northwest Europe was able to embark on the slow process of westward expansion after 1500 which would incorporate the Atlantic into its own orbit.[31] The refinancing of northwest European trade following the post-1689 deregulation of corporate trading helped release resources for Atlantic expansion to a degree which has been seriously underestimated. The movement of Dutch and Huguenot capital into the newly-established English national debt has long been recognised, but the enormous flow of Dutch and German capital into English commodity trade with nearby Europe has passed almost unnoticed. Already by 1695, more than one-third of the value of England's domestic exports was now carried on the accounts of Dutch, German and Scandinavian merchants using London agents. This released metropolitan trading capital for deployment elsewhere: some English merchants withdrew

[28] M. Decker, *An essay on the causes of the decline of the foreign trade of Great Britain* (London, 1744), p. 10.
[29] Ormrod, *Commercial empires*, p. 317.
[30] Emmer, 'The Dutch and the Atlantic challenge', p. 158.
[31] D. Ormrod, 'From seas to ocean. Interpreting the shift from the North Sea-Baltic world to the Atlantic, 1650–1800', in Leonard and Pretel, *The Caribbean and the Atlantic*, pp. 23–4.

from active trade into commission business, while others shifted their interests to the American mainland colonies and West Indies.[32]

The Atlantic, it has often been said, was a European invention.[33] But Europe's drive towards modern economic growth depended on more than colonisation and the transformation of the Americas. It involved making trans-imperial connections within and between the Americas, Africa, the rising entrepot cities of northern Europe, and, above all, the emporia system of the Indian Ocean, described by Chaudhuri as the early sixteenth-century 'cradle of globalisation'.[34]

By the 1590s, Dutch merchants began to circumvent Portuguese contractors for the supply of pepper by trading directly with Asian suppliers, whilst drawing on Amsterdam's active bullion market to make cash payments. Operating as a single trading company from 1602 onwards, the United Dutch East India Company (VOC) rapidly overtook its Portuguese rivals, and its success stimulated enterprising English merchants to follow suit.[35] In comparison, the English East India Company (EIC), chartered in 1600, was undercapitalised and disadvantaged by its dependence on royal favour. Almost from the start, the VOC functioned as a 'company state' in Asia, fully capable of organising its own defence, and prepared to use force to further its own commercial interests to a much greater extent than its English rival. After a promising early start, and modest success in obtaining pepper from Java and Sumatra, the EIC was unable to break the Dutch monopoly of the spice trade of the Moluccas, and entered a period of decline from the 1620s to the 1660s.[36] Military weakness forced the company to rely on largely unsuccessful diplomatic negotiations at home to maintain its viability. By the mid-1630s, the level of Dutch Asian imports was almost four times as valuable as those handled by the English company (Table 1.1).

Although the English lagged far behind the Dutch in the Far Eastern trades before the later seventeenth century, competition to obtain local concessions and efforts to resolve disputed claims between the two companies created a major arena of conflict during the period of the Anglo-Dutch wars. Unfortunately, the Asian dimension of the wars has been largely ignored by historians, while the significance of the Atlantic as a major theatre of conflict

---

[32] Ormrod, *Commercial empires*, pp. 322–33.

[33] D. Armitage, 'Three concepts of Atlantic history', in *The British Atlantic world, 1500–1800*, eds D. Armitage and M.J. Braddick (Basingstoke, 2002), p. 12.

[34] K.N. Chaudhuri, *Trade and civilization in the Indian Ocean. An economic history from the rise of Islam to 1750* (Cambridge, 1985), chapters 1 and 2; idem, *Asia before Europe. Economy and civilization of the Indian Ocean from the rise of Islam to 1750* (Cambridge, 1990), pp. 37–43.

[35] F.S. Gaastra, *The Dutch East India Company. Expansion and decline* (Leiden, 2003), pp. 13–36.

[36] K.N. Chaudhuri, *The English East India Company. The study of an early joint-stock company, 1600–1640* (London, 1965), pp. 3–19 and 56–61.

during the period of the Second Anglo-Dutch War is commonly acknowledged. Not only does this create an unbalanced view of events, it obscures
the global character of the struggle in terms of the interconnectedness of
mercantile interests in the Americas and Asia. It was silver extracted from the
Americas which bought entry into expanding Asian markets, and re-exported
Asian goods, especially light textiles, would in time find ready markets in the
American plantations and colonies.[37] In an increasingly global context, English
and Dutch merchants diversified their investments in portfolios covering
both Atlantic and Asian ventures, as well as trade with the Mediterranean,
the Baltic and nearby Europe. The directors of the VOC were willing investors
in the West India Company (WIC), and by 1613, more than two-thirds of EIC
members also invested in other ventures, especially the Virginia, North-West
Passage, Spanish, and Levant Companies.[38]

In some degree, the neglect of the Asian dimension of the Anglo-Dutch wars
is a reflection of the unhelpful historiographical divide between Asian and
Atlantic studies in understanding European imperial expansion. European
nations chose to resort to war, armed confrontation or peaceful negotiation
as circumstances dictated, and the quest for legitimacy tended to intensify in
proportion to the scale of imperial ambition.[39] Rival claims had to be resolved
back in Europe, through treaties and accords which invariably took account
of earlier recorded agreements. Martine van Ittersum suggests that, for the
Dutch, these 'empires of paper' followed a common approach in both Asia
and the Americas. The VOC and WIC 'literally employed the same personnel,
from the directors down, and routinely copied each other's repertoires of
empire, adapting and changing them along the way'.[40] In the British case,
however, it is difficult to trace a common pattern. In spite of a broadening of
participation from 1698 to 1708, trade to the Far East remained wholly in the
hands of a single monopolistic corporation until the reforms of the 1770s and
1780s. In contrast, the Atlantic trades were conducted by private unincor-
porated merchants, either as sole traders or partnerships, operating under
the umbrella of the Navigation Laws and supported by naval power.[41] The
model was Cromwellian in origin and spirit. It reflected the Commonwealth's

---

[37] A.G. Frank, *ReOrient: global economy in the Asian age* (Berkeley, 1998), pp. 131–51; A.
Attman, *Dutch enterprise in the world bullion trade* (Gothenburg, 1983).

[38] T.K. Rabb, *Enterprise and empire. Merchant and gentry investment in the expansion
of England, 1575–1630* (Cambridge, Mass., 1967), chapter 1; E. Smith, 'The global
interests of London's commercial community, 1599–1625. Investment in the East
India Company', *Economic History Review*, 71:4 (2018), 1131.

[39] A. Pagden, *Lords of all the world. Ideologies of empire in Spain, Britain and France, c.
1500–c. 1800* (New Haven, 1995), pp. 34–54.

[40] See Martine van Ittersum's contribution to this volume.

[41] D. Ormrod, 'Northern Europe and the expanding world-economy. The transformation of commercial organisation, 1500–1800', in *Prodotti e tecniche d'oltremare nelle
economie Europee, secc. XIII–XVIII*, ed. S. Cavaciocchi (Prato, 1998), p. 691.

preference for statutory regulation in place of corporate monopoly privilege, and thus added deeper layers of legitimation for the British Atlantic imperial project. The establishment of the Board of Trade in 1650 added to this, by facilitating metropolitan control

If the British in North America saw themselves primarily as colonists, the African and Asian context was one of forts, factories and commercial exchange. It was arguably one which required little in the way of legitimation of claims on territory or the right to trade until the nineteenth century, when largely commercial activity was overtaken by imperial ambition.[42]

The fiscal-military-naval state

During its long wars to achieve independence, the Dutch Republic had emerged as an extremely efficient fiscal military state, capable of challenging the combined power of Spain and Portugal in the Americas and Asia. The patron–client relationship which had existed with England began to break down after the 1609 truce and the three English garrisons in the Netherlands were returned in 1616 once military support was no longer needed.[43] It gradually dawned upon England's rulers that they were faced by a fully independent state, underpinned by formidable naval and maritime resources.[44]

It was essentially the Republic's military staying power, strengthened after the reforms of Maurice of Nassau in the 1590s, which had secured independence, together with predictable revenues and robust financial services.[45] Its decentralised naval administration, formerly regarded by historians as a weakness, is nowadays recognised as an effective and economical system, in spite of periodic local conflicts of interest. Revenue from customs duties, the *convooien en licenten*, was collected and controlled by each of the five admiralties, to meet naval expenditure as each saw fit.[46] In comparison, the English navy of the 1620s was underfunded, untested, and inadequately managed by a navy office afflicted by corruption. Throughout his reign, James

[42] Pagden, *Lords of all the world*, pp. 37–8.

[43] G. Rommelse and R. Downing, 'Anglo-Dutch mercantile rivalry, 1585–1688. Interests, ideologies, and perceptions', in *Merkantilismus. Wiederaufnahme einer Debatte*, ed. M. Isenmann (Stuttgart, 2014), p. 187.

[44] Anton Poot, *Crucial years in Anglo-Dutch relations (1625–1642)* (Hilversum, 2013).

[45] M. 't Hart, *The Dutch wars of independence. Warfare and commerce in the Netherlands, 1570–1680* (Abingdon, 2014), pp. 4–6.

[46] *Ibid.*, chapter 6; J. Glete, *War and the state in early modern Europe. Spain, the Dutch Republic and Sweden as fiscal-military states, 1500–1660* (Abingdon, 2002), chapter 4; Pepijn Brandon, *War, capital and the Dutch state, 1588–1795* (Leiden and Chicago, 2015), pp. 57–66; L. Gomes, *Foreign trade and the national economy. Mercantilist and classical perspectives* (Basingstoke, 1987), p. 92.

I had promoted an unpopular pro-Spanish peace policy, which nevertheless preserved English neutrality at sea to the benefit of English carriers. By the time of the disastrous Anglo-Spanish war of 1625–30, the inadequate state of the fleet, ill-supplied and -commanded, became apparent to all. For maritime economies with imperial ambitions, sea power was obviously essential for the defence of trade and the state, with the expectation that costs might be balanced against increased revenues from commerce.[47] By strengthening the navy and supporting the armed chartered companies, the Dutch elite succeeded in securing the internalisation of protection costs at an early stage and establishing a new capacity amongst European states for deploying state power and violence on a global scale.[48] The personal government of Charles I, without parliamentary taxation or counsel, struggled to restore even the nation's home defences. Although the proceeds from ship money produced more concrete results than is generally acknowledged, totalling £800,000 from 1634 to 1640, the price in terms of political credibility was unacceptably high.[49]

At the root of England's constitutional crisis which erupted in the 1640s was the repeated failure of the Tudor and Stuart monarchies to make adequate fiscal provision to meet these basic requirements. To this deficiency was added the insistence of the early Stuarts that the regulation of economic affairs should be governed by royal prerogative, a tradition that began to break down with the establishment of committees and councils of trade during and after the economic crisis of the early 1620s. That the Dutch had succeeded in strategising the defence of their economic interests was apparent to the most percipient English observers of the 1640s such as Lewes Roberts, Henry Robinson, and Benjamin Worsley, unanimous in their admiration for the Dutch, who made the 'Care and Protection of Trade abroad in all places their Interest of State'.[50] English mercantilists found their voices during the crisis of the 1620s and developed a 'discourse of trade' which focused on the problems arising from a negative balance of trade rather than its supposedly finite nature.[51] The Cromwellian navigation code embodied these ideas, prompted by a group of London import merchants and articulated especially by Worsley as secretary of the new Council of Trade. Initially, Worsley and his circle, in common with Roberts, Robinson and other writers, argued the case for low customs duties and free ports modelled closely on the Dutch

[47] W. Ashworth, *The Industrial Revolution. The state, knowledge and global trade* (London, 2017), p. 42.

[48] Brandon, *War, capital and the Dutch state*, p. 24; Arrighi, *Long twentieth century*, p. 151.

[49] N.A.M. Rodger, *The safeguard of the sea. A naval history of Britain, 660–1649* (London, 1997), p. 382.

[50] T. Leng, *Benjamin Worsley (1618–1677). Trade, interest and the spirit in revolutionary England* (Woodbridge, 2008), p. 77.

[51] Ibid., 'Commercial conflict and regulation in the discourse of trade in the seventeenth century', *Historical Journal*, 48:4 (2005), 933–54.

staplemarket. This was consistent with a proposal mooted in 1651 for a political union or Protestant confederation of the two countries which would have facilitated a joint Anglo-Dutch entrepot. In fact the union proposal failed and the restrictive side of mercantilist thinking carried the day. The 1651 legislation established regulation of trade as the permanent responsibility of the nation state.

The restructuring of England's public finances was a much slower process and began during the interregnum with a series of borrowing experiments using short-term loans secured with future taxes. Based on assessments and the excise, first introduced in 1643, the new system provided a firm basis for guaranteeing supply for both the army and navy. The practice developed of assigning new revenue ordinances to service public debts incurred for specific purposes.[52] A strong navy was essential to defend the revolution after the execution of Charles I in 1649, and Cromwell reacted quickly. The navy was doubled in size over the next two years and naval expenditure rose to reach nearly £8 million between 1649 and 1660, ten times the figure raised from ship money from 1634 to 1640.[53] Remodelling of the officer corps in 1649 produced greater social cohesion, and naval command became much less prone to internal division. These developments formed the starting point for England's naval revolution of the 1640s and 1650s, involving the creation of a professionalised state navy deploying specialist warships in place of armed merchantmen. This in turn inaugurated a change in naval strategy and tactics which relied on great fleet engagements for which merchant vessels were unsuited.[54] The republican naval system was adopted almost in its entirety at the restoration of Charles II.

The naval revolution of the 1640s and 1650s in both England and the Netherlands represents a significant discontinuity in the longer history of Europe's military revolution. In the latter, a navy of 'precocious efficiency' emerged during the war of independence which drew loans and supplies from local elites and providers, and continued to develop along the lines of what Pepijn Brandon describes as a 'federal brokerage' model. The five admiralties were dominated by the wealth and influence of Amsterdam, which generated just over half the yield of customs duties at the time of the First Anglo-Dutch War, rising to almost two-thirds by the end of the century. But the system remained basically decentralised, dependent on merchant administrators and financial intermediaries. The English navy also relied substantially on brokerage, contracting and the market, but lost its hybrid

---

[52] D. Coffman, *Excise taxation and the origins of public debt* (Basingstoke, 2013), pp. 2–4 and 201–2; J.S. Wheeler, 'Navy finance 1649–1660', *Historical Journal*, 39:2 (1996), 457–66.

[53] N.A.M. Rodger, *The command of the ocean. A naval history of Britain, 1649–1815* (London, 2004), p. 46.

[54] B. Capp, *Cromwell's navy. The fleet and the English Revolution* (Oxford, 1989), p. 6.

public/private character during the Commonwealth period to become a unitary state-funded force. By 1650, English sea power had become a match for that of the Dutch state, capable of acting as an instrument of offensive policy in home and distant waters.[55]

It was during the First Anglo-Dutch War that the English navy shifted decisively away from the deployment of merchant vessels, and 'the transformation of the Dutch war fleet only took place after the limitations of a mostly hired fleet had been shown in battle'.[56] English strategy initially concentrated on intercepting Dutch convoys sailing through the 'narrow seas' rather than confronting the enemy's battle fleet. The Dutch command had other ideas, and both sides soon found themselves drawn into grand engagements. After the English defeat off Dungeness in November 1652, it was realised that a fleet which included unreliable armed merchantmen and civilian captains was no longer fit for purpose. Both were phased out and a new hierarchical command structure was implemented which facilitated the development of new line of battle tactics with the emphasis on broadside gunpower instead of boarding. Fleets were divided into squadrons, as outlined in Blake's 'Instructions' drawn up after the Battle of Portland in 1653, which suited the more heavily armed but smaller English navy. During the course of the first war, the States General, led by Holland's pensionary John de Witt, decided to launch two major naval construction programmes. The Republic emulated the English standing fleet and its tactical focus on line of battle. As in England, the squadron organisation was drastically altered and the officer corps professionalised. These new tactics and organisational changes remained in place until the close of the War of the Spanish Succession, when the Dutch battle fleet was gradually reduced and redesigned for long-distance convoying duties, with greater reliance on cruisers and frigates.[57]

The origins and outcomes of the Anglo-Dutch wars throw into sharp focus the strengths and weaknesses of the 'fiscal military state' as a descriptive term for interpreting the connections between taxation and state formation in Europe. A tide of revisionist writing has added several helpful qualifications, especially in reducing the role of highly centralised bureaucracy as the hallmark of the species, which *inter alia* accommodates more easily the experience of the Netherlands as an efficient federal-brokerage state. The use of private military contractors and the involvement of leading merchant families such as the De Wildts in undertaking navy victualling and supply

---

[55] S.R. Hornstein, *The Restoration navy and English foreign trade, 1674–1688. A study in the peace time use of sea power* (Aldershot, 1991), pp. 1–9.

[56] Brandon, *War, capital and the Dutch state*, p. 87.

[57] *Ibid.*, pp. 316–17; J.K. Oudendijk, *Johan de Witt en de vloot* (Amsterdam, 1944); J.R. Bruijn, *Varend verleden. De Nederlandse oorlogsvloot in de zeventiende en achttiende eeuw* (Amsterdam, 1998), pp. 91–107; Ormrod, 'Institutions and the environment', pp. 160–1.

was paralleled by similar arrangements in Britain, increasingly recognised as a 'contractor state'.[58] More conspicuous in the context of the imperial state was the growing significance of militarised corporate trade in the shape of the two great India companies, the VOC and EIC, along with the comparatively short-lived WIC and the Royal African Company, legally separate from their respective governments but capable, in time, of an unprecedented capacity for unregulated corporate violence.

In the case of the British state, the exemplar for John Brewer's original formulation, many would now accept that the origins of the British tax state lie in the 1640s, arising from financial demands of civil war and the shift towards military dictatorship.[59] A minority of historians continue to reify the 'Glorious Revolution' as the decisive moment in the establishment of the fiscal military state. Steven Pincus and James Robinson have even suggested that such fiscal reforms as did occur before 1688 were associated solely with the civil war rather than major interstate conflicts.[60] The outbreak of the Anglo-Dutch wars clearly rule this out. The first war arose from a combination of economic rivalries coupled with ideologically-driven hopes on the part of English republicans which could not be realised at a time of serious political crisis in Holland after William II's abortive attack on Amsterdam of 1650 and his death three months later. The Holland regents were anxious to avoid war at all costs, but not at the price of a 'full frontal attack on their trade or any attempt to attach or subordinate the Republic politically to England'.[61] In this sense, the subsequent Anglo-Dutch conflicts were a direct outgrowth of the mid-seventeenth-century British crisis and civil war, and played a critical role in generating the naval revolution of the 1640s and 1650s, and its accompanying fiscal demands.

Revisionist writing has underlined the case for a flexible approach to understanding the fiscal military state, indeed Brewer himself never intended

---

[58] A concept first used by R. Knight and M. Wilcox, *Sustaining the fleet 1793–1815. War, the British navy, and the contractor state* (Woodbridge, 2010); Brandon, *War, capital and the Dutch state*, pp. 19, 64–5.

[59] Coffman, *Excise taxation*, p. 1 and chapters 2 and 3; D. Coffman, A. Leonard and L. Neal, 'Introduction', in *idem* (eds), *Questioning credible commitment. Perspectives on the rise of financial capitalism* (Cambridge, 2013), p. 3; P.K. O'Brien and P. Hunt, 'The rise of a fiscal state in England, 1485–1815', *Historical Research*, 66:160 (June 1993), 150–1; P.K. O'Brien, 'The formation of states and transitions to modern economies: England, Europe and Asia compared', in *History of capitalism*, I, eds Neal and Williamson, p. 362; M.J. Braddick, 'An English military revolution?', *Historical Journal*, 36:4 (1993), 965–75.

[60] S. Pincus and J. Robinson, 'Challenging the fiscal-military hegemony: the British case', in *The British fiscal-military states, 1660–c.1783*, eds A. Graham and P. Walsh (London, 2016), p. 259.

[61] J. Israel, Review of S.C.A. Pincus, *Protestantism and patriotism. Ideologies and the making of English foreign policy, 1650–1668* (Cambridge, 1996), *Journal of Modern History*, 71:3 (1999), 680.

to specify the British case as an 'ideal type'.[62] Leaving aside the federal structure of the Dutch state, the British and Dutch cases were in many respects unusual at a European level, but strikingly similar in their common fiscal-*naval* orientation. It was this which enabled them to pursue hegemonic ambitions through a close alignment between the state, merchant elites and trading companies.[63] Hegemony has been variously described as the exercise of power beyond a state's own borders, through coercion, protection, or the market; or, as Immanuel Wallerstein suggested, 'more than mere leadership but less than outright empire', when a hegemonic power is 'able to impose its set of rules on the interstate system'.[64] Arrighi followed Braudel and Wallerstein's attachment to the rhythms of the conjuncture, but in place of the former's emphasis on urban centres of gravity within the system, shifted the focus to the question of hegemonic power and state formation in the expansion of capitalism. As we have already noticed, Arrighi saw a succession of hegemonic core states leading each 'systemic cycle of accumulation' (Figure 1.1). The foregoing suggests that he was substantially right in describing the first two Anglo-Dutch wars as the first and critical point of transition between the Dutch and British cycles.[65] The second was marked by the Treaty of Utrecht of 1713, seen as the point at which Dutch sea power waned, as investors retreated into financing British war-making activities.[66]

As Arrighi realised, the wealth of the Dutch merchant elite rested on its control over world financial networks to an even greater extent than commercial activity, and as with previous and later cycles of accumulation, financialisation and capital export paved the way for the next hegemonic shift, towards newly-united Britain.[67] But in at least one important respect, that of chronology, Arrighi's overview needs revising. Dutch and Huguenot investors indeed made sizeable contributions to English public funds after 1713, although the habit had developed twenty years earlier. Equally significant, as we have already noticed, was the growing contribution of Dutch credit and capital to English commodity trade in the 1690s, and on a smaller scale from the 1660s. David Ormrod has argued elsewhere that this facilitated the refinancing of the North Sea economy, whilst contributing to the capital requirements of the expanding Atlantic trades. For the Dutch, the financial sphere remained uniquely immune from attack at a time when the

[62] J. Brewer, 'Revisiting *The Sinews of Power*', in *The British fiscal-military states*, eds Graham and Walsh, p. 27.
[63] Andrew Lambert, *Seapower states. Maritime culture, continental empires and the conflict that made the modern world* (New Haven and London, 2018), pp. 157–203 and 266–310.
[64] N. Ferguson, 'Hegemony or empire?', *Foreign Affairs*, 82:5 (2002).
[65] The second was marked by the Treaty of Utrecht of 1713.
[66] G. Arrighi and B.J. Silver, *Chaos and governance in the modern world system* (Minneapolis, 1999), p. 54.
[67] Arrighi, *Long twentieth century*, p. 45.

protectionist policies of European nations were undermining the viability of the Dutch entrepot system.[68]

By the close of the seventeenth century, the Dutch merchant elite had succeeded in raising the rate of capital accumulation and extending it far beyond the regional orbit of the state to a much greater degree than the Italian city states had been able to achieve. Internally, as Brandon explains, the formation of a representative federal state served to loosely tie the interests of internationally-oriented merchants and financiers to the larger mass of provincial small businesses. By devolving power downwards and favouring brokerage over bureaucracy, the state enlarged its capacity for waging war. But in the long run, this imposed limits to economic integration and created an inherently unstable coalition of interests.[69] Unsurprisingly, this divergence of interests gave rise to frequent political discourses on the Republic's national interest, debates that were always waged within the context of Dutch national identity.[70]

State and identity

We have suggested that England and the Republic shared a unique experience in seventeenth-century Europe in their common fiscal-naval orientation. In considering the identity of France, compounded of diverse environmental, socio-economic and cultural elements, Braudel recognised that his country had been somehow resistant to capitalism. 'Is it perhaps', he mused, 'both France's tragedy and the secret of its charm that it has never really been won over to capitalism?'[71] The advantages of early political unity were overridden by geography, as the nation was increasingly bypassed by developing trade routes circling around the 'hexagon' from Italy to northern Europe: France failed 'to take effectively to the seas'.[72] England and the Netherlands, on the other hand, shared a common identity as emerging

---

[68] Ormrod, *Commercial empires*, p. 322.

[69] Brandon, *War, capital and the Dutch state*, pp. 29–34.

[70] D. Sturkenboom, 'Amidst unscrupulous neighbours. Amsterdam money and foreign interests in Dutch patriotic imagery', in *Imagining global Amsterdam. History, culture, and geography in a world city*, ed. Marco de Waard (Amsterdam, 2012), pp. 45–65; *idem*, 'Merchants on the defensive. National self-images in the Dutch Republic of the late eighteenth century', in *The self-perception of early modern capitalists*, eds Margaret C. Jacob and Catherine Secretan (New York, 2008), pp. 99–122; G. Rommelse, 'The Dutch Republic. In the shadow of a glorious past', in *Navy officers in the eighteenth century: an international perspective*, eds Anna Sarah Hammar, Jakob Seerup and Evan Wilson (London, 2019), pp. 99–126.

[71] F. Braudel, *The identity of France. Vol. II. People and production* (London, 1990), p. 666.

[72] P. Anderson, 'Fernand Braudel and national identity', *London Review of Books*, 9 May 1991, and reprinted in Anderson, *A zone of engagement* (London, 1992), p. 256; Braudel, *Identity of France. Vol. II*, p. 672.

maritime nations with imperial ambitions, supported by similarities in religious outlook and humanist sensibilities. The rhetorical figure of the *mercator sapiens*, representing the ideals of honesty, wisdom and civic virtue, emerged in Dutch humanist writings of the 1630s, and became equally appealing to English audiences during the republican years and beyond, from Roberts to Child. In practice, merchants and trading companies in both countries became increasingly drawn into fierce competition for every major trade, both inside and outside Europe, and the initial outcome was a naval arms race and a series of fratricidal wars which affected European warfare as a whole.[73]

Insofar as the larger context of Anglo-Dutch relations after 1648 involved a *hegemonic* struggle, all aspects of interstate conflict came into play: politics and diplomacy, ideology and economic interests. Nevertheless, in the historiography of the Anglo-Dutch wars, a false dichotomy has sometimes been drawn between the political, commercial and economic 'causes of war'. Among those commonly regarded as stressing commercial motivations are Nicolaas Japikse, Charles Boxer, Charles Wilson, Peter Klein and Jonathan Israel, though there is considerable variation between them on the place of vested interests, politics and dynastic ambition in shaping the climate of war.[74] Their interpretative grid works well for the First and Second Anglo-Dutch Wars, but is less appropriate for the Third War, which was essentially the project of the absolutist monarchs Louis XIV and Charles II. Other historians, like Johan Elias, Pieter Geyl, Herbert Rowen, James Jones, Simon Groenveld, Ronald Hutton and Paul Seaward, certainly took into account commercial rivalries underlying the Anglo-Dutch conflicts, but chose to put more focus on the diplomatic and political dynamics in both countries.[75] Their work emphasised the importance of partisan and factional rivalries, dynastic agendas, patronage, and personal ambitions and animosities. Finally, a third, radically different, perspective

---

[73] Lambert, *Seapower states*, pp. 157–203 and 272–7.

[74] N. Japikse, *De verwikkelingen tusschen de Republiek en Engeland van 1660–1665* (Leiden, 1900); C.R. Boxer, *The Anglo-Dutch wars of the 17th century, 1652–1674* (London, 1974); C.H. Wilson, *Profit and power. A study of England and the Dutch wars* (London, 1954); P.W. Klein, 'A new look at an old subject. Dutch trade policy in the age of mercantilism', in *State and trade: government and the economy in Britain and the Netherlands since the Middle Ages*, eds S. Groenveld and M. Wintle (Zutphen, 1992), pp. 39–49; J. Israel, 'England's mercantilist response to Dutch world trade primacy,1647–1674', in *ibid.*, pp. 50–61.

[75] J. Elias, *De tweede Engelsche oorlog als het keerpunt in onze betrekkingen met Engeland* (Amsterdam, 1930); P. Geyl, *Oranje en Stuart, 1642–1672* (Utrecht, 1939); P. Seaward, *The Cavalier Parliament and the reconstruction of the old regime, 1661–1667* (Cambridge, 1989); R. Hutton, *Charles the Second. King of England, Scotland and Ireland* (Oxford, 1989); J.R. Jones, *The Anglo-Dutch wars of the seventeenth century* (New York, 1996); S. Groenveld, 'The seventeenth-century Anglo-Dutch wars: economic or political issues?', *Low Countries. A yearbook*, 4 (1995–96), 172–89.

was introduced in 1996, by Pincus.[76] Concentrating on English political and religious discourses, partisan ideologies and anti-Dutch stereotypes, he argued that ideological differences were the primary cause of the wars. Pincus was criticised for his polemical reduction of mercantilist differences and the way he absolutised political polarisation.[77] His politico-cultural approach also attracted a great deal of interest, however, leading up to a reinvigoration of the study of seventeenth-century Anglo-Dutch relations. Elaborating on Pincus's work, historians like Tony Claydon, Charles Levillain, Hugh Dunthorne, David Onnekink, Helmer Helmers and Gijs Rommelse have contributed to a deeper understanding of the politico-cultural dimension of these relations.[78]

Of key importance in the study of this dimension is the concept of national identity. The state, Michael Braddick has argued, is to be understood less as an institutional entity than 'a network of offices exercising political power'.[79] Rather than developing as a result of top-down, deliberate policy, it gradually modernised throughout the early modern age as a result of the interaction between 'social interests – particularly those of class, gender and age'. Describing 'class', Braddick quoted Keith Wrighton, who argued that it should be seen as 'a loose aggregate of individuals of varied through comparable economic positions, who are linked by similarities of status, power, lifestyle and opportunities, by shared cultural characteristics and bonds of interaction'.[80] These classes together formed an 'imagined political community', as Benedict Anderson famously called it, that was bound by a collective identity.[81] This identity, Willem Frijhoff has explained,

---

[76] S. Pincus, *Protestantism and patriotism. Ideologies and the making of English foreign policy, 1650–1668* (Cambridge, 1996); *idem*, 'Popery, trade and universal monarchy. The ideological context of the outbreak of the Second Anglo-Dutch War', *English Historical Review*, 107 (1992), 1–30; *idem*, 'Republicanism, absolutism and universal monarchy. English popular sentiment during the Third Dutch War', in *Culture and society in the Stuart Restoration. Literature, drama, history*, ed. G. MacLean (Cambridge, 1995), pp. 241–66.

[77] J. Israel, 'England, the Dutch Republic, and Europe in the seventeenth century', *Historical Journal*, 40 (1997), 1117–21.

[78] T. Claydon, *Europe and the making of England, 1660–1760* (Cambridge, 2007); D. Onnekink, *The Anglo-Dutch favourite. The career of Hans Willem Bentinck, 1st Earl of Portland (1649–1709)* (Farnham, 2007); H. Dunthorne; *Britain and the Dutch Revolt, 1560–1700* (Cambridge, 2017); C.-E. Levillain, *Vaincre Louis XIV. Angleterre, Hollande, France. Histoire d'une relation triangulaire (1665–1688)* (Champ Vallon, 2010); G. Rommelse, *The Second Anglo-Dutch War (1665–1667). International raison d'état, mercantilism and maritime strife* (Hilversum, 2006); H. Helmers, *The Royalist republic. Literature, politics and religion in the Anglo-Dutch sphere, 1639–1660* (Cambridge, 2016).

[79] M. Braddick, *State formation in early modern England, c. 1550–1700* (Cambridge, 2000), p. 45.

[80] *Ibid.*, p. 1.

[81] B. Anderson, *Imagined communities. Reflections on the origins and spread of nationalism* (London and New York, 1983).

may be considered as a rhetorical construction arising from the interaction between one's own self-image and how one is perceived by others: or between the image that a group has of itself and the conception that others have of it. Stereotyping, clichés, images of heroes and enemies, and similar forms of representation all help to determine identity, which cannot be understood as anything other than a constructed image.[82]

Collective identity was frequently ideologised to legitimise and push political agendas, whether dynastic, commercial, judicial, military or other. Intending to employ the political, diplomatic, fiscal and military resources of the state to further specific purposes, individuals, factions, parties and syndicates sought to present their agenda as congruent with the imagined community's identity and the logical corollary of its collective interest. In other words, ideas, proposals and decisions could only be relevant and valid if presented as beneficial to the nation's interest and inherent in its identity.[83] This was certainly the case in England and especially in the Dutch Republic, where socio-political and judicial relations were much more egalitarian than elsewhere in Europe, and where high literacy rates and high urbanisation ensured a lively public sphere.[84]

The nation's identity developed organically, through social discourses about domestic developments as well as interaction with other nations. This identity, which usually comprised some foundation myth, a pantheon of national heroes, a claim to a specific territory, a more or less coherent cluster of positive character traits, and generally accepted and often repeated parallels with classical or biblical events, served as the prism through which new events and encounters were interpreted. Thus, the nation's collective identity was frequently reconfirmed as well as enriched with new examples, parallels and dimensions. One of the most potent mechanisms of identity formation was mirror imaging, both in a positive and a negative sense. Comparing the

[82] W. Frijhoff, 'Hoe talig is groepsidentiteit? Reflecties vanuit de Geschiedenis', *Taal en Tongval. Tijdschrift voor taalvariatie*, 17 (2004), 9–29.

[83] D. Onnekink and G. Rommelse, 'Introduction', in *Ideology and foreign policy in early modern Europe (1650–1750)*, eds D. Onnekink and G. Rommelse (Farnham, 2011), pp. 1–11; J.D. Davies, A. James and G. Rommelse, 'The ghost at the banquet. Navies, ideologies, and the writing of history', in *Ideologies of Western naval power, c. 1500–1815*, eds J.D. Davies, Alan James and Gijs Rommelse (Abingdon, 2019), pp. 1–14.

[84] F. Deen, D. Onnekink and M. Reinders (eds), *Pamphlets and politics in the Dutch Republic* (Leiden and Boston, 2011); R. Harms, *Pamfletten en publieke opinie. Massamedia in de zeventiende eeuw* (Amsterdam, 2011); S. Groenveld, 'The Mecca of authors? States assemblies and censorship in the seventeenth-century Dutch Republic', in *Too mighty to be free. Censorship and the press in Britain and the Netherlands*, eds A.C. Duke and C.A. Tamse (Zutphen, 1987), pp. 63–86; H. Barker, 'England, 1760–1815', in *Press, politics and the public sphere in Europe and America 1760–1820*, eds H. Barker and S. Burrows (Cambridge, 2002), pp. 48–68.

nation's identity with that of other nations, similarities provided legitimacy and confirmation, while contrasts served to explain and justify a conflict, and also confirmed the positive elements of the collective self-image. These mirror images were given shape in pamphlets, elaborate histories, poems, songs, caricatural etchings, paintings, commemorative medals and sermons.[85]

Negative mirror imaging was a particularly prominent feature of the seventeenth-century Anglo-Dutch wars. Prior to and during the First War, English authors tarnished the Dutch as bad Protestants or even crypto-Catholics who had forsaken the true belief for the worship of Mammon. Their great wealth, it was argued, was ill gotten and essentially parasitic of English natural resources. Their love of the House of Orange, it was claimed, proved that their republicanism was really only skin-deep.[86] Meanwhile, Dutch authors and preachers created a wide gap between their 'justified' Revolt against Habsburg Spain and the recent execution of Charles I, which was consistently referred to as 'regicide' – murder. 'Jealous and thievish', the English were often called 'tailmen', a term that may refer to the devil, a scorpion or the English bulldog. Oliver Cromwell was the archetypical tailman (Figure 1.2).[87] During the Second War, the Dutch were routinely depicted as radical republicans, the natural enemies of all kings and the honourable House of Orange. They were still the parasitic 'bog-dwellers' who kept England from reaching its full commercial and imperial potential. The image of thievish tailmen continued to be employed in the Republic, while the regime of King Charles II was said to be deeply unreliable. The anti-Dutch stereotype employed in England did not change much during the Third War. Dutch authors, however, now added the accusation of Catholic absolutism to their image of Charles II, using his political and familial ties with the Sun King Louis XIV to underpin this claim.[88]

It is obvious that the construction of negative mirror images was closely connected with domestic discourses and political development. Following the Restoration of Charles II in 1660, the English image of 'Dutchness' changed radically. The Dutch were now framed as the enemies of all princes, instead of as crypto-monarchists.[89] At the same time, the Dutch interpretation of 'Englishness' became split. There was a distinctly negative view, held by those in favour of De Witt's True Freedom, and an oppositional Orangist view that

[85] L. Jensen (ed.), *The roots of nationalism. National identity formation in early modern Europe, 1600–1815* (Amsterdam, 2016); K. Kumar, *The making of English national identity* (Cambridge, 2003); R. Stein and J.S. Pollmann (eds), *Networks, regions and nations. Shaping identities in the Low Countries, 1300–1650* (Leiden and Boston, 2010).

[86] Pincus, *Protestantism and patriotism*, pp. 15–82.

[87] G. Rommelse, 'Negative mirror images in Anglo-Dutch relations 1650–1674', in *The roots of nationalism*, ed. Jensen, pp. 199–216.

[88] Pincus, *Protestantism and patriotism*, pp. 195–268; Claydon, *Europe and the making of England*, pp. 132–52; Rommelse, 'Negative mirror images'.

[89] Pincus, *Protestantism and patriotism*.

Figure 1.2 Lord Protector Oliver Cromwell as the despicable tailman. His rapacious jealousy is reflected by the coins falling from his tail. Satirical etching, 1652. Source: Rijksmuseum (Amsterdam), RP-P-OB-79.497.

painted a much more positive picture of the regime of Charles II. Here he was represented as a peace-loving, honourable monarch who only had the best interests of his nephew, the young Prince William III, at heart. Naturally, Charles and his advisors cultivated this Orangist interpretation, because the partisan rivalry in the Republic suited their political agenda.[90]

The resilience of these negative stereotypes is remarkable. The Anglo-Dutch wars of the seventeenth century were followed by a prolonged phase of friendship and of military and diplomatic cooperation. The balance within this alliance shifted fundamentally during the great coalition wars against Louis XIV – in the 1740s the Prussian king Frederick the Great famously compared the Dutch Republic to a humble longboat that was tied to the stern of the proud British men of war – but it lasted until 1780, when the Fourth Anglo-Dutch War broke out. Completely ignoring the ninety years of unequal friendship, Dutch authors and visual artists rehashed the old images of the rapacious, treacherous tailman.[91] Another noteworthy example

[90] Rommelse, 'Negative mirror images'.
[91] D. Onnekink and G. Rommelse, *The Dutch in the early modern world. A history of a global power* (Cambridge, 2019), pp. 183–202 and 238–55.

of this resilience was the German propaganda aimed at winning the Dutch hearts and minds during the Second World War. Aiming to exploit the old animosity, the occupational authorities ordered the issue in 1943–44 of a series of stamps showing the portraits of Michiel de Ruyter and his colleagues. Even more direct was a poster that equated the great admiral's old flagship with a German submarine. Displaying the skyline of London and the Union Jack in the background and raising the call for battle against 'the old enemy', the poster was intended to persuade the Dutch to support the German war effort.[92] A final example is the punning, semi-affectionate use of terms like 'Dutch courage', 'Dutch uncle', 'double Dutch' and 'Dutch treat' by British media, whenever they report about the national football team of the Netherlands or some recent political development. Applied in a completely different, twenty-first-century context, these puns do in fact reflect some of the old stereotypes that had emerged during the Anglo-Dutch wars.

Conclusions

Shifting conceptions of identity and the creation of stereotypes form a common currency in the daily life of most societies, but we should distinguish the habits of contemporaries from debates about the place of collective identity in state formation, a necessarily retrospective activity pursued by historians and social scientists. Within this larger context, several contributions gathered in this volume support a view of the Dutch Republic and England during the period 1652–89 as maritime nations with imperial ambitions, for which the label 'fiscal-naval state' seems the most accurate description. Because of the complex and capital-intensive character of naval organisation, Nicholas Rodger, following Patrick O'Brien, suggests that 'the new concept of the "fiscal-naval state" seems to offer a much more convincing explanation of what really happened [in Britain] than we have yet had available'.[93]

Images of maritime greatness were generated by both societies, and Andrew Lambert has recently emphasised how their self-conscious projection was expressed in both the visual arts and 'architectures of maritime power', such as Amsterdam's Dam Square, Van Campen's Town Hall, and Charles

---

[92] See Daalder's contribution to this volume.

[93] N.A.M. Rodger, 'From the "military revolution" to the "fiscal-naval state"', *Journal for Maritime Research*, 13 (2011), 122–3; P.K. O'Brien, 'The formation of a mercantilist state and the economic growth of the United Kingdom, 1453–1815', World Institute for Development Economics Research, United Nations, research paper 2006/75, July 2006; Graham and Walsh (eds), *The British fiscal-military states*, introduction, especially pp. 7 and 18. From 1689, with the opening of more than a century of intermittent continental warfare, the description 'fiscal-military' state may be thought to retain much validity for Britain, taken to include extensive naval capability.

II's Greenwich Palace.[94] Lambert indeed makes much greater claims than proponents of a distinctive fiscal-naval state form, in designating the Dutch Republic and England as *seapower states* rather than states which merely possessed and deployed navies (sea-states). It was out of weakness, the argument runs, that island or littoral states were driven to exercise their full maritime potential in the face of competition from larger territorial states.[95]

There is some truth in this, though the extent to which 'seapowers' built their whole identity and culture around a maritime existence is debatable. The evidence of the fine arts, even for the province of Holland, suggests a less clear-cut answer. The doyen of the history of the Dutch art market, Michael Montias, showed that maritime subjects formed less than ten per cent of the stock of paintings listed in seventeenth-century Amsterdam inventories, far outnumbered by landscapes, history paintings and portraits.[96] The stock of paintings in England before the 1720s was comparatively small, consisting mainly of portraits, but the well-known arrival of the Van de Veldes in London in the winter of 1672–73 marked the beginning of the Anglo-Dutch school of marine painting.[97] Their arrival was a response to Charles II's general invitation to immigrant craftsmen and artisans, and was triggered by the collapse of the Dutch art market during the catastrophic French invasion of 1672. Insofar as 'marine art was part of the transfer of sea power', it was part of a larger process of import-substitution in the fine arts and luxury trades involving a broad spectrum of Dutch and Huguenot immigrant craftsmen.[98] Marine painting remained a small sector of a growing range of genres introduced by Netherlandish artists after 1660, including still lifes, sporting pictures, house portraits, *trompe l'oeils*, topographical art, cityscapes and, above all, landscape painting which by 1800 had become the pre-eminent British contribution to European art.

Alongside the importance given to the active construction of a cultural identity focused on the sea, Lambert specifically associates seapower states with the export of liberal western values: the 'synergy between inclusive politics and seapower is critical. Progressive political ideologies spread by sea as part of the trading network have always been a primary weapon in the

[94] Lambert, *Seapower states*, pp. 5, 134 and 179–85.

[95] *Ibid.*, p. 8.

[96] J.M. Montias, 'Works of art in seventeenth century Amsterdam', in *Art in history: history in art*, eds D. Freedberg and J. de Vries (Santa Monica, 1991).

[97] M.S. Robinson, *The paintings of the Willem van de Veldes* (London, 1990), pp. xvi and xx.

[98] Lambert, *Seapower states*, p. 275; D. Ormrod, 'The origins of the London art market, 1660–1730', in *Art markets in Europe, 1400–1800*, eds M. North and D. Ormrod (Aldershot, 1998), p. 172; D. Ormrod, Cultural production and import-substitution. The fine and decorative arts in London, 1660–1730', in *Urban achievement in early modern Europe. Golden ages in Antwerp, Amsterdam and London*, ed. P.K. O'Brien (Cambridge, 2001), pp. 210–30.

Table 1.2 Subject categories of paintings
in Amsterdam private inventories (percentages)

Subject	1620–49	1650–79
Landscapes	20.5	25.4
History and Religious	28.7	14.4
Portraits	12.9	14.8
Still lifes	7.8	8.9
Genre	7.3	8.5
Seascapes	4.3	6.0
Allegories	1.4	1.1
Miscellaneous	4.6	4.4
Untitled	12.4	16.5

Source: Montias, 'Works of art', table 2, pp. 350-1

arsenal of seapower.'[99] The sea is perceived, ahistorically, as the handmaiden of freedom, presenting an endless challenge to territorial states with their tendencies towards repression and reactionary aristocratic governance. Elements of the paradigm can indeed be traced in the internal politics of England and the Dutch provinces in our period, in the interplay of landed and mercantile interests. But the uniformly 'progressive' impact of the Dutch and English commercial empires, capable of deploying coercion and violence on a global scale by the mid-seventeenth century, cannot be taken seriously in the light of the intensity of Anglo-Dutch conflict described in these essays. Aside from interstate conflict between the two nations, both conducted 'almost continuous low-intensity warfare on the "periphery"', with scant regard for the rights of indigenous peoples, when not collaborating in the development and protection of the transatlantic slave trade.[100] For more than a century and a half, England's 'seapower status' was nurtured under the umbrella of the Navigation Acts and a constantly rising barrier of mercantilist regulation and protection, representing the antithesis of liberal values.[101]

To some extent, the inadequacy of the 'seapower' paradigm lies in its overemphasis on the purely naval aspect of the fiscal-naval state. It became evident by the Second Anglo-Dutch War that naval hegemony would be secured not primarily by victories at sea but by successive governments' success in revenue-raising. The escalating costs of naval warfare arose less

[99] Lambert, *Seapower states*, p. 8.
[100] Pepijn Brandon, *War, capital, and the Dutch state, 1588–1795* (Leiden, 2015), pp. 4–5; and the essays by Martine van Ittersum and Jaap Jacobs in this volume.
[101] Ormrod, *Commercial empires*, chapters 10 and 11.

from the expense of developing more effective warships and guns than from the need for sustained public investment in onshore infrastructure of ports and coastal defences, dockyards, bureaucratic organisation, manpower requirements and professional command structures.[102] In both countries, private entrepreneurs supported the state's commitments via substantial investment in merchant shipping and brokerage arrangements facilitating networks of naval supply. As Brandon has shown, it was not so much the distinction between Dutch federal administration and England's more centralised system that produced results, but the fact that these were societies in which capitalism had attained more developed forms, so that 'bureaucrats and capitalists interacted on a much more equal footing' than was the case in Habsburg Spain or Bourbon France.[103]

This returns us to the entanglement of histories of capitalism with those of nation states and empires, the large issue raised at the start of this introductory essay. As Arrighi showed, the Anglo-Dutch moment of conflict and its subsequent resolution occupied a period of transition between the Dutch and British cycles of capital accumulation. It occurred during the downswing or B-phase of the European world economy when nation states chose to expand their navies to both withstand and advance mercantilist strategies.[104] After 1689, however, a significant divergence of naval expenditure occurred between the two nations: English outlays had soared to roughly eight times the Dutch level by 1700.[105] This enabled Dutch traders to become free-riders in securing naval protection from their British allies, and surplus capital was increasingly diverted into extending sovereign debt, plantation loans, and the commodity trades of neighbouring states.[106] Amsterdam retained its financial pre-eminence for several decades, and the years from the 1690s to the 1730s were characterised by a diffusion and sharing of entrepot functions with London and Hamburg.[107] At the same time, newly-united Britain pursued increasingly territorial ambitions, taking on the position of an imperial state prepared to wage war in pursuit of national interests, particularly commercial interests.

In these ways, the North Sea economy emerged as the maritime core which led Europe towards 'a plateau of possibilities for precocious industrialisation'

---

[102] P.K. O'Brien and X. Duran, 'Total factor productivity for the Royal Navy from victory at Texel (1653) to triumph at Trafalgar (1805)', in *Shipping and economic growth, 1350–1850*, ed. R.W. Unger (Leiden, 2011), pp. 279–80 and 302; and the essay by Ann Coats and Alan Lemmers in this volume.
[103] Brandon, *War, capital, and the Dutch state*, p. 311.
[104] See above, Table 1.2.
[105] See the essay by Richard Blakemore and Pepijn Brandon in this volume.
[106] Brandon, *War, capital, and the Dutch state*, pp. 316–17.
[107] Ormrod, *Commercial empires*, p. 337; J.A. Faber, 'Structural changes in the European economy during the eighteenth century as reflected in the Baltic trade', in *From Dunkirk to Danzig. Shipping and trade in the North Sea and the Baltic, 1350–1850*, eds W.G. Heeres, L.M.B.J. Hesp and L. Noordegraaf (Hilversum, 1988), pp. 92–3.

during the long upswing of the eighteenth century.[108] The first industrial revolution, we would emphasise, took place within a European zone larger than England, and is best understood as the outcome of policies designed to promote multilateral trade, shipping and commercial services. As O'Brien and Duran have argued, such a narrative 'makes more plausible sense than representation of the outcome as the paradigm case for parliamentary governance, liberty, democracy and private enterprise'.[109]

[108] O'Brien and Duran, 'Total factor productivity', p. 306.
[109] *Ibid.*, p. 307; Ormrod, *Commercial empires*, p. xiii.

II

War in the North Sea

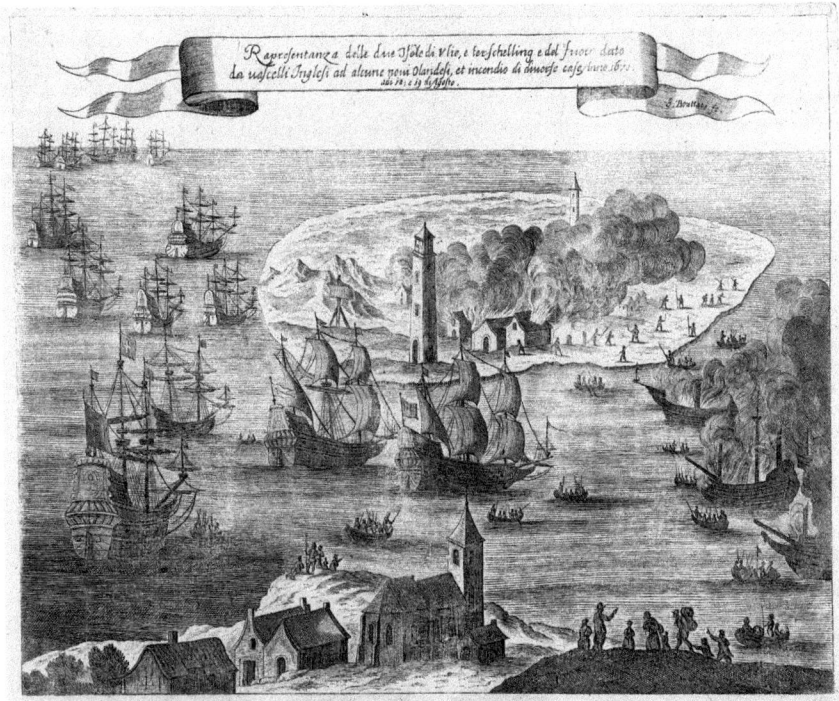

The burning of West-Terschelling in 1666, also known as Holmes's Bonfire.
Etching by Gaspar Bouttatts, 1666. Source: Rijksmuseum (Amsterdam),
RP-P-1908-2092

2

The seventeenth-century Anglo-Dutch Wars in a European context

Gijs Rommelse and Roger Downing[1]

War in the early modern period was endemic; in the entire seventeenth century there were only three years without conflicts between European states.[2] Though some were large-scale conflicts involving several countries, the overwhelming majority were regional, bilateral or internal affairs. These were reported in diplomatic correspondence and in the news media of the period but, as strategic interests of others were little affected, did not receive wide interest. Exceptional in this context were the three primarily sea wars fought between England and the Dutch Republic in the mid-seventeenth century. For a number of reasons, these conflicts were followed with the keenest interest over a wide area. Nevertheless, historians have traditionally tended to take a bilateral viewpoint in their treatment of these wars. This approach overlooks the fact that hostilities between two of the most important economic and maritime powers in Europe could not but have far-reaching consequences, not only for the belligerents' neighbours and close allies, like France, Denmark, Munster and Cologne, but also for the European continent as a whole.[3]

In this contribution the Anglo-Dutch Wars are considered from a Europe-wide perspective. From the beginning of the early modern period the nations of Europe increasingly formed a recognizable economic, political and diplomatic system. One of the most significant drivers for its formation

---

[1] Intending to base this article on a significant number of relevant and representative primary sources, while doing justice to Europe's wide political and linguistic diversity, we have asked a perhaps unusually large number of colleagues for advice and materials. We gratefully acknowledge the help we received from Fadilah Arassi, Michael Clemmesen, Brian L. Davies, Lars Ericson Wolke, Carol Hagen, Alistair Malcolm, Leos Müller, Susana Münch Miranda, Steve Murdoch, Hielke van Nieuwenhuizen, Merlijn Olnon, Luciano Pezzolo, Magnus Ressel, Yolanda Rodriguez Perez, Robert Rowlinson, João Paulo Salvado, Arcadio and Francesco Siciliano, Christopher Storrs, Constantinis Theodoridis and Enrico Zucchi.

[2] G. Parker, *Global crisis: war, climate change and catastrophe in the seventeenth century*, abr. and rev. edn (New Haven and London, 2017), p. 24.

[3] A notable exception is C.E. Levillain, *Vaincre Louis XIV: Angleterre – Hollande – France. Histoire d'une relation triangulaire* (Champ Vallon, 2010).

was the steady expansion, throughout the late Middle Ages and the early modern period, of water-borne commerce. The intensity and volume, and the diversity of the traded merchandise grew spectacularly, while markets and production areas became closely connected in complex distribution networks. These developments in turn required services such as the provision of credit, insurance and trading in securities. City authorities were pleased to encourage these and also to authorize facilities for the minting of specie. National governments also saw the necessity of reacting to these economic developments by regulating and protecting shipping and commerce, at the same time introducing new taxes that were designed to tap into the growing monetary economy. Ambitious merchants established international companies with offices, agents and partners in various European countries. To enable them to anticipate fluctuations in supply and demand, they employed correspondents to provide regular news updates. The Anglo-Dutch Wars, fought primarily in the English Channel and in the North Sea, practically severed the maritime connection between the northern European and the Mediterranean markets. Moreover, they involved two of the most prominent carrier nations. By disrupting the flow of goods throughout Europe and thus affecting fiscal positions, the Anglo-Dutch Wars were bound to attract a significant deal of international interest and invite both governments as well as individuals to consider the strategic implications and to react accordingly.

In analysing the importance of the Anglo-Dutch Wars for the European system, this essay begins by describing the way diplomats functioned as collectors and dispersers of international news and strategic evaluations. They gathered information about the causes and conduct of the wars and frequently provided their own analyses of its consequences. Attention then shifts to the recipients of their letters, the politicians and government advisors involved in foreign politics. The intention is to show how the causes, the conduct and the consequences of the wars were interpreted internationally, and also how these perceptions may have been influenced by English and Dutch government communications and commercial media. The strategic alternatives following from these perceptions are summarized: what dangers and chances did the Anglo-Dutch Wars present to third states and their citizens, and what choices were made to avert these risks or seize upon these opportunities? Finally, the lasting impact of the wars on the European culture of naval warfare is discussed. Their legacy, it will be argued, comprised new models for both naval strategy and tactics, while warship construction underwent revolutionary change.

Diplomatic communication and news gathering

The sixteenth century saw the beginnings of the modern European system of resident diplomatic representation by ambassadors, envoys, residents, consuls and agents. States dispatched individual diplomats or larger embassies on *ad hoc* missions to negotiate alliances or peace treaties. Permanent diplomatic representation in the political centres of other countries also gradually became the custom. This increasingly came to consist of career-diplomats. Pragmatic reciprocity, and the principle that the highest-ranked diplomats were the manifestations of the sovereign powers that dispatched them, brought about the notion of diplomatic immunity. The formal communication between states was conducted by ambassadors, residents and envoys, who generally were also expected to keep their home base informed of political, social and economic developments in the country to which they were assigned.[4]

The Anglo-Dutch Wars generated an intensive correspondence among the envoys of this relatively compact state-system. This was facilitated by fairly well developed lines of communication by road and by water and established postal and courier services. These enabled the diplomats of England and the Dutch Republic to maintain contact with their masters in London and The Hague, employing the packet boat service via Dover. This was not confined to the interbellum periods; at that time, agents tended to remain at their posts for a period, even after the outbreak of hostilities. But more relevant for this chapter, the Anglo-Dutch Wars attracted the interest of the diplomatic networks of many of the other European states. The Swedish envoy Harald Appelboom and the Dane Martinus Tancken, both stationed in The Hague, wrote many letters to their respective governments concerning Anglo-Dutch relations and the conduct and course of the wars. Through their *depêches* and *relazioni*, the Venetian diplomats Lorenzo Paulucci and Alvise Sagredo, based in London and Paris respectively, performed the same service.[5]

Diplomats had various ways of obtaining information. They and their staff members engaged in informal conversations with other diplomats, government officials, courtiers and military officers, in the hope of drawing out items of news, gossip or even state secrets. Sometimes bribes were paid to clerks or other functionaries, while it could also be advantageous to barter with items of information they had received from their own governments. Frequently, the boundary between legitimate news-gathering and downright spying was blurred. In The Hague, the Friesland-born diplomat and historian Lieuwe van Aitzema functioned as the formal representative for the Hanseatic League, while simultaneously using his extensive network to act as paid informer to the Secretary of the English Council of State, John Thurloe. Another minor diplomat and historian, Abraham de Wicquefort, likewise acted as informant to Thurloe's

---

[4] M.S. Anderson, *The rise of modern diplomacy 1450–1919* (London and New York, 1993), pp. viii–x and 149–57; J. Black, *A history of diplomacy* (London, 2010), pp. 59–66.

[5] T. Blanning, *The pursuit of glory. Europe 1648–1815* (London, 2007), pp. 3–39; E. John B. Allen, *Post and courier service in the diplomacy of early modern Europe* (The Hague, 1972), pp. 1–21; P.J. Blok (ed.), *Relazioni veneziane: Venetiaansche berichten over de Verenigde Nederlanden van 1600–1795* (The Hague, 1909), pp. 287–313.

successor, Joseph Williamson, and was also in the pay of others, including the Danish and Swedish sovereigns.[6] Lastly, diplomats benefited from the public press, in the form of newsletters, corantos and pamphlets. The first newspapers appeared in the early years of the seventeenth century, their rapid spread made possible by the contemporary expansion of the postal and courier networks.[7]

In addition to the reports sent by ambassadors, residents and envoys to their sovereign princes and their ministers, they also briefed their colleagues in other capital cities. Political developments in the host country formed their primary concern. They conscientiously reported on significant decisions, current negotiations, partisan struggles, dynastic schemes, religious debates, and rivalries between ambitious courtiers. Of particular importance, and therefore closely followed, were the host country's foreign policy and relations. Aiming to provide a comprehensive picture, they also wrote regarding fiscal developments and the state of the economy. Many of their missives contained detailed information about arriving ships, successful or failed investments, the complaints of merchants, food prices and employment. Some diplomats and news sellers did not restrict themselves to providing factual information; they also provided comprehensive analyses of domestic power shifts, international affairs and the ways by which the strategic interests of their own state or those of its clients were affected or could be promoted. There was thus a considerable body of experience on which diplomats could draw for the monitoring, from a wide variety of European perspectives, of the Anglo-Dutch Wars of the seventeenth century.

Foreign perceptions of causes and responsibility

How, then, did rulers and politicians come to perceive the Anglo-Dutch Wars, their deeper roots, the moral responsibility for their outbreak, and their conduct? Remarkable as it may seem, there are only a few primary sources that shed a direct light on the perspectives of other European rulers and

---

[6] De Wicquefort to Christina of Sweden, 5 June 1652, in H.T. Colenbrander (ed.), *Bescheiden uit vreemde archieven omtrent de groote Nederlansche zeeoorlogen* (2 vols, The Hague, 1919) [hereafter: *Bescheiden*], I, 1–2; De Wicquefort to Frederick III of Denmark, 22 December 1653, in *ibid.*, I, 123; R. Downing and G. Rommelse, *A fearful gentleman, Sir George Downing in The Hague 1658–1672* (Hilversum, 2011), pp. 47–51; G. van der Plaat, *Eendracht als opdracht, Lieuwe van Aitzema's bijdrage aan het publieke debat in de zeventiende-eeuwse Republiek* (Hilversum, 2003), pp. 29–61 and 85–118; A. Marshall, *Intelligence and espionage in the reign of Charles II, 1660–1685* (Cambridge, 1994), pp. 78–95.

[7] J. Raymond and N. Moxham, 'News networks in early modern Europe', in *News networks in early modern Europe*, ed. J. Raymond and N. Moxham (Leiden and Boston, 2016), pp. 1–16; N. Schobesberger, P. Arblaster, M. Infelise, A. Belo, N. Moxham, C. Espejo and Joad R. Schobesberger *et al.*, 'European postal networks', in *ibid.*, pp. 10–63; B. Dooley, 'International news flows in the seventeenth century: problems and prospects', in *ibid.*, pp. 158–77.

politicians. More often, the historian has to make do with indirect evidence, such as specific diplomatic courtesies shown to only one of the belligerents, sudden strategically motivated *renversements* of alliances, the preferential treatment of either Dutch or English merchants and seamen, or diplomatic initiatives undertaken to bring an end to the conflict. These strategic reactions are dealt with in later sections; the present section focuses on the scanty sources from which perceptions of causes and responsibility can be derived.

The Anglo-Dutch Wars were generally seen by neutrals as maritime conflicts. Unlike nearly all other contemporary conflicts, they were fought almost entirely at sea and were believed to revolve around maritime commerce. In January 1652, for example, Giovanni Ambrosio Sarotti, the Venetian resident in Florence, reported that the Duke of Tuscany had stressed that:

> the objects and ideas of these [Dutch] captains, which amount to interrupting the ancient flow of the Levant trade, which the Dutch are persuaded they can take away from the English by combating them in these waters, where the two nations have at stake only ships, not dominions.[8]

Thirteen years later, in March 1665, the Venetian ambassador in Paris, Alvise Sagredo, informed the Doge and Senate that the Dutch were at that stage unlikely to give in to English demands, because they would

> be submitting to a too disadvantageous loss, with respect to what the others wish to exact, while if they resist they place themselves in the obvious necessity of moderating if not abandoning a large measure of that sustenance which in every account depends on liberty of trade, with navigation, so one or more combats will have to decide who will have the worse or the better of it.[9]

Commercial strife, however, was not the only reason. Naval dominance, though obviously intertwined with maritime economic interests, was deemed equally important as a cause. In June 1653, for example, Queen Christina of Sweden received word from her representative in London that

> both parties seem uninterested in your mediation, let them have war since they care not for peace. Both states and nations, but this one in particular, are intolerably arrogant, and it is very well possible that God will break their pride.[10]

It is obvious that the haughtiness displayed by both the English and the Dutch was an expression of their self-confidence as great naval powers, while

---

[8] Giovanni Ambrosia Sarotti to the Doge and Senate, Florence, 11 January 1653, in A.B. Hinds (ed.), *Calendar of state papers Venetian* (London, 1929) [hereafter: *CSPV*], XXIX, 8.

[9] Alvise Sagredo to the Doge and Senate, Paris, 13 March 1665, in *CSPV*, XXXIV, 138.

[10] Count Israel Lagerfeldt to Christina of Sweden, 6 June 1653, in *Bescheiden*, I, 53–4.

their military rivalry at sea, at least in Swedish eyes, could be considered a cause in itself.

The Second and Third Anglo-Dutch Wars were also perceived to have been brought about by the obvious ideological contrast between a republic and a monarchy. Sagredo informed his political masters back in Venice that the position of King Charles II had been much strengthened because the imminent war had caused the politico-cultural rift between England's monarchy and the radically republican regime of John de Witt to widen. Charles had always cultivated the old Anglo-Dutch Protestant connection, for what purposes Sagredo did not mention in his letter, but it now seemed much more opportune to the king to exploit the rift:

> It is therefore generally believed that King Charles will raise his preten-
> sions in proportion to his expenditure and that the justice of his claims
> will be extended to a demand for reparations for all that the Dutch have
> done beyond the line. […] Moreover King Charles, who has always shown
> himself reluctant to break with a power so friendly and of the same religion,
> is not sorry to see that Parliament has spontaneously put such power into
> his hands, with which he arrives at establishing himself upon the throne
> and with its pristine authority.[11]

While Admiral Maarten Tromp has historically been credited for initiating the actual outbreak of the First Anglo-Dutch War, most neutral contemporary observers seem to have been convinced that England was the aggressor in all three cases, even though the English cause may have been justified. In 1665, Sagredo commented that

> the English, strong and vindictive above all others, without the smallest
> imaginable fear of being invaded in their own country, abounding in every-
> thing that serves for the use and delight of man, are pertinaciously resolved
> to settle this point.[12]

And a letter written in June 1672, by the Danish representative in London, Marcus Gjøe Falcksen, to King Christian V, clearly indicated that the third war had been planned in advance by King Charles II, in conjunction with his cousin Louis XIV of France:

> While they [the Dutch] can hardly boast of victory … If one considers the
> whole situation, one may say that they have gained some advantage in as
> much as the king of England must begin again. His plans have been set back
> and obstructed to the great profit of the king of France and his interests.[13]

---

[11] Alvise Sagredo to the Doge and Senate, Paris, 13 March 1665, in *CSPV*, XXXIV, 138.
[12] *Ibid.*
[13] Cited in H.A. Hansen, 'Opening phase of the Third Dutch War described by the Danish envoy in London, March – June 1672', *The Journal of Modern History* 21:2 (1949), 97–108.

Whether or not neutral politicians passed moral judgements regarding the respective roles in the outbreak of the wars, they do not seem to have committed their thoughts to paper. The gradual or rapid deterioration in Anglo-Dutch relations was usually meticulously reported and analysed in objective terms, without showing bias or sympathy. War in itself was deemed tragic because of the loss of human lives. Count Israel Lagerfeldt, Queen Christina's envoy in London, remarked in his letter that 'Your Majesty disapproves of the spilling of Christian blood.'[14] This Swedish concern probably stemmed from the notion that divisions within the Protestant world were unnatural. Testimony to this idea also was the eagerness displayed by the Swiss Cantons to offer their mediation between the two Protestant states. According to the Venetian secretary in Zürich, Gironimo Giavarina,

> The Evangelical Cantons are deeply concerned over the differences and hostilities which are taking place between the republics of Holland and England. Perceiving that the letters they wrote some while ago to both parties urging peace and union have done little good they have decided to make a fresh effort to secure this result and at the same time to win for themselves, if possible, the honour of mediation. Accordingly they have sent to England in their common name, an individual of Sciafusa, of considerable experience, with instructions to present himself to parliament to persuade peace and to learn their will, and then, in conformity therewith, he is to proceed to Holland; in short he is to do his utmost to secure so great a boon.[15]

Most politicians, however, seem not to have acted on this notion of Christian (or Protestant) solidarity; it appears that, to them, war was an entirely natural and acceptable tool the state could choose to employ to serve its interests.

Interestingly, both the Dutch and the English governments, as well as their diplomatic and military representatives abroad, attempted to influence foreign perceptions of the causes and course of the wars. During times of rising tension, both states produced extensive memoranda to justify their positions. Formally presented as diplomatic pleas or complaints, these usually contained long, heavily biased historic overviews of mutual relations. Historical partnerships, cooperation and hostilities were selectively presented in order to 'prove' the righteousness of the claims of the one, or the unjustness of the 'pretentions' of the other. These documents were drafted in Latin or French for presentation to the authorities in London or The Hague. Their real purpose, it seems, was not the submission of the opponent, but to gain the support of the neutral observer or to at least visibly to have laid claim to the moral high ground.

---

[14] Count Israel Lagerfeldt to Christina of Sweden, 6 June 1653, in *Bescheiden*, I, 53–4.
[15] Gironimo Giavarina to the Doge and Senate, Zurich, 19 April 1653, in *CSPV*, XXIX, 81.

Figure 2.1 The Battle of Bergen, on 12 August 1665. The role the Danish/ Norwegian coastal batteries played in the repelling of the English attack is emphasized bottom right. Interestingly, the etching's Italian title, *Atacco Fatto dalli vasccelli Inglesi a quelli de gli Olandesi nel porto di Berge in Norvegia il di 12 di Agosto 1665*, suggests the artist Arnold Bloem aimed to target an international public. Source: Rijksmuseum (Amsterdam), RP-P-BI-1241.

Sometimes these memoranda were directly translated into other languages for the convenience of a neutral readership, but more often they were converted into shorter pamphlets which were then translated.[16] Once the war had commenced, in the Republic the States General would facilitate the publication of allegedly objective accounts of armed encounters. These invariably emphasized the decisive character of Dutch victories or downplayed their setbacks.[17]

The historian cannot possibly assess the impact of this media strategy, but the propagandist publications did not fail to reach their intended political readership. Testimony to this is a report by Lorenzo Paulluci, the Venetian envoy in London:

---

[16] See for example: *Frantzösische Tyrannen, das ist: Umstandlich Wahrhaffte Erzehlung, der unmenschlichen Grausamkeiten, so durch die Franzosen in denen Niederlanden seit hero verübet worden* (1674); *Gespräch über das Interesse des Englischen Staats* (1674).

[17] See for example: *Relatione della battaglia seguita frà l'armate Olandese, & Inglese, a vista del Porto Di Livorno* (Livorno, 1653).

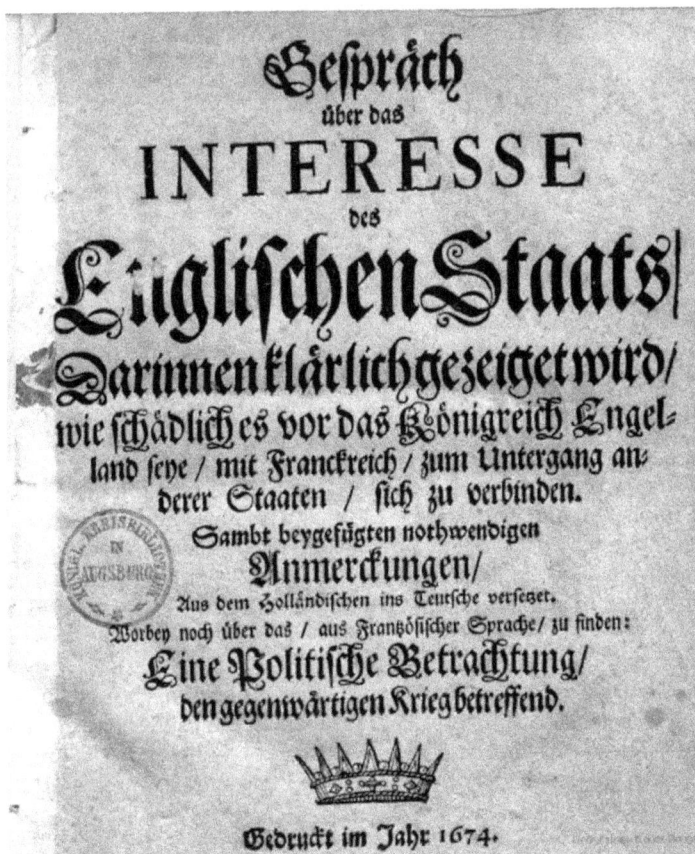

Figure 2.2 *Gespräch über das Interesse des Englischen Staats* (1674).
Source: Google Books.

To add to the extreme animosity [...] the Dutch manifesto has lately appeared here. The enemy shows the weakness of the arguments employed by this side [...]. It accuses the English government of injustice and violence and asserts that after having suffered and done much for a mutual good understanding, Holland had been obliged to take up arms in defence of her own rights and those of her subjects, which had been unjustly attacked by the forces of this Commonwealth. [...] The Dutch also accuse the English of making reprisals while negotiations were in progress, thus proving the evil intentions which compelled the States to repel force by force. They rely on the Almighty and all secular powers admitting the justice of their cause, especially as their object is to check the pernicious designs of the English government, which after wounding Holland in their most vital interests, namely commerce, will treat all other powers in the same way.

45

Figure 2.3 The Battle of Livorno, on 14 March 1653, as seen from the port quay. The monument on the lower left, adorned with the Dutch flag, carries the inscription *'Bataglia secuita tra li vaseli olandesi e inglesi il di 14 Marzo 1653'*. It was previously attributed to Johannes Lingelbach (1622–74). Source: Rijksmuseum (Amsterdam), inv. no. SK-A-1391. 114 x 216 cm, oil on canvas.

So the United Provinces have taken this serious step for the general good as well as for their own liberty, because they will not suffer any longer the wrongs inflicted by their evil neighbours, and relying upon the justice of their cause they anticipate the help of God and man towards ensuring a glorious result.[18]

Both sides also employed theatrical means to emphasize the justness of their respective causes. On 15 July 1665, for example, the ships of an English squadron, at anchor off Livorno, fired their guns in celebration of the English victory during the Battle of Lowestoft. The English 'nation' in the Tuscan town also celebrated ecstatically, staging a bonfire in the central plaza. The central figure in these celebrations was ambassador Sir John Finch. Two years later the tables were turned, when the 'Flemish nation', as Finch referred to the Dutch merchant community in Livorno, organized similar festivities to milk the spectacular Raid on the Medway for publicity. Furious at the local porters and stevedores who joined in these celebrations, mocking the English sailors and traders, Finch issued a formal complaint to the Ducal Court, demanding that impartiality should be more strictly observed or enforced.[19]

---

[18] Lorenzo Paulucci to Giovanni Sagredo, London, 19 September 1652, in *CSPV*, XXVIII, 662.

[19] Constantine Theodoritis, 'Anglo-Tuscan relations and the public sphere of Livorno during the Second Anglo-Dutch War (1665–1667)' (unpublished research paper, Princeton University, 2018), pp. 1–15.

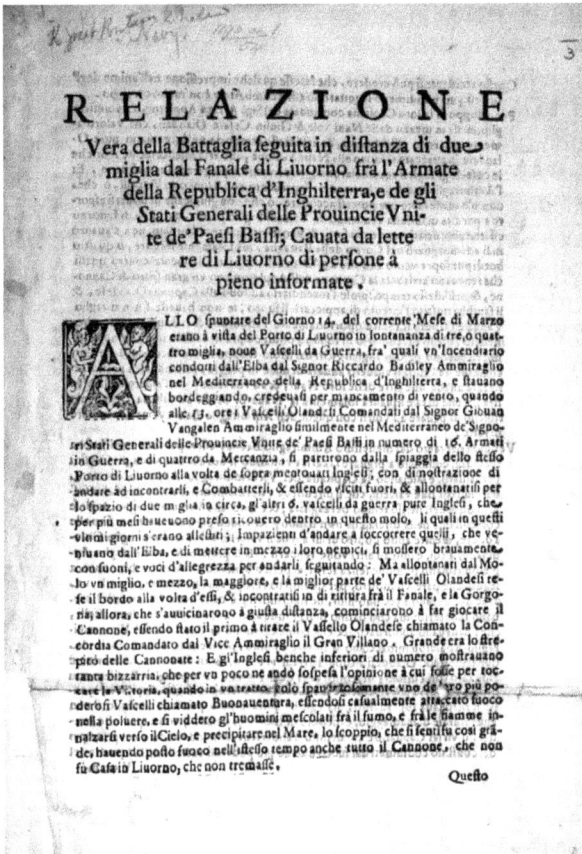

Figure 2.4 *Relatione della battaglia seguita frà l'Armate Olandese, & Inglese, a vista del porto di Livorno* (Livorno 1653). Source: Google Books.

Strategic interests at stake

In the consideration of and reactions to the Anglo-Dutch Wars by European princes and statesmen, the key word is *interest*. Matters that influenced their thinking and their reactions included the preservation of the integrity of their territory and, if possible, its expansion. They sought the consolidation and if possible the increase of their own authority, with which went the need to secure and extend their state's financial and other sources of power. The ostentatious protection of their subjects' own welfare, financial, civic and juridical, formed also an essential component of their interest.

Many European countries became involved in the conflicts. In the first, which was the most entirely a sea war, the effects on other countries were largely indirect, as trading patterns became dislocated, or when their merchant ships fell victim to privateers in the *guerre de course*. The subsequent wars involved states more directly, as allies of one of the belligerents, but also indirectly, when free passage of troops through their territory was negotiated or demanded. In the second war, the Bishop of Munster, Bernhard von Galen, who had a long-running dispute with the Republic concerning the territory of Borculo on the Republic's eastern border, agreed in return for a substantial subsidy to mount a land attack to support the English war at sea. This, however, triggered the participation of France, which in 1662 had concluded a defensive alliance with the Republic. It enabled Louis XIV to fulfil, by having his forces drive the bishop's back across the border, his obligation to the Republic, without needing to confront England at sea and hazarding the ships of his new battle fleet, or provoking Charles II to opposition of his plans for the annexation of the Spanish Netherlands. These he was able to put into effect, following the end of the conflict, in his War of Devolution of 1667.[20]

This represented the first serious act of aggression of Louis XIV, subsequent manifestations of which would affect much of western and central Europe. One who early saw its implications was the Viennese diplomat Baron François Paul de Lisola, who had carried out a number of diplomatic missions in Europe for Emperor Leopold I. Lisola's pamphlet *Bouclier d'Estat et de Justice*, published in England as the *Buckler of State and Justice*, was designed to call attention to Louis's ambitions. It further set out to deny the validity of Louis's claims in the Spanish Netherlands on the basis of his wife's supposed inheritance rights. Lisola saw it as his task to summon the European powers to resist France's assertiveness. The English Secretary of State, Lord Arlington, caused the pamphlet to be translated and published and it was widely read.[21]

It did not take long for the new mood of apprehension of France's growing power to cause the recent belligerents jointly to acknowledge the new danger. Parliament and the English diplomat Sir William Temple negotiated a new Anglo-Dutch treaty, which Sweden proved willing to join, resulting in the Triple Alliance of January 1668.[22] For Louis, this was nothing less than betrayal by the Republic, to which he had faithfully discharged his treaty obligations during the recent war, and he sought an opportunity to break the Alliance at the earliest opportunity. His cousin Charles was smarting from the humiliation of the destruction by the Dutch of a large part of his fleet at Chatham in the closing phase of the second war. Perennially short of money,

---

[20] G. Rommelse, *The Second Anglo-Dutch War (1665–1667). International raison d'état, mercantilism and maritime strife* (Hilversum, 2006), pp. 123–94.

[21] François Paul de Lisola, *Bouclier d'estat et de justice, contre le dessein manifestement decouvert de la monarchie universelle, sous le vain pretexte des pretentions de la reyne de France* (1667); *Buckler of state and justice against the design manifestly discovered of the universal monarchy* (London, 1667); T. Claydon, *Europe and the making of England, 1660–1760* (Cambridge, 2007), pp. 155–7; Levillain, *Vaincre Louis XIV*, pp. 203–6.

[22] K.H.D. Haley, *An English diplomat in the Low Countries. Sir William Temple and John de Witt, 1665–1672* (Oxford, 1986), pp. 142–82.

he proved receptive, in return for a substantial subsidy, to undertake together to settle with the United Provinces once and for all. In the secret Treaty of Dover of 1670 they planned the reduction, in a joint sea and land attack, of the Republic to a puppet state ruled by Charles's nephew, William III of Orange. Lisola's warnings proved accurate in 1672, as the Third Anglo-Dutch War commenced with a joint Anglo-French attack aimed at the dismemberment of the country and the installation of William as puppet king.[23]

Neighbouring territories became involved as Louis sought the cooperation of German states such as Cologne and Munster in permitting free passage of his troops in his land attack on the Republic from the south. Following the reduction of a large part of the country, Louis's attack was checked by the flooding of the country's water defences. Lisola's energetic diplomacy enabled alliances to be concluded between the Dutch, the Empire, Spain and Brandenburg. These latter proved willing to field armies to force the French to abandon their campaign in 1674, while planned Anglo-French cooperative actions at sea failed miserably. A pamphlet, *England's Appeal*, in which the 'incomparable' *Buckler* was cited, awakened public opinion to the inadvisability of being yoked to France in a conflict with the Republic. It proved influential in causing Parliament to bring pressure to bear on the Crown to conclude the war, with no significant gains for Charles.[24] After 1674, *Stadhouder* William III dedicated himself to opposing, in the spirit of Lisola's pamphlet, France's designs. As King William III of England, following the Glorious Revolution of 1688, he would go on to lead the Grand Alliance of European powers until Louis's aggrandisement was checked by the Peace of Rijswijk in 1697.[25]

The conflicts had effects, both political and economic, on regions far removed from the theatres of war, such as the Baltic states. In the second war, the Danes, who had long-running financial obligations to their ally, the Republic, sought to evade these by seeking to ingratiate themselves with England. An attempt to assist the English in the capture of a returning Dutch East Indies merchant fleet, when it sought shelter in the port of Bergen in (Danish) Norway, failed when the Dutch commander occupied the shore batteries and turned the guns on the Earl of Sandwich's English fleet. Sweden, allied to England since its cultivation by Cromwell as a valuable Protestant

---

[23] P. Sonnino, *Louis XIV and the origins of the Dutch War* (Cambridge, 1988); J.R. Jones, *The Anglo-Dutch Wars of the seventeenth century* (New York, 1996), pp. 179–216.

[24] W. Troost, '"To restore and preserve the liberty of Europe". William III's ideas on foreign policy', in *Ideology and foreign policy in early modern Europe (1650–1750)*, ed. D. Onnekink and G. Rommelse (Farnham, 2011), pp. 283–303; Pierre de Moulin (attrib.), *England's appeal from the private cabal at White-Hall, to the great council of the nation, the Lords and Commons in Parliament assembled. By a true lover of his country* (London, 1673).

[25] K.H.D. Haley, *William of Orange and the English opposition 1672–1674* (Oxford, 1953), pp. 5, 52–3 and 88–111.

ally against the Catholic Habsburg powers, accepted a bribe from Louis XIV in return for remaining neutral during the second war. In the third war, Swedish neutrality was once again secured by a bribe.[26]

The Baltic countries were of vital importance, both politically and economically, to both England and the United Provinces, the dominant power in the trade of the region. All shipping from and bound for the west had to pass the narrow entrance formed by the Sound. At periods of tension caused by the periodic conflicts between the Baltic powers, there was always the danger of the closure of the Sound to naval and merchant shipping. In the Baltic as elsewhere, the Anglo-Dutch Wars led to a general depression in sea-borne commerce, as the transport of goods was held up by the uncertainty of a safe passage, while the necessity of convoying led to increased costs. The overall reduction in commercial activity led to a corresponding shrinking in the customs duties that were a major source of national income at the time, necessitating the introduction of new taxes.[27] The malaise is reflected in contemporary correspondence; the Danish resident in The Hague, Tancken, complained to his king that:

> This most unfortunate war at sea disturbs commerce everywhere. From many places and towns of the Baltic, word is received of large stocks of commodities of every kind, which cannot be sold or collected, because the Hollanders do not have the freedom of the seas. Even more do people complain that sorely needed goods cannot be obtained, while those available in abundance cannot be shipped, resulting in the stagnation of commerce and industry, here and in other parts of Europe, and also outside Europe.[28]

His Swedish colleague Harald Appelboom likewise kept his principals informed of the grave situation, though at the same time noting that 'England is able to survive the loss of their trade with the Republic owing to their ally status with Sweden, which gives them secure supplies of naval stores and maintenance materials.' He reported how

> the Dutch warships stationed in the Sound are well positioned to capture neutral ships bound for Flanders and carry them to Holland … they have the cooperation of their ally Denmark, eager to cooperate in any action that can disadvantage Swedish trade.[29]

---

[26] F. Goossens, 'Sweden and the Treaty of Breda in 1667 – Swedish diplomats help to end naval warfare between the Dutch Republic and England', *Forum Navale* 74 (2018), 54–80; Downing and Rommelse, *Fearful gentleman*, 60–8; H.H. Rowen, *John de Witt, Grand Pensionary of Holland, 1625–1675* (Princeton, 1978), pp. 772–8.

[27] Henri Huneken to the Council of Lübeck, 3 December 1672, in *Bescheiden*, II, 204; W. Veenstra and A. Otte, 'Financiering van de oorlogvoering te water. De Admiraliteit van Zeeland, 1597–1795', in *Overheidsfinanciën tijdens de Republiek en het Koninkrijk, 1600/1850*, ed. H. Boels (Hilversum, 2012), pp. 9–38.

[28] Martinus Tancken to Frederik III, 16 July 1653, in *Bescheiden*, I, 67–72.

[29] Harald Appelboom to Prince Karel Gustaf of Sweden, 7 July 1652, in *Bescheiden*, I, 2–5; Harald Appelboom to Oxenstierna, 21 October 1652, in *Bescheiden*, I, 29–30;

This situation proved only temporary, however; during the First Anglo-Dutch War both shores of the Sound belonged to Denmark, then allied with the Republic, whose diplomats succeeded in securing the closure by the Danes of the passage to English shipping, thereby choking off one of England's principal supply routes. Following the war, Denmark, at the request of the Dutch, was included in the Peace of Westminster that ended the war, while subsequently a Swedish diplomatic mission was dispatched to Cromwell's Protectorate for discussions on matters such as a new agreement on reciprocal trade privileges and the re-opening of the Sound.[30]

Producers and shippers described the subterfuges they were forced to employ in order to evade the attentions of potential marauders. Some sailed under false colours such as the flag of Hamburg.[31] Convoys from Holland bound for the Baltic region frequently chose to ship in small craft suitable for navigating the inshore route between the offshore Wadden Islands and the Dutch and German coasts. Following the confiscation by the English of the cargo of the master, one Thering, of a Swedish ship from Stockholm, a proclamation was issued in Göteborg requiring that all cargoes be inspected for items falling under English embargo before departure.[32]

An area that suffered extensive trade disruption and fluctuations of fortune in all three wars was the north German coast and the rivers Elbe and Weser. In the first conflict, Hamburg continued to trade with both England and the Republic, the closing of the Sound even resulting in an increase in English trade. In the second war, the Hamburg merchants' situation also temporarily improved, as they had been exempted from Charles II's 1660 Navigation Act. Convoying was necessary, although it did not succeed in preventing entirely the taking of English merchantmen by Dutch privateers. Bremen's trade was adversely affected by the first war and also by Denmark's war with Sweden, though benefiting in the third by succeeding in supplying both sides with military as well as domestic goods. In the second and third wars, Hamburg and Bremen also operated successfully as the European terminals of Scottish exporters of fish and salt, while Bremen ships were in high demand as neutral carriers.[33]

Harald Appelboom to Queen Christina of Sweden, 23 December 1652, in *Bescheiden*, I, 35–7.

[30] P. Geyl, *Orange and Stuart* (London, 2001), pp. 92–6; M. Roberts (ed.), *Swedish diplomats at Cromwell's court, 1655–1656. The missions of Peter Julius Coyer and Christer Bonde* (London, 1988), pp. 295–301.

[31] E. Baasch, 'Hamburg und Holland im 17. und 18. Jahrhundert', *Hansische Geschichtsblätter* 16 (1910), 45–102.

[32] J. Israel, *Dutch primacy in world trade, 1585–1740* (Oxford, 1989), p. 276; Riksarkivet (Stockholm), E 381: Fran enskilda, 1651–54, Skrifvelser till Gen. Guvernoren Hertig Adolf Johan, 23 July 1652.

[33] K. Zickermann, *Across the German Sea. Early modern Scottish connections with the wider Elbe-Weser region* (Leiden and Boston, 2013).

The intricate relations, bi- and tri-lateral, between England, the Republic, France, Spain and Portugal made it inevitable that the effects of the Anglo-Dutch Wars would be felt, if only indirectly, in the Iberian Peninsula also. War between France and Spain had been concluded with the Peace of the Pyrenees in 1659. Cromwell's war with Spain, which had supported Charles II during his years in exile, ended with the king's Restoration in 1660. For each of the other countries, Portugal, allied with England since 1654, represented a complicating factor. The attempts by the Dutch to relieve Portugal of its remaining possessions in Southeast Asia, and to establish a sugar colony on the coast of Portuguese Brazil, had led to intermittent war between the Republic and Portugal from 1627. The ejection of the Dutch from Brazil had caused the war to flare up again in 1657. This carried the danger that the delicate relations between the Republic and England, at peace since 1654, would deteriorate again. Neither country could afford to become involved in ruinous hostilities again and so Cromwell's offer of mediation between The Hague and Portugal was accepted by De Witt. The English, however, were determined that a peace settlement would not have the result of granting the Dutch trading privileges as favourable to those granted to England in their own treaty with Portugal. A peace treaty acceptable to both was finally concluded in 1661, although implementation was delayed by disputes over the return of islands and property; during the Second Anglo-Dutch War the Dutch were accused of making the conflict an excuse for the delays.

The marriage of Charles II and the Portuguese Infanta Catarina de Braganza in 1662 enjoyed the approval of Louis XIV, who offered help with the financing of the troops to be supplied to Portugal as part of the nuptial settlement. The death of Cardinal Mazarin in 1661 and Louis's assumption of sole power had enabled him to further his aim of isolating Spain. For France, Portugal formed a convenient stick with which to beat the Spanish. Louis XIV hoped, following the death in 1665 of Spain's King Felipe IV, to take advantage of the minority of his feeble heir, Carlos II, to make his bid for the Spanish Netherlands. This he claimed, though it was in breach of the Peace of the Pyrenees, on behalf of the purported inheritance right of his wife, Maria Theresia, the daughter of Felipe's first wife. The distraction to Spain formed by Portugal's resistance to continuing Spanish incursions was welcome to Louis, who was determined to oppose any peace treaty offered to Portugal by Spain. The Portuguese attempted to profit from their temporary usefulness to France by demanding that the value of any help proffered by Louis should exceed that given in the past to Sweden and the Republic.[34] When, during the second war, France entered on the side of the

---

[34] E. Prestage, *The diplomatic relations of Portugal with France, England, and Holland from 1640 to 1668* (Watford, 1925), pp. 142–52 and 215–37.

Republic, thereby entering into war with England, despite their alliance of 1657, Portugal sought to mediate between them, but a proposed treaty was obstructed by both England and France. In 1668 peace was concluded between Spain and Portugal, while that between the Republic and Portugal was finally sealed in 1669, somewhat to the displeasure of the VOC, which would have preferred to continue to challenge the Portuguese for their remaining positions in Asia.[35]

The Mediterranean area saw major naval action only in the first war, with the Dutch victory in the Battle of Livorno of March 1653, which secured the Mediterranean for the Dutch for the rest of the war. The Venetian representative at Florence, Sarotti, wrote of 'the Dutch cruising in these waters for the purpose of attacking English ships'.[36] In the second also, the English were largely displaced by the Dutch. Tuscan trade experienced disruption, and reduced income from tariffs and customs duties. The Duke of Tuscany attempted to safeguard his interests by a policy of neutrality and to search for business opportunities elsewhere. In this he sought the advice of the English ambassador, Finch, regarding a plan for a London outlet for Tuscan manufactures. Although Finch was initially sceptical, the plan was supported by Secretary of State Arlington as a good-will gesture. In the third war, it was the turn of the Dutch to be displaced from the Mediterranean. Tangier, which had formed part of Catarina's dowry on her marriage to Charles II, proved its worth by becoming a well-used shelter for Mediterranean merchants and seemed likely to 'prove the richest port in these parts'.[37]

The Levant trade inevitably suffered during the wars, with exports of Dutch cloth to Turkey falling during the second and even more during the third war. The Ottoman Grand Vizier in Istanbul, Kara Mustafa, was a power to be reckoned with in the Mediterranean. Although not directly involved in hostilities, he was no friend to France and so it was the Republic, in the third war, that enjoyed the benevolence of his neutrality. During the previous conflicts, however, merchant ships of any nation were always liable to be impounded and pressed into service as transport vessels to supply the Turks during their twenty-two-year siege of Candia on Venetian Crete.[38]

---

35 *Ibid.*, pp. 40–98.
36 J.S. Corbett, *England in the Mediterranean, a study of the rise and influence of British power within the Straits, 1603–1713* (2 vols, London, 1904), I, 239–70; Giovanni Ambrosio Sarotti to the Doge and Senate, Florence, 17 August 1652, in *CSPV*, XXVIII, 651.
37 British National Archives (London), SP 98/6, 8 May 1666, fols. 355–6; SP 98/7, 26 October 1666, fol. 297; SP 98/8, 4 January 1667, fol. 390; Corbett, *England in the Mediterranean*, II, 63–82.
38 J. Israel, *Empire and entrepots: the Dutch, the Spanish monarchy and the Jews, 1585–1713* (London and Ronceverte, 1990), pp. 133–62; M. Olnon, 'A most agreeable and pleasant creature? Merzifonlu Kara Mustafa Pasain. The correspondence of Justinus Colyer (1668–1682)', *Oriente Moderno* 22:3 (2003), 649–69.

Naval legacy

The Anglo-Dutch Wars of the third quarter of the seventeenth century fundamentally altered the nature and scale of European naval warfare, as well as
the strategy and tactics employed. No attempt is made here to discuss this
naval dimension in depth – for this, the reader is referred to the contribution
by John Hattendorf in this volume – but the European perspective that this
essay seeks to cover would be incomplete without some brief exposition.

The battle fleets of both England and the Dutch Republic were far larger
than those of any other European power. In 1665, each numbered roughly two
and a half times the French and five times the Danish fleet.[39] International
power relations at sea formed part of the common knowledge base among
Europe's political and diplomatic elites. In June 1665, for example, the Danish
representative in The Hague, Petrus Charisius, wrote: 'finally the time and day
have arrived that all of Europe's potentates and republics have undoubtedly
anticipated for some time, [namely the collision] between the two most
considerable sea powers'.[40] Their two naval organizations, their strategies and
tactics inevitably became matters of intense interest to other powers.

Many European commentators argued that the scale, number and intensity
of the sea battles were the logical consequence of the symbiotic relationship
that existed between the maritime economies and naval capacities of England
and the Dutch Republic. Their sea power served to protect and expand
their economic interests, it was believed, while their commerce and fisheries
generated the financial means to support their great fleets. This symbiosis
enjoyed the intense admiration of Jean Baptiste Colbert, France's Minister of
Finance and, from 1669, also *Secrétaire d'État de la Marine*. Colbert had been
in charge of the navy since the early 1660s and had taken it upon himself to
make France a formidable sea power. He envisioned a great navy that could
help expand and defend France's maritime and colonial economy. It was clear
to him that very substantial investment would be required, but this would
ultimately be the key to a favourable trade balance and a strong treasury. A
powerful navy would, in addition, strengthen France's international standing
and his sovereign Louis XIV's *gloire*.[41]

In 1671, Colbert sent his own son on a tour through the Republic and
England to study every aspect of Dutch and English naval power. The information thus acquired formed the basis of two extensive and complementary

[39] J.B. Hattendorf, 'Navies, strategy and tactics in the age of De Ruyter', in *De Ruyter, Dutch admiral*, eds J.R. Bruijn, R. Prud'homme van Reine and R. van Hövell tot Westerflier (Rotterdam, 2011), p. 100; J. Glete, *Navies and nations. Warships, navies and state building in Europe and America, 1500–1860* (2 vols, Stockholm, 1993), I, 192–5.
[40] Charisius to Frederick III, 15 June 1665, in *Bescheiden*, I, 189–92.
[41] M. Vergé-Franceschi, *Colbert. La politique du bon sens* (Paris, 2003); B. Lutun, *La marine de Colbert. Études d'organisation* (Paris, 2003).

memoranda that served as an impulse for the French naval project. Putting naval power in its wider context, his point of departure in both pieces was the strategic context. It was precisely their understanding of the symbiotic relationship between economy and naval power, Colbert argued, that had allowed the Dutch to transform themselves from 'mere subjects of the King of Spain into one of the foremost powers at sea'.[42] In the English case, he was particularly interested in the political aspirations and glory derived from the strength of the Royal Navy:

> The English [...] claim superiority over all the states of Europe in the waters they refer to as the Narrow Seas [...]. They claim to be the sovereigns over those seas and require all those who sail there to lower their flags and offer the appropriate maritime salute.[43]

Colbert then continued meticulously to describe the Dutch and English naval organisations and officer corps, as well as their shipbuilding, logistical systems and recruitment practices. His long idealization and emulation of English and Dutch sea power also became apparent in 1676, after the spectacularly expanded French navy defeated a Dutch-Spanish force at the Battle of Augusta. Writing to the victorious commander, Vice-Admiral Abraham Duquesne, Colbert stated that 'His Majesty has at last had the satisfaction of seeing a victory against the Dutch, who up till now have always been superior at sea.'[44]

In eighteenth- and nineteenth-century European power politics, ownership of a strong battle fleet became the politico-cultural norm. States employed their fleets to safeguard or expand colonial empires, keep open the sea lanes of communication, fight pitched battles, and exert pressure on their opponents, whose economic assets could be threatened with destruction by blockades or amphibious raids. With European politics being approached and theorized in terms of the 'balance of power', governments routinely and suspiciously monitored construction programmes, and also tactical and technical innovations, being implemented in rival countries. The ownership of a strong and modern battle fleet was also often a matter of national pride. Strategic aims were derived from supposed national interests, while investments for construction, maintenance and operational expenses were explained or justified by appeals to 'the national identity'. The fleet thus became part of this national identity and its operations expressions of it. For an absolutist monarchy like that of the Russian Czar Peter the Great, the fleet could serve as a political symbol. Its magnificent existence bore witness to a regime's political agenda

---

[42] 'Mémoire concernant la marine de Hollande', in *Lettres, instructions et mémoires de Colbert*, ed. P. Clément (9 vols, Paris 1861–82), III, 301–14.

[43] 'Mémoire concernant la marine de Angleterre', in *ibid.*, III, 315–48.

[44] Cited in M. Palmer, *Command at sea. Naval command and control since the sixteenth century* (Cambridge, Mass., 2005), p. 67.

of modernization or globalism, while its military successes strengthened its domestic and international legitimacy. In other countries, such as Britain and the Dutch Republic, the financing, manning and organization of the navy often became the subject of partisan rivalries. These debates were usually waged within the linguistic and metaphorical framework of the national identity.[45] Sea power would probably not have become such a prominent element of the European state- and nation-concepts without the dynamics of the fierce and chronic Franco-British rivalry. It seems fair to say that the roots of this antagonism, certainly as regards its economic, colonial and maritime dimensions, can be traced back directly to the seventeenth-century Anglo-Dutch Wars.

Finally, these wars, with their many pitched battles, also set the tone for the tactics employed by European fleets. The line of battle, with its emphasis on broadside firepower, became and remained the standard stratagem employed during most battles fought by European navies in the age of sail. Not until the second half of the nineteenth century did the line of battle and the ship of the line lose their central role in European sea power to the steam-powered ironclad.[46]

Conclusions

In the three seventeenth-century Anglo-Dutch Wars it was of vital importance for European princes and politicians that they be kept informed, by their own diplomats and also by the emergent commercial news sources, of their progress. They needed to remain abreast, not only of the course of the wars themselves, but also of the fluctuating relations between non-belligerent states, of changes in both their foreign policies and internal politics, and significant developments within their economic and military systems. Diplomatic correspondents differed considerably in their approach, some confining themselves largely to factual accounts, others providing extended reflections and analyses. Contemporary sources yield, in general, little information on how these communications were interpreted.

---

[45] J.D. Davies, Alan James and Gijs Rommelse (eds), *Ideologies of Western naval power, c. 1500–1815* (Abingdon, 2019); R. Harding, *Seapower and naval warfare, 1650–1830* (London, 1999); R. Hobson, *Imperialism at sea. Naval strategic thought, the ideology of sea power and the Tirpitz Plan, 1875–1914* (Boston and Leiden, 2002); J.R. Dull, *The age of the ship of the line. The British and French navies, 1650–1815* (Barnsley, 2009); D. Redford (ed.), *Maritime history and identity. The sea and culture in the modern world* (London and New York, 2013); Alan James, Carlos Alfaro Zaforteza and Malcolm Murfett, *European navies and the conduct of war* (Abingdon, 2019), 59–65 and 81–3.

[46] R. Gardiner, *The line of battle. The sailing warship, 1650–1840* (London, 2004); J.D. Davies, *Pepys's navy. Ships, men and warfare, 1649–1689* (Barnsley, 2008); B. Tunstall, *Naval warfare in the age of sail. The evolution of fighting tactics, 1650–1815* (London, 1990).

On the causes of the wars, in which both ideological and economic provocations played a role, English resentment with the Republic's trade supremacy provided the spur to create a powerful naval capacity with which to mount a challenge to the Dutch. The Dutch, for whom maritime trade was the cornerstone of their existence as a nation, responded by building a fleet of their own in order to challenge England's self-proclaimed right to the dominion of the 'English seas'. While some Protestant states viewed the wars as a tragic brotherly quarrel, for other countries they represented the logical outcome of the conflicting commercial interests.

The effect of the wars on the strategic interests of the European states provides the explanation for the intense interest in them. The continental system was a tangle of overlapping bi- and tri-lateral alliances and contentions. Like the threads of a spider's web set in sympathetic motion when only one is touched, these conflicts between two of the most powerful states inevitably gave rise to reverberations elsewhere. Some countries, with an eye to the dangers of choosing party with one or other of the belligerents, elected to remain neutral, while others from motivations of financial gain or strategic interest allied themselves with one side or the other. An example of the latter was the France of Louis XIV, who sought to seize the opportunity proffered to realize his ambition of annexation of the Spanish Netherlands.

The growing importance of maritime commerce, the increasing interconnectedness of production centres and markets, and the growing economic interdependence of European states together ensured that their own strategic interests were unavoidably affected by the wars. Despite the damage to the trade and shipping of some, for others new chances for enrichment arose. The predominantly maritime character of the wars thus drove rulers and governments to adjust their policies in anticipation of these strategic risks and opportunities.

Much has been written about the 'Westphalian System', that from 1648 seemed to hold some promise of regulating the relations between European states. This article does not pretend to judge the success of this but makes it clear that the period of the Anglo-Dutch Wars was characterized by a high degree of cynicism among third nations. These promoted unashamedly their own interests and showed little concern for the wellbeing of the greater European system. From time to time the Swiss Cantons and Sweden made half-hearted attempts at mediation, but most other powers were concerned only to seek to pluck at the spider's web in order to gain some advantage – territorial, military, or fiscal-economic – for themselves. Regarding the wars from a European perspective shows primarily the absence of any, 'Westphalian' or other, correction mechanism for the creation or restoration of international order.

3

Anglican Royalism and the origins of the Second Anglo-Dutch War

Paul Seaward

The origins of the Second Anglo-Dutch War used to be straightforward. Sir George Clark called it 'the clearest case in our history of a purely commercial war', and Charles Wilson, in his still valuable study of the three Anglo-Dutch wars, now over sixty years old, was struck by the overwhelming consensus of 'royal dukes, timber merchants, gallants of the court, goldsmith money-lenders, peers of the realm, and civil servants', who all agreed on the desirability of war 'undisturbed by social, religious, or political differences'.[1] The clash of commercial interests between the Dutch Republic and the English state from 1648 onwards had already produced the war of 1652–54; since then, new confrontations had arisen, particularly in Africa, and a renewal of war had been talked about from early in the Restoration. The re-enactment of the Commonwealth's Navigation Act, and the adoption of the Interregnum innovation of a Council of Trade, seemed to display the revival in the Restoration of the influence that commercial interests had enjoyed under the Rump Parliament. The Anglo-Dutch Treaty of 1662 surprised many, who had expected war instead; the arrival of war two years later was less remarkable.

Much of the research on the subject published since Wilson's work has looked at the domestic politics of the origins of the war, and has complicated, though not tried entirely to replace, the essentially economic interpretation. The House of Commons Resolution of April 1664, which had given the king confidence that Parliament would back war with the necessary resources, has been shown to have been carefully choreographed by government officials in order to put pressure on Dutch negotiators.[2] J.R. Jones's *The Anglo-Dutch Wars of the Seventeenth Century*, published in 1996, sketched in an interpretation that attributed to James, duke of York, the king's brother and lord admiral, and an enthusiastic advocate of the African trade, the responsibility for escalating the

---

[1] Charles Wilson, *Profit and power. A study of England and the Dutch wars* (London, 1957), pp. 14 and 151.
[2] Paul Seaward, 'The House of Commons Committee of Trade and the origins of the second Anglo-Dutch War, 1664', *Historical Journal* 30:2 (1987), 437–52.

conflict. Jones suggested that 'the court, not the City brought about the war'.[3] The most recent substantial contribution, Gijs Rommelse's *The Second Anglo-Dutch War*, has synthesised newer interpretations, producing a complex picture of the origins of the war in both Britain and the Netherlands.[4]

One book, Steven Pincus's *Protestantism and Patriotism: Ideologies and the Making of English Foreign Policy, 1650–1668*, published in the same year as Jones's, offered a controversial and radically different account of the background to the war. In a formidably well-researched monograph, Pincus challenged the consensus on the economic background to the war, claiming that both it and its predecessor, the First Anglo-Dutch War of 1652–54, had far more to do with ideology than they did with commercial interest. As far as the second war was concerned, he outlined the impact of what he called 'Anglican Royalism' on the management of bilateral relations with the Netherlands during the early 1660s. Anglican royalists – Civil War adherents of the king and the Church of England, and those who adopted their principles after the Restoration – were natural opponents of Dutch republicanism and Calvinism.[5] Their hostility was exacerbated by the ascendancy of the republican faction in Dutch politics and its determination to extinguish the monarchical tendencies represented by the stadholdership of the Princes of Orange, by the consequential arguments over the guardianship of the current Prince, nephew of Charles II, and by the ease with which English political and religious refugees could find asylum in the seven provinces.

Pincus described English diplomatic priorities in the period running up to the war, 1660 to 1664, as amounting to an 'Orangist foreign policy'. The English government offered moral or covert support for Orangists and vigorously protested about the reception of its own enemies on Dutch shores. A treaty between the powers was signed in 1662 only because of English anxiety about an increase in domestic unrest after the introduction of the Act of Uniformity, while alleged links between Dutch republicans and the radical conspiracies of late 1663 continued to poison the relationship. Pincus interprets the Commons Resolution of April 1664 as closely related to a determination to combat radical dissent and its fellow-travellers. It was, he argues, Anglican royalist merchants who 'enthusiastically desired a second Anglo-Dutch war'. The three companies that complained to the House of Commons inquiry about the Dutch were deeply influenced by the Anglican royalist beliefs or associations of some of their leading members.[6] Pincus does not deny a background of economic competition and emphasises a widespread

---

[3] J.R. Jones, *The Anglo-Dutch Wars of the seventeenth century* (London, 1996), p. 151.

[4] Gijs Rommelse, *The Second Anglo-Dutch War (1665–1667). Raison d'état, mercantilism and maritime strife* (Hilversum, 2006).

[5] On 'Anglican Royalism', see below, p. 00.

[6] Pincus, *Protestantism and patriotism. Ideologies and the making of English foreign policy, 1650–1668* (Cambridge, 1996), pp. 195–268.

anger against the Dutch. But key to the descent into war was the animosity against a republican and religiously unsound polity by the partisans of the royal side: 'only when the Anglican royalist reaction of 1663–64 demanded action against Dutch perfidy did war become inevitable'.[7]

Pincus's thesis is part of a broader argument about a fundamental and complex shift in the objectives of English foreign policy in the second half of the seventeenth century: in the 1660s, he suggests, the Dutch Republic was identified as aspiring to 'universal monarchy', a global hegemony previously regarded as being held by the Spanish kingdom, a perception that helped to ensure widespread popular enthusiasm for a confrontation.[8]

Economic interests and English foreign policy

Pincus's book has been the only attempt fully to reconsider the origins in English politics of the Anglo-Dutch conflict of the 1650s and 1660s, and, while controversial, has been influential in forging a new understanding of English foreign policy in the second half of the seventeenth century, emphasising its roots in confessional views and religious attitudes.[9] No one would want to contest the reality of commercial (and extractive, in the case of the fishing industry) competition between the Dutch and the English, and the practical conflicts that resulted, but there is much to be said for Pincus's stress on the part played by religious and political ideas, as opposed to economic interests, in producing the war. Although it is not a point that Pincus himself argues in any detail, it is fair to say that the influence of purely commercial interests on Restoration foreign policy can be exaggerated. The professed interest of Charles II and his brother in promoting international trade, the renewal of the Navigation Act in 1660, the establishment of the councils of trade and foreign plantations and dabbling by many policy-makers and courtiers in schemes for colonial expansion, has been taken to indicate a serious concern with commercial matters.[10] But much of the evidence points to a weakening in practice of commercial representation and influence within government after the Restoration, certainly compared to the very considerable significance of London merchants during the years of the republic.[11] While in its immediate aftermath the role of London in bringing

[7] *Ibid.*, p. 445.
[8] *Ibid.*
[9] See, for example, Tony Claydon, *Europe and the making of England, 1660–1760* (Cambridge, 2007), pp. 132–52. For criticism of the Pincus thesis, see Rommelse, *The Second Anglo-Dutch War*, pp. 199–201.
[10] Rommelse, *The Second Anglo-Dutch War*, pp. 50–64, outlines the structure of political and administrative concern with trade issues during the 1660s.
[11] For which, see Robert Brenner, *Merchants and revolution. Commercial change, political conflict, and London's overseas traders, 1550–1653* (London, 2003), pp. 558–637. See the remarks of Perry Gauci, in *The politics of trade. The overseas merchant in state*

about the collapse of army rule and the calling of free elections as well as financing the borrowing needs of the government bolstered the position of existing City elites, it decayed as the monarchy became more firmly established in power. Some elements within the new regime nurtured considerable prejudices against a group whom they associated with Presbyterian politics; there were many within the City who were out of sympathy with the resurgence of Anglicanism. Gary De Krey's study of the politics of the London corporation after the Restoration has suggested that the more Anglican royalist establishment that gained control of the City as a result of the expulsions, and new religious requirements imposed by the Corporation Act of 1661 were perceived (certainly by those they displaced) to be less committed to advancing trade and poorly integrated with the commercial interests of the City.[12]

Parliament by 1664 reflected a similar decline in mercantile influence. Brenner showed that commercial interests had become a significant force in determining the policy of the English republic.[13] That influence persisted into the Convention Parliament elected in April 1660. But as J.R. Jones has already pointed out, the Cavalier Parliament elected a year later saw a considerable attenuation in their voices.[14] Pepys's remark of 23 March 1664 has been much cited, though not often given the importance it deserves: about a month before the resolution which signalled that war between the two countries had become a serious possibility, he wrote in his diary that his friends at Trinity House had told him that there 'were not above 20 or 30 merchants [in the Commons] which is a strange thing in an island, and no wonder if things of trade go no better nor are better understood'.[15] According to the *History of Parliament*'s calculation, only 28 men with commercial backgrounds had been returned at the 1661 election (two had died before Pepys wrote) compared with 47 in 1660.[16] Forty years earlier, in the 1621 Parliament, there were 49 or 50 Members with commercial backgrounds, though in both the 1624 and 1625 Parliaments the numbers had dropped to 39.[17]

---

  and society, 1660–1720 (Oxford, 2001), pp. 114–16, and in *Emporium of the world. The merchants of the city of London, 1660–1800* (London, 2007), pp. 165–75.

[12] Gary S. De Krey, *London and the Restoration, 1659–1683* (Cambridge, 2005), pp. 79–86.

[13] Brenner, *Merchants and revolution*, pp. 558–637, though Brenner's point is as much on the influence they could bring to bear more generally as on the number of merchants who were members of the Rump Parliament.

[14] Jones, *Anglo-Dutch Wars*, p. 151. See also Gauci, *The politics of trade*, p. 198, and Richard Grassby, *The business community of seventeenth-century England* (Cambridge, 1995), pp. 223–4.

[15] *The diary of Samuel Pepys*, ed. R.C. Latham and W. Matthews (11 vols, London, 1983), V, 95. Pepys does not say who made the remark, though the one person named in the context was Sir William Ryder, who was involved in the promotion of the April 1664 resolution in a number of ways.

[16] *The history of Parliament: The House of Commons 1660–1690*, ed. B.D. Henning (3 vols, London, 1983), I, 7.

[17] *The history of Parliament: The House of Commons 1604–1629*, ed. Andrew Thrush (6 vols, London, 2010), I, 169–70 and 510–14.

Between 1664 and 1666 only eleven members of the House of Commons were at the time or would become members of the East India Company.[18] In 1621 there had been 27 members and officers of the company holding seats, and in the 1624 Parliament there were 25.[19] One new company contradicted the trend: between 1664 and 1666 there were as many Members of the Company of Royal Adventurers trading to Africa in the House of Commons as there were of the East India Company. It was, though, an exception that rather proved the rule: only one of them (Sir Nicholas Crispe) came from a commercial background; the others were all courtiers and royal officials.[20]

Even if the merchant voice was relatively weak among members, the April 1664 Commons resolution may nevertheless have implied a House of Commons with a strong interest in trade issues and a willingness to back commercial voices. But if one thing is clear about the resolution, it is that the committee which heard the evidence on which it was based had been set up (or taken over, since a large number of new members were added to a previously established committee, which was also supplied with new instructions) specifically to provide evidence of anti-competitive activities by the Dutch, and that the people responsible for setting it up were not merchants themselves.[21] Nor, crucially, were they listening very closely to the wishes of the merchants. Pincus provides considerable evidence to show how the trading companies had to be coaxed into submitting evidence against the Dutch. He quotes one of them who did, Edward Adams, remarking in print in 1664 that: 'there is a great rumour flies up and down the world, that in this present conjuncture of affairs, the merchants are the great incendiaries to a war with the Dutch, and if there happen one, 'twill be called the Merchants war, which I suppose is a great mistake'.[22] The merchant and navy contractor George Cocke, who was closely associated with the promoters of the resolution, told Pepys early in the proceedings of the committee that it was designed to get 'underhand'

---

[18] Theophilus Biddulph, Thomas Bludworth, George Downing, Sir Richard Ford, John Frederick, John Joliffe, William Love, John Robinson, Henry Somerset, William Thompson, Roger Whiteley. For details of individual members, see *The history of Parliament: the House of Commons 1660–1690*, at historyofparliamentonline.org.

[19] Maurice Abbott, R. Bacon, R. Bateman, J. Delbridge, Sir George Calvert, Edward Carr, Sir William Cavendish, Sir H. Compton, F. Crane, Dudley Digges, Sir T. Edwardes, William Fanshawe, John Ferrar, Heneage Finch, Thomas Keightley, Sir R. Lovelace, Sir H. Neville, Osborne, Sir Thomas Roe, E. Sandys, Sir E. Seymour, Sir T. Smythe, William Towson, Sir T. Tracy, Sir E. Wardour, Sir R. Weston, Richard Young. For details of individual members, see *The history of Parliament: the House of Commons 1604–1629*, at historyofparliamentonline.org.

[20] William Ashburnham, Sir Charles Berkeley, Lord Brouncker, Sir Nicholas Crispe, William Legge, Matthew Wren, Sir Allen Apsley, John Ashburnham, Henry Bennet, John Denham, Daniel O'Neill.

[21] Seaward, 'House of Commons Committee of Trade'.

[22] *A brief relation of the surprizing several English merchants goods, by Dutch men of war* (1664), quoted by Pincus, *Protestantism and patriotism*, p. 244.

the merchants to present their complaints 'to make them in honour begin a war, which he [the king] cannot in honour declare first, for fear they should not second him with money'.[23] In another conversation with the diarist, the duke of York's secretary, William Coventry, made a similar point – that the resolution had been carefully set up to show the Dutch that the money would be forthcoming to wage war, and to encourage them to back down from confrontation.[24]

Anglican Royalism and ideological war

Who, therefore, was driving the 1664 resolution, and the war? The request to the London livery companies to provide evidence of obstructions to foreign trade produced a variety of complaints, not merely against the Dutch. Those citing the Dutch as obstructing trade were principally the Levant Company, the East India Company and the Royal Adventurers'. In a minute and careful examination of the evidence Pincus argues that both the committee and these companies were dominated by Anglican royalists, largely motivated by ideological rather than commercial considerations, and that the minutes of the meetings at which the three companies decided to put in anti-Dutch evidence to the committee show that those meetings were dominated by men of the same principles.[25] Pincus's conclusion that the resolution 'was not the result of unanimous calculation by English merchants that the Dutch were the sole economic rivals and that those rivals could only be dealt with by a mercantilist war of aggression' can be accepted. But should one also conclude that it was the result of a distinctively Anglican royalist perspective on England's economic interests?[26]

There is much that is attractive about Pincus's argument. He clearly has a point about the Anglican royalist background of the politicians doing most of the work on the committee and of many of the merchants associated with the movement towards the war. Of the committee's leading members, it is reasonable to describe a good number of them as Anglican royalist in the 1660s, including the chairman, Thomas Clifford, and the leading commercial member Sir Richard Ford (a man who was identified by several contemporaries as doing his best to promote a conflict),[27] and as we shall see, Anglican

---

[23] *The diary of Samuel Pepys*, V, 107.

[24] *Ibid.*, V, 121; see also Pincus, *Protestantism and patriotism*, pp. 239–40, for additional contemporary comment on the 'conspiracy for promoting the war with Holland'.

[25] Pincus, *Protestantism and patriotism*, pp. 237–55.

[26] *Ibid.*, pp. 252 and 255.

[27] *Ibid.*, p. 238. Apart from Clifford and Ford, Pincus cites Sir Thomas Bludworth, Sir Theophilus Biddulph, Sir Thomas Strickland, Sir Thomas Littleton and Sir John Shaw. Two of these men, Clifford and Strickland, subsequently became Catholics. In fact De Krey refers to Biddulph as a 'presbyterian' (De Krey, *London*

Royalism ran like a thread through one of the companies concerned in particular.

Yet the equation between Anglican Royalism and the pressure for the war does not quite work. One immediate doubt is the term itself. 'Anglican Royalism', though used at least as far back as the 1930s, has become a common phrase as a result of the work of Mark Goldie in the 1980s, though Goldie's focus was mainly on the clerical supporters of episcopacy and a powerful monarchy.[28] It has become normal to apply the term also to laymen who showed their commitment to both the Church and the monarchy; but it might be argued that it implies a doctrinaire attitude that was not necessarily shared by all of these. Not all of the men who fought for the king and were conformists in religion can be assumed to have been hostile to the Dutch Republic (or, indeed, necessarily in favour of religious persecution). A second concern is the presence among the most prominent voices strongly raised against the war of a number of men, including the lord chancellor, Edward Hyde, earl of Clarendon, and the lord treasurer, Thomas Wriothesley, earl of Southampton, whose credentials as both Anglicans and royalists were impeccable. They were certainly no friends to the Dutch Republic; but they also regarded the idea of war as politically and financially reckless. Pincus also cites Anglican royalists who were deeply dubious about the war. George Oxenden, for example, an East India merchant, thought the war would be potentially ruinous, although he argued that he thought a war was 'inevitable' because it was 'state policy and the nation's right'. This might be taken to suggest support for the war in spite of its economic effects: it sounds more like reluctant acceptance by one inclined to assume that the powers that be knew what they were doing.[29] On the other hand, among the most hawkish of those egging on a confrontation with the Dutch was the English envoy to The Hague, Sir George Downing: previously a preacher in the parliamentary army, a Cromwellian civil servant who worked against royalists in the Netherlands, Downing was no Anglican royalist, and clearly more of an economic warrior than an ideological one.[30]

---

and the Restoration, p. 13). Men such as Sir Winston Churchill, Bullen Reymes, Edward Seymour, and Henry Coventry. For more details of the membership of the committee, see Seaward, 'The House of Commons Committee of Trade', pp. 444–6.
[28] Mark Goldie, 'John Locke and Anglican Royalism', *Political Studies* 31:1 (1983), 61–85, esp. 77.
[29] Pincus, *Protestantism and patriotism*, p. 245.
[30] Downing's career is described in Jonathan Scott, '"Good night Amsterdam". Sir George Downing and Anglo-Dutch statebuilding', *English Historical Review* 118 (2003), 334–56. The role of George Monck, duke of Albemarle, the former Cromwellian military and naval commander, may also have been significant: see William Coventry's memorandum in the Coventry Papers, Longleat, vol. 102 (cited from British Library, M874/9), f. 7.

Thirdly, there were indeed Anglican royalists closely involved in the affairs of the three companies (Levant, East India and Royal Adventurers') who complained most bitterly about the activities of the Dutch. Pincus's evidence for their importance in preparing the statements of the Levant Company, however, is not quite compelling,[31] and he offers no backing for the suggestion that they were significant in bringing forward the complaints of the East India Company. Indeed, he accepts that the East India Company was concerned that their evidence should not be seen to be promoting a war, and made clear subsequently that they were hostile to it. Of the three, the Company of Royal Adventurers trading to Africa displays both the clearest relationship between its members and Anglican Royalism, and the clearest enthusiasm for war.[32]

The Royal Adventurers' Company is, indeed, at the centre of the question of the reason why England went to war in 1664.[33] Its interest in provoking conflict in order to challenge Dutch trade on the west coast of Africa has been recognised since before the outbreak of the war itself; the expedition of Sir Robert Holmes against Dutch interests on the Guinea Coast in early 1664 – on behalf of the company but with ships loaned by the king – was designed to inflame the situation.[34] Sir George Carteret, the treasurer of the navy, told Pepys in December 1664 that the African trade 'brought all these troubles upon us between the Dutch and us'. Sir Orlando Bridgeman, then lord keeper, in 1668 blamed the company too.[35] The formation of the company in 1660 was just as much a new element brought into Anglo-Dutch relations as was the change of regime and the arrival in power of Anglican Royalism: the two factors were, indeed, closely related. But was the company's determination to

---

[31] Pincus, *Protestantism and patriotism*, p. 242, n. 16. Pincus lists fourteen members of the committee of the Levant Company entrusted with making the report to the Commons committee, of whom he says two (Joliffe and Love) were 'the only known dissenters', and he provides evidence for the Anglican and royalist affiliations of seven of them: George Smith, John Buckworth, Nicholas Penning, John Langley, Thomas Bludworth, Thomas Vernon, Francis Clarke. Of these seven, however, De Krey lists Langley (whom Pincus links to Anglican Royalism through his relationship to Paul Rycaut) as one of the contributors to the Dissenting Loan of 1670 (De Krey, *London and the Restoration*, p. 408: see also pp. 129 and 131), which makes Anglican Royalism unlikely. Of the remaining five not identified by Pincus, another, John Gould, contributed to the same loan.

[32] Pincus, *Protestantism and patriotism*, pp. 247–8.

[33] See G.F. Zook, *The Company of Royal Adventurers trading into Africa* (Lancaster, 1919), for an account of the company's history; its successor is dealt with in K.G. Davies, *The Royal African Company* (London, 1957), and William Pettigrew, *Freedom's debt. The Royal African Company and the politics of the Atlantic slave trade, 1672–1752* (Chapel Hill, NC, 2013).

[34] See Rommelse's account of the expedition and its sequel, in *The Second Anglo-Dutch War*, pp. 93–4 and 105–8.

[35] Both cited by Pincus, *Protestantism and patriotism*, pp. 247–8. See also the remark of James Ralph, quoted on p. 293.

provoke a conflict an ideologically-driven struggle against Dutch hegemony or the result of an ambition to make money in the highly profitable, but highly risky, business of the West African slave trade?

Pincus argues that the company by 1664 was 'solidly Anglican royalist'.[36] Among its members were Lord Berkeley, its sub-governor, Thomas Grey, its deputy governor, Ellis Leighton, its secretary, Sir Richard Ford, a former deputy governor, Captain George Cocke, Sir William Ryder, John Bence, Sir Nicholas Crispe, John Buckworth, Henry Brouncker, Sir John Shaw, Sir John Wolstenholme, John Cutler, and Colonel William Ashburnham, all classified as Anglican royalist. Though there were men of a different persuasion among its members – including the former Cromwellian associate Lord Ashley, later the earl of Shaftesbury, and the earl of Pembroke – these wielded little influence. Whether 'Anglican royalist' is quite the right term is a moot point, for two of those listed were, or were suspected of being, Catholic, and another came from a parliamentarian background.[37] It might be added that Pincus finds it hard to prove Sir William Ryder's Anglican royalist credentials or his support for the war.[38] But Pincus is right in arguing that many of the most active members of the company were strongly associated with Royalism and the cause of the Church.

Many of these men were also, however, close associates of the duke of York, its founder, and of the court. Of the fourteen listed by Pincus, six – the three officers Berkeley, Grey and Leighton, plus Brouncker, Shaw and Ashburnham – are defined as Anglican royalists largely through their association with the duke. As for the others, they clearly included Anglican royalists, but just about all of them are known to have had business interests closely interwoven with the court.[39] Crispe, whether Anglican royalist or not, had a particularly

---

[36] Pincus, *Protestantism and patriotism*, p. 248.

[37] *Ibid.*, pp. 248–52: Henry Brouncker and Sir Ellis Leighton were regarded as Catholic. Pincus suggests that Thomas Grey was too, but there is no evidence of this: he was the elder son of the first Lord Grey of Warke, who was of a puritan disposition and had served as Speaker of the House of Lords in the Civil War; Grey's own Anglican Royalism should therefore be doubted. See Pepys, *The diary of Samuel Pepys*, V, 300, for the likely source of the confusion.

[38] Pincus, *Protestantism and patriotism*, p. 250, and n. 36.

[39] Sir John Shaw and Sir John Wolstenholme were farmers of the customs, and therefore essentially dependent on a financial relationship with the government. George Cocke, Richard Ford and Sir William Ryder were all naval contractors, and therefore had a personal interest in a war. 'John Cutler', listed by Pincus, is puzzling. The John Cutler he refers to at p. 252 and n. 43 is not noted by *The history of Parliament* as a member of the Royal Adventurers'. William Cutler is listed on the company's 1663 charter (British Library, Sloane MS 205) as a member. William Cutler was warden of the Drapers' Company in 1660 and 1664 and was a supplier to the navy, often in association with Sir William Ryder. I have not been able to establish anything about his religious and political stances. See *The diary of Samuel Pepys*, X, 69 (Cocke), 84 (Cutler), 354 (Rider).

strong reason to be involved in the company, since his property in West Africa was incorporated into the Adventurers' initial investment, although the circumstances under which this happened remain cloudy.[40] It might be added that of the eleven members of the Royal Adventurers' who sat in the House of Commons in 1664, eight of them – William Ashburnham, Sir Charles Berkeley, Lord Brouncker, William Legge, Matthew Wren, Sir Allen Apsley, Sir Henry Bennett, Daniel O'Neill – were associated with York in some way, and most of the others were courtiers.

York's patronage of the Royal Adventurers' Company is well known. It was referred to by J.R. Jones in the book published the same year as Pincus's, who was not therefore able to discuss it, although he did contest the suggestion of the 'Marxist literary critic Michael McKeon', 'that rather than seeking to advance the national interest the company was trying to line the pockets of the courtiers and their select merchant allies'.[41] For Pincus, Anglican royalist affiliation was a much more precise way of describing these men than their relationship with York and the court. This was certainly a network with a strong Anglican royalist flavour; but there seems no particular reason to assume that this flavour was of particular importance, or more than a symptom of the fact that they moved in circles that were close to the court and the duke. It is not surprising that York's circle was dominated by royalists and anti-presbyterians, particularly the former exiles who had been his close associates during the Interregnum. But *these* Anglican royalists were probably enthusiastic about a war not because they were Anglican royalists, but because they were closely associated with York.

Anglican Royalism and the court

On the face of it, this might be taken as evidence that the supposed link between Anglican Royalism, as such, and backing for the war, does not really exist. But it might be countered that York's views on foreign policy were, essentially, Anglican royalist: that York's associates were with him not because they were courtiers, but because they shared his anti-presbyterian and anti-republican outlook on the world – that his aims, and therefore theirs, were not primarily concerned with commercial profit, but with a determination, driven by religious and political prejudice, to damage the Dutch Republic.

Pincus says relatively little about York's own motives, though he does emphasise the duke's hostility to Dutch republicanism, and his natural interest in reinstating his nephew (and later his son-in-law), the Prince of

---

[40] See Zook, *The Company of Royal Adventurers*, pp. 15–16, for an account of the complex relationship between Crispe and the company.
[41] Pincus, *Protestantism and patriotism*, p. 248.

Orange, as Stadholder.[42] No doubt this was true; but contemporaries were more inclined to notice his commitment to English sea power, his interest in the African trade, and sheer belligerence.[43] Most of what we know about York's interest in the war comes from three well-known contemporary accounts, two from men who were particularly well-acquainted with York politically, and the third from James himself. The first is in the memoir of his father-in-law, the earl of Clarendon. Clarendon's account of the origins of the war describes the approach of 'some merchants and seamen' to York via his secretary William Coventry, proposing the erection of a joint stock company with monopoly rights of trade in West Africa, to profit from trade with, and the enslavement of, Africans. York reacted with alacrity to the proposal and became the company's governor. The company, which 'consisted of persons of honour and quality', would, Clarendon predicted, become highly successful as long as it 'be not broken or disordered by the jealousy that the gentlemen adventurers have of the merchants, and their opinion that they understand the mysteries of trade as well as the other'. He recalled how the company pressed the government for help in confronting aggressive Dutch competition, and extolled the case for a wholesale war. Its members and supporters stressed the ease with which the Dutch could be beaten, how successfully Cromwell had challenged them, and the old list of grievances against Dutch competitors across the globe. These arguments, Clarendon wrote,

> made a very deep impression in the duke; who having been even from his childhood in the command in armies, and in his nature inclined to the most difficult and dangerous enterprises, was already weary of having so little to do, and too impatiently longed for any war, in which he knew he could not but have the chief command.[44]

Clarendon's account tallies closely with that derived from York himself, in James Clarke's *Life of James II*.[45] York described in this memoir how he promoted the interests of the trading companies,

> and moreover he set up a new one for Guinea, which was absolutely necessary for the support of the foreign plantations, and for hindering the Dutch from being absolute masters of the whole Guinea trade: to this end he made use of the advice and industry of Sir Richard Ford, and some other merchants, who had got the secret which the Dutch had, of dying the Sayes of such a colour as the Blacks liked.

---

[42] *Ibid.*, pp. 221, 304–5 and 397.

[43] There is a discussion of York's attitudes on this subject in John Callow, *The making of King James II* (Stroud, 2000), pp. 207–13.

[44] Edward Hyde, earl of Clarendon, *The life of Edward, Earl of Clarendon* (2 vols, Oxford, 1857), II, 2–5.

[45] See Callow, *The making of James II*, pp. 1–7, for a discussion of the history of and problems with this source.

He went on to say, that the confrontations with the Dutch in Africa and

> the several complaints of our merchants of the injuries they received from
> the Dutch, by their depredations of them during the late disturbances in
> England, were a sort of preamble and introduction to the war which soon
> after follow'd against Holland; for it now grew to be the sense of the whole
> Nation, and of the House of Commons in particular, that satisfaction ought
> to be given to our merchants for the injuries and losses they had sustain'd
> by the unjust encroachments of the Hollanders.[46]

The third contemporary account of York's attitudes is William Coventry's
remarkable memorandum on the origins of the Dutch war, written probably
just after the war, perhaps just after he had been sacked by the duke in 1667.
It tells a very similar story:

> The Guinea Company of which his R[oyal] H[ighness] was governor (and
> in promoting which he took great delight) the company being then much
> steered by Sir Rich[ard] Ford Cap[tain] George Cock and Sir William Rider
> of the merchants and Sir G[eorge] Carteret and Mr Gray of the court party
> as they called it. The first [i.e. Carteret] (though underhand) governing the
> merchants by the dependence they had on him for trade and payment,
> the latter (Mr Gray) steered by the merchants partly without perceiving
> it (being zealous for the company) and partly out of a desire to maintain
> a popularity with the merchants as well as court party, that so he might
> be chosen the next year sub-Governor, of which he was ambitious, partly
> having nothing else to do and partly for the opportunity it gave him to
> make his court to his R[oyal] H[ighness] I say the Guinea Company in this
> condition and thus supported grew very violent in their debates against
> the Dutch.[47]

All three of these accounts suggest that it was the potential for profit and
glory that persuaded York to promote a highly dangerous and aggressive
policy against the Dutch. And while York was clearly more willing to
contemplate conflict against the Dutch Republic than he was against (say)
monarchical France, nothing suggests that the Republic's religion and
politics took more than a background role in his determination to press for
war. York's motives were conventionally princely, and of a piece with his
martial interests. Anglican royalists may have been preponderant in the
intersecting networks of the court, the Royal Adventurers' and the servants
of the duke of York, but the principal conclusion that should be drawn is
that Anglican royalists were the most influential voices at court and the

[46] J.S. Clarke, *The life of James the Second, King of England, etc. Collected out of memoirs writ of his own hand* (2 vols, London, 1816), I, 401.
[47] Coventry Papers, Longleat, vol. 102 (cited from British Library, M874/9), ff. 3–8. The paper itself may imply that the war is still continuing, referring to 'the war with the Dutch in which his Majesty hath been engaged since 1664'.

most likely companions of York, rather than that they were, by virtue of their religious and political stances, more keen on war with the Dutch than anyone else.

A similar point can be made concerning the links between Anglican royalists and the leading figures involved in the work of the Commons committee. Pincus refers to the 'overwhelming dominance of Anglican royalists at the committee meetings'. And indeed, many of the most significant members of the committee – people like Henry Bennet, Joseph Williamson, Henry Coventry, Thomas Clifford and many others – can be characterised as Anglican royalists. But they were all agents of, and clearly acting on behalf of, the court. Not all of the 'Anglican royalists' appointed to the committee were government agents, and Pincus provides a list of other regular attendees who were not so closely involved in promoting royal business: Sir Richard Ford, Sir Thomas Bludworth, Sir Theophilus Biddulph, Sir Thomas Strickland, Sir Thomas Littleton and Sir John Shaw. But of these, two (Sir Richard Ford and Sir John Shaw) were members of the Royal Adventurers' Company, and a third, Sir Thomas Strickland, was probably already (as he was later) a close associate of the secretary of state, Henry Bennet.[48]

As indicated above, these men were so heavily involved in promoting the April 1664 resolution because it was, at the time, the policy being pursued by ministers (including those who were not particularly keen on a war) to secure a strong statement indicative of the House of Commons' willingness to support the king in a conflict against the Dutch. As William Coventry (a member of the Commons committee) put it:

> Sir G[eorge] Downing then negotiating in Holland found the Dutch to condemn the kings power in all parts of his negotiation, and the Dutch did well know the king was poor, and little thought he could maintain a war with them, Sir G[eorge] Downing therefore (the Parliament then sitting) wrote over wishing the Parliament would make a vote of assistance to the king in case the Dutch were and continued injurious, whether he received this lesson from hence I will not affirm but it is not improbable.[49]

In the end, of course, the Dutch were unconvinced, and in any case events off the coast of Africa rapidly closed the door to a peaceful settlement.

---

[48] For the details of their (and other members') involvement in the committee and the government, see Seaward, 'House of Commons Committee of Trade', pp. 444–6. Thomas Clifford ended up a Catholic, but can probably be assumed to be still a member of the Church of England in 1664. Sir Thomas Littleton was a man of complex views, and despite an equivocally royalist background, he was fully prepared in 1668 to talk about the Calvinist tradition in the Church of England: see his entry in historyofparliamentonline.org.

[49] Coventry Papers, Longleat, vol. 102 (cited from British Library, M874/9), f. 5.

Anglican Royalism and public opinion

The argument of *Protestantism and Patriotism* does not wholly depend on the identities of the individuals most directly concerned in preparing the way for war. Pincus emphasises the evidence for popular support for the war in 1664 and 1665 based on a common resentment of what was perceived as the arrogance and aggression of Dutch commercial activities and their ambition to engross all of the world's trade.[50] He and others have picked apart English polemic against the Dutch, showing that it ranges well beyond the immediate complaints at issue in 1664–65: there were plenty of attacks on Dutch republicanism and religious diversity in ways that display royalist and conformist sensibilities, although it has also been suggested that war propaganda was 'so diverse it verged on confusion', failing to choose between the threats of Dutch republican principles and commercial competition.[51]

All of this is quite true. Two points about the propaganda war, though, might be recognised. The first is that (as Pincus acknowledges) the identification of Dutch aggression and ambition to dominate international trade was not exclusive to Anglican Royalism. Anglican royalist commentators may have linked it to republicanism and opposition to monarchy and to the religious culture of the Dutch. Such views may also have made them rather more keen on armed conflict than those who were closer to the religious sensibilities of the United Provinces. As Pincus argues, the war itself helped to deepen the confessional and ideological splits in English political society, which persisted well into, and beyond, the 1690s.[52] But it was not essential to accept this link to share the idea that the Dutch aimed at 'ingrossing the universal trade not only of Christendom, but, indeed, of the greater part of the known world', as Benjamin Worsley had put it in 1652.[53] Pincus recognises that the analysis of Dutch aggression and ambition had been initially developed under the English Commonwealth regime in the early 1650s, though then, he argues, it was linked to an apocalyptic narrative of Dutch religious corruption, which reflected a preoccupation with the Orangist challenge to the republic. But the fact that this analysis could be fitted into such differing narratives might rather be taken to imply that the latter were

---

[50] Pincus, *Protestantism and patriotism*, pp. 289–91 and 299–317.

[51] Claydon, *Europe and the making of England*, p. 140.

[52] See Pincus, *Protestantism and patriotism*, pp. 273–5.

[53] [Benjamin Worsley], *The advocate: or, a narrative of the state and condition of things between the English and Dutch nation, in relation to trade* (London, 1652), p. 1. See Pincus, *Protestantism and patriotism*, pp. 48–51, for his interpretation of Worsley's piece, particularly its 'apocalyptic' preface, as related to the Council of State's religious and political opposition to the Orangist elements within the Dutch state. Thomas Leng, *Benjamin Worsley (1618–1677). Trade, interest and the spirit in revolutionary England* (Woodbridge, 2008), pp. 75–9, reads the preface as largely irrelevant to the secular argument presented in the main text.

rhetorical cover for the true quarrel, rather than themselves the cause of the quarrel. The second point is that a good deal of this thinking was called into existence by the war and the period of confrontation that led up to it: indeed much of it was incited by statements emanating from the court and from those particularly interested in the war.[54] The resolution of 1664 was in itself designed to promote the notion that Dutch commercial competition was unfair and aggressive. Where hostility to the Dutch was expressed through Anglican and royalist sentiments, this was as likely to have been the result of the war, and the propaganda effort that accompanied it, as its cause.[55]

The war, as Coventry put it, was the result of 'strange accidental things concurring from several parts and parties without any intent to help each other'.[56] The principal 'accidental things' were the intrigues of the Royal Adventurers', the adventurism of the duke of York, and the effort to encourage the House of Commons into a belligerent anti-Dutch attitude. The prominence of 'Anglican royalists' in these events, and their distaste for the Dutch Calvinist Republic, was not irrelevant to the origins of the war: this was a community that was much more predisposed to be contemptuous of the Dutch than had been the English republic or the Protectorate in the early 1650s. But it is hard to see it as central.

Risk and vigour in business and war

Nevertheless, if Anglican Royalism was not in itself the cause of the war, by pointing out the Anglican royalist flavour of the drive towards it Pincus has done much to enhance our understanding of the meaning and significance of the war in terms of English commercial and foreign policy, and to make us aware of the political and religious undercurrents to the conduct of foreign affairs from the Restoration onwards. In particular, Pincus's book has forced the recognition of a crucial point in relation to the politics of English international trade. Like some contemporary commentators, we have tended to regard 'merchants' as a single class, with essentially the same interests and the same attitude towards the Dutch trade: as a consequence we have, in the past, accepted that competition with the Dutch united the commercial community into support for a war.[57] Pincus has shown emphatically that this

---

[54] See especially Pincus, *Protestantism and patriotism*, p. 278 (commenting on the Williamson newsletter).

[55] Compare this to Rommelse, *The Second Anglo-Dutch War*, pp. 199–200.

[56] Coventry Papers, Longleat, vol. 102 (cited from British Library, M874/9), f. 5.

[57] Clarendon, especially, used the word 'merchants' indiscriminately, referring to their support for the war, though he possibly meant to refer solely to the merchants involved in the African trade. See *Life*, II, 5 ('The merchants took much delight to enlarge themselves upon this argument'), pp. 48–9.

was far from the case. Indeed, his evidence indicates that those involved in the more settled forms of international trade, probably where a rough *modus vivendi* now operated with the Dutch, were keen to avoid the destructive and disruptive effects of war.[58] But for those anxious to develop risky new areas of trade, disruption was precisely what was required. Moreover, for these businesses, state backing was essential, since the sort of aggressive action they wanted would require diplomatic cover and military support. It made sense to seek the patronage of the king's brother and head of the navy and to secure the involvement of many in the court circle. Those involved in the Africa trade deliberately built up a network of supporters which was naturally Anglican royalist in flavour, possessed sufficient interest at court to swing policy, and, with little experience and high and probably unrealistic expectations, would have had a rather different attitude towards risk than ordinary merchants.[59]

Wars do not happen by themselves. Any observer would have recognised that war between the English and the Dutch in 1665 was hardly unlikely: the two countries had fought ten years before, and the tensions between them, new and old, were numerous, structural and impossible to resolve to everyone's satisfaction. But the fact that two countries compete for resources and in markets, even very vigorously, does not mean that they are bound to come to blows. Nor does the fact that their elites revile one another. What is necessary is that key policy-makers believe – whether accurately or recklessly – that the benefits to them of going to war outweigh the risks. Coventry, in his memorandum on the origins of war, wrote that York, keen on beating the Dutch out of Africa, eager to have a chance to show his military prowess, and advised that the Dutch were easily beatable, 'was willing to oblige the king and the nation with the hazard of his life, and the truth is the vigour of his Royal Highness broke the measures of those ministers who would otherwise have preserved the peace at any rate'. English policy-makers, as he underlined, consistently under-estimated their antagonists. 'The Dutch', he went on, 'are not to be trampled on, if you do they will kick, their trade is their God, if you depress that by any force they will venture all for it, and therefore when you apply force to protect your trade or oppress theirs, prepare for a war'.[60]

---

[58] Pincus, *Protestantism and patriotism*: see, particularly, the comments given at pp. 292–6.

[59] One might add that the issue highlighted by Clarendon about the management of the Royal Adventurers' – the conflict between professional businessmen and courtiers – mirrored the issue much debated within the contemporary navy (also, of course, headed by the duke of York) about whether professionals or gentlemen should be the principal commanding officers, for which, see J.D. Davies, *Gentlemen and tarpaulins. The officers and men of the Restoration navy* (Oxford, 1991), pp. 27–66.

[60] Coventry Papers, Longleat, vol. 102 (cited from British Library, M874/9), f. 7.

4

War, foreign relations and politics in the Netherlands from the Second Anglo-Dutch War to the Revolution of 1688

Elizabeth Edwards

The commemoration or, for the Dutch, celebration of the raid on the Medway in June 1667 drew a narrow focus on Anglo-Dutch relations in the second half of the seventeenth century.[1] This dramatic episode was, however, just one of many encounters between the two states between 1650 and 1689 encompassing, *inter alia*, trade conflict and war, diplomacy and espionage, and religion.[2] To a greater or much lesser extent all these elements were endemic during the period of the Second Anglo-Dutch War of 1665–67. The aftermath and impact of the war on the Dutch and the English reflected the complexities of international relations in early modern Europe and had significant implications for their internal politics. Priorities for the years 1667–72 and the outbreak of the Third Anglo-Dutch War were determined by a variety of often conflicting interests raising the question of how far the principal players were in control of these interests. Beyond the natural euphoria of a victory over the English at sea, and the conclusion of the treaty at Breda a few weeks later, the Dutch had to react quickly to political developments at home, challenges to their maritime trade and shifting international interests and allegiances. The English by contrast had to come to terms with a peace which confirmed their overseas conquests, but exposed the limits of the Stuart state, raising the crucial issue of the nature and role of the fiscal and administrative state under Charles II. To quote J.R. Jones, 'One of the characteristics of the Anglo-Dutch wars that made them unique in the context of the seventeenth century was that governments in both countries had to rely on the co-operation of representative institutions.'[3]

---

[1] Elizabeth Edwards, 'The Dutch in the Medway 1667. Commemoration and reflection', *Archaeologia Cantiana*, 139 (2018), 155–61.

[2] Political and religious migrants had moved between the two states throughout the century as internal political reactions to theological disputes changed according to the theo-political views of the governments.

[3] J.R. Jones, *The Anglo-Dutch Wars of the seventeenth century* (New York and London, 1996), p. 64.

In the Dutch Republic one of the most visible and immediate effects of the successful enterprise was a temporary rise in the reputation of Cornelis de Witt, older brother and confederate of John de Witt, grand pensionary of the province of Holland since 1653. As a representative of the Holland city of Dordrecht, Cornelis played an active role in the management of military and naval actions and in 1664 had been scapegoated for the military withdrawal from the threat of incursions in the eastern provinces by the prince bishopric of Munster.[4] Following their crucial role in the Medway raid of 1667, the De Witts enjoyed a surge of popularity, helped by their own propaganda.[5] But underlying tensions and issues soon resurfaced. By 1671 Cornelis was once again being blamed for the failure to achieve a rapprochement with Cologne and Munster who in 1672 joined forces with France to invade the Dutch provinces of Gelderland, Overijssel and Utrecht.[6] But it was the eventual downfall of his brother's administration in 1672 that was more decisive, and in the end, fatal for them both.

The real significance of the events of 1667 for the Dutch can therefore be seen in the play of internal political alignments and their influences on foreign and economic policy both before and after the war. The States' political interests were underpinned by two major issues facing the Dutch for the twenty-two years of the first stadholderless period from 1650 to 1672: the potential future role(s) of the young Prince of Orange and the struggle for satisfactory alliances with other European powers. It was the double catastrophe in 1672 of naval war with England and a French land invasion which set in train the balance of power struggles both within the Dutch States government and in the European arena. Looking at the potential political role of the young Prince of Orange and Dutch foreign relations with France and/ or England will show that in the long term the major significance of 1665–67 was either to accelerate events along a trajectory already signalled, or to stall them for a while. Despite wide ideological differences between interest groups, they were bound together by the course of events and these two closely interlinked issues as well as the complexities of the economic implications implicit in almost all matters within the States.

Foreign relations and politics 1650–67

The peace John de Witt had concluded with Cromwell's England in April 1654 at the end of the First Anglo-Dutch War was unpopular and caused rifts in the States. The conditions, kept secret until the ratification, included the Act

---

[4] J.I. Israel, *The Dutch Republic. Its rise, greatness and fall 1477–1806* (Oxford, 1995), p. 770.
[5] The most notable piece of propaganda was probably the painting, *The apotheosis of Cornelis de Witt, with the raid on Chatham in the background*, by Jan de Baen (1633–1702).
[6] Israel, *The Dutch Republic*, p. 774.

of Exclusion preventing the infant Prince of Orange being accorded the title of stadholder, and it was not until the following year that De Witt persuaded the Orangist province of Zeeland to accept it.[7] These events, justified by De Witt in his *Deductie* of 1654,[8] helped to establish Holland's grand pensionary as the *de facto* director of the States' foreign policy and strengthened the domination of Holland over the other Dutch provinces. The supporters of the House of Orange were forced to accept the situation, but remained a potent force within the Republic able to take advantage of the changes in international relations and internal politics after 1666/7. Jill Stern's study of the crisis of Orange and its recovery between 1650 and 1675 explores the evidence of an Orangist ideology which developed as a counter to the 'attacks' by the supporters of De Witt.[9]

Throughout the 1650s and 1660s the Dutch were torn between the potential advantages of an alliance with either France or England, or possibly both.[10] At the same time they were balancing their policy decisions alongside the known, or unknown, negotiations between France and England as well as other European states including Spain.[11] In relation to France, there was a large core led by De Witt who believed in maintaining peace through negotiation, attempting to work out compromise agreements based on the Treaty of the Pyrenees of 1659 and the alliance of 1662. But at the same time there was a strong threat from French expansionism and the issues became joined in the Spanish Netherlands. Before the deterioration in relations with England finally led to war in 1665, the Dutch continued to strive for working alliances with both the English and the French. With England the negotiations were mainly over trade disputes dating back to the aftermath of the First Anglo-Dutch War. A treaty was finally signed in September 1662. In April of

[7] For comparative interpretations of the exclusion of Orange from political power, see H.H. Rowen, *John de Witt. Grand pensionary of Holland* (Princeton, 1978), pp. 215–37; and Wout Troost, *William III, the Stadholder-King. A political biography* (Aldershot, 2005), pp. 29–34.

[8] *Deductie, ofte Declaration van de Staten van Hollandt ende West-Frieslandt; Behelsende Een waerachtich, ende grondichbericht van De Fondamente der Regieringe vande vrye Vereenichde Nederlanden … Ingestelt ende dienende tot Justificatie van't verlenen van seckere Acte van Seclusie, Raeckende 't employ vanden HEERE Prins van Oraigne …* (The Hague, 1654).

[9] Jill Stern, *Orangism in the Dutch Republic in word and image, 1650–1675* (Manchester, 2010).

[10] Charles-Edouard Levillain, *Vaincre Louis XIV, Angleterre-Hollande-France, histoire d'une relation triangulaire, 1665–1688* (Champ Vallon, 2010).

[11] See J.C. Boogman, 'The *raison d'état* politician Johan de Witt', *Acta Historiae Neerlandica*, 2 (1978), 55–78; M.A.M. Franken, 'The general tendencies and structural aspects of the foreign policy of the Dutch Republic in the latter half of the seventeenth century', *Acta Historiae Neerlandica*, 3 (1968), 1–42; and Gijs Rommelse, *The Second Anglo-Dutch War (1665–1667). Raison d'état, mercantilism and maritime strife* (Hilversum, 2006), pp. 22 ff.

the same year De Witt had succeeded in concluding a treaty with the French to preserve the strength of the Dutch Republic, which included terms for military support in the event of threats from England and an agreement on a satisfactory tariff policy. But crucially, it omitted discussion of the status of the Spanish Netherlands.[12] In the event, although the French, under the terms of the 1662 treaty, were nominally an ally of the Dutch in the Second Anglo-Dutch War, they offered only minimal support,[13] but did assist in the repulse of Munster troops in 1665/6 when the military resources of the Dutch were in dire straits.[14] The economic growth of the Dutch Republic owed much to the failure of Antwerp to preserve its international role as the major port for the Low Countries during the Eighty Years War of independence from Spanish rule. Aggressive French territorial gains in 1667 and further ambitions in the Spanish Netherlands were therefore not only a threat to the frontiers of the newly consolidated republic with the spectre of dominance by another major power, but also a potential threat to the economy which underpinned it. Trade with the Spanish Netherlands and France, and the importance of the inland river trade with the European hinterland, as well as the Baltic trade, may not have had the glamour and potential of global colonial trade, but it was bread and butter, and drink, for many Dutch people.

With the English, mutual interest arising from common religious and republican sympathies counted for little in 1652 and maritime competition predominated. Yet the peace treaty which the English forced on the Dutch at Westminster in 1654 was underlined in part by Cromwell's motives for keeping the House of Stuart, through its connections and sometime refuge in the Netherlands, in a powerless position and of establishing a common protestant cause.[15] The peace treaty was signed, but the terms of the consequent maritime trading negotiations were more difficult to settle and the repercussions of the treaty were to be far-reaching beyond the lifetime of the first stadholderless period. As De Vries and Van der Woude put it, 'The First Anglo-Dutch War ... ushered in a twenty-five-year period of repeated attacks – both military and economic – on Dutch commercial hegemony.'[16] The further deterioration of relations between England and the Dutch Republic has generally been ascribed to the resurgence of economic warfare, the renewal of the Navigation Acts and the introduction of a ten-mile fishing limit around the coast of England. This consensus by historians naturally has

---

[12] Rowen, *De Witt*, pp. 465–70.

[13] Jones, *Anglo-Dutch Wars*, p. 166; Israel, *Dutch Republic*, pp. 776–7.

[14] Rowen, *De Witt*, pp. 598–9.

[15] For a particularist view on the causes of the war, see Simon Groenveld, 'The English Civil Wars as a cause of the First Anglo-Dutch War, 1640–1652', *The Historical Journal*, 30:3 (1987), 541–66.

[16] Jan de Vries and Ad van der Woude, *The first modern economy. Success, failure and perseverance of the Dutch economy, 1500–1815* (Cambridge, 1997), p. 409; Rowen, *De Witt*, p. 257; Jones, *Anglo-Dutch Wars*, pp. 142–3.

its nuances,[17] but whether it was primarily caused by the machinations of the newly appointed ambassador to The Hague, Sir George Downing,[18] the negotiations by De Witt with the French or the colonial struggles across the Atlantic, the Second Anglo-Dutch War (1665–67) can justifiably be described as a trade war.[19] Only Baxter in his study, strongly underpinned by the importance of dynastic conflict, saw the war as a direct result of the purely personal/political breakdown between Charles II and De Witt. And although Pincus denies economic causes for the war he argues that to the English, Dutch trading practices were another manifestation of the republicanism which was a threat to the restored monarchy. Elsewhere in this volume Paul Seaward revisits the arguments over the causes of the Second Anglo-Dutch War through a balanced analysis of Pincus's discussion of the significance of 'Anglican Royalism'.[20] Nevertheless, soon after the peace treaty of Breda in July 1667, Downing's successor as English ambassador, Sir William Temple, observed that Amsterdam traders appeared to be fairly pragmatic about the English as their mutual trade recovered, but were very concerned about France's continued 'designs' on Flanders spreading north to the Dutch Republic.[21] The territories making up the Spanish Netherlands had long been seen by the English as the buffer against French northward expansion and continued to be watched with increasing care as the intentions of Louis XIV became more apparent during the latter half of the seventeenth century, leading up to the War of the Spanish Succession.

Concurrently, from 1665, one of the major issues within the Dutch Republic was the role that the Prince of Orange might eventually fill. William III was born in 1650, a week after the untimely death of his father whose short stadholdership had been both provocative and divisive. The stadholder threatened military reprisals against Amsterdam's opposition to his rearmament proposals and on 30 July 1650 he assembled troops to march on the city, but was foiled by the information from a Hamburg postal rider allowing the city to organise resistance. On the same day he imprisoned six of the most outspoken of his opponents among the leading Holland

---

[17] Among the most recent, Rommelse, *The Second Anglo-Dutch War*.

[18] Roger Downing and Gijs Rommelse, *A fearful gentleman. Sir George Downing in The Hague, 1658–1672* (Hilversum, 2011), and Jonathan Scott, 'Downing, Sir George, first baronet (1623–84)', in *Dictionary of National Biography* (2004), https://doi. org/10.1093/ref:odnb/7981, provide the background to the complex personality and the political and economic acumen of Downing.

[19] S. Baxter, *William III and the defense of European liberty 1650–1702* (London, 1966), pp. 32–3; Steven C.A. Pincus, *Protestantism and patriotism. Ideologies and the making of English foreign policy, 1650–1668* (Cambridge, 1996), p. 441.

[20] See above, pp. 00.

[21] K.D. Haley, *An English diplomat in the Low Countries. Sir William Temple and John de Witt 1665–1672* (Oxford, 1986), p. 142.

regents (including the father of John de Witt) in the Castle of Loevenstein.[22] These actions of William II shifted simmering discontent with the apparent dynastic and quasi-monarchic tendencies of the House of Orange to an open split between Statists/Republicans and Orangists. The Dutch had rejected monarchical rule during the Eighty Years War and it should be noted that both those termed Statists or Republicans, and those identified as Orangist, were defenders of the independence of the state implicit in the republican form of government. After the Act of Exclusion, the main branch of the House of Orange was effectively excluded from a functional role within the States government, but their presence and historical importance to the very existence of the Republic could not be ignored.[23] Nor could their relationships with the noble and royal houses of Europe, with the often ambivalent English Stuarts, but also with the German state of Brandenburg, which gave some minor semblance of international acceptability, particularly for the Holy Roman Emperor and the emerging absolutist monarchy in France. That the Dutch and English, both republican protestant states in the 1650s, had gone to war in 1652, and were to do so twice more in spite of their strong dynastic connections, indicates that very complex issues were at stake, in terms of both global trade and the balance of power in Europe. Throughout the 1660s, and with the establishment of the personal rule of Louis XIV in 1661, sustained *inter alia* by Colbert's economic policy, the potential threat from France began to emerge as a challenge to the security of the Dutch state both territorially in the Spanish Netherlands and in the maritime trades. In many quarters this threat was seen as almost equal to that of the English.

The brief civil strife in the Dutch Republic in 1650 does not sit easily with the theory of a mid-seventeenth-century European crisis. This long-running debate was put into perspective as far as the Dutch Republic was concerned by Franken in his introductory chapter to his thesis, *Coenraad van Beuningen's politieke aktiviteiten in de jaren 1667–1684*: 'The political crisis in the Republic … should be explained rather from a point of view of the specific relationships and the situation in the [country] rather than as a common problem.'[24] Its importance was the impact on the administration which followed during the

---

[22] 'Loevesteiner' became a commonly used name for opponents of the Orangists. Willem Frijhoff and Marijke Spies, *Dutch culture in a European perspective. 1650 hard-won unity* (London, 2004), pp. 73–7.

[23] The stadholder had been the representative (viceroy) of the Spanish monarchy before the Revolt against Spain in the mid-sixteenth century, led by the then stadholder William I (the Silent), Prince of Orange. After the establishment of the United Provinces of the Dutch Republic the stadholder was the highest noble representative of the constituent provinces.

[24] E.J. Hobsbawm, 'The general crisis of the seventeenth century', in *Crisis in Europe 1560–1660*, ed. T. Aston (London, 1965), pp. 87–8; M.A.M. Franken, *Coenraad van Beuningen's politieke aktiviteiten in de jaren 1667–1684* (Groningen, 1966), 'Introduction' translated in Franken, 'The general tendencies', p. 2, n. 2.

minority of William III, domestically and in international relations, together with the continuing influence it had on relations between the prince on his restoration and the regents of the leading towns, in particular the powerful city of Amsterdam. From the beginning of the Revolt against Spain in the late sixteenth century, the Princes of Orange had, until 1650, established themselves firmly as the appointees to the role of stadholder in five of the seven provinces and also to the posts of Captain- and Admiral-General for the military and naval forces.[25] However, as a republic, the Dutch state was formally governed by the States General. The three-tier system, city, provincial and States General, was cumbersome and balanced in favour of Holland whose provincial estates met in the Binnenhof in The Hague alongside the States General, and who made the largest contribution to the States' coffers.[26] The leading political administrative role was increasingly taken by the grand pensionary of this largest and richest province. From 1653 John de Witt's skilful statesmanship steered the Dutch successfully through their period of greatest economic and cultural achievements in the face of war and challenges on all sides. Respect, tempered by competition, was paid to these achievements by the French and the English and led to Dutch involvement in international conflicts on an almost equal footing with the developing major powers. However, by the mid-1660s pressures were beginning to mount and discontent was becoming overt. The Orangists saw their chances of political revival in the person of the Prince of Orange, now nearing adulthood. And it was during the Second Anglo-Dutch War that both sides were striving to achieve the outcome they deemed best for the Dutch Republic.

Although the prince was too young to be involved in all the events of these years, they were to be part of his legacy. On the restoration of Charles II in 1660, the Act of Exclusion was revoked, but the English king vacillated and no strong moves were made to restore the House of Orange in the person of the young prince to a position of power in the Dutch Republic. When his mother, Charles II's sister Mary, died suddenly on a visit to England in 1661, the fortunes of the child were dependent on confrontation or consultation between his German grandmother together with the States, and the King of England whom Mary had named as his guardian, contrary to previous understandings with De Witt. Proposals for making William a Child of State foundered and he remained under the influence of the Orangists until 1666 when he had reached an age at which his potential participation in the government of the country could not be ignored. He was made Child of State in 1666, but the plans of De Witt were not wholly successful, and when the Perpetual Edict was passed in Holland in 1667, compromises were already

---

[25] The stadholder of Friesland and Groningen was usually a member of the junior Orange-Nassau family.

[26] See J.L Price, *Holland and the Dutch Republic in the seventeenth century. The politics of particularism* (Oxford, 1994).

being made. The Edict acknowledged that there would eventually be a role for the prince by admitting him to the Council of State in due course, but it curbed his potential powers by prohibiting tenure of the office of Captain- and Admiral-General together with that of stadholder. Potentially this allowed both the supporters and opponents of the House of Orange to see benefits in passing the Perpetual Edict. By the time Holland had persuaded Zeeland to accept this by the Act of Harmony in 1670, Zeeland had already accorded the prince the ritual acknowledgement of his status as First Noble in 1668, and it was too late for De Witt to have effective control over his future. Events were moving too fast for the grand pensionary, but his impressions on the prince, with whom he had almost daily meetings during the late 1660s, were added to William's earlier Orangist education and gave him an insight into the *raison d'état* of the States as they had been guided under De Witt.

If the role of the Prince of Orange was the most overt issue dividing the government at local, provincial and States level, the play of foreign policy and its repercussions on trade were the crucial day-to-day matters exercising them. Throughout the 1660s the role of De Witt dominated Dutch politics at home and abroad. In his 1978 magisterial work *John De Witt, Grand pensionary of Holland*, Rowen provided an almost blow-by-blow account of the ever changing internal and international relationships that De Witt was facing up to. However, it is apparent that despite the three-tiered structure of representative government and the dominance of Holland and Amsterdam, there was an effective centralised system of decision-making. This could work independently of the restrictions imposed on it by the system, and not solely because the complexities of the system precluded easy consultation. Thus it was that De Witt was able to arrange the Triple Alliance of 1668 almost single-handed.[27]

One of the outcomes of the diplomacy of the First Anglo-Dutch War had been the beginnings of the friendship between De Witt and Coenraad van Beuningen, then pensionary of Amsterdam, which was to last until 1668 when they were unable to reconcile their divergent views of the potential of French or English friendship.[28] Van Beuningen's career as a politician spanned many years from the 1650s and, until the mid-1670s, he also acted from time to time on behalf of the States as a diplomat in Paris and London, but, although he

---

[27] Franken, *Coenraad van Beuningen's politieke aktiviteiten*, pp. 31–2; J.H. Grever, 'The structure of decision-making in the States-General of the Dutch Republic 1660–68', *Parliaments, Estates and Representation*, 1 (1981), 13–33, cites particular examples of how De Witt overcame the 'official' processes to achieve swift decisions. See also Price, *Holland and the Dutch Republic*, p. 213.

[28] De Witt had great respect for Van Beuningen's political methods because he '*meer oog had voor het algemeen belang van de Republiek dan de particularistisch Amsterdamse faktieman die Valckenier was*' (had a better eye for the affairs of the Republic than the factional particularism of the Amsterdammer Valckenier): Franken, *Coenraad van Beuningen's politieke aktiviteiten*, p. 77.

was seen as the representative of his city, his strongly ingrained anti-French sentiments, his independent views and his frequent absences in the service of the States distanced him from his peers who often rejected his views. His character has been neatly summarised by Peter Burke: 'Van Beuningen is a fascinating but not an isolated sample of the coexistence of new science, Cartesianism, astrology and millenarianism inside one man's head.'[29]

The internal divisions of the States, which continued throughout the whole period from the 1650s, were often encouraged by the intervention of the foreign powers, by their ambassadors and their agents, while the ideological differences between Orangists and republicans and the religious divisions between Arminians and Contra-Remonstrants could be exploited to manipulate factional interests within the regent class. In a period of complex international relations with serious unresolved internal political divisions, normal diplomacy was much informed by networks of informal agents on all sides. The well-established merchant and trading networks in the maritime states, with relatively close, easy transport links, provided an alternative and regular means for communication to supplement the more formal diplomatic links. In 1650 the Amsterdammers had dismissed earlier rumours from foreign merchants about William II's planned attack as propaganda,[30] but had acted successfully on the eye-witness account of the Hamburg messenger. Negotiators would be aware and in some cases responsive to the large output of propaganda which was published in the Dutch Republic where censorship was minimal, whereas in England the licensing laws were not relaxed until 1695 and in France strict controls were enforced. In addition to Dutch writers, 'The 'Republic of Letters' centred in Rotterdam published works from authors based in other European countries or by refugee opposition writers, providing them with a platform for promulgating opposition ideas.

From Breda to the Third Anglo-Dutch War (1667–72)

For all its maritime strength and superiority and the apparent glorious end to the Second Anglo-Dutch War, the Dutch Republic remained in its vulnerable geographical position, with its relatively small population. Not only was its republican status barely respected among the crowned heads of Europe, it was also becoming increasingly clear that its continued existence as a political force to be contended with was founded principally on the basis of economic wealth and the advantages it had established in international maritime

---

[29] P. Burke, *Venice and Amsterdam. A study of seventeenth century elites* (2nd edn, London, 1994), p. 103; E.C. Edwards, 'Amsterdam and William III: the role of influence, interest and patronage on policy-making in the Dutch Republic, 1672–1684' (unpublished PhD thesis, University College London, 1988), pp. 162–7.
[30] Frijhoff and Spies, *1650 hard-won unity*, p. 75.

trade.[31] That by 1667 the Republic could not be sure of any treaty with either France or England only served to increase this vulnerability.

De Witt's support from Amsterdam had already diminished during the latter part of the 1660s. In addition to the breach with Van Beuningen, the death in 1665 of his powerful close ally in the Amsterdam regency, his father-in-law, Cornelis de Graeff, had reduced much of his influence. From the late 1660s the political alignments in the city underwent seismic shifts with pragmatic and opportunist politicians such as Gillis Valckenier gaining ascendancy over those led more by ideological politics.[32] It was Valckenier, not Van Beuningen, who was a member of the group responsible for the education of the Prince of Orange as Child of State. At the same time De Witt was becoming very much aware that his ablest subordinate was Gaspar Fagel, pensionary of the largely Orangist town of Haarlem and from 1670 *griffier* (secretary) to the States General. Fagel succeeded De Witt as grand pensionary in 1672 and became a faithful servant of William III until his death on the cusp of the expedition to England in December 1688.[33]

French success against Spain in the Spanish Netherlands, after the invasions of 1667 and the acquisition of strategic towns, led to the creation of the incongruent Triple Alliance between the Dutch Republic, England and Sweden in 1668. Its consequences released France from any lingering responsibilities to the Dutch under the terms of the 1662 alliance. Colbert believed that an attack on Dutch economic strength was one sure way of continuing the promising trends in French economic expansion. Since 1667, therefore, the French and the Dutch had in effect been in a state of economic cold war with punitive tariffs imposed by the French on Dutch imports. Added to

[31] J.W. Smit, 'The Netherlands and Europe in the seventeenth and eighteenth centuries', in *Britain and the Netherlands in Europe and Asia. Papers delivered to the third Anglo-Dutch historical conference*, eds J. Bromley and E.H. Kossman (London, 1968), p. 23, quotes Pieter de Groot writing in 1673: 'What constitutes the wealth of the Republic? The opulence of its trade. And what is the source of that trade? Good government. For nothing is more attractive for the whole world than freedom of conscience and security of possessions. It is impossible that this freedom and this security of possessions would survive the government of a monarch.' See also 'Considerations Upon the Present State of the United Netherlands, composed by a lover of his countrey for the encouragement of his countreymen, in this troublesome time. Exactly translated out of Nether-dutch into English by a most cordial lover of both the nations', in *The Somers tracts*, ed. Walter Scott (13 vols, London, 1809–15), VIII (1812), 1–26, and 'Delenda est Carthago, or the true Interest of England in relation to France and Holland. By the Earl of Shaftesbury', speech made by Shaftesbury at the opening of the English Parliament on 5 February 1673: 'The interest and life of Holland, all the world knows is trade. It is advantageous to others; but it is necessary to them ...', in *ibid.*, VIII, 37.

[32] Edwards, 'Amsterdam and William III', chapters 6 and 7.

[33] E.C. Edwards, 'An unknown statesman. Gaspar Fagel in the service of William III and the Dutch Republic', *History*, 87:287 (2002), 358–79.

these growing threats was the landward threat from the French alliance with Cologne and Munster. However, the fragility of the Triple Alliance made prevention of the signing of the (Secret) Treaty of Dover between England and France in 1670 impossible. The motives of the English king, after the fall of Clarendon in 1667, have often been rehearsed and, to put a partially favourable spin on them, he was in a similar position to that his nephew the Prince of Orange was to find himself in after 1672. He had lost and been restored to his inheritance and had to walk a political tightrope for survival in the face of opposition within a parliamentary system which had defeated his father. However, although Charles and William had a common Stuart heritage, the English king was steeped in his own brand of quasi-catholic 'Anglican Royalism' (as more critically was his brother and successor James, duke of York), but William was brought up in Calvinist republicanism. If by negotiation and sleight of hand Charles was able to exploit the hand of friendship from Louis XIV at the expense of his nephew for his immediate purposes, and at the same time win round Parliament in the short term, that was the path that he would choose to follow. The recall of Sir William Temple early in 1672 and the appointment of Downing once again as ambassador to The Hague soon disabused the Dutch of all English promises that they would stand by the terms of the Triple Alliance.[34] Thus the final negation was achieved of all the diplomacy of the Dutch with France and England during the preceding ten years. Success in achieving the signing of the Triple Alliance quickly turned to failure and the Treaty of Dover in 1670 between the French and the English was once more a sign of the increasing power of the King of France. In 1672 the invasion of the Dutch Republic by the forces of France, Munster and Cologne in parallel with the sea war with England sealed De Witt's fate.

With England there was an element of sympathy, particularly among the Orangists, who saw the possibility of exploitation of Stuart links and religious confraternity; but there was also an element of tension because of what was perceived as a greater economic threat than France, and the obverse of the Orangist view, that the Stuart link was a threat to the sovereignty of the provinces supporting such dynastic monarchist and militarist ambitions as William II had displayed. Hence an alliance between France and England, aimed principally at the Dutch, deprived them of the possibility of help from either. Therefore when Cologne and Munster, who had threatened in 1665/6, joined forces with the two powerful allies, the vulnerability of the Dutch Republic was quickly evident with the fall of the provinces of Gelderland, Overijssel and Utrecht, disasters which changed the motivation of the pacifists who now saw a combined military and economic threat as likely to destroy their hard-won independence for ever.

---

[34] Haley, *An English diplomat*, p. 283.

The specific causes of the war of 1672 can be traced back no further than the Triple Alliance of January 23, 1668, in which the Dutch republic joined with the kingdoms of Great Britain and Sweden to oppose the conquest of the Spanish Netherlands by France. In no sense whatever was the war the culmination of a long enmity between the two states of France and the United Provinces. They were, to the contrary, traditional friends and allies.[35]

Rowen's rather dogmatic statement at the beginning of his 1957 essay on the Triple Alliance has become more nuanced in the succeeding years, not least by himself in *John de Witt*,[36] and more particularly by Haley in *An English Diplomat in the Low Countries*.

The maxim that 'my enemy's enemy is my friend' is quickly discredited once the original enemy is no longer a critical threat. And this was certainly true of the deterioration in relations between the Dutch and the French in the 1660s (after the Peace of the Pyrenees between France and Spain in 1659) where there was no common ideology of the state, no religious confraternity and an increase in maritime and commercial competition.[37] Added to which they did both have a common, but conflicting, interest in the control of trade and security of territory within and through the Spanish Netherlands. It would probably be true to say that the origins of French aggression towards the Netherlands should be seen in the end of the mid-century crises in France, the death of Mazarin and Louis XIV's assumption of personal rule in 1661. Although the impact of this critical change in French rule may have matured slowly, into the melting pot came the accession in 1665 of the weakly four-year-old Carlos II as ruler of the now declining Spanish empire, who clearly looked to be the last Habsburg king and whose imminent death was awaited for the next thirty-five years; the Spanish Netherlands featured highly in the possible division of his inheritance when he died. Adding England into the mix with its politico-religious issues and its increasingly dominant colonial trade as well as historical dynastic links to the French monarchy, this was a very volatile period in international relations between the major three emergent western European maritime trading states. The nuances of this debate continue as contemporary historians challenge shifting historical approaches to the ideological causes of war in the seventeenth century.[38]

---

[35] H.H. Rowen, 'The Triple Alliance', in *The ambassador prepares for war* (International Scholars Forum Series) (The Hague, 1957), p. 18.

[36] Rowen, *De Witt*, pp. 465–90.

[37] Haley, *An English diplomat*, p. 25; Israel, *The Dutch Republic*, p. 779.

[38] See in particular David Onnekink, 'The ideological context of the Dutch War (1672)', in *Ideology and foreign policy in early modern Europe (1650–1750)*, ed. David Onnekink and Gijs Rommelse (Aldershot, 2011), pp. 131–44.

War and peace 1672–88

In this case the prescience of Van Beuningen was seen to be justified, but did little to undermine the essentially pro-French views of the majority of the Amsterdam regents. As the 1670s progressed, it was peace and trade, rather than friendship or alliances with the French, that those opposing William III's policies were more concerned about. Disaffection with the prince after 1674 and an increasing push for peace in Amsterdam brought together the more radical and moderate members of the city's government, who agreed a *Concept tot Eenigheit* (Concept for Unity) in 1676.[39] Van Beuningen maintained his anti-French views until 1684 when his opposition to military finance in the end was greater than his opposition to Amsterdam's pro-French views.

The troubles of 1650 had been stimulated by fears of excessive demands for rearmament and the supporters of De Witt were acutely aware that the army was synonymous with Orangist power. But it was the coming of age of William III which provided an Orange symbol in February 1672 to take over as Captain-General in an *'ad expeditionem'* compromise with the Wittians.[40] It was only the delay of war from the summer of 1671 to the spring of 1672 which gave the Dutch time to overcome their internal struggles over military expenditure and meet the coordinated French and English attacks with anything like a prepared army. The war with England started officially in March 1672 and with the French a month later. In the event, the Dutch acquitted themselves creditably against the English at sea, but this was little defence against the combined land forces led by France. The enemy advances in the east and the subsequent Dutch retreat, first to Utrecht and then into Holland, the heart of the Republic's wealth and power, were halted only by the success of the waterline defences.

The provincial states began to believe that they would have to give in to the might of France and make concessions acceptable to Louis XIV, but critically these were rejected. The initiative in forming Dutch policy began to shift from the ruling class. De Witt was now the villain of the piece as the principal formulator of the unsuccessful Triple Alliance. Early rioting was directed at local town council level, where each town determined its own policy, rather than at central policy. But after Louis XIV's rejection of the Dutch terms in June 1672 and his retaliation with more excessive ones, attention began to focus on changing the balance within the Republic. Latent Orangism became blatant and restoration of the prince to the stadholdership was the rallying cry. The Dutch did not have to look far for a scapegoat or a saviour. After

---

[39] Hans Bontemantel, *De Regeeringe van Amsterdam soo in't civiel als crimineel en militaire*, ed. G.W. Kernkamp (2 vols, The Hague, 1897), II, 246–63.

[40] Charles-Edouard Levillain, 'William III as military dictator', in *Redefining William III. The impact of the King-Stadholder in international context*, ed. Esther Mijers and David Onnekink (Aldershot, 2007), p. 161.

twenty years of power, De Witt had at last become exposed to an effective opposition. His persistence with a pro-French attitude was seen to have been misguided and his completion of the Triple Alliance totally ineffective, undermining trust in his ability to direct foreign policy. Having lost the confidence of his peers and vilified in pamphlets, De Witt now fell victim to the anger of the masses. The attack on him and his brother on 21 June 1672 resulted in effective loss of control of the power of state and, more sinisterly, in the execution of his attacker, interpreted by the people as a martyrdom,. Calls for the elevation of the prince were strengthened. The civil unrest, often sustained rather than controlled by the civic militias, forced the hands of the towns and eventually all the Holland representatives agreed to the revocation of the Perpetual Edict on 3 July and the appointment of William as stadholder six days later.[41] Following the events of 1672, an informal form of censorship restricted pamphlet literature to support of the Orangist regime until the end of the Third Anglo-Dutch War in 1674, after which 'The Arminians, and fifth monarchy men ... continue printing pasquilles against the Prince of Orange, and Pensioner Fagel', reflecting the precarious fragility of Dutch unity during the war.[42]

Less than two weeks after the appointment of the prince as stadholder, the final overthrow of De Witt was brought about, first through accusations of treason against his brother and, after his sentence fell short of death, the violent reaction of the crowd on the night of 20 August and the murder of both the De Witt brothers. Three days later, Gaspar Fagel was appointed grand pensionary, and the internal conflict began to subside as major changes (*wetsverzettingen*) were made to many town governments removing overtly anti-Orangist regents from office. In most cases the lists of replacements were drawn up by the prince and his advisors, but in the case of Amsterdam, the city itself undertook many of the changes but submitted the final lists to the stadholder for approval. This not only allowed several anti-Orangists to retain their office, but also gave the influential members of the town council the opportunity to select those most likely to be useful politically. And it gave Amsterdam the power to act, from time to time, as an effective opposition to the aims of the prince and influence their relationship with him until 1688.[43]

---

[41] D.J. Roorda, in *Het rampjaar 1672* (Bussum, 1971), and, *idem, Partij en factie. De oproeren van 1672 in de steden van Holland en Zeeland, een krachtmeting tussen partijen en facties* (Groningen, 1961), gives a full account of events in the Dutch Republic in 1672.

[42] British National Archives (London), SP84/199, f. 6; Roorda, *Partij en factie*, p. 12. The majority of the pamphlet literature published in the Dutch Republic in the late seventeenth century can be found through W.P.C. Knuttel, *Catalogus van de pamfletten-verzameling berustende in de Koninklijke Bibliotheek* (9 vols, The Hague, 1889–1920).

[43] There is some doubt about the origin of the list for replacements in the top level of Amsterdam's city government: I.J. Brugmans (ed.), *Geschiedenis van Amsterdam*

In contrast to the fall and death of De Witt was the dramatic rise to favour and power of the Prince of Orange, whose education De Witt had tried to direct, but who was also strongly influenced by his family and its history. He was reaching his majority with a keen interest in military matters and had a core of supporters with political momentum on their side. But in the long term his stadholdership was to be fraught with internal tensions. The events of 1650, and more particularly the Act of Exclusion of 1654 and De Witt's justification of it, had established a *raison d'état* which brought political theory nearer to reality. The ideas expounded in de la Court's *Het Interest van Holland* of 1662[44] reflected the core working ideology of the True Freedom[45] which could not be undone by the changes of 1672, when the powers of the grand pensionary to guide and determine States policy were acknowledged in the *'Instructie raadpensionaris'*.[46] The degree of input and influence from De Witt in the book has been discussed often, but the significance of the publication is the impact it made on political reality in the Dutch Republic. The years of De Witt's power had altered the political state for the long term and it was one of the major restraints on William III that he could never assert himself in the way his forefathers had done, despite being granted many of their privileges in perpetuity for his family. In effect, this concession was emptier than their lifetime appointments and in the face of opposition and frustration, particularly with Amsterdam, he drew back pragmatically from the kind of actions employed by his father.

In the Treaty of Westminster in February 1674, barely two years into the Third Anglo-Dutch War, the English negotiated peace with the Dutch Republic. By 1673 it had become clear to the English that the war was a vehicle for French ambition, and the new Parliament in the same year, sustained by the propaganda of *Englands Appeal*, put pressure on the king, to which he finally succumbed in early 1674 and the Peace of Westminster was signed in February of that year.[47] Added to the propaganda of *Englands Appeal*, the activities of the agent Du Moulin strengthened the case for those arguing for

---

[44] P. de la Court, *Het Interest van Holland, ofte Grond van Hollands welvaren* (Amsterdam, 1662).

[45] For discussion on the theory of True Freedom see: G.O. van de Klashorst, 'De Ware Vrijheid, 1650–1672', in *Vrijheid. Een geschiedenis van de vijftiende tot de twintigste eeuw*, ed E.G.O. Haitsma Mulier and W.R.E. Velema (Amsterdam, 1999), pp. 157–85; Gijs Rommelse and Roger Downing, 'The fleet as an ideological pillar of Dutch radical republicanism, 1650–1672', *The International Journal of Maritime History*, 27:3 (2015), 388–92; and Smit, 'The Netherlands and Europe', pp. 22–8.

[46] Edwards, 'An unknown statesman', 356.

[47] *Englands Appeal from the private cabal at White-hall to the great council of the nation, the Lords and Commons in Parliament assembled. By a true lover of his country* (London, 1673); Jones, *Anglo-Dutch Wars*, p. 199.

(6 vols, Utrecht and Antwerp, 1972–73), p. 182; Bontemantel, *De Regeeringe van Amsterdam*, II, 196.

a peace with the Dutch. Haley's thesis on this affair of 1672–74 drew on the comprehensive correspondence of English agents in the Netherlands during the Third Anglo-Dutch War to demonstrate the range, styles and effectiveness of secret correspondences.[48]

In this context it is perhaps more useful to look at the war of 1672 as two independent struggles against allies with widely differing war aims: the predominantly naval Anglo-Dutch war of 1672–74, and the land-based Franco-Dutch conflict of 1672–78. Each contributed eventually to the breakdown of Anglo-French relations, and the gradual shift to the alliance with England resulting from the events of 1688/9. While the English king and Parliament were engaged in their own power struggles, the Dutch war with France continued until the Peace of Nijmegen in 1678 and sowed the seeds of the fairly ill-assorted coalition which grew up in opposition to the France of Louis XIV and the new balance of power which emerged at Utrecht in 1713. Military success for William III did not last beyond 1674 as the war became a series of stalemate events and a strong peace party emerged in 1675, dividing the towns of Holland and creating an alliance between, among others, the Holland pacifist towns and the province of Friesland. The prince's dalliance with the proffered dukedom of Gelderland in 1675 was pragmatically rejected, but had raised again the spectre of monarchic and dynastic ambitions. As an English observer wrote to secretary of state, Sir Joseph Williamson, in 1675:

> The people in Amsterdam half mad, it is not be believed how strongly the peoples' affections are alienated since that attempt of making the Prince, Duke of Gelderland. This country dayly decayes in politiques and traide and the suffrable taxes make the people made [*sic*]. If the war last one year more, this land will be ruined.[49]

From the late 1660s, the French ambassadors, first the Comte D'Estrades, the Marquis de Pomponne and then the Comte D'Avaux, carried out their formal diplomatic duties in the name of Louis XIV with the official representatives of the States General, but worked with the opposition within Amsterdam with varying degrees of success.[50] D'Avaux extended his contacts to the province

---

[48] K.H.D. Haley, *William III and the English opposition 1672–74* (Oxford, 1966); Dutch National Archives (The Hague), 10.10.29/547.

[49] British National Archive, SP84/199, f. 6.

[50] Godefroy D'Estrades, *Lettres, mémoires et négociations de M. le Comte d'Estrades*, ed. P. Marchand (9 vols and supplement, The Hague, 1743). Vols 7, 8 and 9 specifically include the correspondence of the three French ambassadors (D'Estrades, D'Avaux and Colbert) at Nijmegen from 1676 to 1678; Jean Antoine de Mesme, Comte d'Avaux, *Négociations de Monsieur le Comte D'Avaux en Hollande depuis 1679, jusqu'en 1684*, ed. E. Mallet (6 vols, Paris, 1752); Charles-Edouard Levillain, 'French diplomacy and the run-up to the Glorious Revolution (1688): a critical reading of Jean-Antoine d'Avaux' correspondence as ambassador to the States General', *The Journal of Modern History* 88 (2016), 130–50.

of Friesland in the 1680s.[51] To counteract his activities, particularly in the 1670s and 1680s, grand pensionary Fagel developed a network of internal agents within the States who reported on the opposition and their contacts with the French ambassador.[52]

The final French victory consolidated some of their gains in the Spanish Netherlands, but it can also be seen that the very survival of the Dutch state against the ambition of Louis XIV was a victory for the future of the Republic which had looked into the face of a new autocratic overlord and come away with its borders and institutions intact.[53] The politics behind the marriage of William III with Mary Stuart in 1677 were shaped by several influences: closer English and Dutch ties, the ambition of William as a potential claimant to the English throne, the breakdown of Anglo-French relations, and Charles II's desire to strengthen his own image as a protestant Stuart as opposed to the duke of York's obvious catholicism. However it had taken five years of planning, having been viewed negatively by both the Dutch and English, and was finally made in a rather low-key manner, but eventually not only strengthened William's standing in relation to the English crown, but also consolidated his perceived role in the eyes of France.[54]

The English were somewhat restrained in European matters after the final peace between the French and Dutch at Nijmegen in 1678 as they became embroiled in the Popish Plot episode and the consequent exclusion crisis of 1679–83 with all its ramifications for the eventual denouement of James II's reign. Meanwhile in the Dutch Republic matters nearly reached breaking point between the prince and Amsterdam from 1682 to 1684, as the urgency of relieving the siege of Luxembourg and containing French expansion was driving the Orangist cause and funds were required for a force of up to 16,000 men. In late 1683, William and his advisors made a week-long visit to the city to secure their support for increased military finance, but in the end left in total frustration. Kurtz's definitive work, *William III en Amsterdam 1683–5*, provides a useful source for this crisis, and her examination of the contemporary pamphlet literature demonstrates the level of propaganda which it

[51] J.F. Gebhard, *Het leven van Mr Nicolaas Cornelisz Witsen (1641–1717)* (2 vols, Utrecht, 1881), I, 209–10.
[52] Edwards, 'An unknown statesman', 366–70; and E.C. Edwards, 'Amsterdam and the ambassadors of Louis XIV 1674–85', in *Louis XIV outside in: images of the Sun King beyond France, 1661–1715*, eds Tony Claydon and Charles-Edouard Levillain (Farnham, 2015), pp. 187–208.
[53] D.J. Roorda, 'The Peace of Nijmegen, the end of a particular period in Dutch history', in *The Peace of Nijmegen 1676–1678/9. International congress of the tricentennial Nijmegen 14–16 September 1978*, ed. J.A.H. Bots (Amsterdam, 1980), pp. 17–28.
[54] Baxter, *William III*, pp. 144–5 and 148–50; Israel, *Dutch Republic*, pp. 841–2; Troost, *William III*, pp. 137–8.

created.[55] The following year, letters from the French ambassador to Louis XIV, giving details of his contacts with Amsterdam, were passed to the prince and, despite the city being censured, support for their views eventually won out in the States General and William was forced to admit defeat.

However, the issues became joined against the ambitions of Louis XIV exacerbated by the *dragonades* from 1681 and the revocation of the Edict of Nantes in 1685, when religious refugees in both the Netherlands and England provided a visible sign of the effect of Louis XIV's policies, together with the actions of James II after 1685. The tensions between William and Amsterdam, for whom peace had become the watchword for economic recovery and any attempts to increase military expenditure anathema, had to be addressed through negotiation and compromise. Foremost among the arbitrators of consensus between the prince, the grand pensionary Fagel and Amsterdam in late 1688 was the burgomaster Nicholas Witsen. In service with the prince in the field in 1676, Witsen emerged as the leading politician in Amsterdam during the 1680s as 'the most influential of the then Amsterdam burgomasters and a man who was by no means an uncritical accomplice of the Stadholder ...'.[56] This is not the place to rehearse the events leading to the Dutch expedition to England in November 1688, but suffice it to say that among the major elements in the Dutch decision to support the Prince of Orange were the renewed trade war with France, the collapse of the Amsterdam stock exchange in August 1688, and both the threats to, and potential for, maritime trade.[57]

[55] G.H. Kurtz, *Willem III en Amsterdam 1683–5* (Utrecht, 1928). See also, Edwards, 'An unknown statesman', 367; Franken, *Coenraad van Beuningen's politieke aktiviteiten*, pp. 220–38; Israel, *Dutch Republic*, pp. 830–4; Wout Troost, 'William III, Brandenburg, and the construction of the anti-French coalition, 1672–88', in *The Anglo-Dutch moment. Essays on the Glorious Revolution and its world impact*, ed. Jonathan I. Israel (Cambridge, 1991), p. 327.

[56] The only full study of Witsen remains: Gebhard, *Het leven van Mr Nicolaas Cornelisz Witsen*; P.J.A.N. Rietbergen, 'A fateful alliance? William III and England in Dutch historiography, 1688–9', in *The Anglo-Dutch moment*, ed. Israel (Cambridge, 1991), p. 470.

[57] Jonathan I. Israel, *Spain, the Low Countries and the struggle for world supremacy 1585–1713* (London, 1997), pp. 330–43.

5

Competing navies: Anglo-Dutch naval rivalry, 1652–88

John B. Hattendorf

The period of acute Anglo-Dutch rivalry in the seventeenth century involved three maritime economic wars and wide-ranging peacetime competition at sea, but ended with a transformation in international politics and mutual relations that turned those same rivals into the close allies that became known as 'The Maritime Powers'. The three naval wars in 1652–54, 1665–67 and 1672–74, as well as the Dutch invasion of England in 1688, were separated by periods of maritime, economic, and colonial rivalry. The navies of both countries operated primarily in European waters, but there was a gradual increase in naval activities in the wider Atlantic world in this period. Although the immediate causes and contexts for each of the periods of conflict were different, these conflicts were each incremental stages in an Anglo-Dutch naval arms race that established navies as permanent standing forces among the major European powers. At the same time, navies created basic approaches to warship design, naval operations, and naval tactics that dominated European naval warfare into the early nineteenth century.

Competition in the maritime shipping world

The gradual ending of the Thirty Years' War and the Eighty Years' War between 1646 and 1648 transformed the international security and economic situations of Europe. For the Dutch Republic, these changes heralded a new phase in the Dutch economy that brought its maritime trade and dominance at sea to new heights. The Dutch advantage made English shipping rates no longer attractive and English shipping firms found themselves suddenly undercut in trading to the Baltic, Caribbean, Flanders, Italy, Ottoman Empire, Spain, and Portugal. England was not alone in feeling the brunt of Dutch commercial success. The merchants of Denmark, Genoa, the Hanseatic League, and Venice were also hurt, but the English losses were higher than others. In particular, the English resented

Dutch success.[1] Strongly objecting, the English ambassadors complained to the States General in March 1651 that Dutch shipping companies had been keeping the 'foundation to themselves for ingrossing the universal trade not only of Christendom, but indeed, of the greater part of the knowne world'.[2] This widening gap in maritime trade is one of several factors that led to war between England and the Dutch Republic, but it was only indirectly reflected in the corresponding naval developments in each country.

Navies in the early modern period[3]

In studying Swedish history, the British historian Michael Roberts set off a widespread debate among military historians with his 1956 inaugural lecture at Queen's University in Belfast on 'The Military Revolution, 1560–1660'.[4] He argued that technical developments in military tactics created a revolution in military affairs that 'exercised a profound influence upon the future course of European history. It stands like a great divide separating medieval society from the modern world.'[5] Some naval historians have sought to find a similar naval revolution. The historiographical discussion first moved toward changing technology as a reflection of a revolution in naval affairs. The pacifist scholar Carlo Cipolla, who thought revolutions an impolite and irrational way of settling issues, led the way with his study of technological innovation and the early phases of European imperial expansion.[6] Historians such as John Guilmartin, Richard Barker, Geoffrey Parker and Andrew Thrush all pointed to technological innovations that marked vital turning points in early modern naval history.[7] Parker went much further to argue that 'a revolution in naval warfare occurred in early modern Europe which was no less important than that by land, for it opened the way to the exercise of European hegemony over most of the world's oceans for much

---

[1] Jonathan I. Israel, *The Dutch Republic. Its rise, greatness and fall* (Oxford, 1995), pp. 610–11; *idem, Dutch primacy in world trade, 1585–1740* (Oxford, 1989), pp. 197–207.

[2] English Ambassadors to the States General, 30 March 1651. Quoted in Israel, *Dutch primacy*, p. 207, from the Dutch National Archive (The Hague), 1.01.02/5899/i.

[3] The following section is based on John Hattendorf, 'Navies and naval operations', in *The Routledge research companion to marine and maritime worlds, 1400–1800*, eds Claire Jowitt, Craig Lambert and Steven Mentz (London, forthcoming).

[4] Michael Roberts, 'The Military Revolution, 1560–1660', in *Essays in Swedish history*, ed. Michael Roberts (London, 1967), pp. 195–225.

[5] Roberts, 'Military Revolution', p. 195.

[6] Carlo Cipolla, *Guns, sails and empires. Technological innovation and the early phases of European expansion, 1400–1700* (New York, 1966).

[7] John Guilmartin, *Gunpowder and galleys. Changing technology and Mediterranean warfare at sea in the sixteenth century* (New York, 1975); the principal articles are gathered in Jan Glete (ed.), *Naval history, 1500–1680* (Aldershot, 2005), pp. 3–97.

of the modern period'.[8] Another line of historiography linked the revolution in military affairs to navies with the development of bureaucracies and the fiscal-military state.[9] In a precursor to Roberts's 1956 military revolution argument, the economist Joseph Schumpeter had argued that the power of the state to tax stemmed from the need in early modern Europe to support standing armies. Looking back to this argument in 2004, a group of scholars suggested that navies found a variety of other sources of sustainment. These factors included the interrelationship of navies with overseas trade, indirect taxation, royal patronage, and more efficient and adaptable bureaucracies.[10] Additionally, there are critical links between naval developments and the nature of the national societies that supported navies, the character of those governments, and the types of naval operations involved.[11] More recently, Louis Sicking has argued that none of this made for a revolution in naval affairs. While there were fundamental technological, organizational, operational, and tactical changes for navies, these changes took place through evolution over three centuries and constituted a transformation, not a revolution.[12]

---

[8] Geoffrey Parker, *Military Revolution. Military innovation and the rise of the West* (Cambridge, 1988), pp. 82–114, quotation at p. 83.

[9] Jan Glete, *War and the state in early modern Europe. Spain, the Dutch Republic and Sweden as fiscal-military states* (Abingdon, 2005), pp. 140–73.

[10] N.A.M. Rodger, 'From the "military revolution" to the "fiscal-naval state"', *Journal of Maritime Research*, 13:2 (2011), 119–28; *idem*, 'Introduction. Navies and state formation', in *Navies and state formation. The Schumpeter thesis revisited and reflected*, eds J.G. Backhaus, N. Kyriazis and N.A.M. Rodger (Munster, 2012), pp. 9–20.

[11] Rodger, 'Introduction', pp. 9–20; Ole Felbaek, 'Navy, army, and state finances. Denmark, 1500–1700', in *Navies and state formation*, eds Backhaus, Kyriazis and Rodger, pp. 108–10; Jan Glete, 'The Swedish fiscal-military state and its navy, 1521–1721', in *ibid.*, pp. 158–62; Holger Herwig, 'Navalism and state building. The Tirpitz Plan 1897–1914', in *ibid.*, pp. 205–13; P.K. O'Brien, 'State formation and economic growth. The case of Britain, 1688–1846', in *ibid.*, pp. 271–2; Karel Davids and Marjolein 't Hart, 'The navy and the rise of the state. The case of the Netherlands, c. 1570–1810', in *ibid.*, pp. 306–8; Ian Thompson, 'Navies and state formation. The case of Spain (1500–1800)', in *ibid.*, pp. 350–1; Jürgen Backhaus, 'Financing the navy – the Schumpeter hypothesis refuted', in *ibid.*, p. 361.

[12] Louis Sicking, 'Naval warfare in Europe, c. 1330 – c. 1680', in *European warfare, 1350–1750*, eds F. Tallett and D.J.B. Trim (Cambridge, 2010), pp. 236–63; *idem*, 'European naval warfare', in *Oxford handbook of early modern European history, 1350–1750. Volume 2: Cultures and power*, ed. Hamish Scott (Oxford, 2015), pp. 591–611. See also, Beatrice Heuser, *Strategy before Clausewitz. Linking warfare and statecraft, 1400–1830* (Abingdon, 2017), pp. 48–64; Gijs Rommelse, 'An early modern naval revolution? The relationship between "economic reason of state" and maritime warfare', *Journal of Maritime Research* 13:2 (2011), 138–50.

The English and the Dutch navies in the mid-seventeenth century

During the reign of King Charles I from 1625 to 1649, the Royal Navy reflected within itself the opposing social and political divisions of Britain's three kingdoms. Naval officers from the aristocracy – the gentlemen officers – supported the king's navy as a symbol of the monarchical state and the navy's use as a symbol and weapon of the king's power and royal purpose on the high seas. In contrast, the naval officers from other social classes who had risen solely on merit within the service – the tarpaulin officers – represented merchant trade that the king had shown little interest in protecting and the parliamentary politics that the king was stifling. On top of this, the king represented a 'high church' Anglicanism that some thought was only a disguised form of Roman Catholicism. In opposition, the merchant community showed strong support for Presbyterianism and a range of puritanical protestant views.[13] In this situation, the navy became a point of national political contention over the constitutional issue of parliamentary funding for the king's navy.

As the political divisions within the British Isles grew into a civil war between the king and Parliament in 1642, the use of the sea for the political and economic purposes of the opposing sides became increasingly important. Early on, the parliamentary forces took control over most of the navy, placing the Earl of Warwick as commander-in-chief and, later, lord admiral. At the same time, the parliamentarian John Pym began to strengthen the financial foundations for the navy and improve naval administration through a series of interlocking parliamentary committees. As a result, the earlier constitutional tension over the navy that had existed between king and Parliament disappeared.[14] Although events on land, rather than at sea, determined the results of the Civil War, the uses of sea power provided essential aspects to the conflict. The ability of parliamentary naval forces to impose a degree of control in British coastal waters was a crucial factor to the success of parliamentary forces. The Civil War laid the basis for future naval development on a global basis with the deployment of naval forces to the Mediterranean and West Indies and with the incremental development of dockyards, victualling facilities, and warship construction. These developments during the Civil War were erratic and uncoordinated. They contributed to the centralization of naval direction in England and the overall sustainment and effectiveness of the growing experience and professionalization of naval officers and ratings, preparing them for the future naval conflicts.[15]

---

[13] N.A.M. Rodger, *The safeguard of the sea. A naval history of Britain, 660–1649* (London, 1997), p. 410.

[14] *Ibid.*, pp. 417 and 421–2.

[15] Richard Blakemore and Elaine Murphy, *The British civil wars at sea, 1638–1653* (Woodbridge, 2018), pp. 173–8.

From the establishment of the Dutch Republic and the beginning of the Eighty Years' War, naval forces were essential for the protection of local waters as well as the trade that expanded rapidly from 1590 onwards. In contrast to the English navy, the navy of the Dutch Republic was a decentralized organization that utilized local networks for mobilizing resources for national maritime defence. Since 1626, the Dutch navy had developed a permanent corps of naval captains. Due to the local network connections of the admiralties, the navy benefited from the rapid advances in technology and rational shipbuilding that provided the foundation for Dutch maritime supremacy in the seventeenth century. The admiralties each had the function of enforcing maritime law, authorizing privateers, and selling the licences for convoy and foreign trade. In the period before the Anglo-Dutch wars, the navy's principal source of financial support was the sale of licences tied to the navy's major function to protect maritime trade.[16]

Table 5.1 The major European navies, 1640–50,
compared in total displacement tonnage

Year	England	Dutch Republic	France	Denmark-Norway	Sweden	Portugal (estimated)
1640	38,000	45,000	29,000	20,000	28,000	18,000
1645	39,000	-	20,000	16,000	35,000	18,000
1650	49,000	29,000	21,000	23,000	28,000	26,000
1655	90,000	64,000	18,000	21,000	23,000	17,000

Source: Jan Glete, *Navies and nations. Warships, navies and state building in Europe and America, 1500–1860* (2 vols, Stockholm, 1993), I, 179 and 186.

The statistics of the size of European navies between 1640 and 1650 reflect both the general effect of the peace in continental Europe and the growth of the English navy during the Civil War. In 1640, the Dutch navy was 118 per cent the size of the English navy. Five years later in the mid-1640s, the Swedish navy temporarily surpassed the Dutch. By the end of the decade, however, the Dutch navy had regained a slight relative edge in size over the Swedish navy but had dropped to only 59 per cent of the size of the English fleet. By 1650, the English navy had rapidly grown in size during the English Civil War, while the Dutch navy had declined in total tonnage as it divested itself of hired shipping and was no longer the largest navy in Europe.

---

[16] Glete, *War and the state*, 165–7; Jaap R. Bruijn, 'The raison d'être and the actual employment of the Dutch navy in early modern times', in *Strategy and the sea. Essays in honour of John B. Hattendorf*, eds N.A.M. Rodger, J. Ross Dancy, Benjamin Darnell and Evan Wilson (Woodbridge, 2016), pp. 77–8; Davids and 't Hart, 'Case of the Netherlands', pp. 285–8.

In 1648, the Dutch navy settled into a peacetime routine. The principal mission of the Dutch navy was convoying merchant ships in dangerous waters and being the general protector of Dutch maritime supremacy. For these purposes, the Dutch fleet was made up of smaller-sized warships, under a thousand tons displacement. Approximately one-third of the Dutch fleet was between 500 and 1,000 tons displacement while the other two-thirds was between 100 and 500 tons displacement.[17] These ships lacked uniformity in design, creating marked differences in speed and manoeuvrability among them. At this point, the Dutch navy had given little thought to standardization in warship design as a component for a fleet in battle.[18]

Despite the fluctuations over the decade of the 1640s, the English navy had become the largest in Europe by 1650, with a notable superiority in size over the Dutch navy, now in second place. Sweden and Portugal had become close contenders to the Dutch with a rough parity in size among those navies. At the end of the decade in continental Europe, there was no indication that a significant naval armaments race might be brewing.

In England, the parliamentary naval forces had acquired a large number of ships through capture, purchase and construction between 1645 and 1650. These acquisitions reflected a fundamental change in the nature of the English fleet which, like the Dutch, had been a combination of hired merchant ships and purpose-built warships. By the early 1650s, purpose-built warships dominated the English navy.[19]

There were both external and internal reasons why Parliament needed to strengthen its navy.[20] The leaders of the new Commonwealth saw the need for a strong navy to complete the revolution and to eliminate the royalist forces that remained both at home and abroad, where they were harboured in the Dutch Republic and in colonies such as Barbados, Virginia, and elsewhere. At the same time, some had a desire to export the English revolution. As the radical Puritan preacher Hugh Peter told Parliament in December 1648, 'This army must root up Monarchy, not only here, but in France and other Kingdoms round about; this is to bring you out of Egypt: this army must dash the powers of the earth to pieces.'[21] Moreover, with the active support of the merchant shipping community

---

[17] Glete, *Navies and nations*, I, 201. For lists of ships, see James Bender, *Dutch warships in the age of sail 1600–1714. Design, construction, careers and fates* (Barnsley, 2014), pp. 140–79.

[18] Jaap Bruijn, *The Dutch navy of the seventeenth and eighteenth century* (Columbia, 1993), pp. 60–1.

[19] Hans Christophe Junge, *Flottenpolitik und Revolution. Die Entstehung der englishen Seemacht während der Herrschaft Cromwells* (Stuttgard, 1980), p. 133. For details, see J.D. Davies, *Pepys's navy. Ships, men and warfare, 1649–1689* (Barnsley, 2008); and Rif Winfield, *British warships in the age of sail 1603–1714. Design, construction, careers and fates* (Barnsley, 2009).

[20] Glete, *Navies and nations*, I, 179–80.

[21] Quoted in Junge, *Flottenpolitik*, p. 121

behind the Commonwealth, there was a continuing desire to rebalance the trade advantage that the Dutch had gained after the Peace of Westphalia in 1648.

Pressure from the Eastland and Levant merchants involved in European trade along with the Hamburg Merchant Adventurers and some influential merchants involved in the West India trades led to Parliament passing the Navigation Act of 1651. This Act revived earlier ideas to challenge Dutch commercial interests by requiring goods imported into England to be carried directly from their point of origin in English ships. The assumptions and motivations behind the Act were not purely commercial in nature. Merchant shipping and the fisheries were traditionally associated with maintaining a nursery for seamen upon which the navy depended. Additionally, the regulation of trade required some naval means to enforce the law at sea. Furthermore, having a strong navy in place gave the Commonwealth the armed strength to back diplomatic negotiations with other countries as well as to challenge the Dutch at sea, if necessary. At the same time, the navy provided a means to export some degree of control to overseas colonies and the protection of colonial trades.[22]

The Commonwealth's decision to expand its navy created a major governmental crisis between 1649 and 1652. From a national management perspective, there was too much work needed and too few to do it with too few resources. Also, there were extensive logistical and financial needs for expanding the fleet in 1649 and then maintaining that fleet. Operations extended first to support military expeditions in the Downs, Ireland and Scotland, then Portugal and the Western Mediterranean in 1650–51, with additional squadrons sent to Barbados and Virginia in 1651. In response, the Commonwealth began as early as 1649 to re-organize the administrative and fiscal management of the navy to meet these mounting challenges.[23]

The First Anglo-Dutch War, 1652–54[24]

When war finally erupted between the Dutch and the English in the spring of 1652, it happened suddenly. War followed the breakdown of the Anglo-Dutch diplomatic negotiations over England's Navigation Act and the Dutch rejection

---

[22] David Ormrod, *The rise of commercial empires. England and the Netherlands in the age of mercantilism 1650–1770* (Cambridge, 2003), p. 310; Charles Wilson, *Profit and power. A study of England and the Dutch wars* (London, 1957), pp. 53–9; Michael Braddick, 'The English government, war, trade and settlement, 1625–1688', in *The Oxford history of the British empire. Volume 1: The origins of empire* (Oxford, 1998), pp. 302 and 306.

[23] James Scott Wheeler, 'Prelude to power. The crisis of 1649 and the foundation of English naval power', *The Mariner's Mirror* 81:2 (1995), 148–55; *idem, The making of a world power. War and the military revolution in seventeenth century England* (Stroud, 1999), pp. 43–6.

[24] This section is a revised version of the similar section in: John Hattendorf, 'Navies, strategy and tactics in the age of De Ruyter', in *De Ruyter. Dutch admiral*, eds J.R.

of England's proposal for a union between the English Commonwealth and the Dutch Republic. England's immediate objective in going to war was to compel the Dutch Republic to stop the Dutch claim to immunity from a search at sea and to stop harbouring enemy royalists. Dutch maritime trade and fisheries were the obvious Dutch vulnerabilities that England could strike. Even while negotiations were in progress, the Dutch immediately mobilized a fleet of 150 ships under Lieutenant-Admiral Maarten Harpertszoon Tromp to protect Dutch shipping between the Strait of Gibraltar and the Sound. At the time, the five Dutch admiralties had seventy-nine warships collectively available to them, most of which were old and not ready for battle. As typical of practice in the past, the mobilization brought in a variety of ships to the fleet that were essentially armed merchantmen on lease. The English saw this mobilization as a threat. The very fact of naval mobilization added a volatile element to the situation.

The geostrategic maritime relationship between the Dutch Republic and the British Isles gave England an advantage. All Dutch Atlantic and Asiatic trade had to pass either south of the British Isles through the narrow waters of the Channel, or 'north about' around Scotland, to the North Sea. Additionally, the prevailing southwesterly winds made it more difficult for Dutch ships to approach England directly, while it was easier for the English to approach the Dutch coast.

The situation in which the conflict arose did not present opportunities for any extensive thinking about strategy, that is to say, comprehensively using naval force to control an enemy force to achieve broader political objectives. Although the Dutch fleet was numerically superior, the English navy was in a better condition to fight. In 1652, the Dutch preferred their well-tried approach in using a limited number of ships, operating from a windward position, to quickly sail downwind to attack enemy ships and to grapple and board them for immediate hand-to-hand combat. When operating in large fleets with a wide variety of ship-types, they had developed an organization of five squadrons that each sailed from the windward position in a line-ahead formation to approach the enemy, then immediately moved to attack individual ships with initial gunfire, then grappled and overwhelmed them with a large boarding party.[25]

Initial English attacks on the Dutch fisheries north of Scotland and returning Dutch East Indiamen in the Channel failed. From this approach, English naval strategy shifted to attacking Dutch naval vessels with the

---

Bruijn, R.B. Prud'homme van Reine and R. van Hövell tot Westerflier (Rotterdam, 2011), pp. 97–118.

[25] Bruijn, *Dutch navy*, pp. 53–4; *idem*, *Varend verleden. De Nederlandse oorlogsvloot in de zeventiende en achttiende eeuw* (Amsterdam, 1995), pp. 92–3. See also 'The resolution of Admiral Tromp on the distribution of the fleet in case of its being attacked', in *Fighting instructions 1530–1816*, ed. J.S. Corbett (London, 1905), p. 91.

object of removing them as a preliminary to destroying Dutch trade. Battles were typically fought as opposing fleets encountered one another. The initial tactical preference of English naval commanders involved choosing to use their warships in gunnery duels in a line-of-battle against opposing Dutch warships that were protecting convoys of merchant vessels. The Dutch acceptance of this challenge with a similar type of naval force created a kind of operational reasoning that led eventually to a strategic rationale for naval power.[26]

The English General at Sea, Robert Blake, encountered the Dutch fleet off Dover on 19/29 May 1652 and demanded a salute in recognition of Britain's sovereignty of those seas.[27] Gunshots were exchanged and a battle ensued in which two Dutch ships were lost. The incident marked the beginning of the open conflict between the two states. This action illustrated little change from earlier practices. As chance encounters, there is no indication of pre-planned approaches on either side, either from a strategic or a tactical point of view. The surviving accounts of subsequent engagements – including those in the Channel near Plymouth when De Ruyter had a minor victory over Sir George Ayscue in action on 16/26 August 1652; the battle of the Kentish Knock in the Thames estuary in which Blake and Vice-Admiral Sir William Penn defeated Admiral Witte de With on 28 September/8 October 1652, the battle of Dungeness in which Tromp defeated Blake on 30 November/10 December 1652 – suggest that no new or distinctive tactics were in use. At Dungeness, Tromp's numerical superiority had won the day for the Dutch. The battle demonstrated to the Council of State in England that the naval administrative crisis that had begun in 1649 had not yet been resolved. Parliament had voted no additional funds for the navy since the beginning of the war and was not matching requests for rising English naval expenditures. Changes in parliamentary direction along with new admiralty and navy commissions improved the administrative situation for a time until Cromwell's coup of April 1653 and his subsequently becoming Lord Protector in December 1653. From that point, the army-dominated government failed to appreciate some critical naval needs.[28]

The following year, Blake and his fellow General at Sea, Richard Deane, were able to attack the Dutch convoy under Tromp's protection off Portland in a three-day battle that had begun on 18/28 February 1652/3. Similarly, the English defeated the Dutch at the Gabbard off the North Foreland on 12–13/22–23 June 1653, and off Terheide, south of Scheveningen, on 10/20

[26] Herbert Richmond, *Statesmen and sea power* (Oxford, 1946), pp. 39–41.
[27] See Thomas Wemyss Fulton, *The sovereignty of the sea. An historical account of the claims of England to the dominion of the British seas, and of the evolution of the territorial waters* (Edinburgh and London, 1911).
[28] N.A.M. Rodger, *The command of the ocean. A naval history of Britain, 1649–1815* (London, 2004), pp. 35–7; Wheeler, *Making of a world power*, pp. 47–56.

August 1653, when Tromp died in action. The English suffered a severe loss when Commodore Jan van Galen destroyed the four-ship English squadron of Richard Badiley at Livorno (Leghorn) in the Mediterranean on 13/23 March 1652/3, leaving English trade unprotected in the Mediterranean. In response, the Council of State detached twenty ships from the main fleet and sent them to the Mediterranean. The Council's decision was an English strategic error that allowed Tromp's larger fleet to defeat Blake off Dungeness in December 1652, but it taught a lesson for the future not to divide the fleet.

The first minor evidence of any change taking place in tactical ideas occurred on 10/20 February 1652/3, just eight days before the battle of Portland. Vice-Admiral Sir William Penn issued instructions to his squadron directing the smaller ships to stand to windward to observe and to protect the larger fighting ships from an attack by enemy fireships.[29] The major change came on 29 March/8 April 1653 at Portland, where the English were refitting after the three-day battle off that port. Preparing for the next encounter, the three English Generals at Sea – Robert Blake, Richard Deane, and George Monck – issued two complementary documents, 'Instructions for the better ordering of the Fleet in Fighting'[30] and 'Instructions for the better ordering of the Fleet in Sailing'.[31] While much of these were a compilation of standard and existing directives, they included some innovations. First, issued together they established a connection between cruising formations and tactical formations in a battle that naval officers developed later. Despite their limitations, these documents were to be acted upon at sea in the context of preparation for battle, giving the English fleet a degree of discipline under the control of its flag officers that it had not previously seen.

Although the evidence from surviving documents is vague, from this point forward the English fleet began to conduct itself differently than it previously had. The next major battle was at the Gabbard on 2–3/12–13 June 1653, in which Deane died in action. Despite that loss, both English and Dutch sources report that the English ships were under better control and that their broadside gunnery while in a line was effective in preventing the Dutch from approaching for grappling and boarding. While this is suggestive of new tactical thinking, there is no evidence that it was employed in the final major battle of the war off Terheide.

These experiences of naval warfare between 1652 and 1654 led naval leaders to think differently and to prepare for future wars. For the Dutch, the reverses at sea led to an immediate commitment to build a larger fleet of purpose-built warships to replace the traditional dependence on leasing

---

[29] B. Tunstall, *Naval warfare in the age of sail. The evolution of fighting tactics, 1680–1815* (London, 1990), p. 18.

[30] Corbett, *Fighting instructions*, pp. 99–103; J.R. Powell (ed.), *The letters of Robert Blake, together with supplementary records* (London, 1937), pp. 467–71.

[31] Powell (ed.), *Letters of Blake*, pp. 471–6.

armed merchantmen. While the war was still in progress, the States General authorized in February 1653 the construction of thirty purpose-built warships carrying up to fifty-four guns. As the peace negotiations were in progress at the end of the year, thirty more similar warships were ordered, and soon they were declared as public property that could not be demobilized and sold off at the end of a war.[32] The Dutch Republic's need to replace hired ships with purpose-built warships created costs that forced the States General to subsidize the five admiralties with funding from the provinces beyond the admiralties' traditional funding source in convoy fees and selling licences. During the First Anglo-Dutch War, the admiralties had 33 per cent of their funding from the provinces with only 27 per cent from convoys and licensing. A new tax of shipping and trade supplied 23 per cent to supplement the funding. The key figure in making this permanent shift of financial and political support for the navy was *raadpensionaris* Johan de Witt.[33]

With this series of decisions, the most powerful navy in Europe shifted to adopt the new international standard of permanent national navies; others nations followed this lead. At the same time, this led to the tacit acceptance of a strategic corollary: the protection of one's own merchant trade and the security of one's coast from invasion – two central functions for navies – was best achieved by fighting and defeating a similar type of enemy naval force in a battle between warships. The presence of an undefeated enemy naval force gave that opposing nation an ability to oppose one's use of the seaways for either peaceful trade or military use.

The interwar period, 1654–65

In the dozen years that lay between the First and Second Dutch Wars, both the Dutch and English navies continued to grow and to develop, as did other navies. The displacement figures reflect not only the increase in numbers of major warships but also the increase in the size of warships as the ship of the line developed to carry increasing numbers of guns.

Across the two decades during which the Second and Third Dutch Wars took place, one can see a significant development taking place. On the one hand there is the rapid rise of the English and Dutch navies as they faced each other, but there is also the sudden appearance of France as a significant naval power. Cardinal Richelieu had established a firm basis for the French navy. With the end of the Fronde and the Franco-Spanish War of 1635–59 in the Mediterranean, France began to concentrate on developing her navy for

---

[32] Bruijn, *Dutch navy*, pp. 53–4; *idem, Varend verleden*, pp. 95–7.

[33] Davids and 't Hart, 'Case of the Netherlands', pp. 291–3 and 303; see also: J.K. Oudendijk, *Johan de Witt en de vloot* (Amsterdam, 1944), pp. 43–57; H.H. Rowen, *John de Witt. Grand pensionary of Holland* (Princeton, 1978), pp. 79–82.

Table 5.2 The major European navies, 1660–90,
compared in total displacement tonnage

Year	England	Dutch Republic	France	Denmark-Norway	Sweden
1660	88,000	62,000	20,000	16,000	23,000
1665	102,000	81,000	36,000	26,000	31,000
1670	84,000	102,000	114,000	32,000	34,000
1675	95,000	89,000	138,000	29,000	35,000
1680	132,000	66,000	135,000	38,000	20,000
1685	128,000	76,000	123,000	38,000	33,000
1690	113,000	58,000	122,000	35,000	37,000

Source: Glete, *Navies and nations*, I, 192, 195, 220 and 235.

Table 5.3 Comparison in numbers of warships over 700 tons displacement

Year	England	Dutch Republic	France	Denmark-Norway	Sweden
1660	57	51	15	11	11
1665	69	70	25	16	18
1670	60	88	75	20	20
1675	68	73	87	19	21
1680	89	62	83	25	13

Source: Glete, *Navies and nations*, I, 204.

operations in the Atlantic and beyond. With Mazarin's death in 1661, Louis XIV and Colbert moved France to the front rank of European navies within a decade. The French navy quickly adopted and intellectualized the new approaches to warship design, purpose-built warships, and tactics.[34]

In the wake of the First Anglo-Dutch War, the two rivals experienced an uneasy peace. Cromwell was once again rebuffed in his desire to unite with the Dutch and other Protestant powers. The threat of naval clashes continued over fisheries and inspection of shipping.[35] At the same time, Cromwell's navy presented a significant threat to European states at home as well as to their

---

[34] Alan James, *The navy and government in early modern France 1572–1661* (Woodbridge, 2004), pp. 148–65. See also: Daniel Dessert, *La Royale. Vaisseaux et marins du Roi-Soleil* (Paris, 1996); Rif Winfield and Stephen Roberts, *French warships in the age of sail 1626–1786. Design, construction, careers and fates* (Barnsley, 2017), pp. 13–14 and 53.

[35] Timothy Venning, *Cromwellian foreign policy* (New York, 1995), pp. 172–89.

Atlantic empires. Keeping England's navy in service, Cromwell launched his 'Great Design' in 1655 and used the English navy to capture Jamaica from Spain, if failing to achieve his broader imperial vision.[36] Meanwhile, the Dutch war with Portugal and the deployment of the Dutch navy to Lusitanian waters precluded any direct Dutch attempt to regain Brazil.[37] At the very end of this interwar period of mounting tensions, in 1664–65, De Ruyter made an expedition to West Africa, the Caribbean, and Newfoundland that demonstrated Dutch determination to fight for their trading interests and overseas possessions.[38]

By 1660, when King Charles II was restored to the British throne, he acquired a navy with a total of 156 ships, of which 75 carried 40 to 64 guns. Moving to even larger vessels, Peter Pett built the 80-gun *Naseby* at Woolwich in 1655, while his brother, Christopher, built the 70-gun *Richard* at Woolwich in 1658. Two years later, the 100-gun *Sovereign* was built at Chatham.[39] As a war between the two maritime countries approached in the early 1660s, the Dutch also began to strengthen their fleet in a three-year period of warship construction that brought in 60 more warships of 80 and more guns.

In the Dutch Republic, the *raadpensionaris* in Holland from 1653, Johan de Witt, reflected the commercial interests of the Amsterdam merchants and became the dominant political force in helping to modernize the Dutch navy.[40] In both countries, notable naval administrators were placed to come to the fore. In Holland, the father and son team of David and Job de Wildt, whose tenures stretched from the 1640s to 1704, and, in England, the young Samuel Pepys began his notable career as a novice only in 1660.[41]

England's Royal Navy was now under the command of the lord high admiral, a young and inexperienced, but firm, leader in the king's brother, the twenty-seven-year-old James, Duke of York. Having seen many actions ashore, James had an able advisor for naval matters in the experienced Admiral Sir William Penn and his secretary Sir William Coventry.

---

[36] Carla Gardina Pestana, *The English conquest of Jamaica. Oliver Cromwell's bid for empire* (Cambridge, Mass., 2017), pp. 248–56.

[37] Wim Klooster, *The Dutch moment. War, trade and settlement in the seventeenth-century Atlantic world* (Ithaca, 2016), pp. 89 and 93.

[38] Henk den Heijer, 'Michiel de Ruyter's expedition to West Africa and America, 1664–1665', in *De Ruyter. Dutch admiral*, eds Bruijn, Prud'homme van Reine and van Hovell tot Westervlier (Rotterdam, 2011), pp. 162–81.

[39] Brian Lavery, *The ship of the line. Volume 1: The development of the battle fleet 1650–1850* (London, 1984), pp. 30–2 and 59–60.

[40] Rowen, *John de Witt*, pp. 78–83; Bruijn, *Dutch navy*, pp. 75–82; *idem, Varend verleden*, pp. 103–7.

[41] For a study on this subject, see C.S. Knighton, *Pepys and the navy* (Stroud, 2003).

The Second Dutch War, 1665–67[42]

The second war between England and the Dutch was caused by a complex set of complementary, and occasionally contradictory, motives involving commercial rivalry, national prestige, politics, foreign and imperial policies.[43] England's broad strategic aim on entering the war was to isolate the Dutch from their vital trade sources. The way the English intended to do this was to force the Dutch navy out to fight by threatening Dutch commerce, then win a naval battle decisively that destroyed the fighting capability of the Dutch, and then establish an economic blockade of the Dutch coast.[44]

As war approached in late 1664, the Duke of York took direct command of the English fleet at Portsmouth on 9/19 November. Moving quickly on 11/21 November, he set a new tone for employing heavily armed ships by immediately organizing the fleet by dividing it into three squadrons. While the surviving documentation does not provide all the details, this seems to have been the creation of the English terminology that would last well past the age of sail. The Red squadron was the senior, followed by the White, and then the Blue, and with each squadron flying a flag to denote this: White in the van, Red in the centre, and Blue in the rear. In turn, each squadron had three divisions, each commanded by an admiral in the centre, with a vice-admiral in the van, and a rear-admiral in the rear. This arrangement made a total of three flag officers for each squadron and a total of nine in the fleet.

Over the next two weeks, the Duke of York issued separate sailing and fighting instructions that largely reflected those that the Commonwealth had issued. The fighting instructions contained two very important new articles. One required the formation of a line ahead on either a starboard or larboard tack. The other required ships' captains to hold their fire until their guns came within a distance that their gunfire could affect. Further innovations seem to have taken place between November 1664 and 1 February 1665, when the Duke of York issued signals that made it clear that ships were expected to take up pre-planned positions in the line of battle. These orders established a naval order of battle. In the coming months, several iterations of the orders appeared, along with additional instructions.[45]

On the opening of the war, the English and Dutch fleets immediately took up positions from which they could aggressively use their battle fleets to protect and defend their merchant trade. In April, the Duke of York moved to intercept Dutch homeward-bound convoys and to try to force a battle by luring the Dutch war fleet out to protect their commerce. The English had no

---

[42] This section is a revised version of: Hattendorf, 'Navies, strategy, and tactics'.

[43] Gijs Rommelse, *The Second Anglo-Dutch War (1665–1667). International raison d'état, mercantilism and maritime strife* (Hilversum, 2006), pp. 198–201.

[44] Richmond, *Statesmen and sea power*, p. 46.

[45] Tunstall, *Naval warfare*, pp. 22–4; Corbett, *Fighting instructions*, pp. 122–30.

margin of superiority which would allow them to maintain a superior force in Dutch waters for any length of time and they eventually withdrew for supplies and repairs, allowing the Dutch navy to put to sea.[46]

The effect of the improved English tactical dispositions showed in the battle of Lowestoft on 3 June 1665, when the Duke of York defeated the Dutch. In the course of the battle, the English flagship *Royal Charles* and the Dutch flagship *Eendracht* had engaged. During the action, *Eendracht* received a hit in the powder room and exploded, killing the Dutch commander, Jacob van Wassenaer, lord of Obdam. This accident in combat led to the Dutch withdrawal from the action and was the fortuitous event that cleared the way for De Ruyter's promotion to replace Wassenaer as lieutenant-admiral of Holland and West Friesland.[47]

The conduct of the English ships in actual combat differed somewhat from the ideals that had been laid out on paper in the instructions issued beforehand. The plans did not work out as intended. Some ships luffed up to windward and were in three, four, and even five ranks, instead of a single line of battle, even causing some casualties in English ships by friendly fire.[48]

Several months after the battle, the Earl of Sandwich reflected on their actions and came up with detailed and practical recommendations for improvement in future operations.[49] The Dutch, too, reflected on their defeat in the battle of Lowestoft. But their official investigation into the defeat stressed the importance of grappling and boarding an enemy ship, while the admiralty of Zeeland encouraged its officers to think innovatively about how to defeat the English tactics and to avoid 'the long and disadvantageous gun-battle with the English and to bring about the early laying aboard at the first opportunity …'.[50] However, the English tactic of staying in a close-ordered line and using heavy broadside gunnery fire precluded the use of the Dutch tactics of a group attack for grappling and boarding.

Despite these official conclusions, new ideas about tactics were brewing in the minds of the Dutch admirals. After lengthy discussions with sea officers during August 1665, Johan de Witt reflected the results of those conversations in the correspondence and directives coming from the States of Holland. Their thoughts centred on several vital conclusions, based on recent experience: (1) the long-acknowledged need to maintain discipline in battle with a well-ordered fleet; (2) the fighting should be done in a single line-of-battle, close-hauled, with three squadrons, positioned to windward

---

[46] Richmond, *Statesmen and sea power*, p. 47.

[47] Bruijn, *Dutch navy*, p. 77; idem, *Varend verleden*, pp. 100–1.

[48] R.C. Anderson (ed.), *The journal of Edward Montagu first Earl of Sandwich, admiral & general at sea, 1659–1665* (London, 1929), p. 224: 3 June 1665.

[49] *Ibid.*, pp. 269–70: 29 August 1665.

[50] R.E.J. Weber, 'Introduction of the single line ahead as a battle formation by the Dutch 1665–1666', reprinted in Glete, *Naval history*, p. 317.

of an enemy; (3) the flag officers needed to be less exposed at the beginning of an action; and (4) a reserve corps was necessary. A new order embodying these ideas was issued to the Dutch fleet under Cornelis Tromp on 15 August 1665 and had some variant alternatives included. One of these had the centre squadron slightly further from the enemy than the other two squadrons.[51] This order produced the so-called 'snake-shaped line' that remained in the instructions for more than twenty years, but was rarely, if ever, used. Some further changes to the instructions were made on De Ruyter's return, after more than a year away from home waters in Africa and the West Indies, on his appointment as commander-in-chief on 11 August 1665. For the Dutch admirals, much remained to be resolved and clarified in their tactical ideas.

Meanwhile, the English victualling and shore-based naval support system had broken down. At about the same time, the overall strategic situation changed in January 1666, when both France and Denmark declared war against England. The situation placed even great stress on English logistical support in the naval war, as Denmark closed the Sound, and with it, access to the Baltic, to English merchant vessels, creating a further significant shortage for England of the essential naval supplies from this region for shipbuilding and repair. England, as well as the Dutch Republic, faced a major shortfall in seamen to man their warships. As for France, Louis XIV had only a peripheral interest in the war and had agreed, with growing embarrassment, to meet a 1662 treaty obligation with the Dutch. In the event, France secretly instructed her admirals to avoid battle, if possible.[52]

In the Dutch navy, the issues concerning tactics, the numbers of squadrons, and the presence of a reserve squadron continued to remain issues of debate for some time. Finally, after extensive discussions that involved De Ruyter and De Witt as well as representatives of the States General and representatives of the five provincial admiralties of the Dutch Republic, it was agreed that De Ruyter could have the discretion to command the fleet in battle in an arrangement of three squadrons divided into squadrons under vice-admirals and rear-admirals. Just one week after this decision was made, the Dutch and English fleets met off the Thames estuary in the Four Days' Battle (1/11–4/14 June 1666).[53]

This huge, prolonged action has earned the reputation for being the largest and bloodiest battle in the age of fighting sail. The experience of the battle, although it included boarding, grappling, and the use of fireships, showed a marked improvement in Dutch tactics and the Dutch navy's ability to do

---

[51] *Ibid.*, 320–1.

[52] Gaston Zeller, *Histoire des relations internationales. Les temps modernes, de Louis XIV à 1789* (Paris, 1955), p. 25.

[53] See: H.A. Foreest and R.E.J. Weber, *De Vierdaagse Zeeslag 11–14 juni 1666* (Amsterdam, 1984); and Frank Fox, *A distant storm. The Four Days' Battle of 1666* (Rotherfield, 1996).

damage with gunfire to the English with their new 70- and 80-gun ships sailing in the newly adopted line-of-battle.

An equally interesting aspect of the battle was the English estimate of the strategic situation that led the English to divide their fleet. Earlier in the year, Admiral Lord Sandwich had sailed with thirty ships to protect English trade in the Mediterranean. Now, while De Ruyter was approaching with his large force of eighty-four ships, the English received intelligence – false intelligence, as it turned out – that the French Toulon squadron under the Duke of Beaufort was approaching the Channel to join the Dutch. Leaving Albemarle with fifty-four English ships of the line, Prince Rupert took twenty ships and spent three of the four days of the battle guarding against the possibility of the French landing ashore in Britain or attacking England's coastal trade. The situation illustrated England's strategic dilemma in not knowing whether to concentrate her battle force to defeat De Ruyter's fleet or to deal with the multiple smaller threats that she faced on other fronts.

After the action, the Four Days' Battle bought time for the English to reflect on tactics while repairing their battle damage. On 16 July 1666, Prince Rupert and the Duke of Albemarle issued their 'Additional Instructions for Fighting', which emphasized the need to 'keep up with the admiral of the fleet and to endeavour the utmost that may be the destruction of the enemy, which is always to be the chiefest care'.[54] Moreover, it instructed that 'all the best sailing ships are to make what way they can to engage the enemy, that so the rear of our fleet may the better come up ...'.[55]

At the same time, the Duke of York first issued one of the most important and influential English instructions of the era in July 1666, intended to ensure that the English fleet maintained the weather gage:

> In case we have the wind of the enemy, and the enemy stands toward us and we towards them, then the van of our fleet shall keep the wind, and when they are come to a convenient distance of the enemy's rear shall stay until our whole line is come up within the same distance of the enemy's van, and then our whole line is to stand along with them the same tacks on board, still keeping the enemy to leeward, and not suffering them to tack in the van, and in case the enemy tacks in the rear first, and the whole line is to follow, standing all along with the same tacks on board as the enemy does.[56]

The thought expressed here stood for more than a century as the mandatory Article XVII of the eighteenth-century Royal Navy's permanent *Sailing and*

---

[54] Corbett, *Fighting instructions*, pp. 129–30.

[55] *Ibid.*

[56] Corbett, *Fighting instructions*, pp. 148–9, misdated as 1672, but 18 July 1666 as documented in Tunstall, *Naval warfare*, pp. 27–30.

Fighting Instructions. Additional points in this document expressed the importance of keeping the line and dividing an enemy's fleet by tacking through the enemy's battle line to gain the windward position.

Just over a week after these additional instructions appeared, the English under the Duke of Albemarle, and the Dutch fleet, under De Ruyter, met again in the Two Days' Battle of St James's Day on 25–26 July/4–5 August 1666. In this action, the two relatively equal fleets exchanged heavy gunfire, but the English maintained the advantage with a disciplined van and centre. The aftermath of this defeat for the Dutch provided the opportunity to think again about fleet tactics. In this period, De Ruyter pointed out that it was necessary for ships to keep in their assigned station, 'otherwise the train of ships would be too extended, and the ships would be left unsupported'.[57] In the weeks and months that followed, Johan de Witt played a crucial role in institutionalizing further changes. He incorporated De Ruyter's signal to form the battle line into the general signal book, organizing the battle fleet firmly into three squadrons with three divisions each, and even established a standard diagram for the navy, making sure that these procedures and copies of the orders were distributed for reference among those who issued orders to the fleet.[58]

By late 1666, the English were encountering severe difficulties in finding the financial resources and the supplies to keep their fleet at sea. Seamen protested, and dockyard workers mutinied as peace negotiations began. In early 1667, King Charles II decided not to attempt to put the fleet to sea and opted instead to have only two small squadrons at sea to serve as coastal guard ships. Instead of maintaining full English naval strength against the Dutch, English leaders assumed that the Dutch were on the verge of surrender and sent a twenty-ship squadron to the Mediterranean, making the same error that had led to Tromp's victory in 1653. This unexpected and egregious strategic error removed England's main naval defence and gave the Dutch navy an opportunity of an entirely different kind that had little to do with the tactical discussions for fleet battles. It was at this point that De Ruyter made his raid on the English coast in the Thames estuary and the Medway River, famously capturing the 86-gun ship named after the king, *Royal Charles*, and towing it back as a prize to Holland.[59]

Aside from firmly establishing the line-of-battle tactics in both the Dutch and English navies, the Second Dutch War left both countries exhausted. The experience of the first two wars continued to urge on the increase in the size of warships. In ship design, the stability that went toward a firm platform for

---

[57] Weber, 'The single line ahead', p. 325.

[58] These changes were reflected in De Ruyter's instructions of 6 August 1667, in R.E.J. Weber, *De seinboeken voor Nederlandse oorlogsvloten en konvooien tot 1690* (Amsterdam, 1982), Doc. 21: pp. 102–14.

[59] P.G. Rogers, *The Dutch in the Medway* (Oxford, 1970).

gunnery had come to outweigh the importance of speed, as did a stiffness that prevented a ship from heeling too far so that its lower gun ports could not be used. The 70-gun third rate ship of the line became a recognized success in the Royal Navy and the three-deck, 100-gun first rates were returning to favour. Across the North Sea, consideration of the shallow waters and sandbanks led the Dutch to avoid building three-deck ships and to prefer beamy vessels, but their large 60-, 70- and 80-gun warships were fully capable of dealing with the English. Additionally, as the French began to emphasize their navy in the early 1660s, they initially turned to the Dutch to supply some major warships. These French ships of Dutch design were more substantial than their English counterparts and more stable two-deckers with their lower tier of guns higher off the water.[60]

The Third Dutch War, 1672–74[61]

From a strategic perspective, the Third Dutch War was significantly different from the others. The origins of the war lay in the personal enthusiasms of the young Louis XIV and not the more careful judgements of his ministers.[62] This involved a *volte-face* from previous French policy in the Second Dutch War with France's decision to invade and to overwhelm the Dutch Republic. It meant a *volte-face* for England as well, who had agreed in 1668 with Sweden and the Dutch Republic to prevent French occupation of the Spanish Netherlands.[63] France actively sought to embroil England in the war for its objectives to destroy the Dutch Republic. On the English side, King Charles II's motives for entering into the secret Treaty of Dover and in the Third Dutch War in alliance with France against the Dutch Republic lie fundamentally in internal English politics and the king's struggle for maintaining the Crown's controlling power over Parliament.[64]

The immediate outbreak of the war resulted from the English initiative in sending out two squadrons of frigates, one under Sir Edward Spragge and the other under Robert Holmes, to contrive an incident by asserting English 'sovereignty of the sea' and use this as a rationale to attack the homeward-bound Dutch convoy from Smyrna. Although the Dutch forces defended themselves effectively and repulsed the English squadrons, nevertheless, the incident became the *casus belli*. On receiving the news, Charles II declared war

---

[60] Lavery, *Ship of the line*, I, 32–6.
[61] This section is a revised version of: Hattendorf, 'Navies, strategy, and tactics'.
[62] Paul Sonnino, *Louis XIV and the origins of the Dutch war* (Cambridge, 1988), p. 176.
[63] For details of this negotiation and agreement, see Birger Fahlborg, *Sveriges yttre politik, 1664–1668* (2 vols, Stockholm, 1949), II, 465–547.
[64] J.R. Jones, *The Anglo-Dutch Wars of the seventeenth century* (New York and London, 1996), pp. 179–88.

on the Dutch Republic on 18/28 March 1671/2, followed by Louis XIV on 6 April 1672.[65]

From a naval perspective, this situation in policy and strategy created a distinctive aspect of this war that contrasted with the earlier two conflicts. In retrospect, it implied the need for the English navy to begin to develop means to cope with a coalition naval force and also to complement military operations ashore. While the English initially anticipated a naval war, the French quickly developed plans of their own for aggressive military operations to invade the Republic. French soldiers with troops from England, Cologne and Munster moved from the south and the east. These troops occupied much Dutch territory, but the English were not directly part of these operations.

The naval actions were similar to the earlier wars but showed the more mature tactical development that emerged from the experience of the first two Dutch wars. Moreover, in every one of the four significant actions in this war, a French squadron joined with two English squadrons to create the line of battle. Anglo-French naval strategy focused on blockading the Dutch coasts to establish a position from which an invasion from the sea could be launched. To counter the Anglo-French plan, the Dutch responded by flooding the polders of Holland to prevent occupation and creating a formidable naval defence to avoid any such landing.

In this war, De Ruyter had the advantage of having the Dutch fleet in an excellent state of readiness with the new warships from the 1664–66 building programme available. In addition, De Ruyter had trained his commanding officers in procedures for meeting a superior enemy force in battle. In particular, he had finally succeeded in doing away with the earlier ideas about group tactics for grappling and boarding, concentrating on training his fleet in the practical use of the 'single line ahead' formation that the English had pioneered and the Dutch had taken over after the battle of Lowestoft in 1665. Also, he built further on this approach with innovative tactical thinking on how to counter the Anglo-French use of these tactics, although this was done by word of mouth and in practice rather than in formal written instructions.[66] In contrast, the Duke of York, who commanded the combined Anglo-French fleet, issued fighting instructions to the fleet that were fundamentally the same as those released in 1666.[67]

The first fleet engagement of the war occurred on 28 May/6 June 1672 when De Ruyter with 62 ships attacked the allied fleet of 82 ships as they lay at anchor in Solebay, off Southwold, Suffolk. Although the English and French had expected an attack, they were still at anchor when De Ruyter appeared. The French squadron, under the comte d'Estrées, and the English separated, and two separate actions ensued, in which the Dutch prevailed in

[65] Sonnino, *Louis XIV*, p. 191.
[66] Bruijn, *Dutch navy*, p. 88; idem, *Varend Verleden*, p. 115.
[67] Tunstall, *Naval warfare*, p. 32; Corbett, *Fighting instructions*, pp. 133–63.

both. De Ruyter's attack successfully served to force the English and French to postpone their plans to make a landing in Holland and, at the same time, created a feud between d'Estrées and his second in command, Abraham Duquesne, whom d'Estrées accused of failing to support him. Similarly, the English admirals traded recriminations.[68]

Late in 1672, the Amsterdam and Zeeland admiralties sent separate secret naval expeditions to America under Jacob Binckes and Cornelis Evertsen the Youngest. Meeting at Martinique in 1673, they joined forces to attack English and French shipping. In the process of operating in the West Indies, raiding Virginia and in the Chesapeake Bay, reconquering New York, and attacking the Newfoundland fisheries, they captured 650 ships.[69]

Following this, the focus of events shifted ashore with the lynching of the De Witt brothers in The Hague and the military defence of Holland under the stadholder Prince William III, which even utilized some guns and men taken from Dutch warships to defend the homeland. In the meantime, De Ruyter planned to make an aggressive attack on England to sink ships and block the channels to Portsmouth and London.[70] Thwarting this plan in May 1673 just as De Ruyter appeared off the Thames, the new commander of the English fleet, Prince Rupert of the Rhine,[71] forced De Ruyter's fleet back into Dutch waters. Forced to take the defensive, De Ruyter took his fleet to the Schooneveld flats off Walcheren Island, where he made brilliant use of his local knowledge of the sandbanks in two actions, the first on 28 May/7 June and the second on 4/14 June 1673.

Outnumbered 76 to 52 ships, De Ruyter used the restricted conditions to advantage. Prince Rupert expected to use his numerical superiority to deliver a decisive blow, but De Ruyter came out to windward of the shoals to gain a tactical advantage and was able to manoeuvre to avoid the advance squadron and the fireships that the allies deployed. Instead of retreating as Rupert expected, the Dutch formed a line to defend their position. Rupert had placed the French squadron in the middle of his line to prevent the situation that had occurred at Solebay. In the van, Rupert engaged with Cornelis Tromp's squadron, while De Ruyter's and Adriaen Banckert's squadrons dealt with Spragge's and d'Estrées', and then rejoined Tromp to engage Rupert. The general action successfully prevented the allied English and French fleet from making any gains. Although neither side lost any ships, the English

---

[68] R.C. Anderson (ed.), *Journals and narratives of the Third Dutch War* (London, 1946), pp. 13–22, 95–101, 156–7 and 164–84; Michel Vergé-Franceschi, *Abraham Duquesne. Huguenot en marin de Roi-Soleil* (Paris, 1992), pp. 254–60; J.D. Davies, *Gentlemen and tarpaulins. The officers and men of the Restoration navy* (Oxford, 1991), p. 171.

[69] Bruijn, *Dutch navy*, p. 77; D.G. Shomette and R.D. Haslach, *Raid on America. The Dutch naval campaign of 1672–1674* (Columbia, 1988).

[70] Rodger, *Command of the ocean*, p. 83; Bruijn, *Dutch navy*, p. 89; idem, *Varend verleden*, p. 117.

[71] Frank Kitson, *Prince Rupert. Admiral and general-at-sea* (London, 1998), pp. 246–89.

and French were unable to approach the Dutch ports and were baffled by the sandbanks.[72]

A week later on 4/14 June 1673, the opposing fleets met again off Schooneveld with similar results. The lack of communication between Rupert and d'Estrées confused the allied fleet, and the allies withdrew to the Nore at the mouth of the Thames, concluding that they could not reach the coast by challenging De Ruyter at Schooneveld.[73]

Meanwhile, the allied fleet cruised off the Texel to draw De Ruyter out into open water and clear an avenue for landing. The two fleets engaged on 11/21 August in the battle off Kijkdown (Texel). With the same commanders, the fleets were slightly larger, with the Dutch outnumbered, 86 ships to 60. In the end, the battle divided into separate squadron actions, with the French taking little part. De Ruyter's manoeuvres forced the allies back to the English coast and broke their blockade of the Dutch coast.[74] The misunderstandings that arose in the battle between d'Estrées and Rupert became recriminations in a public dispute that showed the strains within the alliance, helping to contribute to ending allied operations and to concluding that the war had been a failure for France and England.[75]

The Anglo-French fleet had consistently tried to break through the Dutch naval defences but failed in all their attempts to do so. De Ruyter's success in this was the most significant naval achievement of the era, and the prevention of an enemy landing in Holland and Zeeland was the critical element for Dutch defence. In this, De Ruyter's actions in the Third Dutch War marked the firm implementation of the range of new European naval developments.

The Anglo-Dutch peace of 1674 to the Dutch invasion of England in 1688

Although England had made peace with the Dutch Republic, the Dutch war with France did not end for another four years, not until 1678. Dutch naval operations shifted from the North Sea to the Baltic, the Channel, and the Mediterranean. The Dutch enemies now included the Dunkirk privateers, whom the French encouraged to attack Dutch shipping. The Republic

[72] J.C.M. Warnsinck, *Admiraal De Ruyter, de zeeslag op Schooneveld juni 1673* (The Hague, 1930); Tunstall, *Naval warfare*, p. 35; Jaap Bruijn, *De oorlogvoering ter zee in 1673 in journalen* (Groningen, 1966), pp. 55–6 and 114–15; Anderson, *Journals and narratives*, pp. 32–6, 300–2, 319–20, 334, 377, 386 and 387.

[73] Jones, *Anglo-Dutch Wars*, p. 206; Tunstall, *Naval warfare*, p. 36; Bruijn, *Oorlogvoering*, pp. 60 and 118–20; Anderson, *Journals and narratives*, pp. 37–40, 303, 322, 336, 378, 379 and 389.

[74] Bruijn, *Oorlogvoering*, pp. 89–90, 152–4, 184–5 and 205–9; Anderson, *Journals and narratives*, pp. 46–53, 311, 355–62, 381, 386 and 390–4.

[75] Carl Ekberg, *The failure of Louis XIV's Dutch war* (Chapel Hill, 1979), pp. 161–70.

joined with the Spanish to fight the French in the Mediterranean. There, De Ruyter died in combat against Duquesne's French fleet in 1676.[76] The war against France spread to the Baltic, where Sweden had made an alliance with France against Denmark. The Republic sent squadrons of ten to fifteen ships to assist the Danes each year for three years between 1675 and 1677. The combined Dutch and Danish fleet under Cornelis Tromp won a major victory off Öland's southern tip in 1676, and Tromp even served as head of the Danish navy. Across the Atlantic in the Caribbean, the Dutch also fought the French with Jacob Binckes's squadron's attack on Cayenne in French Guiana, Guadeloupe, and Tobago. Following the 1678 Peace of Nijmegen, the Dutch navy settled into a peacetime role. The Republic reduced its active naval forces and limited naval operations to the protection of trade in the Mediterranean.[77] Meanwhile, the English navy had been operating in a similar peacetime mode since 1674. King Charles II had died in 1685, and his brother, the Duke of York, came to the throne as King James II. Throughout this period, English naval operations were also mainly in the Mediterranean. The English navy developed an extensive system of trade protection, regional squadrons deterring attacks, combating the Barbary corsairs using bases at Lisbon, Gibraltar, Port Mahon, and also at Tangier, which did not mature as a naval base as had been hoped.[78]

James II's predilection for the Catholic Church aroused protests in England over his government's policies, but the Civil War and Cromwell's military dictatorship were too vivid in living memory for any immediate desire for revolution. Across the North Sea, however, Prince William III was gravely concerned about the survival of the Dutch Republic as Louis XIV led France to what appeared to be ever expanding influence and power on the continent. In this context, England would become a severe threat to the Dutch Republic if James II were to ally with France in an anti-Dutch foreign policy. In early 1688, William III began to think seriously – and secretly – about asserting his claim to the English throne, as well as that of his wife, Mary, James II's eldest daughter. If successful, this would make him both the unrivalled leader in the Dutch Republic as well as king of England. William skilfully worked to exploit the anti-Catholic sentiments among key Englishmen to develop opposition to James. Among the supporters whom William brought to his side was Admiral Arthur Herbert, who had publicly opposed James's policies and had been passed over for command of the main English fleet. Between June and October 1688, the Dutch gathered ships at the Rotterdam admiralty

---

[76] Vergé-Franceschi, *Duquesne*, pp. 268–78; *idem*, 'De Ruyter versus Duquesne. A battle to the death', in *De Ruyter. Dutch admiral*, eds Bruijn, Prud'homme van Reine and van Hövell tot Westerflier (Rotterdam, 2011), pp. 183–98.

[77] Bruijn, *Dutch navy*, pp. 77–9.

[78] Sari R. Hornstein, *The Restoration navy and English foreign trade, 1674–1688. A study in the peacetime use of sea power* (Aldershot, 1991).

that eventually included 48 ships of the line and frigates, with 28 smaller warships, manned by 9,500 seamen. Also, the Dutch navy hired some 300 merchantmen and 60 fishing boats to carry 15,000 armed troops, 4,000 horses, and extensive supplies for their support. Under the command of Admiral Arthur Herbert, the massive fleet of 463 ships left Hellevoetsluis on 20/30 October, but heavy westerly winds drove them back to port. Trying again about noon on 1/11 November 1688, with the benefit of an easterly gale that later became legendary as the 'Protestant Wind', the fleet set a northwesterly course toward the open North Sea, and the large force gradually came into an ordered formation. About midnight that day, William and Herbert changed their apparent intention to land the expeditionary force on the northeast coast of England. Instead, they altered course and sailed down the Channel, taking advantage of the easterly wind that kept Lord Dartmouth and James II's opposing fleet in the Thames estuary. On 3/13 November, Dartmouth's flagship moored in the Gunfleet sighted William's fleet directly to windward. Later that day, the Dutch fleet passed through the Straits of Dover and were off Dungeness that night and off the Isle of Wight on 4/14 November. Unable to get around the sandbanks and to overcome the tide, Dartmouth could not get to sea until 4/14 November, by which time the Dutch were far ahead of them down the Channel. On 5/15 November, the wind shifted back to prevailing southwesterly, slowing Dartmouth's chase further, but remaining advantageous for William and Herbert to sail handily into the east-facing Torbay on the coast of Devon. On the same day, William with the embarked troops and horses landed at Brixham, on the south side of the bay. Over the next two days, the seas were unseasonably calm and there was no opposition, allowing the 15,000 troops and 4,000 horses with their supplies to get ashore safely.[79]

Conclusion

Over the twenty-four-year period of the three Anglo-Dutch naval wars between 1652 and 1674, navies first employed the offensive and aggressive naval tactics with heavily gunned, large warships operating in a line of battle. Supported by the growing complex administrative and governmental organizational structures ashore, tactics, ships, and gunnery were further refined and developed over the following century to become the hallmarks of the European sailing navies through the period of the Napoleonic Wars. William III's invasion force in 1688 demonstrated a further step in the transformation of fleets in more effectively and efficiently organizing and launching in a

---

[79] Rodger, *Command of the ocean*, pp. 136–9; Bruijn, *Dutch navy*, p. 80; A. Pearsall, 'The invasion voyage: some nautical thoughts', in *1688. The seaborne alliance and diplomatic revolution*, eds C. Wilson and D. Proctor (London, 1989), pp. 165–74.

short period of time an amphibious expeditionary force. Such characteristics dominated naval history for the remainder of the age of sail and continued in spirit for centuries. These steps over a thirty-six-year period between 1652 and 1688 were but a part of the more substantial and continuing evolutionary transformation of navies across the centuries, both before and after these events.

6

The Dutch and English fiscal-naval states: a comparative overview

Richard J. Blakemore and Pepijn Brandon

Warfare at sea defined the relationship between the Dutch and English states during the second half of the seventeenth century. The ships of these two nations encountered one another again and again, in vast battles and in small skirmishes, in European waters and around the world. Many thousands fought in these conflicts, which had an impact upon the entire populations of both countries, as well as having significant consequences for global politics.[1] Mobilising the naval forces that fought these wars was an enormous undertaking, and naval administration and operations occupied much government time and resources in England and the Dutch United Provinces throughout this period. Both countries can therefore be considered as fiscal-naval states, a concept which has emerged from debate around the existence of an early modern military revolution by land and by sea, and which draws on John Brewer's description of England as a fiscal-military state in the eighteenth century.[2] Fiscal-naval states were, as N.A.M. Rodger

---

[1] For an accessible overview of these wars, see J.R. Jones, *The Anglo-Dutch wars of the seventeenth century* (New York and London, 1996).

[2] John Brewer, *The sinews of power. War, money, and the English state, 1689–1783* (Cambridge, 1989); and for a more recent reflection on the term, see Rafael Torres Sánchez (ed.), *War, state and development. Fiscal-military states in the eighteenth century* (Pamplona, 2007). For the maritime dimension of the military revolution debate, see Geoffrey Parker, *The Military Revolution. Military innovation and the rise of the West, 1500–1800* (Cambridge, 1988), chapter 3; Jaap R. Bruijn, 'States and their navies from the late sixteenth to the end of the eighteenth centuries', in *War and competition between states*, ed. Philippe Contamine (Oxford, 2000), pp. 69–98; Jan Glete, *Warfare at sea, 1500–1650. Maritime conflicts and the transformation of Europe* (London, 2000); Jeremy Black, *Naval power. A history of warfare and the sea from 1500* (Basingstoke, 2009); Louis Sicking, 'Naval warfare in Europe, c. 1330–c. 1680', in *European warfare, 1350–1750*, eds Frank Tallet and D.J.B. Trim (Cambridge, 2010), pp. 236–63; the roundtable of articles by Gijs A. Rommelse, John F. Guilmartin, and N.A.M. Rodger, in *Journal for Maritime Research*, 13 (2011), 117–50; Jürgen G. Backhaus (ed.), *Navies and state formation* (Berlin, 2012); Richard Harding, *Modern naval history. Debates and prospects* (London, 2016); David Plouviez, 'Marines Européennes, développements

puts it, 'distinguished by [their] commitment to a capital-intensive, high-technology mode of warfare demanding long-term state investment', and both the Dutch and English states easily fit this definition.[3]

As we will explore in this chapter, this commitment and this investment had profound implications for the shape of these two states as they developed across the seventeenth century, with consequences for domestic as well as foreign policies. The Dutch and English navies influenced government revenue, expenditure, and taxation, which affected a wide swathe of society; they directly employed large numbers of people; and they drew on extensive networks of suppliers and contractors. These navies held a key place not only in maritime warfare but also in national identity formation, even while such identities coexisted (sometimes uneasily) with local loyalties, which also featured heavily in naval ideology, especially in the Dutch case. While our purpose here is primarily to examine how these two fiscal-naval states developed over the seventeenth century, and to establish similarities and divergences, we also wish to offer some comments on the broader significance of these developments. We will pursue this comparison by exploring, in turn, the organisation of the two navies; the structures of revenue and expenditure which financed them; and the scope and scale of private involvement in and alongside state activities.

The organisation of the two navies

As we have noted, navies held an important position in the ideologies of early modern states, especially those, like England and the United Provinces, which relied upon seaborne trade and pursued imperial ambitions. The concept of 'naval theatre', developed by historians of twentieth-century empire, provides a useful starting point for considering early modern naval policy, as it emphasises that navies' role in advertising and thus reinforcing the idea of state authority is vitally important as well as their actual military activities.[4] Dutch and English rulers both sponsored scholarly disquisitions

---

administratif, économique et financier', in *The sea in history. The early modern world*, eds Christian Buchet and Gérard le Bouëdec (Woodbridge, 2017), pp. 773–84.

[3] N.A.M. Rodger, 'From the "Military Revolution" to the "Fiscal-Naval State"', *Journal for Maritime Research*, 13 (2011), 122; see also Patrick O'Brien, 'State formation and economic growth. The case of Britain, 1688–1846', in *Navies and state formation*, ed. Backhaus, pp. 217–72; N.A.M. Rodger, 'Introduction: navies and state formation', in *Navies and state formation*, ed. Backhaus, pp. 9–20; N.A.M. Rodger, 'Social structure and naval power. Britain and the Netherlands', in *The sea in history*, eds Buchet and Bouëdec, pp. 679–85.

[4] For a discussion of this concept, see Daniel Owen Spence, *Colonial naval culture and British imperialism, 1922–67* (Manchester, 2015), pp. 2–3, and the historiography cited there.

on maritime sovereignty which supported their imperial agendas.[5] They also paid for large and lavishly decorated warships as an immediately accessible statement about their power. The *Sovereign of the Seas*, built in 1637, the *Naseby*, built in 1655 and renamed the *Royal Charles* in 1660, and the *De Zeven Provinciën*, built in 1665, all served the same propagandistic purpose, and the Dutch seizure of the *Royal Charles* in 1667 was one of the most dramatic and symbolic moments in the wars between these two states. Even though neither country's might at sea ever matched up to the grand claims made for it, the well-publicised association of the state with naval power was nevertheless a key component in their political legitimacy, and this wider dimension is an aspect of early modern fiscal-naval states which deserves further investigation.

The ideological position was not contradictory to, but overlapped with, the obvious implications of these navies for international power-projection and economic success. Dutch political and economic elites were committed to maintaining naval power as a central plank of state policy. An aggressively trade-oriented strategy of naval interventions in the Baltic, Mediterranean, and Atlantic basins underpinned mid-seventeenth-century Dutch primacy in international trade.[6] The self-perception of the Dutch state as a mighty maritime republic, even surpassing Venice at its prime, simultaneously became deeply engrained in public consciousness.[7] An incipient culture of veneration around successful admirals like Michiel de Ruyter helped to establish the figure of the 'sea-hero' as an important protagonist in patriotic narratives, prefiguring the central role of maritime history in the construction of nineteenth-century Dutch nationalism.[8] However, the Dutch Republic also participated on a major scale in continental wars, from the Eighty Years' War with Spain that continued through the first half of the century, to the string of conflicts sometimes referred to as the Forty Years' War between the Dutch Republic and France, which the country found itself in the middle of by the end of the century.[9] As a result, Dutch rulers always had to balance their priorities between warfare on land and at sea.

---

[5] Martine Julia van Ittersum, *Profit and principle. Hugo Grotius, natural right theories and the rise of Dutch power in the East Indies, 1595–1615* (Leiden and Boston, 2006); Richard J. Blakemore, 'Law and the sea', in *Routledge research companion to marine and maritime worlds, 1400–1800. Oceans in global history and culture*, eds Claire Jowitt, Craig Lambert and Steve Mentz (Abingdon, forthcoming 2020).

[6] Jonathan I. Israel, *Dutch primacy in world trade 1585–1740* (Oxford, 1989).

[7] Classical statements are C.R. Boxer, *The Dutch seaborne empire 1600–1800* (London, 1965); Simon Schama, *The embarrassment of riches. An interpretation of Dutch culture in the Golden Age* (London, 1987).

[8] Ronald Prud'homme van Reine, *Zeehelden* (Amsterdam, 2005).

[9] Marjolein 't Hart, *The Dutch wars of independence. Warfare and commerce in the Netherlands, 1570–1680* (Abingdon and New York, 2014); David Onnekink, *Reinterpreting the Dutch Forty Years War, 1672–1713* (London, 2016).

For England, not only was international warfare conducted largely by sea throughout this period, but the navy was intimately tied to the monarchy; indeed, except for the interregnum of the 1650s, the navy was the personal possession of the crown. While this relationship has sometimes been characterised as a misplaced interest on the part of the Stuarts in grandiose decoration and unwieldy magnificence with little concrete value, such an assessment is problematic.[10] The rulers of England were personally concerned with the practical side of naval affairs as much as the lustre it might lend to their reign, though to differing degrees. James VI and I, Oliver Cromwell, and William III largely relied on their subordinates, though all of them intervened at times, while Charles I and his two sons took a much more direct role in running the navy. Charles I's reign collapsed and the navy largely sided with his opponents in the subsequent civil wars, but this was probably the result of the political tensions that disrupted his reign, rather than his naval policy itself.[11] Charles II and James II were more successful in their management of the navy, and kept a tight control over decision-making, though as with their father this did not prevent James's eventual downfall.[12] At times a lord high admiral held office, but they were often assistants to, not independent deputies of, the sovereign; at other times, commissioners carried out the functions of the admiral, usually with the monarch at their head.[13] In 1679–84, rather exceptionally, the admiralty commissioners sought to take over direction of the navy and diminish the king's role, but by the end of his reign Charles II was back in command.[14] Throughout much of this period, then, England's rulers themselves oversaw the management of the navy, though parliament played an increasing role from the 1650s onwards, and especially after 1689.[15]

The practical activities of English naval administration were carried out by various forms of 'navy board', originating in the Tudor era. Initially known

[10] Kenneth Andrews, *Ships, money and politics. Seafaring and naval enterprise in the reign of Charles I* (New York, 1991), pp. 130–8; N.A.M. Rodger, *The safeguard of the sea. A naval history of Britain, 660–1649* (London, 2004), pp. 380–1; Richard J. Blakemore, 'Thinking outside the gundeck: maritime history, the Royal Navy, and the outbreak of British civil war, 1625–42', *Historical Research*, 87 (2014), 259; J.D. Davies, *Kings of the sea. Charles II, James II and the Royal Navy* (Barnsley, 2017), pp. 14–15.
[11] Brian W. Quintrell, 'Charles I and his navy in the 1630s', *Seventeenth Century*, 3 (1988), 159–79; Andrew Thrush, 'The navy under Charles I: 1625–1640' (unpublished PhD thesis, University of London, 1991), pp. 23–44; Andrews, *Ships, money and politics*, chapter 6; Blakemore, 'Thinking outside the gundeck'.
[12] J.D. Davies, *Pepys's navy. Ships, men and warfare 1649–1688* (Barnsley, 2008), pp. 26–7; idem, *Kings of the sea*, chapter 6.
[13] Rodger, *Safeguard of the sea*, pp. 372 and 391–2; idem, *The command of the ocean. A naval history of Britain, 1649–1815* (London, 2004), p. 87.
[14] J.D. Davies, *Gentlemen and tarpaulins. The officers and men of the Restoration navy* (Oxford, 1991), pp. 189–98; idem, *Pepys's navy*, pp. 25–32; idem, *Kings of the sea*, pp. 113–25; Rodger, *Command of the ocean*, pp. 109–10.
[15] Rodger, *Command of the ocean*, pp. 181–7.

as the four principal officers of the navy, these were augmented and then replaced by a sequence of navy commissioners and committees during the 1640s and 1650s, and reinstated in 1660 but with additional officials.[16] Most of these positions were personal appointments by the king or the admiralty, and were sometimes held for life. While this reflected another close tie between ruler and navy, it also provoked repeated accusations of corruption.[17] There were also separate organisations for specific tasks. Victualling was carried out alternately by the surveyor of the navy, by a specific victualling board, or by a syndicate of contractors, and the Ordinance Office was also independent, although placed under admiralty oversight in 1653.[18] Though all administrators across this period faced similar limitations, there was a general trend of increasing institutional efficiency, at least in relative terms.

The highest tier of naval organisation thus remained closely tied to the monarch and became more effective at realising the ruler's wishes as the century went on, but it was also relatively small in terms of personnel, even at the end of the century. Beyond the central administration the English navy relied on locally placed officers, such as dockyard commissioners or squadron commanders; the navy's most important dockyards were those on the Thames at Deptford and especially Chatham, the largest dockyard in Europe, but Portsmouth also grew in size and activity.[19] The admiralty issued ever more detailed regulations to govern the actions of these officers, both general codes like the Articles of War of 1652 and General Instructions of 1663, and specific commands on a plethora of naval matters.[20] Nevertheless,

---

[16] Arthur W. Tedder, *The navy of the Restoration. From the death of Cromwell to the Treaty of Breda; its work growth and influence* (London, 1916), p. 42; Thrush, 'Navy under Charles I', pp. 66–85; Andrews, *Ships, money and politics*, pp. 188–9; Robert Brenner, *Merchants and revolution. Commercial change, political conflict, and London's overseas traders, 1550–1653* (Cambridge, 1993), pp. 389, 432–4, 553 and 582–4; Bernard Capp, *Cromwell's navy. The fleet and the English Revolution 1648–1660* (Oxford, 1989), pp. 44–50 and 156–62; Rodger, *Safeguard of the sea*, pp. 331–3 and 370–4; *idem, Command of the ocean*, pp. 33–7 and 103–6; Richard J. Blakemore and Elaine Murphy, *The British civil wars at sea, 1638–1653* (Rochester, 2018), pp. 87–91.

[17] A.P. McGowan (ed.), *The Jacobean Commissions of Enquiry, 1608 and 1618* (London, 1971); Thrush, 'Navy under Charles I', pp. 85–102 and 171–8; Andrews, *Ships, money and politics*, pp. 190–5; Rodger, *Safeguard of the sea*, pp. 364–8; *idem, Command of the ocean*, pp. 99–102; Blakemore and Murphy, *Civil wars at sea*, pp. 90–3.

[18] Tedder, *Navy of the Restoration*, pp. 112–14; Alan P. McGowan, 'The Royal Navy under the first Duke of Buckingham, Lord High Admiral 1618–1628' (unpublished PhD thesis, University of London, 1967), chapter 8; Thrush, 'Navy under Charles I', chapters 6 and 7; Davies, *Pepys's navy*, pp. 200–2; Rodger, *Command of the ocean*, pp. 42–3, 46 and 188–96.

[19] Davies, *Gentlemen and tarpaulins*, p. 14; *idem, Pepys's navy*, pp. 178–85; Rodger, *Command of the ocean*, pp. 103–4 and 188–9; *idem, Safeguard of the sea*, pp. 335–7.

[20] Tedder, *Navy of the Restoration*, pp. 67–71, and see also pp. 48–54; Davies, *Gentlemen and tarpaulins*, pp. 43–50 and 87–8; Capp, *Cromwell's navy*, pp. 219–25; Rodger, *Command of the ocean*, pp. 59–60.

some degree of independence to interpret these orders, if not to disregard them entirely, remained. The administration of the English navy, therefore, was in principle under the close personal supervision of the monarch, and was increasingly bureaucratic and authoritarian, but presided over an organisation in which there was flexibility at all levels.

By contrast, the Dutch navy maintained a strictly federal administration. Naval direction was subdivided between five separate admiralty boards located in Holland, Zeeland, and Friesland. They operated under the States General and worked out common policies during meetings in The Hague (called the *Haagse Besognes*), but retained administrative independence in the execution of their tasks.[21] The roots of this federal naval organisation lay in the Habsburg period, when the Zeeland town Veere acted as the seat of the imperial fleet in the Low Countries, but armed trade protection largely remained within the purview of the different trading towns.[22] The Dutch Revolt led to the establishment of a state navy and the five admiralty boards, of which those for Amsterdam, Rotterdam, and Zeeland became the most important. Attempts to bring these five local boards under a unified central administration faltered on the particularism of Dutch provinces and towns.[23] Instead, a complicated system of cross-representation was erected, in which towns and the nobility retained seats on the admiralty boards. For example, in 1606–1795 there were twelve seats on the Amsterdam admiralty board, of which six were filled by representatives of the province of Holland, and the other six by representatives of each of the other provinces that made up the Republic. The six seats of Holland in turn were divided between the nobility, Haarlem, Leiden, Amsterdam, Gouda, and Edam. Meanwhile, the city of Amsterdam had one permanent representative on the admiralty board of Zeeland and one on the board located in Holland's Northern Quarter.[24]

This federative organisational structure made naval administration itself a terrain of conflict between competing regional interest-groups, and between the admiralty towns and the States General.[25] For example, in 1621, the wish of the States General to put into action a fleet of over one hundred ships failed

---

[21] For a general overview see Jaap R. Bruijn, *The Dutch navy of the seventeenth and eighteenth centuries* (St John's, Newfoundland, 2011).

[22] Louis Sicking, *Neptune and the Netherlands. State, economy, and war at sea in the Renaissance* (Leiden and Boston, 2004), chapter 6; J.P. Sigmond, *Zeemacht in Holland en Zeeland in de zestiende eeuw* (Hilversum, 2013), pp. 86–110.

[23] C.A. Davids and M.C. 't Hart, 'The navy and the rise of the state. The case of the Netherlands c.1570–1810', in *Navies and state formation. The Schumpeter hypothesis revisited and reflected*, eds J. Backhaus, N. Kyriazis and N.A.M. Rodger (Munster, 2012), pp. 282–7; Pepijn Brandon, *War, capital, and the Dutch state 1588–1795* (Leiden and Boston, 2015), pp. 58–9.

[24] Brandon, *War, capital, and the Dutch state*, p. 62.

[25] Bruijn, *Dutch navy*, p. 27.

because of local opposition against the costs of such an operation, as well as the preference of the admiralty towns to prioritise convoying missions to protect their immediate trading interests.[26] On the other hand, it could also lead to an exceptional level of direct investment of local political and economic elites in the making and execution of naval policy, especially in the towns that housed one of the admiralty boards.[27] Thus, throughout the seventeenth century the Amsterdam mayors regularly acted as intermediaries between the admiralty board and rich Amsterdam houses to secure emergency loans when inland provinces proved reluctant to pay their share of the agreed subsidies.[28] Undoubtedly, the readiness with which Amsterdam regents responded to emergencies was enhanced by the fact that on the admiralty board 'that city was always represented by one of its foremost elder burgomasters … [while] close relatives of city council members occupied the permanent positions of secretary, advocate fiscal and collector general'.[29]

Overlap between admiralty boards and other local or regional institutions of power was not limited to direct representation and familial ties with urban magistrates. Out of the 287 admiralty councillors sent to fill one of the seats for the province of Holland on the Amsterdam admiralty board before 1795, 52 also at some points of their lives served as directors of the Dutch East India Company (VOC) or the West India Company (WIC), or as governors of the Society of Suriname. From the last quarter of the seventeenth century onward, the Amsterdam admiralty board usually included at least one councillor who simultaneously acted as a director in the Amsterdam chamber of the VOC.[30] The Dutch navy therefore did not experience the kind of efforts at centralisation that in the English case emanated from the crown and national parliament, but there was still a degree of coordination between the different federal institutions which constituted the Dutch fiscal-naval state.

Beyond their administrations, both the Dutch and the English navies were substantial employers – among the largest in both countries. At its peak during wartime, the English navy employed more people than populated any city in England apart from London, and the crews of its largest warships

---

[26] Olaf van Nimwegen and Ronald Prud'homme van Reine, 'De organisatie en financiering van leger en vloot van de Republiek', in *De Tachtigjarige Oorlog. Van opstand naar geregelde oorlog 1568–1648*, ed. Petra Groen (Amsterdam, 2013), pp. 384–5.

[27] Jan Glete, *Navies and nations. Warships, navies and state building in Europe and America, 1500–1860* (2 vols, Stockholm, 1993), I, 154.

[28] Van Nimwegen and Prud'homme van Reine, 'De organisatie en financiering van leger en vloot', p. 384.

[29] Bruijn, *Dutch navy*, p. 27. The close connection is further substantiated in Brandon, *War, capital, and the Dutch state*, p. 63, and annex 1 and 2.

[30] Pepijn Brandon, 'Global power, local connections. The Dutch admiralties and their supply networks', in *The contractor state and its implications, 1659–1815*, eds Richard Harding and Sergio Solbes Ferri (Las Palmas de Gran Canaria, 2012), p. 59.

were equivalent in number to the residents of a village.[31] In terms of employees and estates, as well as expenditure, the navy was easily the largest single department of government in England. This highlights another aspect of the fiscal-naval state worthy of more investigation: the navy brought government directly into the lives of hundreds of thousands of people, just as central and local authorities did.[32] The hierarchy of naval personnel reflected contemporary social status. In England, the high command were generally aristocrats or gentlemen, as were many captains; the expansion of the navy during the 1640s–50s brought in many 'tarpaulin' (non-aristocratic) officers, which provoked debates after 1660 about their suitability, although this was as much about political allegiance as it was about social standing, and these divisions should not be exaggerated.[33] Over the course of the century various government initiatives, such as the introduction of the examination for lieutenant in 1677, led to professionalisation and a greater sense of identity among the English naval officer corps regardless of their background.[34]

The rest of the navy's employees probably did not share this sense of professional identity tied to the navy as an institution, as opposed to a more general identification as part of a global sector of maritime workers. Although some seafarers spent their lives in the navy, especially warrant or petty officers, the majority of sailors moved in and out of naval employment throughout their careers.[35] The government introduced a distinction between 'ordinary' and 'able' seamen in 1652, the latter more experienced men who received higher pay, as one of many measures throughout this period to encourage skilled seafarers to enlist.[36] Volunteers generally met the English

---

[31] Capp, *Cromwell's navy*, p. 213.

[32] For an overview, see Michael J. Braddick, *State formation in early modern England c. 1550–1700* (Cambridge, 2000).

[33] Davies, *Gentlemen and tarpaulins*, pp. 5, 27–33, and chapter 3; *idem, Pepys's navy*, pp. 94–9; *idem, Kings of the sea*, pp. 126–80; Capp, *Cromwell's navy*, pp. 171–9.

[34] Davies, *Gentlemen and tarpaulins*, pp. 40 and 52–4; *idem, Pepys's navy*, pp. 98–9; *idem, Kings of the sea*, pp. 141–50; Capp, *Cromwell's navy*, pp. 179 and 195–201; Rodger, *Safeguard of the sea*, p. 409; *idem, Command of the ocean*, pp. 119–23; Daniel Baugh, 'The professionalisation of the English navy and its administration, 1660–1750', in *The sea in history*, eds Buchet and Bouëdec, pp. 852–66.

[35] On warrant and petty officers see: Thrush, 'Navy under Charles I', pp. 163–70; Capp, *Cromwell's navy*, pp. 201–11 and 230–43; Davies, *Pepys's navy*, pp. 100–4; Rodger, *Command of the ocean*, p. 124.

[36] Davies, *Gentlemen and tarpaulins*, pp. 79–82; Capp, *Cromwell's navy*, pp. 258–62; see also Thrush, 'Navy under Charles I', pp. 204–5 and 207–12; Andrews, *Ships, money and politics*, pp. 221–4; Rodger, *Safeguard of the sea*, pp. 327–8; *idem, Command of the ocean*, pp. 46–8, 104–5, 194–6, 210 and 312–13; Andrew Little, 'British seamen in the United Provinces during the seventeenth-century Anglo-Dutch wars: the Dutch Navy – a preliminary survey', in *Trade, diplomacy, and cultural exchange. Continuity and change in the North Sea area and the Baltic c. 1350–1750*, ed. Hanno Brand (Hilversum, 2005), pp. 75–93; Geoffrey L. Hudson, 'The relief of English disabled ex-sailors, c. 1590–1680', in *The social history of English seamen, 1485–1649*, ed. Cheryl

navy's requirements during peacetime, but in wartime, demand repeatedly outstripped supply, a situation not helped by low naval wages and poor-quality victuals (usually the result of the navy's financial difficulties), and by harsh naval discipline.[37] The English navy therefore turned to compulsion to fill its ships, and though impressment might not fully match the image of the violent and indiscriminate pressgang which was popular in later centuries it was nevertheless predictably unpopular with sailors.[38] The Dutch navy faced similar problems and also put considerable pressure on sailors to sign up, though preferring economic means such as embargoes on merchant shipping barring alternative routes for employment.[39] While their naval administrations reflect the different political structures of the two states, there are thus significant similarities in the way that both navies employed large numbers of their states' subjects, and in the coercive authority they claimed over these subjects.

Structures of revenue and expenditure

Both naval administration and naval employment depended upon, and impacted upon, another essential area of state activity: revenue and taxation. Comparing the costs and effectiveness of early modern fiscal-military and fiscal-naval arrangements is notoriously difficult, as figures are incomplete and often denote wildly different things. Moreover, while competing directly and on more or less the same terms in some areas, states also pursued very different strategies and aims, creating their own highly specific demands and criteria for determining what amounted to the effective deployment of manpower and strategic resources. Nevertheless, when embedded in long-term narratives of state development, such comparisons can enlighten us about structural trends in state formation.[40] Naval organisation and

---

A. Fury (Woodbridge, 2012), pp. 229–75; Richard J. Blakemore, 'The legal world of English sailors, c. 1575–1729', in *Law, labour, and empire: comparative perspectives on seafarers*, eds Maria Fusaro, Bernard Allaire, Richard J. Blakemore and Tijl Vanneste (Basingstoke, 2015), pp. 104–5.

[37] Tedder, *Navy of the Restoration*, pp. 63–6; Davies, *Gentlemen and tarpaulins*, pp. 79–80, 82–4; *idem*, *Pepys's navy*, pp. 122–4; Capp, *Cromwell's navy*, pp. 272–82; Rodger, *Safeguard of the sea*, p. 403; *idem*, *Command of the ocean*, pp. 19–20, 40 and 60.

[38] Thrush, 'Navy under Charles I', pp. 214–47; Davies, *Gentlemen and tarpaulins*, pp. 71–8 and 136–8; *idem*, *Pepys's navy*, pp. 108–13; Capp, *Cromwell's navy*, pp. 272–82; Rodger, *Safeguard of the sea*, pp. 398–403; *idem*, *Command of the ocean*, pp. 55–9 and 126–32; Blakemore and Murphy, *Civil wars at sea*, pp. 98–104.

[39] Jaap R. Bruijn, 'Career patterns', in *'Those emblems of hell'? European sailors and the maritime labour market, 1570–1870*, eds Paul C. van Royen, Jaap R. Bruijn and Jan Lucassen (St John's, Newfoundland, 1997), p. 29.

[40] For some recent examples, see David Ormrod, *The rise of commercial empires. England and the Netherlands in the age of mercantilism, 1650–1770* (Cambridge, 2003); Marjolein

operations in the seventeenth century were expensive activities, and both the Dutch and English navies repeatedly faced problems in securing the funds they needed; the response to these problems in large part determined the shape and nature of each fiscal-naval state.

Both the Dutch and English states initially relied on revenues from trade to pay for their navies. Following a plan formulated at the end of the 1580s at the same time as the five admiralties were established, the main source of revenue (the 'ordinary income') earmarked for the Dutch navy was from customs. The admiralty boards themselves organised the collection of this tax.[41] Similarly, in England under the early Stuarts, as in the medieval and Tudor periods, the navy (like other departments of government) was funded out of the monarch's ordinary revenue drawn from customs duties, as well as their own estates and a few other sources.[42] The underlying principle seems to have been that since the navy's primary function was to protect trade, it should be funded by a tax on trade. The main hitch for the Dutch system was that through the federal structure of the Republic, as we have seen, local merchant communities could exert great pressure on admiralty officials. They predictably tended to employ this influence to ensure that custom tariffs remained low overall, and there were strong incentives for the local admiralty boards to give their 'own' trading communities comparative advantages by consistent under-taxation.[43]

For both navies, moreover, rising costs and greater activity meant that demand repeatedly outstripped supply. The English crown occasionally supplemented their revenues by levying direct taxation on the approval of parliament, especially in times of war – but, like their Dutch counterparts, the members of the landed gentry and merchant elite who sat in the English parliament were reluctant to levy high taxes. This precipitated a series of crises and provoked tensions between the crown and parliament during the

---

't Hart, 'Mobilising resources for war. The Dutch and British financial revolutions compared', in *War, state and development*, ed. Sánchez, pp. 179–200; Patrick O'Brien and Xavier Duran, 'Total factor productivity for the Royal Navy from victory at Texel (1653) to triumph at Trafalgar (1805)', in *Shipping and economic growth, 1350–1850*, ed. Richard W. Unger (Leiden, 2011), pp. 279–308; Wantje Fritschy, *Public finance of the Dutch Republic in comparative perspective. The viability of an early modern federal state (1570s–1795)* (Leiden and Boston, 2017); Plouviez, 'Marines Européennes', pp. 777–84.

[41] Davids and 't Hart, 'The navy', pp. 287–91.

[42] James Scott Wheeler, *The making of a world power. War and the Military Revolution in seventeenth-century England* (Stroud, 1999), pp. 94–8 and 120–7; Rodger, *Safeguard of the sea*, pp. 341–4.

[43] Marjolein C. 't Hart, *The making of a bourgeois state. War, politics and finance during the Dutch Revolt* (Manchester and New York, 1993), pp. 100–8; Wietse Veenstra, 'Tussen gewest en generaliteit. Staatsvorming en financiering van de oorlog te water in de Republiek der Verenigde Nederlanden, in het bijzonder Zeeland (1586–1795)' (unpublished PhD thesis, Free University Amsterdam, 2014), pp. 78–98.

first half of the seventeenth century, and inadequate financing was the main cause of several humiliating naval defeats during the 1620s.[44] The Dutch navy, too, had to find additional funds to carry the costs of naval operations beyond immediate trade protection, and, as with the English parliament, for these 'extraordinary expenses' petitions were put to the States General for approval. Once approved, provinces paid these subsidies from their tax incomes according to set quota, but the federal structure of the Dutch Republic again led to great variations in the level of commitment to the actual payment of these approved sums by the various provinces. In 1635, the provinces in total were in arrears by approximately £400,000,[45] which at that time amounted to total naval expenses for an entire year. By 1685, arrears had almost doubled to over £700,000, and by 1700 had reached almost £1 million. However, about half this sum accrued to the admiralty board of Zeeland alone. Amsterdam suffered such underpayment to a far lesser extent, with provincial arrears amounting to £140,000 in 1635 and £170,000 half a century later.[46]

Mainly due to this support in Holland, and building on the sixteenth-century 'financial' revolution which had created a relatively efficient fiscal and credit system there, customs revenues and subsidies did provide consistent funds for most of the seventeenth century.[47] Yearly naval expenditure remained at wartime levels of around £400,000 in most of the early decades of the century. About 75 per cent of these expenses went to operational costs: outfitting fleets and hiring and feeding men. The most costly elements of naval policy were the maintaining of the blockade of the Flemish coast, and the outfitting of convoys (principally in the North Sea, the Baltic, and the Mediterranean), which cost just below £100,000 each.[48] After the Peace of Westphalia/Munster that ended the eight decades of armed conflict with the Habsburg Empire, a clear popular sentiment existed to cut back on war expenses, shared by substantial sections of the Dutch ruling class. This partially explains why the Dutch came quite unprepared into the First Anglo-Dutch War that broke out in 1652. With average annual expenditures of around £600,000 during the war years 1652–54, the Dutch fell well behind the English during this war.

---

[44] McGowan, 'Royal Navy', chapter 4; Thrush, 'Navy under Charles I', pp. 123–63 and 198–200; Wheeler, *The making of a world power*, pp. 26–33; Rodger, *Safeguard of the sea*, pp. 357–63 and 373–6.

[45] The exchange rate between the guilder and the pound at this time fluctuated roughly between 10:1 and 11:1. To make comparison easier, we have consistently used 10:1 as the rate here, rounding figures downwards.

[46] Davids and 't Hart, 'The navy', pp. 273–5, 302–4; Veenstra, 'Gewest en generaliteit', pp. 99–102.

[47] 't Hart, 'Mobilising resources', pp. 181–6; Davids and 't Hart, 'The navy', pp. 276–80.

[48] 't Hart, *Bourgeois state*, pp. 52 and 54; Van Nimwegen and Prud'homme van Reine, 'De organisatie en financiering van leger en vloot', pp. 384–5.

This level of English expenditure in the 1650s was only possible because of substantial changes in the structure, basis, and level of English naval financing which had already occurred, contrasting to the continuity visible in the Dutch case, and which reconfigured the navy's place within the English state as a whole. In response to the failures of the 1620s, Charles I tried to improve naval finances in 1635–39 with 'Ship Money', a direct levy which he imposed by his own authority rather than through parliament. Though it initially raised funds which were indeed used for the navy, it proved controversial in subsequent years and has often been regarded as a cause of the civil wars of the 1640s.[49] Ironically, however, parliament's victory in those wars led to a far higher level of taxation than Charles had ever imposed. Parliament introduced excise taxes on several commodities and levied direct taxes through the monthly Assessment, which were as unpopular as 'Ship Money' had been, but which parliament were more successful at carrying out. The income from specific goods was directed to the naval fleet, which had largely sided with parliament in 1642, and which aided parliament's eventual victory.[50] Parliament spent more on the navy, and set out larger fleets, than Charles I was ever able to, and this continued into the 1650s: expenditure rose from £200–300,000 a year during the 1640s to over £1 million a year in 1653–54.[51] Between 1649 and 1660 the navy received a total of £8 million from the government, compared with £3.5 million in 1625–29 and less than £1 million in 1634–40.[52] This system also meant that a much wider range of Britain's population contributed to naval expenditure through taxation, and established a much closer association between parliament and the navy.

The interregnum regimes could not ensure consistent support for the navy, due to reduced taxation and political disruption in the later 1650s, and in 1660 Charles II inherited a navy that was deep in debt. Even so, he maintained some of the interregnum's taxes, which also enabled him to continue another fiscal innovation of the 1640s–50s: securing loans at better rates by assigning

[49] Andrews, *Ships, money and politics*, chapter 6; Andrew Thrush, 'Naval finance and the origins of the development of ship money', in *War and government in Britain, 1598–1650*, ed. Mark Charles Fissel (Manchester, 1991), pp. 133–62; Braddick, *State formation*, pp. 241–4; Rodger, *Safeguard of the sea*, pp. 381–3; see also David D. Hebb, *Piracy and the English government, 1616–1642* (Aldershot, 1994), pp. 30–41, for a smaller and earlier levy to fund a naval expedition.
[50] Wheeler, *Making of a world power*, pp. 102–19, 127–43, 148–67 and 179–94; Braddick, *State formation*, pp. 213–21; Patrick K. O'Brien, 'Fiscal exceptionalism: Great Britain and its European rivals from civil war to triumph at Trafalgar and Waterloo', in *The political economy of British historical experience, 1688–1914*, eds Donald Winch and Patrick K. O'Brien (Oxford, 2002), pp. 245–66; Rodger, *Command of the ocean*, pp. 37–40; Blakemore and Murphy, *Civil wars at sea*, p. 91.
[51] Capp, *Cromwell's navy*, pp. 9–10; see also J.S. Wheeler, 'Navy finance, 1649–1660', *Historical Journal*, 39 (1996), 457–66; idem, *Making of a world power*, pp. 39–42, 45–52 and 204–5.
[52] Capp, *Cromwell's navy*, p. 4; Rodger, *Command of the ocean*, p. 46.

predicted future taxation to their repayment. The navy faced problems with liquidity in each subsequent war, but there were improvements in cost-effectiveness, and it still had a sounder financial base than at any previous time.[53] Throughout Charles II's reign it cost around £300–400,000 annually in peacetime, and up to £1 million annually in war, generally representing over one-fifth of government expenditure.[54] An additional £600,000 was provided for a ship-building programme in 1677, even though it was peacetime.[55] Overall, Dutch and English naval expenditure continued to stand at quite similar levels in the three decades that followed the First Anglo-Dutch War. During the second war, the Dutch doubled their naval expenses to about £1.2 million per year, slightly more than the outlays on the navy by the English government.[56] Moreover, it has to be kept in mind that the Dutch state simultaneously footed the bill for massive involvement in continental warfare, which the English state managed to avoid for most of the seventeenth century.

As Wantje Fritschy has shown, a real divergence of naval expenditure levels only occurred after the Glorious Revolution in 1689. This event brought the two states into an alliance, but also shifted the balance of naval strength between them. In the two major European wars that followed, the War of the League of Augsburg and the War of the Spanish Succession, the Dutch maintained annual levels of naval expenditures of around £1 million and £900,000 respectively (the latter for the years 1702–09).[57] However, English annual expenditure at the beginning of the eighteenth century briefly peaked at just below £8 million, roughly equivalent to Dutch naval expenditure for the entire decade. During most of the eighteenth century, the Dutch state accepted the role of junior partner in a naval alliance with Britain, concentrating their expenses on financing long-distance convoying of the merchant fleet and cutting back expenditure levels.[58] British naval expenditure, meanwhile, continued to increase in leaps and bounds, supported by a British 'financial revolution' that in some ways copied, but eventually outstripped, the Dutch system, and

---

[53] Tedder, *Navy of the Restoration*, pp. 3–6, 45–8 and 54–6; Davies, *Gentlemen and tarpaulins*, pp. 148–9 and 163; *idem, Pepys's navy*, p. 36; Capp, *Cromwell's navy*, pp. 333–65; Rodger, *Command of the ocean*, pp. 40–1, 95–102 and 108–10; Patrick O'Brien, 'The sea and the precocious transition of the British Isles into a hegemonic political and economic power', in *The sea in history*, eds Buchet and Bouëdec, pp. 756–62.

[54] Davies, *Gentlemen and tarpaulins*, p. 15, n. 18; Michael J. Braddick, *The nerves of state. Taxation and the financing of the English state, 1558–1714* (Manchester, 1996), pp. 30–2; Wheeler, *Making of a world power*, pp. 54–8, 143–6, 167–72, 195–6 and 204.

[55] Rodger, *Command of the ocean*, pp. 108–9.

[56] Fritschy, *Public finance*, p. 268.

[57] Veenstra, 'Gewest en generaliteit', p. 126.

[58] 't Hart, 'Mobilising resources', pp. 193–200; Bruijn, *Dutch navy*, pp. 127–40; Davids and 't Hart, 'The navy', pp. 304–8; Brandon, *War, capital, and the Dutch state*, pp. 130–5; Fritschy, *Public finance*, pp. 268–9.

in which indirect taxes played an increasingly important role.[59] Though there were some resemblances between the two states in the sources of funding, both in customs revenues and direct taxation, and in the level of expenditure, the two states had very different fiscal underpinnings which unsurprisingly mirror their political and naval organisation: one centred on the crown and parliament, the other decentralised and under the strong influence of local commercial elites. The Dutch fiscal system of customs revenue and additional provincial taxes was established early and remained fairly stable throughout this period, despite the problems of limited taxation and underpayment. The English system developed more slowly and fitfully, was driven in part by political turbulence, and resulted in a shift in public attitudes: while 'Ship Money' and parliament's excise taxes provoked intense resistance, by the end of the century the idea of increased taxation in support of the navy had largely been accepted by the political nation.[60] Moreover, this comparison of long-term trends shows that there is no clear link between the 'tactical revolution' at sea during the first half of the seventeenth century, or the increase of Anglo-Dutch naval competition in the mid-seventeenth century, and the centralisation of fiscal-naval arrangements. The decentralised Dutch state spent more on its navy and was overall more successful financially than England before the 1650s, and largely kept pace with English spending up until the 1690s, suggesting that no one model of the early modern fiscal-naval state was automatically more effective at extracting and deploying resources.[61] In a similar way, these states depended on varying levels of private involvement to achieve the same objectives.

Naval power and private enterprise

While standing navies expanded in terms of infrastructure and administration, operations, and personnel, they remained only one (albeit the most important) component of an early modern fiscal-naval state. Private enterprise continued to play a significant role both in support of navies and as an alternative to them throughout the seventeenth century and into the

---

[59] Brewer, *Sinews of power*, pp. 34–42, and chapter 4; Patrick O'Brien, 'Inseparable connections. Trade, economy, fiscal state, and the expansion of empire, 1688–1815', in *The Oxford history of the British empire, volume 2: The eighteenth century*, eds P.J. Marshall and Alaine Low (Oxford, 1998), pp. 53–77; Patrick O'Brien and Philip A. Hunt, 'England, 1485–1815', in *The rise of the fiscal state in Europe, c. 1200–1815*, ed. Richard Bonney (Oxford, 1999), pp. 53–100; O'Brien, 'State formation'.

[60] Braddick, *State formation*, pp. 271 and 284–5. Sarah Kinkel has argued, however, that the navy remained a topic of considerable political debate: see *Disciplining the empire. Politics, governance, and the rise of the British navy* (Cambridge, Mass., 2018).

[61] See also Louis Sicking, 'Le maritime, fondement de la prédominance commerciale et économique des Provinces-Unies', in *The sea in history*, eds Buchet and Bouëdec, p. 464.

eighteenth. However, there were significant shifts in the nature and extent of this participation, which resulted from naval expansion. For example, from the medieval period until the mid-seventeenth century, naval warfare had relied to a large degree on the state hiring merchant ships to supplement the relatively small number of state-owned warships.[62] Yet the hiring of merchant ships created tensions between private interests and the strategic and tactical priorities of the state. For example, employing merchant ships for martial purposes benefited those who hired out their ships – often at high rates, exploiting wartime urgency – and established a close link between the navy and certain merchants, which could be problematic. In 1647, critics accused English parliamentarian naval administrators, most of whom were merchants, of hiring their own ships for state service at exorbitant rates even if they were unsuitable for naval service.[63]

This approach also created a route to bypass central state institutions in the organisation of protection, as the Dutch case illustrates well. In 1631, the States General, under pressure from a number of trading towns, had given its approval to the formation of new institutions, the *Directies*. These committees existed in several ports, and were headed by burgomasters and representatives from different groups of traders. Their task was to hire and arm merchant ships on their own account, in order to organise additional convoys which were financed through a separate tax, levied only on the merchants who profited directly from their employment.[64] Though these *directie*-ships acted under the formal command structures of the navy during operations, they were organisationally independent, and during the First Anglo-Dutch War they attracted criticism for their low quality, their reluctance to take risks during battle that endangered valuable private assets, and the disreputable conduct of their captains. Several mutinies broke out on *directie*-ships during the 1650s, showing 'that the old axiom was untenable that the merchant fleet, as a reserve for the state navy, should be seen as the backbone of protection at sea'.[65]

In the English case, the increase in naval resources across the 1630s and 1640s, and especially during the 1650s, eventually removed the need for hired merchant ships. By the end of the First Anglo-Dutch War, the English naval fleet was largely state-owned, a development that, like the changes in English naval finances to which it was closely linked, owed much to

[62] Andrews, *Ships, money and politics*, pp. 25–9; Rodger, *Safeguard of the sea*, pp. 118–20; Bruijn, 'States and their navies', pp. 73–6 and 78–80; Sicking, 'Naval warfare', pp. 255–8.
[63] Andrews, *Ships, money and politics*, pp. 190–202; Blakemore and Murphy, *Civil wars at sea*, pp. 92–3.
[64] Bruijn, *Dutch navy*, p. 27.
[65] Johan E. Elias, *De vlootbouw in Nederland in de eerste helft der 17de eeuw 1596–1655* (Amsterdam, 1933), p. 90. On the mutinies, see Brandon, *War, capital, and the Dutch state*, p. 88.

the circumstances and demands of civil war and revolution.[66] The Dutch navy, which had employed the strategy of arming merchant ships with great success in the preceding period, was slower than the English state in adapting to this new approach. The thrust towards what Jaap Bruijn has called the transition from the 'Old' to the 'New' navy came only with the poor performance of the Dutch fleet in the First Anglo-Dutch War.[67] Out of a total of 154 ships constituting the Dutch fleet, 88 had been hired merchant-men (about half of them *directie*-ships), which were regarded as less effective in battle.[68] The naval commander Maerten Harpertszoon Tromp lobbied intensively for a large building programme of custom-made warships, to bring the Dutch standing navy to the level of their English adversaries. A competing attachment to the traditional strategy of using merchant ships as a second tier of the naval fleet is apparent from the Amsterdam city council's proposal, around the same time, to instead formulate a set of rules for the building of merchant-men that would allow them to be more easily trans-formed into men-of-war.[69] However, Tromp's line won out in the end. At the instigation of Johan de Witt, the leading Dutch statesman at that moment, the aftermath of the First Anglo-Dutch War saw a major transformation of naval facilities, allowing for building programmes for specialised warships run by the admiralty boards themselves. The imposing Amsterdam naval storehouse and admiralty shipyard, erected in 1656, were the visible result of this change in approach.[70] The Dutch navy reaped the benefits during the Second Anglo-Dutch War, when the balance of naval power between the two nations had been more or less restored.

Both navies continued to rely on private enterprise in other ways. One of them was the dependence of these enhanced facilities for the building and outfitting of warships on private ship-builders and extensive supply networks. The English navy was 'far and away the largest industry in the country ... at the heart of a web of sub-contractors that extended the navy's reach far inland'.[71] The royal dockyards relied on private suppliers for their building and maintenance programmes, and the navy also purchased victuals from merchants, drawing large numbers of producers and artisans into the fiscal-naval state, and perhaps boosting the British economy.[72] During the 1640s and 1650s, at least, this often involved women, usually widows, some of

---

[66] Capp, *Cromwell's navy*, pp. 6–9 and 80; Davies, *Pepys's navy*, pp. 16 and 57; Rodger, *Command of the ocean*, pp. 45, 59 and 216–18.

[67] Bruijn, *Dutch navy*, pp. 59–63; see also Bruijn, 'States and their navies', pp. 83–90.

[68] J.C. de Jonge, *Geschiedenis van het Nederlandsche zeewezen* (2nd rev. edn, 5 vols, Haarlem, 1858–62), I, 762–3.

[69] Elias, *Vlootbouw*, p. 94.

[70] Brandon, *War, capital, and the Dutch state*, pp. 146–7.

[71] Davies, *Pepys's navy*, p. 33; Rodger, *Command of the ocean*, pp. 112–18.

[72] Davies, *Pepys's navy*, pp. 69, 78 and 200–1; Rodger, *Command of the ocean*, pp. 45–6, 98–100, 105–7 and 188–95; *idem*, '"Fiscal-naval state"', p. 123.

whom ran considerable businesses which supplied the navy with hammocks, flags, and other goods.[73] The Dutch admiralty boards utilised decentralised market-mechanisms to an even greater extent, especially for provisioning. The Dutch navy did not take responsibility for organising victualling centrally; instead, captains received a lump sum per crewmember, with which they had to procure a set list of supplies. This created large possibilities for private gain, provided that captains managed to buy their hard tack, salted meat, and other daily necessities on the cheap.

Michiel de Ruyter himself provides one of the famous examples of captains who acquired a small fortune in this way. According to calculations by Prud'homme van Reine, who certainly is not a hostile biographer of De Ruyter, this successful merchant-turned-admiral managed to retain one-third of the seven *stuyvers* per man per day that he received for the crew of his flagship *De Zeven Provinciën*. Extrapolating from his extant account books, Prud'homme van Reine estimates that De Ruyter received £32,000 from the admiralty board for victuals between 1652 and 1667, on which he could have made a profit of as much as £7,000.[74] With victualling making up 14 per cent of total naval expenditure, this must have created a lush market. Of course, such windfalls were not confined to captains. Either through their personal businesses, through family members, or through underhand deals, the higher echelons of naval administration in both England and the United Provinces were routinely (and not always legally) involved in the costly provisioning of wood, rope, hemp, and other naval necessities. Next to them stood many of the leading merchants of the seventeenth century. The 'contractor state' which historians have identified in the late eighteenth century was already in existence, although perhaps less systematically organised and not always as effective as it later proved.[75]

Beyond the navy itself, these fiscal-naval states employed privateers as a substantial and continuous part of their wartime strategy, but here there was more wide-reaching change in their purpose and activities.[76] In the

---

[73] Blakemore and Murphy, *Civil wars at sea*, pp. 89–91.

[74] Ronald Prud'homme van Reine, *Rechterhand van Nederland. Biografie van Michiel Adriaenszoon de Ruyter* (Amsterdam and Antwerpen, 1996), pp. 219–20.

[75] Roger Knight and Martin H. Wilcox, *Sustaining the fleet, 1793–1815. War, the British Navy and the contractor state* (Woodbridge, 2010), especially pp. 8–16; Christian Buchet, *The British Navy, economy and society in the Seven Years War*, trans. Anita Higgie and Michael Duffy (Woodbridge, 2013). For an international comparative perspective, see: H.V. Bowen, 'Round table. The contractor state, c. 1650–1815', *International Journal for Maritime History*, 25:1 (2013), 239–74; and the special issue 'Extending the state. The business of war and the eighteenth-century contractor state', eds Pepijn Brandon, Marjolein C. 't Hart and Rafael Torres Sánchez, *Business History*, 60:1 (2018).

[76] Janice E. Thomson, *Mercenaries, pirates, and sovereigns. Extraterritorial violence in early modern Europe* (Princeton, NJ, 1994), pp. 21–6 and 44–54; Gijs Rommelse, 'An early

Elizabethan period and again in the 1620s England had deployed large numbers of privately-owned warships in both European waters and further afield.[77] During the 1640s parliamentarians, royalists, and Irish confederates all employed privateers, and this was especially important for the royalists and confederates who possessed no regular naval forces.[78] After the 1650s, with the increased naval fleet, English privateers became less numerous in European waters but remained important to the expanding American colonies, which depended on privateering to bring in specie and goods, and for their defence.[79] In the Dutch case, too, privateering continued to form an important part of commercial warfare. It retained an especially strong foothold in the province of Zeeland, where privateering and later the participation in the illegal slave trade partially compensated for the loss of other trading opportunities to Holland.[80] Beyond European waters commercial companies like the VOC, WIC, and English East India Company also performed essential, though gradually shifting, roles in trade protection and naval conflict throughout the seventeenth century and long into the eighteenth.[81]

As with hired merchant ships and private suppliers, the profit-seeking of privateers and the objectives of the state could align, but did not always do

---

modern naval revolution? The relationship between "economic reason of state" and maritime warfare', *Journal for Maritime Research*, 13 (2011), 143–4.

[77] Kenneth R. Andrews, *Elizabethan privateering. English privateering during the Spanish War, 1585–1603* (Cambridge, 1964); John C. Appleby, 'English privateering during the Spanish and French Wars' (unpublished PhD thesis, University of Hull, 1983).

[78] Ben Coates, *The impact of the English Civil War on the economy of London, 1642–50* (Aldershot, 2004), pp. 97–9 and 125–32; Blakemore and Murphy, *Civil wars at sea*, pp. 104–7, 110–12 and 117–20.

[79] Rodger, *Command of the ocean*, pp. 23–4, 79 and 92–3; Susan Dwyer Amussen, *Caribbean exchanges. Slavery and the transformation of English society, 1640–1700* (Chapel Hill, NC, 2007), pp. 38–42; Douglas R. Burgess, *Politics of piracy. Crime and civil disobedience in colonial America* (Lebanon, NH, 2014), chapter 2; Mark Hanna, *Pirate nests and the rise of the British empire, 1570–1740* (Chapel Hill, NC, 2015), chapter 3; Kris Lane, *Pillaging the empire. Global piracy on the high seas, 1500–1750* (Abingdon, 2016), chapter 4; John C. Appleby, 'Pirates, privateers, and buccaneers. The changing face of English piracy from the 1650s to the 1720s', in *The social history of English seamen, 1650–1815*, ed. Cheryl A. Fury (Woodbridge, 2017), pp. 217–22.

[80] J.Th.H. Verhees-Van Meer, *De Zeeuwse kaapvaart tijdens de Spaanse Successieoorlog 1702–1713* (Middelburg, 1986); Davids and 't Hart, 'The navy', pp. 298–302; Sicking, 'Le maritime', p. 464.

[81] Thomson, *Mercenaries, pirates, and sovereigns*, pp. 31–40, 59–68 and 97–105; Femme S. Gaastra, *The Dutch East India Company. Expansion and decline* (Zutphen, 2003); Helen Julia Paul, 'Joint-stock companies as the sinews of war. The South Sea and Royal African Companies', in *War, state and development*, ed. Sánchez, pp. 277–94; Philip J. Stern, *The company-state. Corporate sovereignty and the early modern foundation of the British empire in India* (Oxford, 2011); Henk den Heijer, *Geschiedenis van de WIC* (Zutphen, 2013); Philippe Haudrère, 'Les compagnies de commerce. Instruments de la puissance maritime', in *The sea in history*, eds Buchet and Bouëdec, pp. 763–72.

so. The career of the most famous English buccaneer, Henry Morgan, reveals the uneasy relationship between these fiscal-naval states and the semi-independent privateers they employed. Morgan led several successful and brutal campaigns against Spanish America during the 1670s, and was then tried for piracy, but was exonerated and made deputy governor of Jamaica, in which role he displayed a rather ambivalent attitude towards his former comrades.[82] His experiences were part of a wider trend whereby the English state sought to circumscribe and control privateers, and eradicate piracy, starting with parliamentary and colonial legislation in the 1670s, and intensifying with further legislation and more vigorous prosecution from the 1690s onwards.[83] Piracy resurged in the early eighteenth century, and privateers continued to feature in England's (and other countries') maritime strategy throughout that century, but under much stricter control than before: another way in which fiscal-naval states flexed their muscles and dictated the terms of their authority over their subjects, this time on a global scale.[84]

Conclusions

One of the more interesting dimensions highlighted by this comparison is the internationally interactive nature of fiscal-naval state development: the extent to which change in one state drove change in others, especially those which, like the Dutch and English states, repeatedly came to blows. In some ways this happened as a blunt arms race – as when the Dutch navy were forced to adapt from merchant ships to state-owned warships, because the English had already done so – but it also occurred in a more subtle and complex fashion, such as the connections between the 'financial revolutions' which occurred first in Holland and later in England. The various similarities between the Dutch and English navies, such as their ideological associations, their employment of large portions of the population, their level and sources of funding, and the overall shift towards greater state control while preserving some role for private agents, owe much to both the competition and the connections between these two states. Fiscal-naval

[82] Hanna, *Pirate nests*, p. 123; Lane, *Pillaging the empire*, pp. 113–14.

[83] Robert C. Ritchie, *Captain Kidd and the war against the pirates* (Cambridge, Mass., 1986), pp. 152–5; Burgess, *Politics of piracy*, chapters 3–6; Margarette Lincoln, *British pirates and society, 1680–1730* (Farnham, 2014), chapter 3; Hanna, *Pirate nests*, chapters 5–7; Lane, *Pillaging the empire*, pp. 176–90.

[84] Ritchie, *Captain Kidd*, pp. 233–7; David J. Starkey, *British privateering in the eighteenth century* (Exeter, 1990); Thomson, *Mercenaries, pirates, and sovereigns*, pp. 108–18; Marcus Rediker, *Villains of all nations. Atlantic pirates in the Golden Age* (London, 2012), especially chapter 7; Burgess, *Politics of piracy*, chapters 7–11; Hanna, *Pirate nests*, chapters 8–10; Lane, *Pillaging the empire*, pp. 190–202; Appleby, 'Pirates, privateers, and buccaneers', pp. 222–35.

states must be understood within the international political ecosystem in which they evolved.

At the same time, it is important not to obscure the individual character-istics of each state. There were significant differences between the Dutch and English fiscal-naval states and their development, especially in political terms: one was a localised federal republic, the other a centralising monarchy; one was relatively politically stable, albeit with various factional and provincial rivalries, the other riven by internal turmoil with long-lasting consequences. These differences affected the shape and direction of the two navies, but they did not guarantee greater success, in fiscal-naval terms, until the start of the eighteenth century. Although Britain became the dominant maritime power thereafter, this was certainly not a predetermined trajectory. Perhaps the greatest strength of the concept of fiscal-naval states for historians, therefore, is in opening up discussion of the various ways in which warfare at sea and naval organisation are both a consequence of, and have an impact upon, wider patterns of early modern state-formation.

7

Dutch and English dockyards and coastal defence, 1652–89

Ann Coats and Alan Lemmers

Dutch and English trade and naval rivalry was enduring and embittered as both nations contested the resources and routes of the North Sea. Their multi-dimensional competitiveness, counterbalanced by common expertise of North Sea navigation, recurrent naval personnel interchange, and aspects of political and religious culture, underpinned the Anglo-Dutch wars, determining their defensive and offensive infrastructures.[1] In the mid-seventeenth century Dutch financial and political institutions were better placed than the English to support their navies, dockyards and defence.[2] Naval organisation was highly fragmented and its shore facilities (bases, stores, yards) divided among five regional admiralties: one in Zeeland, one in Friesland and three in Holland (Northern Quarter, Amsterdam and Rotterdam/Maas). Although accountable to the States General, the admiralties in many ways were tied to local customs, economy and political influence. On their provisional recognition in 1597, future unification had been intended, but in the end the arrangement of five separate admiralties endured until 1795. Each admiralty was presided over nominally by the admiral-general of the republic, usually the stadtholder, but this custom lacked constitutional foundation, as two stadtholder-less eras demonstrated (1650–72, 1702–47).[3] Meanwhile the

---

[1] P.G. Rogers, *The Dutch in the Medway* (Oxford, 1970), pp. 22–5 and 66–7; Andrew R. Little, 'British seamen in the United Provinces during the seventeenth century Anglo-Dutch Wars: the Dutch navy – a preliminary survey', in *Trade, diplomacy and cultural exchange. Continuity and change in the North Sea area and the Baltic c.1350–1750*, ed. Hanno Brand (Hilversum, 2005), pp. 76–92.

[2] 'English' denotes government and navy before the 1707 Act of Union between England and Scotland. However, James I and II, Charles I and II, Cromwell and William III were also rulers of Scotland and Ireland, which had separate admiralties, but the navy operated in 'British' seas, protected British merchants, obtained supplies from the British Isles and contained many Scots and Irish personnel. See J.D. Davies, *Pepys's Navy. Ships, men and warfare 1649–1689* (Barnsley, 2008), pp. 12, 30–1, 33–4 and 36.

[3] In the Republic there were five theoretically equal admiralties, so 'admiralty' is used generically. 'Admiralty of Amsterdam' is capitalised as a proper noun, but

logistical organisation of the navy remained largely as before, scattered across a dozen bases.

In the period 1650–70 the traditional Dutch fleet, until then reliant largely on recruiting merchantmen, was replaced by a standing fleet with purpose-built men-of-war, to be maintained in peacetime. A permanent Dutch fleet entailed expansion of existing shore facilities, previously rudimentary. It also had far-reaching consequences for Dutch society, as naval shipbuilding grew exponentially while separating itself from private enterprise. With the development of line tactics, the sea officers became professionalised, warships were specialised and both civilian commanders and merchantmen disappeared from the fighting fleet. Finally, from 1672 naval deployment followed the changes in defence policy due to growing external threats and alliance obligations, which at the national level further separated the fleet from maritime enterprise, as we shall see.

English aspirations to counter or emulate the Spanish, Portuguese and Dutch overseas expansion were supported from the sixteenth century by permanent naval dockyards at Portsmouth, Deptford, Woolwich and Chatham, the largest and most expensive state-funded installations. Private yards on the Thames and southern coasts provided supplementary shipbuilding. Dockyards focused defensive operations, mounting guardships and coastal cruises. Naval anchorages at Harwich, the Nore, the Downs, Spithead and St Helen's required shore defences, while the vulnerable narrow channel between Hurst Castle and the Isle of Wight required extra defensive works and forces during wartime.

The 1650s republic invested funds derived from sales of Dean and Chapter lands, royal and royalist estates and fee farm rents in dockyards and shipbuilding to defend England's coasts against piracy and to protect trade.[4] In December 1652, a new admiralty commission mobilised naval resources to deliver a decisive victory in the First Anglo-Dutch War (1652–54), mustering 20,000 seamen and 2,000 dockyard workers.[5] But in April 1653 Oliver

otherwise referred to as the 'Amsterdam admiralty', etc. In England there was only one Admiralty, capitalised as a proper noun. For the Republic's state institutions, see R. Fruin and H.T. Colenbrander, *Geschiedenis der staatsinstellingen in Nederland tot den val van de Republiek* (The Hague, 1901), *passim*.

[4] 'April 1649: An Act for abolishing of Deans, Deans and Chapters, Canons, Prebends and other offices and titles of or belonging to any Cathedral or Collegiate Church or Chappel within England and Wales', in *Acts and Ordinances of the Interregnum, 1642–1660*, ed. C.H. Firth and R.S. Rait (London, 1911), pp. 81–104; 'March 1650: An Act for the selling Fee-farm Rents belonging to the Commonwealth of England, formerly payable to the Crown of England, Dutchy of Lancaster, and Dutchy of Cornwall', in *ibid.*, pp. 358–62. Fee farm rents: ground rents formerly paid to the crown.

[5] V.A. Rowe, *Sir Harry Vane the Younger* (London, 1970), pp. 158–90, 255, 257–60 and 279.

Cromwell dissolved the Long Parliament and removed influential admiralty commissioners Sir Henry Vane Jr and Colonel George Thompson, eliminating their political influence to fund this larger navy.[6]

Cromwell's death in September 1658 signified the end of the Interregnum. The restored Stuarts subsequently manipulated dockyard towns through political patronage, enforced new charters and oaths and imposed manned fortifications and military governors.[7] The navy and naval administration became fragmented by royalist/republican and 'gentlemen and tarpaulin' differences, while inefficient tax collection prevented significant naval outlay before the 1670s and large-scale investment before the 1690s.[8]

In view of these multiple difficulties, it seems clear that Dutch and English coastal defences were compromised in some degree by national leadership and economic and manpower issues. Secure defence (and offence) required an efficient and well-supplied infrastructure and loyal dockyard and naval workforces. Defence also required investment in shipbuilding, naval technology and contractors providing cost-effective and proficient naval ordnance, while dockyards needed timely naval supplies imported on protected merchant ships. This interconnectedness of dockyards, fortifications, naval shipbuilding, ordnance and manning had to function well to provide an effective coastal defence. Naval defeats revealed weaknesses and disconnections in the system in ways which we describe below. These ideal conditions were most obviously found wanting in the Chatham raid of 1667, the episode with which we close this review.

Dutch naval facilities 1648–52

From 1588 the admiralties established annual requirements for naval defence. There was no long-term planning or commitment and vessels that were likely to remain idle for a year were usually sold to economise on maintenance. At the outset of the First Anglo-Dutch War (1652–54), raising and owning a large and permanent naval force was beyond anybody's vision. With the Spanish threat gone after 1639 and no French or English fleet to speak of, there had been little need. Men-of-war were built either in admiralty shipyards or under contract by private shipbuilders.[9] Admiralty facilities were modest: Amsterdam, the

---

[6] C. Hill, *God's Englishman* (Harmondsworth, 1970), p. 139.

[7] Ann Coats, 'L'arsenal de Portsmouth: contrefort contesté de la marine, de la monarchie et de l'église au XVIIe siècle', in *Les arsenaux de Marine, du XVIe siècle à nos jours*, ed. C. le Mao (Paris, forthcoming).

[8] P.K. O'Brien, 'Fiscal and financial preconditions for the rise of British naval hegemony 1485–1815', Working Paper No. 91/05, Department of Economic History, London School of Economics (2005), 9, 14, 18 and 21–32.

[9] Nicolaes Witsen's famous treatise on shipbuilding contains several contracts for men-of-war, with a (private) shipbuilder. Ab Hoving, *Nicolaes Witsens Scheeps-Bouw-Konst open gestelt* (Franeker, 1994), pp. 316–33.

richest of all admiralties, until 1660 had a shipyard with two slipways in a restricted terrain, launching two ships a year at the most.[10] The far smaller and poorer Frisian admiralty had moved from Dokkum in 1645, where it had no shipyard at all, to Harlingen, where it was allotted sizeable premises with two building slips. The yard was to become quite productive during the first two Anglo-Dutch wars, but at other times the admiralty would buy or lease vessels from colleague admiralties and the slips were little used.[11] Rotterdam and as far as we know all the towns of the Northern Quarter each possessed a modest building yard, as did Flushing and Veere in Zeeland.[12] However, many, if not most, men-of-war were built at private shipyards, which stimulated the local economy and fattened the admiralty council members' purses.

Figure 7.1 Amsterdam naval facilities c. 1600, facing southwards. One of the large shipyards on the island, top middle, belonged to the Amsterdam chamber of the Dutch East India Company, the other to the Amsterdam Admiralty. B.F. van Berckenrode, *Amstelredamum emporium…*, 1625, detail. Source: Amsterdam City Archives.

[10] Alan Lemmers, *Van werf tot facilitair complex. 350 jaar marinegeschiedenis op Kattenburg* (The Hague, 2005), pp. 19–24.
[11] Thea Roodhuyzen, *De Admiraliteit van Friesland* (Franeker, 2003), pp. 9–12. After 1667 Harlingen production had two more peaks, in the 1690s and the 1780s. C.W.J. Schaap, 'De Admiraliteit van Friesland, haar vlagofficieren en schepen', in *Jaarverslag Fries Scheepvaartmuseum en Oudheidkamer* (1982), pp. 54–77.
[12] A.F. Franken, *Scheepswerven in Zeeland. Een onderzoek naar de geschiedenis en relicten van Zeeuwse scheepswerven* (Goes, 1996), pp. 34–5, 55, 58–60 and 78–9; Benoit Strubbe, 'Oorlogsscheepsbouw en werven in Zeeland tijdens de Engels-Staatse oorlogen (1650–1674)' (unpublished MA thesis, University of Ghent, 2007), pp. 56–62.

The English fleet until 1650 had also relied on the merchantmen reserve in times of war, but English commercial vessels were substantially built and well-armed, to serve mercantile purposes as well as privateering and warfare if necessary.[13] This made them less suited for some trades, which gave the Dutch highly diversified commercial fleet an important lead. The downside of the Dutch situation was that the great variety of specialised commercial vessels left few convertible to warfare. The shortage of proper fighting vessels was a structural problem existing from the early seventeenth century and decried repeatedly by perceptive admirals after each peace was concluded and most of the fleet discarded. At the outbreak of the First Anglo-Dutch War, when the regular fleet was at another low due to the peacetime cutbacks, some even proposed (belatedly) copying the English practice and demand that all future commercial vessels be built to minimal battle requirements, but the idea was not followed up.[14]

English naval and dockyard administration 1650s to 1680s

During the Interregnum, the Council of State undertook the monarch's Privy Council executive functions. Admiralty and naval commissions included army officers, salaried merchants, shipbuilders, government clerks, dockyard commissioners and naval officers with discharged administrative functions, with an emphasis on expertise.[15] In 1660 the navy was again administered by the monarch and the Privy Council, conveying policy to the Lord High Admiral. He commanded the Navy Board, which directed dockyard resident commissioners and officers and organised supplies. The Navy Board built, fitted out, manned and repaired naval ships in naval dockyards and bases. It also administered dockyards and overseas bases, leased transports, purchased and distributed naval stores and issued ordnance. It appointed

---

[13] Ralph Davis, *The rise of the English shipping industry in the 17th and 18th centuries* (Newton Abbot, 1962, 2nd printing 1972), pp. 12–13, 45–8 and 50–4.

[14] J.E. Elias, *De vlootbouw in Nederland 1596–1655* (Amsterdam, 1933), pp. 92–4; L.C.E. van 't Zand, 'De oorlogsvloot van Johan de Witt. De bouw van oorlogsschepen door de admiraliteit van de Maze in de eerste (1652–1654) en tweede (1665–1667) Engels-Nederlandse oorlog' (unpublished MA thesis, Leiden University, 1996), pp. 39–40; J.R. Bruijn, *Varend verleden. De Nederlandse oorlogsvloot in de zeventiende en achttiende eeuw* (Amsterdam, 1998), p. 95.

[15] W.N. Hammond, 'The administration of the English Navy 1649–1660' (unpublished PhD thesis, University of British Columbia, 1974); B. Spring, 'The administration and its personnel under the Protectorate of Oliver Cromwell, 1653–1658' (unpublished MA thesis, University of British Columbia, 1968); B. Capp, *Cromwell's navy* (Oxford, 1992), pp. 44–52, 80, 156, 264 and 363; R.C. Anderson, 'Operations of the English Fleet 1648–52', *English Historical Review*, 21 (1916), 409; Alfred C. Dewar, 'The naval administration of the Interregnum 1641–59', *Mariner's Mirror*, 12:4 (1926), 406–30.

and paid warrant officers, dockyard and naval personnel and at times fed seamen and cared for sick seamen.[16] The Corporation of Trinity House (1514), a complementary maritime institution of sailing masters, regulated Thames pilots, ships' masters, navigational buoys and lighthouses, and monitored coastal channels, hazards and markings.[17]

Charles II confirmed James Duke of York as Lord High Admiral and the Privy Council appointed a new Navy Board on 4 July 1660, a blend of royalists and experienced former parliamentarians.[18] Apart from Clerk of the Acts Samuel Pepys, all had considerable naval, shipbuilding, or military experience.[19] They were paid by the Commonwealth practice of fixed salaries, rather than fees and allowances.[20] 'Thus the new form of administration was a compromise between the systems of the Commonwealth and pre-Commonwealth times.'[21] The comptroller was normally the senior naval officer, had the widest remit and coordinated all activities.[22] After James resigned as Lord High Admiral in 1673, admiralty commissioners were political appointees, mostly aristocrats allied closely to the king, whereas navy commissioners were salaried merchants, shipbuilders, naval officers and government officials, leading to occasional disputes. Relations within the Navy Board were also far from harmonious, with rivalries between naval and civilian members.

Late Stuart dockyards were 'economic by-products of the state in pursuit of war', undertaking industrial production, apprentice entry and time-work discipline. From 1660 to 1688, the navy consumed around a quarter of government outlay, half of which was allocated to civilian dockyards, rising to one-third during the war years 1673–74. While these proportions fell slightly during the longer period ending in 1711, we must bear in mind that total government expenditure rose almost seven-fold. Nationally, the

---

[16] J.G. Coad, *The royal dockyards 1690–1850* (Aldershot, 1989), pp. 23–4; *idem, Support for the fleet. Architecture and engineering of the Royal Navy's bases 1700–1914* (Swindon, 2013), pp. 4 and 53; J.M. Collinge (ed.), *Navy Board officials 1660–1832. Office-holders in modern Britain* (12 vols, London, 1978), vol. 7, 1–2 and 18.

[17] G.G. Harris, *The Trinity House at Deptford, 1514–1660* (Oxford, 1969).

[18] J.R. Tanner (ed.), *A descriptive catalogue of the naval manuscripts in the Pepysian Library* (4 vols, London, 1903), I, 6–7. Charles I had declared before the Privy Council on 18 March 1638 that his son James would be the future Lord Admiral. W.G. Perrin, 'The Lord High Admiral and the Board of Admiralty', *Mariner's Mirror*, 12:2 (1924), p. 133.

[19] C.H. Firth, revised by C.S. Knighton, 'Carteret, Sir George, first baronet (1610?– 1680)', in *Oxford Dictionary of National Biography* (Oxford, 2008) [hereafter: *ODNB*]; C.S. Knighton, 'Batten, Sir William (1600/01–1667)', in *ibid.*, 2008; C.S. Knighton, 'Pepys, Samuel (1633–1703)', in *ibid.*, 2004; J.D. Davies, 'Montagu, Edward, first Earl of Sandwich (1625–1672)', in *ibid.*, 2004.

[20] G.E. Aylmer, *The king's servants 1625–1642* (London, 1961), pp. 437–8.

[21] A.W. Tedder, *The navy of the Restoration* (Cambridge, 1916), p. 43.

[22] Collinge, *Navy Board officials*, p. 5.

Table 7.1 Naval expenditure as a percentage of total
English government expenditure (annual averages)

	Naval expenditure (pounds sterling)	Total government expenditure (pounds sterling)	%
1661–65	323,126	1,311,326	24.6
1665–67	628,651	2,725,202	23.1
1667–72	No adequate figures available		
1673–74	865,312	2,565,134	33.7
1674–88	447,767	1,693,653	26.4
1688–97	2,147,008	7,483,843	28.7
1697–1702	1,022,411	5,299,781	19.3
1702–11	1,925,356	8,935,722	21.5

Source: D.C. Coleman, 'Naval dockyards under the later Stuarts', *Economic History Review* 6 (1953), 135–7. Shaded rows represent years affected by war.

dockyard workforce rose from 980 to 2,263 from 1654 to 1689. Dockyards required extensive naval stores not only from the British Isles, but also from the Baltic, India and the Americas, underlining merchant navy ties.[23]

As Lord High Admiral, James prioritised naval debts and funding, his personal secretaries becoming naval administrators.[24] In 1660 the wages of 40 'unnecessarily kept' ships and 3,695 men totalled £129,981, increasing by £11,085 monthly. Parliament voted a £420,000 assessment to pay off the army and 'some part of the Navy' (65 non-commissioned ships, 36 commissioned ships and dockyard wages), but this was future money, yet unavailable.[25] On 25 August 1660 the debts of the navy were estimated at £678,000, including

---

[23] *Ibid.*, pp. 135–42, 145–50 and 155; R. Latham and W. Matthews (eds), *Diary of Samuel Pepys* (11 vols, London, 1995), vol. 10, 289 [www.pepysdiary.com/diary/].

[24] Sir William Coventry 1660–67, Matthew Wren 1667–72, Sir John Werden 1672–73, Samuel Pepys 1673–79, Thomas Hayter 1679–80, John Brisbane 1680–85 and Pepys 1685–89. S. Lee and S. Kelsey, 'Sir William Coventry (1627–86)', in *ODNB*, 2004; Stuart Handley, 'Matthew Wren, (1629–72)', in *ibid.*, 2008; T. Venning, 'Sir John Werden (1640–1716)', in *ibid.*, 2004; C.S. Knighton, 'Samuel Pepys (1633–1703)', in *ibid.*, 2015.

[25] *Journal of the House of Commons. Vol. 8, 1660–67* (London, 1802), 16 May 1660, pp. 27–33: www.british-history.ac.uk/commons-jrnl/vol8/pp27–33; 'Charles II, 1660: An Act for granting unto the Kings Majestic Fower hundred and twenty thousand pounds by an Assessment of three score and ten thousand pounds by the moneth for six moneths for disbanding the remainder of the Army, and paying off the Navy', in *Statutes of the Realm. Vol. 5, 1628–80*, ed. John Raithby (s.l., 1819), pp. 269–77.

£195,075 wages due to ships at sea and £111,953 wages due to ships in port.[26] Only 8 of the 109 Commonwealth ships were paid by the end of 1660, the rest in July 1661.[27] In June 1662, when the Privy Council ordered '20 ships be forthwith set out', Pepys knew the navy was unprepared, 'we neither having money, credit, nor stores'.[28] Government functions were also disrupted by plague, with the king and Privy Council in Oxford July–January 1666.

Resident commissioners oversaw dockyard officers for the Navy Board. Interregnum commissioners Phineas Pett, William Willoughby and Nathaniel Bourne, at Chatham, Portsmouth and Harwich, were private shipbuilders or merchants as well as state employees. Deptford and Woolwich were administered directly by the Navy Board, and Sheerness by Chatham. Commissioners continued at Chatham and Portsmouth after 1660. Dockyard master shipwrights built and repaired ships (shipwrights comprised a third to half the workforce), the master attendant, an ex-naval officer, moved and docked ships, and the master house-carpenter built and repaired docks and wharves. Foremen and quartermen, leading a gang or shoal of twenty men, were promoted from the workforce.

Personnel were organised into the ordinary: permanent officers, warders and shipkeepers who maintained the ships in reserve; and the extraordinary: constructing new ships or rebuilds. Experienced shipwrights trained apprentices for seven years. Dockyard wages were fixed in 1650. Shipwrights, the highest paid and most numerous, received 2s 1d a day plus a weekly lodgings allowance of 2½d. Other trades included caulkers, joiners, house-carpenters, wheelwrights, scavelmen, blockmakers, sawyers, treenail-mooters, oarmakers, pitchheaters, coopers and masons. Labourers were employed seasonally as required. At busy times or when a ship docked or undocked at night, a Night was 5 hours' overtime for a day's pay, thus double time; a Tide was 1.5 hours at 7/8d.[29] Dockyard workers were paid at least six months, sometimes two years in arrears.[30] Workmen subsisted within a variable debt economy,

---

[26] British Library (London) [hereafter: BL], Additional Ms. 9302, fols. 114, 115v and 116.

[27] British National Archives (London) [hereafter: BNA], ADM 106/3, fol. 212; ADM 106/2, 21.9.1660; ADM 2/1745, fol. 9v, 11.6.1660; ADM 106/3, 24.6.1660, 2.2.1660[1]; 11.3.1660[1]; *The Diary of Samuel Pepys*, 18 September 1660; 15 October 1660; 10 and 30 November 1660; 4 December 1660; 21 January 1660/61; 4 February 1660/61; 27 February 1660/61; 14 August 1661; 28 December 1661; Capp, *Cromwell's navy*, pp. 374–5.

[28] *The Diary of Samuel Pepys*, 28 June 1662.

[29] National Maritime Museum (London) [hereafter: NMM], SER/131, Abstracts of the numbers of workmen weekly employed in His Majesty's several yards, 1686–1718; D.A. Baugh, *British naval administration in the age of Walpole* (New Jersey, 1965), p. 309; D.A. Baugh (ed.), *Naval administration 1715–1750* (London, 1977), p. 267. Scavelmen shovelled out the docks and treenail-mooters shaped treenails, large wooden dowels which joined timbers.

[30] BNA, ADM 42/1047, Portsmouth ordinary paybook, January–March 1662.

dependent on dockyard colleagues, landlords, local shops and alehouses (whose credit was limited), to whom workers had to pay debt interest. Strong dockyard communities were united by close family ties and indebtedness. Dockyard workers also had by-employments, working in private shipyards and in harvests. Chips, a customary waste perquisite of pieces of wood less than three feet long, carried from the yard three times a day, were used for house-building, fuel or sale items, providing subsistence money.[31]

During the Interregnum, many officers were puritans or presbyterians. Some continued after 1660, like the Petts, a dynasty of master shipwrights dominating the Thames and Medway yards, and John Tippetts at Portsmouth: master shipwright 1650–67, then resident commissioner 1668–72.[32] The loyalty of all dockyard employees (4,658) to the new regime was imposed by swearing oaths of allegiance to Charles II by July 1660, James ordering refusers to be discharged. In August 1660 Portsmouth dismissed 116 workmen, mostly nonconformists, but some returned.[33] Dockyards thus retained a strong nonconformist thread from the Interregnum to the 1690s.

Dutch naval shipbuilding, 1653 to 1664

In the years running up to the First Anglo-Dutch War, the English government had thus acquired a substantial, specialised battle fleet. From the first hostilities, the inadequacy of the hurriedly thrown together Dutch sea forces, although quite numerous, was apparent to all in the

---

[31] J.R. Tanner (ed.) *Hollond's discourses of the navy & Sir R. Slyngesbie, Discourse of the navy 1660* (London, 1896), pp. ix and 99; A.D. Thrush, 'The navy under Charles I 1625–1640' (unpublished PhD thesis, London University, 1991), 119–21; A.J. Marsh, 'The navy and Portsmouth under the Commonwealth', in *Hampshire Studies*, eds J. Webb, Nigel Yates and Sarah Peacock (Portsmouth, 1981), p. 130; M. Oppenheim, *A history of the administration of the Royal Navy* (London, 1988), p. 365; Peter Guillery, Andrew Donald, Mark Fenton, George Wilson and Mike Hesketh-Roberts, *The Block Mills, Portsmouth Naval Dockyard, Hampshire. An analysis of the building*, Report B101612003, Historic England, Historic Buildings and Areas Research Department (2003), pp. 40–1.

[32] See Peter Pett above; Stuart Rankin, 'Pett, Peter (*d.* 1589)', in *ODNB*, 2008; J.K. Laughton, revised by Sean Kelsey, 'Pett, Sir Peter (*bap.* 1630, *d.* 1699)', in *ibid.*, 2008; Roy McCaughey, 'Pett, Phineas (1570–1647), in *ibid.*, 2008; Philip MacDougall, 'Tippetts, Sir John (*d.* 1692)', in *ibid.*, 2012. See Hammond, 'Administration of the English navy', pp. 124 and 131, for Petts in the Thames and Medway.

[33] *Calendar of state papers: domestic series, of the reign of Charles II, 1665–1666* [hereafter: *CSPD*], ed. M.A. Everett (London, 1864), p. 182; BNA, SP 29/143, fol. 172, 13–16 June 1667; ADM 42/1215; ADM 42/1215; ADM 106/2, 22 December 1660; ADM 106/2, 19 December 1660; ADM 2/1745, 11 June 1660; ADM 42/1047; ADM106/1, 29 June 1660; Bodleian Library (Oxford), Carte Ms. 73, fol. 402r (my thanks to Dr J.D. Davies for his transcript); Capp, *Cromwell's navy*, pp. 372–4; *CSPD, Interregnum, 1650*, ed. M.A. Everett (London, 1876), p. 542; NMM, Dockyard officers lists.

Dutch Republic. With its barrage of gunfire, the English fleet surprised everyone. In consequence, before the war was eight months old, a building programme of thirty fighting ships was unanimously voted in the States General (February 1653). Partly because of the haste and the limited admiralty building capacity, partly with an eye on cost-efficiency, the States General insisted on a public call for tender: even the existing admiralty yards had to submit their bids alongside private shipbuilders. With their minds on their purse, the States General also interfered with the dimensions of the ships, reducing them considerably against the wishes of naval officers.[34]

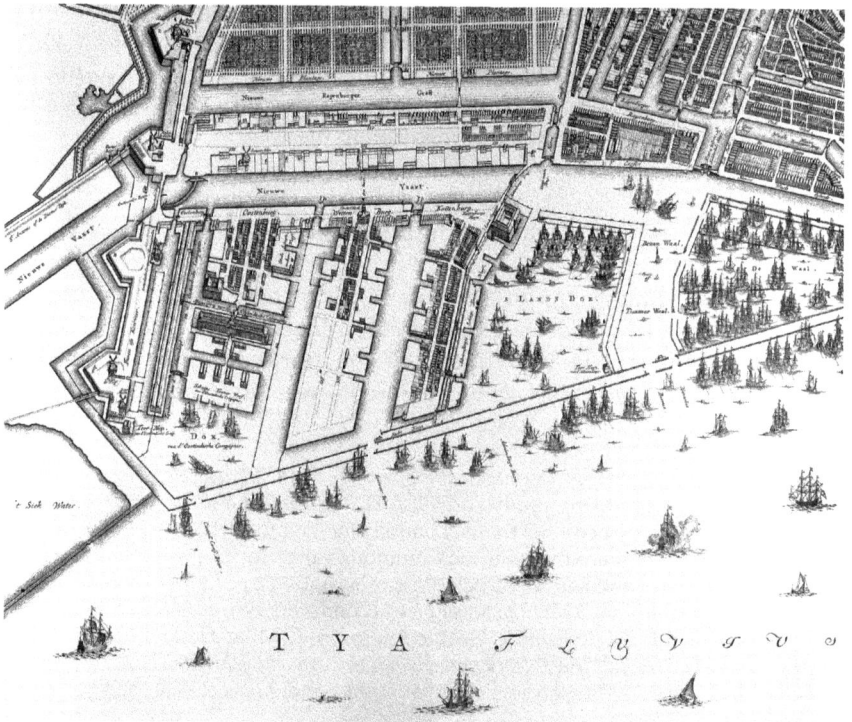

Figure 7.2 Amsterdam naval quarter after 1655, facing southwards. Three new islands have been created and the defence bulwarks moved to an outer layer. The admiralty yard occupies the right-hand shore of the island on the right, with the basin in front of it. The ropery is located on a fourth island on the far left. Source: Netherlands Institute of Military History (The Hague).

[34] Elias, *Vlootbouw*, pp. 99–123 and 126–7; Bruijn, *Varend verleden*, p. 95.

Figure 7.3 J. Mulder, *Amsterdam Admiralty Yard*, c. 1700, view from the city.
Photo: Alan Lemmers.

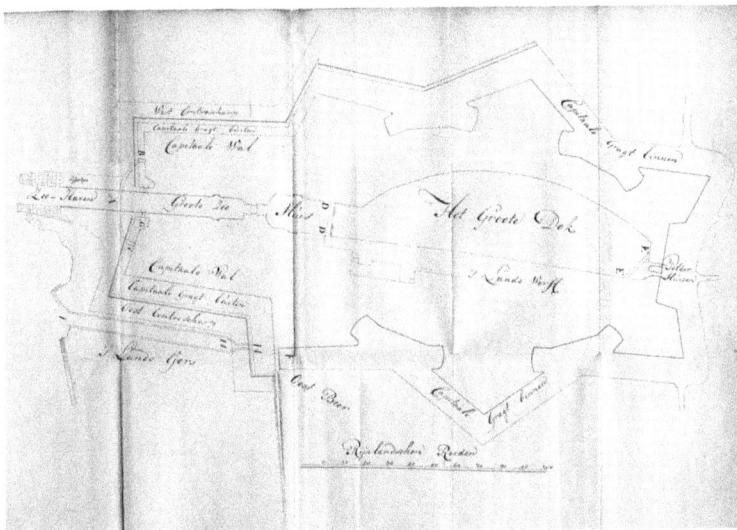

Figure 7.4 Hellevoetsluis naval base c. 1675–1800. Hellevoetsluis, lying in the
Haringvliet near the coast, had no building slips, but served as equipment
facilities for the Rotterdam Admiralty. The building slips were in Rotterdam itself.
Manuscript plan inserted in *Rapport wegens den staat van 's Lands schepen van oorlog…*
(The Hague, 1796). Source: Netherlands Institute of Military History (The Hague).

147

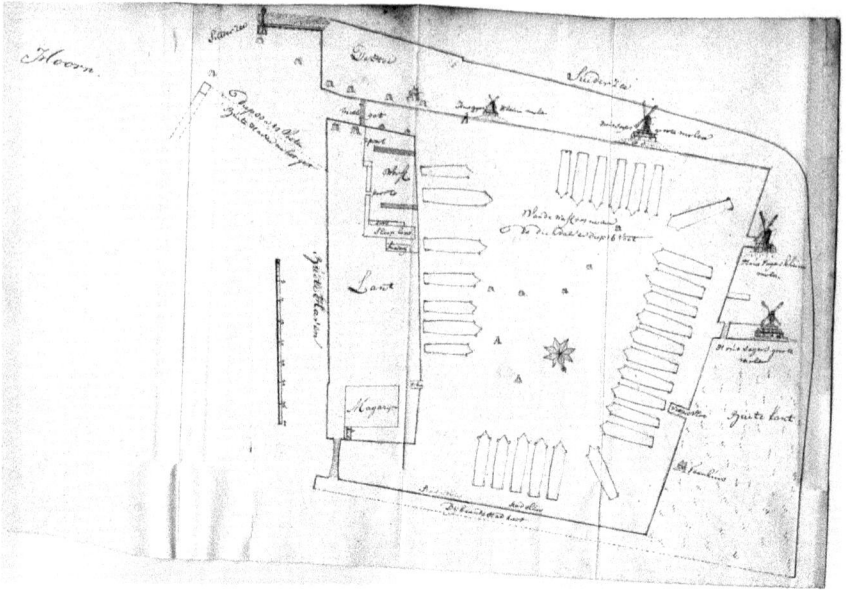

Figure 7.5 Hoorn naval base c. 1650–1800. This plan shows the situation in 1795, but it had apparently not changed since the mid-seventeenth century. Manuscript plan inserted in *Rapport wegens den staat van 's Lands schepen van oorlog…* (The Hague, 1796). Source: Netherlands Institute of Military History (The Hague).

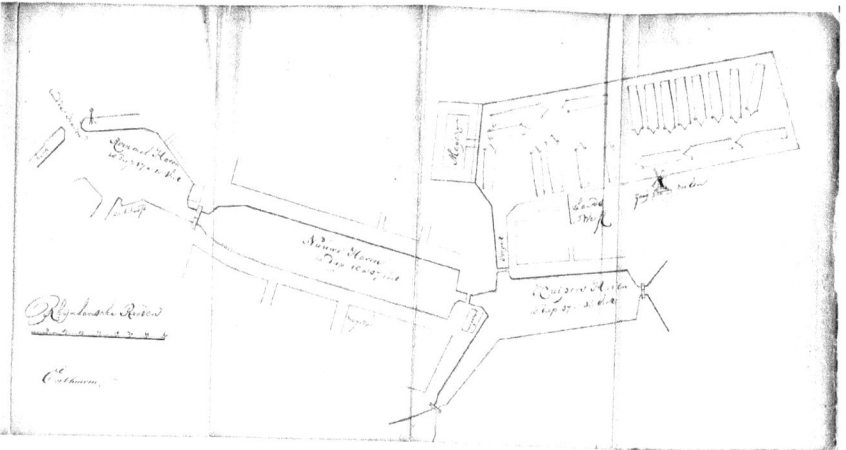

Figure 7.6 Enkhuizen port and naval base c. 1650–1800. This plan shows the situation in 1795, but it had apparently not changed since the mid-seventeenth century. The entrance to the harbour is at the far left, and the naval facilities are located top right. The awkward accessibility of the naval facilities was a problem. Manuscript plan inserted in *Rapport wegens den staat van 's Lands schepen van oorlog…* (The Hague, 1796). Source: Netherlands Institute of Military History (The Hague).

148

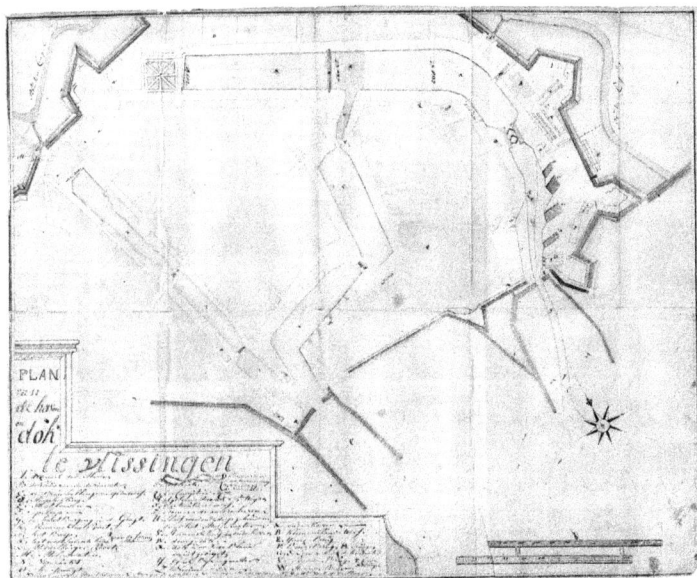

Figure 7.7 Flushing naval base after 1688. The plan is from 1795, but the situation was the same in the seventeenth century. The entrance to the naval part of the harbour is at the right and the dock continues along the top. Manuscript plan inserted in *Rapport wegens den staat van 's Lands schepen van oorlog...* (The Hague, 1796). Source: Netherlands Institute of Military History (The Hague).

Meanwhile, large numbers of ships were lost and the emergency grew. A second construction programme of thirty men-of-war was approved in December 1653, this time including considerably larger hulls.[35] Finally grand pensionary de Witt succeeded in passing a bill prohibiting the sale or discarding of vessels in peacetime, unless with unanimous consent (January 1654). This bill had far-reaching consequences. From now on the admiralties would maintain their unemployed ships, which meant that the Dutch Republic, for the first time, possessed a 'standing fleet'.[36] More ships also meant more guns, examined later. All this cost much money and shipping taxes increased considerably. In all, sea-trade remained a highly lucrative sector, which is one reason why most citizens accepted the changes without grumbling too loudly – another was that most people believed these changes to be temporary at most.

In the event, none of the new ships served during the war, as peace was signed before they were finished. Thus, the admiralties in 1654 found

---

[35] J.E. Elias, *Schetsen uit de geschiedenis van ons zeewezen* (6 vols, The Hague, 1918–28), VI, 149–50; *idem, Vlootbouw*, pp. 131–44; Bruijn, *Varend verleden*, p. 96.

[36] Bruijn, *Varend verleden*, pp. 96, 97.

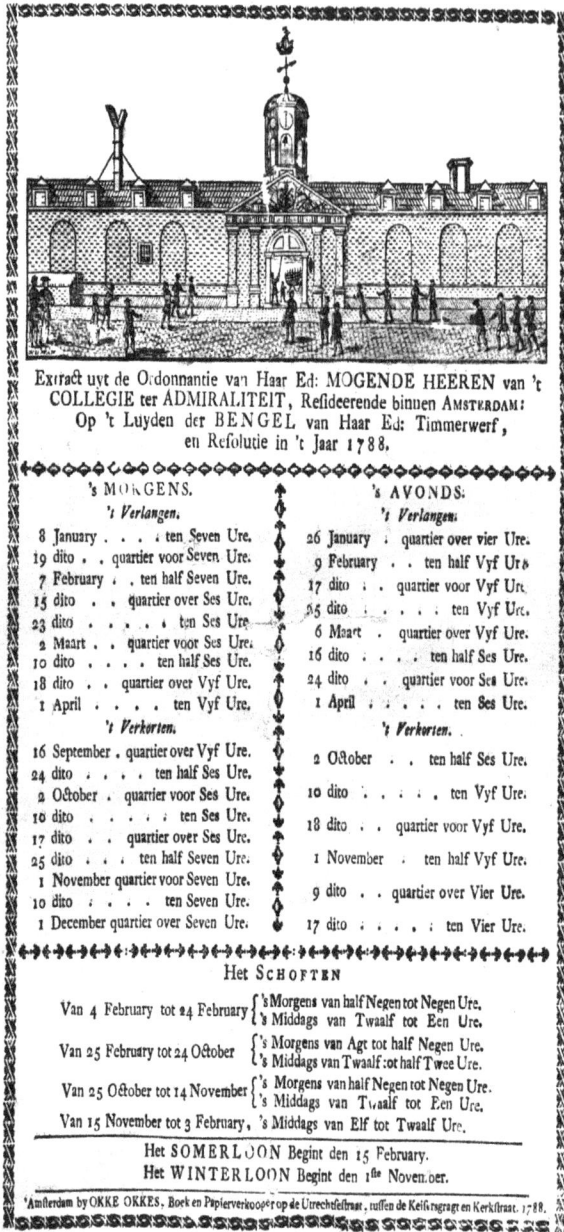

Figure 7.8 Shifts of the labourers of the Amsterdam Admiralty Dockyard. The hours varied with the hours of daylight, and the pay the workmen received accordingly. Source: Het Scheepvaartmuseum (Amsterdam).

themselves in possession of a brand new fleet, which they had furthermore pledged to maintain. The Amsterdam admiralty was the first to recognise that it now needed substantial docking and repair facilities, besides ample building capacity to replace old and worn vessels, and an administration to run all of it. As the war was being concluded, the admiralty bought a substantial plot on Kattenburg island, one of three artificial islands newly created in the IJ. A huge storehouse was built for ships to come alongside and to be provisioned directly from every storey. The shoreline gained five building slips, two for large ships and three for medium-sized vessels. The terrain was sealed off from the street by a row of storehouses and offices, a large smithy and other workshops. For regular town dwellers the site was off limits. When not in service the ships were laid up in a basin facing the yard. The admiralty ropery was located nearby. The yard was begun in 1655 and completed by 1660. As far as we know the first ship was launched from its slips in 1662.[37]

As we saw, the two shipbuilding programmes of the First Anglo-Dutch War were executed largely by private shipyards. However, the admiralties increasingly objected to public tender. It was impossible to daily oversee the construction if ships were built at locations dispersed across the nation. Control was imperative because private shipbuilders tended to interpret the building contracts to their individual custom, while military demands became ever more rigorous.[38] To keep the building process under control, it had to be kept close at hand, which required admiralty construction sites. Yet on the eve of the Second Anglo-Dutch War only the Amsterdam admiralty had as yet enhanced its shore facilities to a level where it no longer needed to outsource building contracts. The Rotterdam armoury and warehouses were doubled after the First Anglo-Dutch War and its base at Hellevoetsluis much improved, but the admiralty made no move yet to expand its building facilities, which consisted of two building slips.[39] We have no information on any changes in the shore facilities of the admiralties of the Northern Quarter and Zeeland.[40] The Frisian admiralty in 1665–67

[37] Lemmers, *Van werf tot facilitair complex*, pp. 31–49.
[38] Elias, *Vlootbouw*, pp. 115 and 142–3; Bruijn, *Varend verleden*, p. 102.
[39] S.J.M. Dorré, 'Onverschrokken door alle stormen heen. Inleiding tot de geschiedenis van 's Lands werf te Rotterdam (1795–1813)' (unpublished MA thesis, Leiden University, 1993), pp. 14–20; J.P. Sigmond, *Nederlandse zeehavens tussen 1500 en 1800* (Amsterdam, 1989), pp. 121–2.
[40] For a description of the shore facilities of the Northern Quarter (Hoorn, Enkhuizen and Medemblik), see: Hendrik Aeneae, Samuel Story, Engelbert Lucas and Pieter Glavimans, *Rapport wegens den staat van 's Lands schepen van oorlog en kleinere vaartuigen tot den zeedienst betrekkelyk, mitsgaders den staat der havens, scheeps-timmer-werven, magazynen, arsenaalen etc., zo als zich die, by inspectie van de ondergeteekende leden eener door Hun Hoog Mogenden daar toe aangestelde commissie bevonden, in het voorjaar, of in de maanden van Maart en April, des Jaars 1795* (Den Haag, 1796).

would contribute considerably to the fleet, thanks to its prior move to Harlingen, but this was one of the few periods it produced any numbers.[41] As always, Amsterdam dwarfed the other admiralties: after all their income largely depended on trade volume, which made the Amsterdam admiralty the richest by far.

English shipbuilding, 1650s to 1680s

The Commonwealth remodelled its navy. New sailing instructions issued in 1653 excluded hired armed merchantmen from the operational fleet, apart from victuallers, convoyers or fireships, such as the *Barbadoes Merchant*, *Constant John* and *John & Sarah* fireships in the 1667 Chatham ordinary.[42] The Venetian ambassador reported in 1655 that 'although the Dutch fleet has the greater numbers the English maintain that one of theirs will always be a match for four or five Dutchmen, owing to the quality of their timber, their build and their solidity'.[43] Barbour asserted that by 1650 the navy had developed two 'distinctive fighting types: the great ship and the frigate'.[44] The former was described by the Venetian Secretary in 1655: 'They have recently invented a colossal kind of ship, carrying as many as 120 bronze guns, which may, without exaggeration be called floating fortresses. They put on board 700 to 800 men in each and any one of them would meet the attack of 100 light galleys.'[45]

The Venetian exaggerated. The Commonwealth's one 'colossal' ship built in 1655, *Naseby*, named after Cromwell's victory, only ever had 82 guns. In 1654, following the First Anglo-Dutch War, the Council of State ordered the Admiralty Committee to build four second-rate ships, the first since the 1630s. Two were launched in 1656, *London* at Chatham and *Dunbar* at Deptford, and *Richard* at Woolwich in 1658, named after Cromwell's son and successor. They were two-deckers: *London* had 64 guns, mostly brass, in the proportion

---

Although this inspection report dates from 1795, little seems to have changed since the mid-seventeenth century.

[41] J.C. de Jonge, *Geschiedenis van het Nederlandsche zeewezen* (2nd rev. edn, 5 vols, Haarlem 1858–62), I, 637–8; Schaap, 'De Admiraliteit van Friesland', *passim*; Roodhuyzen, *De admiraliteit van Friesland*, pp. 1 and 6–7.

[42] Violet Barbour, 'Dutch and English merchant shipping in the seventeenth century', *Economic Historical Review* (1930), 261; Davies, *Pepys's Navy*, pp. 57 and 248–50; BNA, ADM 42/1, Lady Quarter January–March 1667.

[43] 'Venice: July 1652', in A.B. Hinds (ed.), *Calendar of state papers Venetian* (London, 1927) [hereafter: *CSPV*], vol. 28, 1647–1652, pp. 254–63.

[44] Cromwell's Protectorate, http://bcw-project.org/timelines/the-protectorate, British Civil Wars, Commonwealth and Protectorate website; Barbour, 'Dutch and English merchant shipping', p. 261.

[45] 'Venice: November 1655', in *CSPV*, vol. 30, *1655–1656*, pp. 131–46.

of 10 tons of ordnance to 100 tons of ship weight.[46] *Naseby* and *Richard* were renamed *Royal Charles* and *Royal James* (classified as a first-rate) at the Restoration and targeted by the Dutch for capture/burning on the Medway in June 1667. Fifteen *Speaker*-class third-rate/frigates of c. 750 tons were built in 1650–54, carrying 48–56 guns for speed and offence, and seventeen fifth-rates as scouts.[47]

The Commonwealth's impressive shipbuilding investment increased the fleet from 67 to 280 ships in 1649–60, but naval expenditure exceeded income during the Spanish War (1654–60). By spring 1659 admiralty commissioners needed £2,157,883 (including £300,000 owed to seamen and £378,000 for shipyards and stores) to send out a summer guard.[48] With no effective leadership since Cromwell's death in 1658, government employees, creditors and contractors hoped that Charles Stuart's restoration would restore their finances.[49]

The Stuart government was penurious, however. Parliament granted Charles an annual income of £1,200,000 from grants and subsidies, but this was not money in the Treasury, and was insufficient for the navy.[50] Nevertheless, it inherited 'a well-run royal navy': 109 ships including four first-rates (more than other navies) with three decks, 82–102 guns and weighing 1,550 tons. Second-rates in the 1660s had 72–80 guns, with only two complete tiers of gunports. Third-rates had two decks, 60–74 heavier guns than fourth-rates, which had 46–52 guns and included frigates. Modified hired merchantmen of 500 tons were also classed as fourth-rates. Outside the battle-line, fifth-rates supported fireships and sixth-rates were used for coastal defence and commerce raiding.[51] English hull forms were more tapered than the Dutch, for faster sailing and manoeuvring, but their smaller storage capacity was adequate for short-term campaigns. Shipbuilding programmes of eight ships were ordered in 1664 and ten in 1666 (both incomplete). French successes in 1676 prompted parliamentary funding to complete thirty ships in 1677. These shared standardised

---

[46] Frank Fox, 'The *London* of 1656. Her history and armament', in *Pepys and chips. Dockyards, naval administration and warfare in the seventeenth century* (Transactions of the Naval Dockyards Society, vol. 8, Portsmouth, 2012), pp. 60 and 62–5.

[47] Davies, *Pepys's Navy*, pp. 47, 49, 51 and 55.

[48] C.D. Chandaman, *The English public revenue 1660–1688* (Oxford, 1975), pp. 196–7.

[49] Hammond, 'Administration of the English navy', pp. 22, 25–6, 48, 52–6, 75, 106, 117, 159 and 371–2; Capp, *Cromwell's navy*, pp. 363–6.

[50] At first this only yielded about a third of this, due to inefficient tax farming and economic slumps. By the 1680s, extra parliamentary funds and improved tax collection produced an average annual £1,200,000 throughout his reign. This adversely affected credit and prices of naval provisions. Chandaman, *The English public revenue*, pp. 200–1, 263–4, 268 and 270.

[51] J. Glete, *Navies and nations. Warships, navies and state building in Europa America, 1500–1860* (2 vols, Stockholm, 1993), I, 204; Davies, *Pepys's Navy*, p. 36; Frank Fox, *The Four Days' Battle of 1666* (Barnsley, 2009), pp. 39 and 42–6.

dimensions but varied in detail. Bows had become shorter since 1652 and keels longer. Forecastles were added to the first- and second-rates. Dutch and English fleets had roughly comparable ship numbers, but English ships were more heavily armed and constructed than the Dutch, which had to navigate shallower coastal waters.[52]

By 1674, after the attrition of the Second and Third Anglo-Dutch Wars, England had 92 warships, many in disrepair, compared with 136 Dutch, although 9 were first- and second-rates which the Dutch lacked. English Barbary campaigns in the 1670s and 1680s also required three galley frigates.[53] From 1666 to 1674 English broadside weight ratio to hull tonnage reached its maximum extent, then declined as the navy campaigned regularly in the Atlantic, dictating higher freeboard and smaller calibre guns. In the switch from a Dutch to a French enemy in 1689, fourth- to sixth-rates, neglected since the 1670s, were again considered necessary to protect Britain's coastal shipping. James II began his reign with 24 commissioned warships and 10 yachts; in April 1688 he had 26 operational ships, increased to 48 by October.[54]

English naval ordnance

In the 1640s ships used muzzle-loading guns of cast bronze ('brass') or cast iron. Gunners favoured brass guns for their beauty and for earlier warning of bursting, therefore safety. Administrators preferred iron because it was much cheaper. As iron-founding techniques improved, iron guns increasingly replaced brass in both English and Dutch fleets through the second half of the seventeenth century. Royal gunfounder John Browne experimented with cheaper lightweight iron guns, drakes, with narrower chambers, using less metal and a smaller charge of gunpowder; but they had a fierce recoil, limited range, and shot could jam in the chamber. He supplied the *Sovereign of the Seas* with 96 of her 102 guns, mostly drakes, but these were replaced systematically from the 1650s with heavier but more satisfactory true-bored 'fortified' guns. The largest English naval guns from the mid-1650s were the 42-pounder 'cannon of seven', with a 7-inch bore, weighing a massive three tons.[55]

[52] Fox, *Four Days' Battle*, pp. 37–9 and 41–2; Davies, *Pepys's Navy*, pp. 41, 44 and 47–50.
[53] Davies, *Pepys's Navy*, pp. 49 and 63.
[54] Fox, *Four Days' Battle*, pp. 47–8; Davies, *Pepys's Navy*, pp. 39, 49–50 and 54; J.D. Davies, *Kings of the sea. Charles II, James II and the Royal Navy* (Barnsley, 2017), chapter 11.
[55] Ruth Brown, 'John Browne, gunfounder to the Stuarts. Part 2, bronze and iron guns, 1630–1645', *Wealden Iron Research Group Bulletin*, 25, Second Series (2006), pp. 46–50; Fox, 'The *London* of 1656', p. 59; *idem, Four Days' Battle*, pp. 51–3. My thanks to Frank Fox for advice on this section.

In the 1660s, the admiralty and ordnance boards favoured very heavy naval armament, so ships became bigger platforms. Utilising heavy lower guns in battle gave a 20–25 per cent gunpower advantage to the English, and stronger hull construction gave endurance.[56] By the 1680s, gun batteries on first-rates totalled 165 tons, and c. 130 tons on large third-rates, with a proportion of guns to ships' tonnage of about 1:8 or 1:9. Ships also carried the weight of forty rounds of powder and shot, necessitating a larger build. Guns were used mainly in broadsides one side at a time. Lower gundecks were only a few feet above the waterline, reducing their use in rough weather. First-rates in the 1680s had 90–100 guns, with main gundecks up to 170 feet long, second-rates had 64–90 guns, third-rates 60–74 guns, fourth-rates 30–56 guns, fifth-rates 28–38 guns and main gundecks 90–110 feet long, and one-deck sixth-rates had 4–18 guns.[57]

The English aimed roundshot at the hull on the down roll of the ship to batter the enemy into submission, whereas the Dutch aimed bar and chain shot at the rigging on the up roll. The Dutch sought to board, but from 1653 the English preferred sole artillery duels resulting from the introduction of the line-of-battle. Fireships, old small ships loaded with combustible materials, were used by both sides. Fifth-rates aided their fireships and cut out enemy fireships.[58] In 1677 the ordnance establishment set a ratio of guns to ships' tonnage of 1:8, but the 1685 establishment increased the ordnance weight ratio slightly in larger ships and was more flexible.[59]

Essential gunpowder supplies were focused in the south of England and London in the 1640s. The process required sulphur, charcoal and saltpetre, imported from India by the East India Company, guaranteed by naval protection of trade routes. Production was boosted by new sites in the Midlands and parliamentary control of powder works, aided by taxes and loans.[60] The Stuarts benefited from these improvements.

Dutch guns

While in tactics the emphasis shifted to artillery, the number of cannon during the First Anglo-Dutch War ran alarmingly low due to wear and ship losses, and it proved hard to replenish stocks. Bronze guns could be cast in Dutch foundries, but cheaper cast-iron guns had to be procured from elsewhere. Since the early seventeenth century, a small number of Amsterdam

---

[56] Fox, *Four Days' Battle*, pp. 43 and 47–9; Davies, *Pepys's Navy*, pp. 47–9.
[57] Davies, *Pepys's Navy*, pp. 39–44.
[58] Fox, 'The *London* of 1656', p. 66; Fox, *Four Days' Battle*, pp. 53–8.
[59] Davies, *Pepys's Navy*, p. 86; Glete, *Navies and nations*, I, 27–8.
[60] Stephen Bull, *The Furie of the ordnance. Artillery in the English Civil Wars* (Woodbridge, 2008), pp. 74 and 77–80.

entrepreneurs had established a powerful iron and gun industry in Sweden.[61] But in February 1653 a contract with three of those arms manufacturers for 1,200 cast-iron guns was blocked by the Swedish government, forbidding gun export in favour of domestic use. Threatening to turn to foreign competition, the Dutch sought supplies in Spain, the Ruhr, Liège, Geneva and Russia. Eventually Sweden allowed the purchase of a limited number, but the two shipments totalling 380 heavy guns (18- and 12-pounders) were seized by the enemy (7 July 1653). The new ships completed in 1654–55 could not therefore be armed and lay idle at the quays.[62] Only after the war did they receive their armament.

Swedish gun production became an issue of conflict between the Swedish crown and the Dutch owners of the foundries, and even played a part in the Dutch involvement in the Second Northern War (1655–60). The last reference we have to an arms deal with Sweden concerns a delivery of 600 iron guns in 1664.[63] In its continued effort to break the Dutch industrial and commercial dominance of domestic gun production and exports, Sweden in 1665 exchanged the United Provinces for England as its main commercial ally. Thereupon the Dutch reverted swiftly to other foreign suppliers and increased domestic production of bronze guns, even though they were much more expensive. A state gun foundry was erected in The Hague, while elsewhere local brass founders were employed. During the ensuing war between the Republic and England, Sweden lost millions in arms deals because it switched to England, which had a strong ordnance industry of its own.[64] There is no mention of a gun shortage in the Republic. After the war Sweden re-opened its gun export to the Dutch Republic.

Dutch coastal defence and naval shipbuilding, 1665–72

The First Anglo-Dutch War was purely maritime, as the second would be: the English attack was solely directed at breaking Dutch commercial success at sea. The Dutch never really feared invasion and in consequence we read little of counter-incursion measures. The Zeeland estuary, the straight stretch of Holland coast and the Wadden Islands were notoriously dangerous sailing waters and the coastal area was densely populated. The villages and towns

---

[61] J.E. Elias, 'Contract tot oprichting van een Zweedsch factorie-comptoir te Amsterdam in 1663', *Bijdragen en Mededeelingen van het Historisch Genootschap*, 24 (1903), 356–400; P.W. Klein, *De Trippen in de 17e eeuw. Een studie over het ondernemersgedrag op de Hollandse stapelmarkt* (Assen, 1965), *passim*.
[62] Elias, *Vlootbouw*, pp. 129–30 and 164–73.
[63] De Jonge, *Zeewezen*, I, 656–7.
[64] Elias, 'Contract tot oprichting', pp. 379–90. As far as we know The Hague foundry was also limited to brass founding. Dutch gun production and acquisition (iron guns) after 1655 needs more research.

were alert and erected provisional redoubts in the dunes once war had been declared, manned by civic guards or peasant volunteers. In February 1665 Johan de Witt ordered a signal service to be raised along the coast to monitor shipping movements, but this seems to have been normal in times of war.[65] The naval bases lay relatively far inland or behind treacherous shallows and were hard to reach in an attack; only Flushing and Hellevoetsluis were directly accessible from the sea and therefore had fortifications. Most ports and estuaries had one or two perfunctory guns in redoubts guarding their roads, but they have never been reported to see any action. In wartime the defence of ports and roads was augmented with guardships and floating batteries. Some ships were assigned to act as fire watch, keeping an eye on all incoming shipping to prevent a disguised enemy fireship from approaching the vulnerable ships at anchor; they would also intercept and question foreign fishermen and merchantmen passing the coast.[66] A so-called 'inner watch' prevented merchantmen from leaving the roads without permission.[67] Setting a fire watch was not a specifically Dutch practice but common in Europe. However, the fire watch did not prevent Holmes's Bonfire (August 1666) taking the Republic completely unawares. Following the St James's Day Fight, the English admirals directed Sir Robert Holmes, whose force included five fireships and 1,170 marines, to capture, burn, or sink the Dutch merchant fleet in the Vlie anchorage, where it was awaiting escort before venturing out to sea. Holmes fired 150 vessels and plundered and burnt the town of West Terschelling.[68]

In the Third Anglo-Dutch War (1672–78) and the subsequent Guerre de Hollande (1672–78) De Ruyter repeatedly thwarted Anglo-French invasion attempts with naval action, placing the fleet in the first line of coastal defence. In theory this approach would not change for a century, but it was never tested again before 1799.

In the growing tensions of 1664 a new building programme of forty-eight men-of-war had been voted by the Dutch Estates General and again private shipbuilders were called upon.[69] In the meantime twenty Dutch East Indiamen and fifteen large merchantmen (with captain and crew) completed the fleet in the first year of the war, but this was the last time. The battle of Lowestoft in May 1665 was a sad lesson in the incompatible sailing qualities and military discipline of a mixed fleet. The forces with which De

[65] J.C.M. Warnsinck, *Van vlootvoogden en zeeslagen* (Kampen, 1940), p. 256; P.J. Blok, *Michiel Adriaensz. de Ruyter* (The Hague, 1928), p. 240. The issue requires more research. No more mention is made of coastal signal services until the Fourth Anglo-Dutch War (1780–84): De Jonge, *Zeewezen*, IV, 454.
[66] A.L. van Schelven, *Philips van Almonde, admiraal in de gecombineerde vloot, 1644–1711* (Assen, 1947), p. 161.
[67] H.A. van Foreest and R.E.J. Weber (eds), *De Vierdaagse Zeeslag 11–14 juni 1666* (Amsterdam, 1984), pp. 15–16.
[68] Fox, *Four Days' Battle*, pp. 296–7.
[69] Another twelve were ordered in 1666.

Ruyter fought the Four Days' Battle in 1666 and raided Chatham in 1667 consisted exclusively of purpose-built men-of-war (apart from troopships, fireships and supply vessels).[70] In the next war (1672–74) Dutch naval forces consisted entirely of men-of-war in regular service, largely built in admiralty dockyards. Meanwhile the ships had also grown from 36/44 guns in 1653 (with a singleton of 56 guns) to a two-thirds majority of 60-gun ships or larger in 1667–74, six even counting more than 80.[71] The Dutch fleet now matched the Royal Navy, almost: on both counts – the number of ships and their armament – the English fleet remained superior.

Shore facilities did not change greatly in this second phase. Besides construction, their work consisted largely of war repairs and maintenance. As we saw, the Amsterdam admiralty yard was in operation by the early 1660s, but production only slowly came to full power. Just two ships were built at the yard in 1662–63, but in 1665–67 sixteen ships were launched with six carrying more than 60 guns; three even had more than 80 guns. In its subsequent history the yard employed a daily workforce of 1,000 labourers in peacetime to 3,000 in peak times, i.e. war. For 250 years it was the largest local employer in the country. The department of shipbuilding was headed by the master shipwright, the department of equipment by the dockyard superintendent. Except for raw materials and semi-manufactured products like linen, the yard was self-sufficient: every part of the ship (except ordnance) was produced onsite. The division of labour was extreme, partly due to the guild system in force in the city of Amsterdam. The labourers were organised in gangs of ten to twenty with a headman, and occupations varied from ship carpenters to sawyers, cleavers, pumpdrillers, wainscotters, pulley makers, sailmakers, gun carriage makers, smiths, tinsmiths, plumbers, painters, masons, tool makers, carriers, cleaners and many more.[72]

We have no data on the Amsterdam master shipwrights of the time. The first names we have are Hendrik Jacobszoon Cardinael (active 1676–1704) and Jan van Rheenen (active 1704–22), both originating from the Zaan area.[73]

---

[70] For De Ruyter's fleets, see H.A. van Foreest, 'De vierdaagse zeeslag en zijn betekenis voor de nazaat', in *De vierdaagse zeeslag 11–14 juni 1666. Engelse en Nederlandse voordrachten gehouden in het kader van de manifestatie '1666 Nederland ter Zee 1966'*, ed. J.W.F. Nuboer (The Hague, 1966), pp. 43–63; C.J.W. van Waning and A. van der Moer, *Dese Aengenaeme Tocht. Chatham 1667 herbezien door zeemansogen* (Zutphen, 1981), pp. 84–9 and 111. However, during the Third Anglo-Dutch War (1672–74) the Dutch navy did occasionally hire privateers for reconnaissance and as dispatch vessels. J.R. Bruijn, 'Kaapvaart tijdens de Tweede en Derde Engelse Oorlog', *Bijdragen en Mededelingen betreffende de Geschiedenis der Nederlanden*, 90 (1975), 419.

[71] Data derived from the appendices to De Jonge, *Zeewezen*, I, 760–88, and II, 774–8.

[72] Lemmers, *Van werf tot facilitair complex*, pp. 56–7; A.J. Deurloo, 'Bijltjes en klouwers', in *Economisch Historisch Jaarboek*, XXXIV (The Hague, 1971), pp. 4–71.

[73] De Jonge, *Zeewezen*, III, 146–8, S. Lootsma, *Historische studiën over de Zaanstreek* (Koog-aan-de-Zaan, 1939), pp. 183–4.

The 'Zaanstreek' was the most industrialised region of the Republic, with a booming shipbuilding industry that supplied half of Europe. Thanks to the sawmill, which the Amsterdam sawyers' guild opposed for many decades, it outstripped the Amsterdam private shipbuilding sector by far. The position of master shipwright with the other admiralties is even less documented: most likely local shipwrights of repute were employed, such as the master shipwright of the local chamber of the East India Company, as occasion and need arose. Fortunately, we have more information on the 'oldest' admiralty, as it provided the admiral's flagship: from the mid-seventeenth century the Rotterdam yard was ruled by the Van den Tempel dynasty.[74]

As other admiralties followed the Amsterdam example, the transformation of shore facilities continued for three more decades. The third stage of development coincided with William III's occupation of the English throne. In 1689 the Rotterdam yard moved from the Nieuwehaven to the Reuzeneiland and expanded to four slipways.[75] William III personally supported the expansion of the Zeeland naval facilities, which were concentrated at Flushing. They covered the entire eastern harbour, with a building yard near the harbour entrance. The basin could berth more than eighty ships and was, for a while, the largest of the Dutch navy. Finally, in 1700–05 the Zeeland admiralty built a drydock (of English design!) at Flushing, the first and only one in the United Provinces for the next century. This concluded the modernisation of the Dutch shore facilities for this period. As far as we know, Friesland and the Northern Quarter had not followed suit, probably from lack of finances.[76]

Professionalism and manning in the English navy

The restored navy retained many 'tarpaulins', experienced merchant captains and warrant officers, but also recruited young cavalier officers.[77] Tension between these two professional groups persisted until the 1690s. The 'tarpaulin' viewpoint was articulated by Richard Gibson, Pepys's clerk, in his account of a Dutch skipper's 1659 analysis of the First Anglo-Dutch War: 'Wee came to Fight the English with Gentlemen Comãnders at Sea; And you us with Seamen Comãnders of your Shipps; and by this meanes you came to Beate the Dutch.' The skipper warned: 'if ever hereafter Wee should Fight

---

[74] Jan Salomonsz. van den Tempel on his death in 1657 was succeeded by his son Salomon Jansz. van den Tempel, active 1657–73 or 1691? – the genealogical and historical data are contradictory. See also Van 't Zand, *De oorlogsvloot van Johan de Witt.*

[75] Dorré, *Onverschrokken door alle stormen heen*, pp. 14–20.

[76] The next upgrade of shore facilities occurred in the context of the Fourth Anglo-Dutch War (1780–84).

[77] J.D. Davies, *Gentlemen and tarpaulins. The officers and men of the Restoration navy* (Oxford, 1991), pp. 5–6 and 16–18.

with the English for the Mastery of the Sea with Seamen Comãnders and you us with Gentlemen Comanders Wee should Beate you'.[78]

In wartime, merchant ships raised their wages to attract naval seamen. To lure volunteers, the Commonwealth had increased pay for able seamen to 24s a month from 1 January 1653; ordinary seamen's wages remained at 19s. Impressed merchant seamen supplied the shortfall.[79] Fox estimated that in 1665–66, 28,000 men were required, and English ships often had short complements with soldier substitutes, who were a last resort as seamen disliked them. To retain professional skills, the navy began keeping some captains on half-pay from 1667, gradually extending this to all. From 1676 Admiralty Secretary Samuel Pepys introduced training for young midshipmen as volunteers per order, with a compulsory two years of sea service, then three years for lieutenants before they took an exam to qualify for a commission.[80]

Andrew Little calculated that the Dutch and English navies each sought 25–30,000 men every spring during the Anglo-Dutch wars, and 3,000 English and Scots were serving, by force or choice, in the Dutch navies in 1667.[81] As ships grew larger, more men were required. After 1671, a wartime fourth-rate needed up to 170 men, a third-rate 360, a second-rate 530 and a first-rate 850.[82] Although Charles II could not pay promptly, men did volunteer for popular captains. Additionally, experienced seamen were pressed from merchant ships and coastal communities.[83] However, with no embargo on merchant recruitment in 1667, Pepys noted in his Diary on 22 June that 10–15,000 seamen were taken up by merchant ships at the beginning of the year, making 'it impossible for us to have set out a fleet this year (if we could have done it for money and stores)'.

Due to pay arrears, seamen's mutinies and riots bedevilled the fleet and the Navy Ticket Office in 1667, despite Parliament providing money to pay them in January 1667.[84] In March, Pepys described 'a poor seaman, almost starved for want of food, lay in our yard a-dying; I sent him half-a-crown – and we ordered his ticket to be paid'. In August he recorded, 'the desperate

---

[78] BL, Additional Ms. 11684, fols. 31–31v.
[79] Fox, *Four Days' Battle*, pp. 32–4; *CSPD: Interregnum, 1652–53*, ed. M.A. Everett (London, 1878), p. 42.
[80] Capp, *Cromwell's navy*, pp. 18, 45–6, 54, 56–7 and 162–211; Davies, *Pepys's Navy*, pp. 95–9; M. Duffy, 'The foundations of British naval power', in *The Military Revolution and the state 1500–1800* (Exeter, 1980), p. 63; Davies, *Gentlemen and tarpaulins*, pp. 16–18.
[81] Little, 'British seamen in the United Provinces', pp. 76–91.
[82] Davies, *Pepys's Navy*, p. 41.
[83] Fox, *Four Days' Battle*, pp. 22–3 and 37; Fox, 'The *London* of 1656', pp. 57 and 59; Davies, *Pepys's Navy*, pp. 108, 123 and 125.
[84] *The Diary of Samuel Pepys*, 2 January 1666/67; 13–16 February 1666/67; 28 September 1667; Capp, *Cromwell's navy*, pp. 278–82; Fox, *Four Days' Battle*, p. 34.

condition that we put men into for want of their pay makes them mad, they ... would as readily serve the King again, were they but paid'.[85] Two-part tickets had been used since 1654 which postponed payment and deterred men from re-enlisting.[86] Pepys reported on 14 June that:

> ... several seamen came this morning to tell me that if I would get their tickets paid, they would go and do all they could against the Dutch; but otherwise they would not venture being killed and lose all they have already fought for – so that I was forced to try what I could do to get them paid.[87]

The Chatham Storekeeper highlighted the critical consequence of delayed ticket payments to Pepys on 14 June. He 'did hear many Englishmen on board the Dutch ships, speaking to one another in English, and that they did cry and say, "We did heretofore fight for tickets; now we fight for Dollers!"' One such was Captain Robert Holland, who piloted Dutch ships through Thames and Medway sandbanks. Another was Thomas Tobiaszoon, Irish captain of *Harderwijk* in the Four Days' Battle (1666). In command of the 50-gun *Beschermer*, he piloted Dutch boats to Gillingham Reach and led the capture of *Royal Charles*, accompanied by an English trumpeter.[88]

Dutch recruitment and professionalisation

Like its opponent, the Dutch fleet in January 1665 faced a serious personnel problem, as in every other war. Unlike the army, the admiralties did not offer fixed contracts, but then neither did the East India Company or other commercial employers in the seafaring business. Plans for the creation of a regular workforce with year-round contracts were proposed on several occasions, but never taken up: it was simply too expensive.[89] Besides, able seamen were always on hand, even more so in times of war when commercial shipping would slacken. But sea service with the navy was not popular. The rate of pay was low, the duration of contracts uncertain and bodily risks high. If left to choose, sailors preferred commercial employers.

---

[85] *The Diary of Samuel Pepys*, 12 March 1667; 14 and 22 June 1667; 22 August 1667; Capp, *Cromwell's navy*, pp. 57, 258–74, 281–2 and 288–92; *CSPD: Interregnum, 1652–53*, p. 43.

[86] *The Diary of Samuel Pepys*, 14 February 1666/67.

[87] *Ibid.*, 14 June 1667.

[88] *Ibid.*, 14 June 1667; 22 June 1667; Rogers, *The Dutch in the Medway*, pp. 63–4 and 98–9; Little, 'British seamen in the United Provinces', pp. 88–9; Fox, *Four Days' Battle*, p. 338. The Ticket Office was put under Brounker's supervision in December 1668. See *The Diary of Samuel Pepys*, 28 September 1667.

[89] De Jonge, *Zeewezen*, I, 667–8. Propositions were made in 1627, 1659, 1665 and 1666. G.J.A. Raven, *Het personeelsprobleem bij de marine 1750–1950*. Netherlands Institute of Military History (The Hague), manuscript collection, I, pp. 4 and 6.

Recruitment was therefore a recurring problem, and no less at the beginning of the Second Anglo-Dutch War. Captains, who were personally responsible for the assembly of the crew, could offer a premium for enlistment, which varied with the experience of the candidate. But the need for crew became so acute, some even started to top up wages, against which Johan de Witt voiced his disapproval, as such practices put the government at the mercy of the common sailor. With recruitment officers hunting for destitute sailors and campaigning in foreign ports, underhand methods were not eschewed. However, forced enlisting or pressing was not done. That did not mean the authorities were averse to other coercive or 'tempting' measures, such as a pardon for deserters, the demand of every ship owner and privateer to contribute a share of their workforce, a general trade embargo forcing seamen to seek employment in the navy, or a transfer of soldiers to sea service.[90] Apparently these and other measures were effective, for in May 1665 the personnel problem was largely solved. Only a few ships of the fleet with which Admiral Wassenaer van Obdam engaged the English near Lowestoft were poorly manned.[91]

Besides sailors, the fleet was always in want of sea soldiers. The battle of Lowestoft demonstrated, not for the first time, the unfitness of landlubbers on board. De Witt and Admiral de Ruyter in December 1665 solved this by the creation of a permanent regiment (4,000) of marines, soldiers with sea legs. The cost of this regiment in permanent pay was more acceptable than the employment of sailing personnel on a yearly basis, as marines could also be deployed on land in any season. They answered to expectations with their first exploit, the Chatham expedition, and a second regiment was created in 1669. On land they played an important role in the repulsion of the French invasion in 1673–74, but the service was dissolved in the army at the conclusion of war with France in 1678.[92]

From 1626 the navy employed sixty captains on a permanent basis. As a result of the appalling performance of civilian commanders during the battle of Lowestoft and the introduction of new fighting instructions thereafter, naval officers professionalised. Merchant captains were untrained in line tactics and often lacked the discipline to keep formation in the face of danger or when seduced by easy prey. Thus the fleet switched to professional manpower commanded by men experienced in sea battle and receptive to

[90] Bruijn, *Varend verleden*, pp. 163–4; Raven, *Het personeelsprobleem*, pp. 31–3.
[91] This was due, of course, to a combination of measures: the sailors' pay, for instance, had risen significantly by that date. Bruijn, *Varend verleden*, pp. 163–4; Raven, *Het personeelsprobleem*, I; Warnsinck, *Van vlootvoogden en zeeslagen*, pp. 255–6; De Jonge, *Zeewezen*, I, 776 (Bijlage XXVIII).
[92] In 1694 a new regiment of marines was created at the instigation of the city of Amsterdam; they would play an important role in Spain during the War of Spanish Succession. C.J.O. Dorren, *De geschiedenis van het Nederlandsche Korps Mariniers van 1665–1945* (The Hague, 1948), p. 26.

military discipline. Whereas before merchantmen had been hired to join the warring fleet, from 1666 they mostly lay idle in times of conflict. Their owners not only lost out on the rent, but additionally suffered increased shipping taxes to pay for men-of-war to be built and maintained, even in times of peace. Their captains were out of work for much of the duration of the hostilities, while a quota of the crew was forced to enlist with the fleet. In the admiralty boards the number of merchants decreased markedly, to be replaced by patricians and notables. The rift between private enterprise and the war fleet would thereafter grow.[93]

English dockyards and coastal defences threatened

London was the hub of commerce and state. The Thames estuary, 'bounded by Aldeburgh (Suffolk), Southend-on-Sea (Essex) and Margate (Kent)' and the River Medway, contained one Essex and four Kentish dockyards: Harwich, Deptford and Woolwich (the main building and research and development yards), Chatham and Sheerness.[94] As dockyards gained assets or strategic roles they acquired fortifications, sometimes more symbolic than tangible.

Portsmouth was England's oldest dockyard with the first drydock (1495–1623), victualling and fitting out a third of the fleet in the 1630s.[95] In 1648 the 'eight ships lying at Portsmouth remained staunch' to the parliamentary cause.[96] Even before the first Anglo-Dutch battles fought offshore, its use was increased. Shipwrights were sent from the Thames for winter refitting in the 1650s and in 1652–53 it victualled 2–3,000 seamen.[97] In May 1656 navy

---

[93] This process is brilliantly analysed in: J.R. Bruijn, 'Mars en Mercurius uiteen. De uitrusting van de oorlogsvloot in de zeventiende eeuw', in *Bestuurders en geleerden. Opstellen over onderwerpen uit de Nederlandse geschiedenis van de zestiende, zeventiende en achttiende eeuw, aangeboden aan Prof. Dr. J.J. Woltjer bij zijn afscheid als hoogleraar aan de Rijksuniversiteit te Leiden*, eds S. Groenveld, M.E.H.N. Mout and I. Schöffer (Amsterdam, 1985), pp. 102–3; and Bruijn, *Varend verleden*, pp. 140–2.

[94] H. Burningham and J. French, *Historical changes in the seabed of the greater Thames estuary* (The Crown Estate/National Maritime Museum, 2008), p. iv, www.thecrown-estate.co.uk/media/5746/historical_changes_in_thames_estuary_seabed.pdf; Jonathan Coad, *Support for the fleet. Architecture and engineering of the Royal Navy's bases 1700–1914* (Swindon, 2013), p. 4.

[95] William Page (ed.), *Victoria County History Hampshire* (London, 1912), vol. 5, pp. 371, 372, 375 and 381–2; N.A.M. Rodger, *The safeguard of the sea. A naval history of Britain, 660–1649* (London, 1997), p. 377; Oppenheim, *A history of the administration*, pp. 296–7; BL, Additional Ms. 9297, fol. 75; BNA, SP 16/195, fol. 6, 25 June 1631; Additional Ms. 9301, fol. 33v.

[96] Page (ed.), *Victoria County History Hampshire*, vol. 5, p. 380.

[97] Marsh, 'The navy and Portsmouth', p. 121; *CSPD: Interregnum, 1650*, pp. 177, 199 and 545; NMM, REC/1, fol. 73; *CSPD: Interregnum, 1653–1654*, ed. M.A. Everett (London, 1879), p. 145.

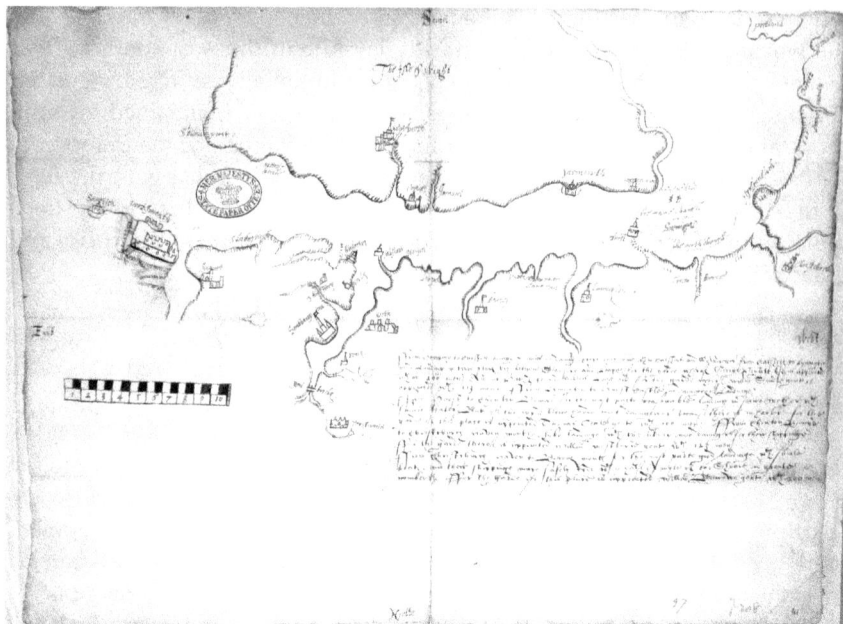

Figure 7.9 Coastal defences of Hampshire & Isle of Wight, 1585. The description of the haven of Portesmouth [*sic*]: map of the coast of Dorset and Hampshire from Portland to Southsea, including the Isle of Wight, showing churches and fortifications. With a note indicating landing places, guard commanders and numbers of men. Scale: 1 inch to slightly over 3 miles. Cardinal points [north at the bottom], MPF 1/208. Source: British National Archives (Kew).

commissioners Francis Willoughby, Nehemiah Bourne and John Taylor from Chatham surveyed a site for a new drydock at Portsmouth.[98] They found 'that there is convenience for the erection of a drydock, at a cost of 3,200*l*., and that it may be extended for 500*l*. more'.[99] Admiralty commissioners approved its construction in August.[100] Portsmouth was considered 'equipped for all purposes' in June 1659. Nine ships were built 1649–59: four third-/fourth-rates, two fifth-rates, one sixth-rate, a pink and a hoy.[101]

---

[98] Marsh, 'The navy and Portsmouth', p. 120.

[99] *CSPD, Interregnum, 1655–1656*, ed. M.A. Everett (London, 1882), p. 552.

[100] Marsh, 'The navy and Portsmouth', p. 120. Portsmouth Borough contributed £500 for its extension to increase Portsmouth contracts.

[101] Page (ed.), *Victoria County History Hampshire*, vol. 5, pp. 381–2; NMM, REC/1, fol. 73; *CSPD, Interregnum, 1653–1654*, p. 145; *CSPD: Interregnum, 1650*, pp. 177, 199, 545; J. Coad, 'Historic architecture of H.M. Naval Base, Portsmouth, 1700–1850', *Mariner's Mirror*, 67:1 (1981), 9; Marsh, 'The navy and Portsmouth', pp. 120–1 and 130–2; A.J. Willis and M.J. Hoad (eds), *Borough sessions 1653–1688* (Portsmouth, 1971), p. xxxi; Oppenheim, *A history of the administration*, p. 363; C. Donnithorne, Naval biographical database: www.navylist.org/.

To improve capacity, an estimate was prepared for a new third-rate drydock costing £2,597 in December 1661.[102] Sir Bernard de Gomme extended the town's fortifications between 1662 and 1682, fulfilling Henry VIII's design to surround Portsmouth fully by moats or the sea, and enclosed the dockyard with an earthen rampart and palisade in 1667.[103] Only one great ship was moored in the ordinary in June 1667: *Royal Sovereign*, with the third-rate 60-gun *Slothany*, *Galloone* and *Ostrich* hulks and *Marygold* hoy; but the Dutch only advanced within gunshot of Southsea Castle on 12 July and a signaller was arrested on the beach.[104] After the Second Anglo-Dutch War Parliament funded thirty ships, of which Portsmouth built second-rates *Vanguard*, *Ossory* and *Coronation* and third-rates *Eagle* and *Expedition*. During Charles II's reign Portsmouth built on average a ship a year, peaking in the 1670s, when sixteen were built, totalling thirty-four ships between 1660 and 1688.[105]

In December 1688 James II's son the Duke of Berwick, Portsmouth governor, allowed Irish soldiers to terrorise the town to preserve it as James's bastion. Commissioner Beach feared the soldiers would set fire to the storehouses, but dockyard workers and watchmen 'kept them off' until the county militia relieved the borough.[106] With only one building slip and one double dock for William III's increased navy, commissioner Willshaw argued in 1690 that another drydock at Portsmouth would save time, ships and money.[107] In October 1691 the Admiralty approved navy surveyor Edmund Dummer's basin, a great stone drydock for first-rates with revolutionary stepped stone

---

[102] BL, Additional Ms. 9302, fol. 127v, 18 December 1661.

[103] N. Pevsner and D. Lloyd, *The buildings of England. Hampshire and the Isle of Wight* (London, 1990), pp. 418–19; G. Williams, *The western defences of Portsmouth harbour 1400–1800* (Portsmouth, 1979), pp. 8 and 14–23; J. Webb, 'Port and garrison town', in *The Spirit of Portsmouth*, eds. J. Webb, Nigel Yates and Sarah Peacock (Chichester, 1989), pp. 73–4; R. East, *Extracts from records in the possession of the Municipal Corporation of the Borough of Portsmouth* (2nd edn, 1891), pp. 635–6, 673–4 and 793–4; H. Arthur Doubleday and William Page (eds), *Victoria County History Hampshire*, vol. 2 (London, 1903), p. 190; S. Quail, 'Stone towers: the fortifications of Portsmouth', in *The Spirit of Portsmouth*, eds Webb *et al.*, pp. 54–5 and 58–9; S. Quail, *The origins of Portsmouth and the first charter* (Portsmouth, 1994), p. 19; *CSPD, Interregnum, 1651–52*, ed. M.A. Everett (London, 1877), p. 300; A. Corney, *Fortifications in old Portsmouth* (Portsmouth, 1980), pp. 8–10; A. Corney, *Southsea Castle* (Portsmouth, 1968), p. 11; Andrew Saunders, *Fortress builder. Sir Bernard de Gomme, Charles II's military engineer* (Exeter, 2004), pp. 133–48 and 155–7.

[104] BNA, ADM 42/1047, Portsmouth ordinary paybook. *Slothany*, https://threedecks.org; BNA, SP 29/209, fol. 129, 14 July 1667; fol. 127, 14 July 1667.

[105] B. Pool, 'Pepys and the thirty ships', *History Today*, 20 (1970), 489–95; John Ehrman, *The Navy in the war of William III, 1689–1697* (Cambridge, 1953), pp. 430–9 and 632; Donnithorne. Naval biographical database: www.navylist.org/.

[106] BNA, ADM 106/387, fol. 41, 26 January 1688/9.

[107] BNA, ADM 106/402 part 1, fols. 151v and 152, 14 August 1690; ADM 7/335, 30 September 1699.

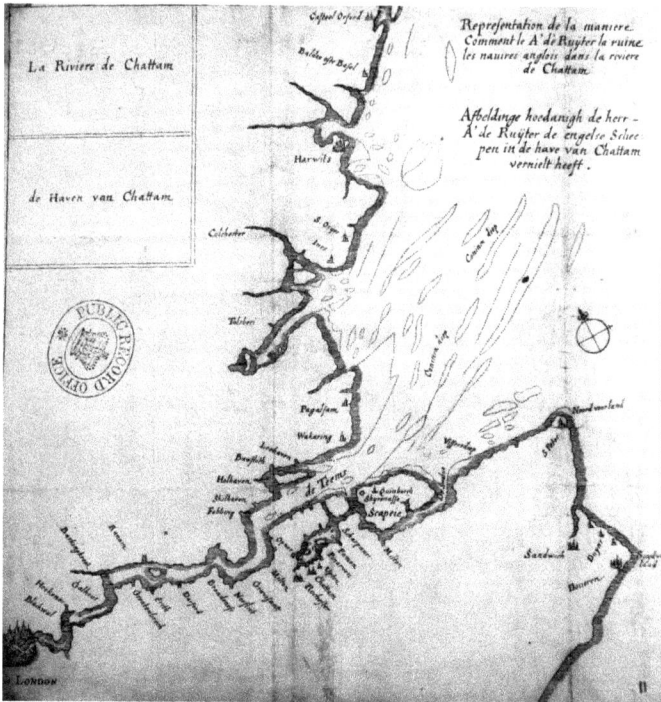

Figure 7.10 Marcus Doornick, Afbeeldinge van de Reviere van London/Picture of the River of London the Haven of Chatham, Sheppey & ca. 9–13/19–23 June 1667, MPF 1/231. Source: British National Archives (Kew).

sides, a wet dock for docks to drain into and a wooden drydock which enabled more ships to be repaired and fitted out more effectively.[108]

Chatham became a mooring and storehouse facility in 1547 after the French attacked Portsmouth in 1545. In the mid-seventeenth century it was a major shipbuilding and repairing dockyard, with a double dock, accessible from London and strategic for Netherlands campaigns.[109] By the end of the seventeenth century it was 'the country's premier naval base' with four docks, a double dock and a slip. It had the highest number of employees in 1689: 1,100 out of the total 2,263, twice that of Portsmouth (507).[110] However, the security

[108] BNA, ADM 7/169, 5 September 1691; BL, King's Ms. 43, fol. 105; Coad, *The royal dockyards*, p. 96.

[109] Coad, *The royal dockyards*, pp. 1 and 91.

[110] Jonathan Coad, 'Historic architecture of Chatham dockyard,1700–1850', *The Mariner's Mirror*, 68:2 (1982), 135; *idem, The royal dockyards*, p. 91; BNA, ADM 42/1, Chatham yard ordinary paybook, 1660–80; NMM, SER/131, Abstracts of workmen weekly employed in His Majesty's several yards, 1686–1718.

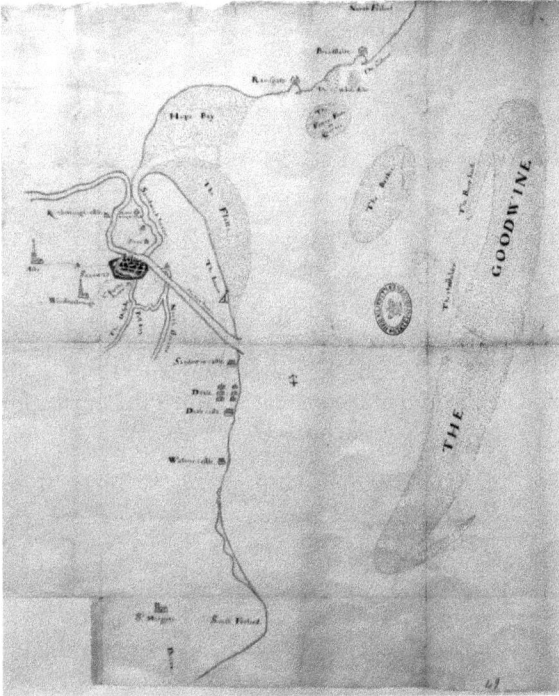

Figure 7.11 On the Kentish coast, Sandwich, Deal and Walmer castles protected the Downs anchorage, where ships heading for the Channel took refuge from the enemy, the weather and the treacherous Goodwin Sands. A small naval base at Deal replenished ships with emergency stores. The Downs: Goodwin Sands and Sandwich, Deal and Walmer Castles 1640, drawn by Robert Jager, Town Clerk from November 1640, MPF 1/280. Source: British National Archives (Kew).

of Chatham's naval ships had been threatened in 1644–45 by the pay arrears of mutinous shipkeepers and seamen. They also supported the 1648 Kentish and naval revolt, when seven royalist naval ships seized Walmer, Deal and Sandown castles protecting the Downs anchorage.[111] New commissioner Peter Pett failed to manage workforce expectations amid conflicting sectarian ideologies and low funds. This dockyard rebellion was prompted not by disloyalty but pay grievances and a desire for the civil war to end.[112] Ignoring advice, Pett delayed posting extra guards on *Sovereign* and *Prince*, which were

[111] *CSPD, Charles I, 1648–49*, ed. W.D. Hamilton (London, 1893), pp. 85 and 87; BL, Additional Ms. 9300, no. 36, fol. 95. 4 July 1648.
[112] Catharina Clement, 'Political and religious reactions in the Medway towns of Rochester and Chatham during the English Revolution, 1640–1660' (unpublished PhD thesis, Canterbury Christ Church University, 2013), pp. 122 and 285–6.

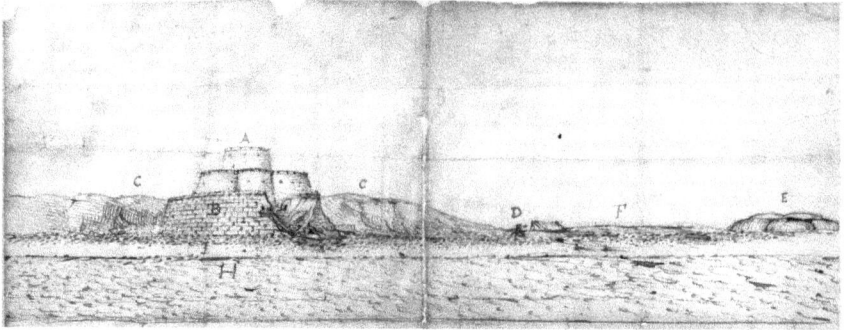

Figure 7.12 View of Walmer Castle, Kent, 1640, showing breaches in the sea wall, and land claimed by the lord of the manor, MPF 1/281. Source: British National Archives (Kew).

Figure 7.13 Inset view of Dover Castle and town by W[enceslas] Hollar. Surveyed by Philip Symonson, Rochester. Engraved by P. Stent at the White Horse in Giltspur Street, London, 1659, MPF 1/224. Source: British National Archives (Kew).

taken by the rebels.[113] Nevertheless, Pett prevented them from taking over the dockyard and by September 1648 the parliamentary navy had retaken the Downs castles and Dover.[114]

By the 1660s the silting and winding Medway restricted access to Chatham. At its junction with the Thames, Sheerness dockyard was designed as Chatham's deepwater satellite harbour.[115] In August 1665 Pepys and commissioner Peter Pett 'walked up and down, laying out the ground to be taken in for a yard to lay provisions for cleaning and repairing of ships, and a most

[113] *CSPD, Charles I, 1648–49*, pp. 78 and 85–7; BL, Additional Ms. 9305, fols. 62, 62v, 69v, 71–4, May 1648; Additional Ms. 9299, fol. 206, 12 April 1648; Additional Ms. 9305, fol. 69, 9 May 1648; Additional Ms. 9300, no. 30, fol. 83, 28 May 1648, no. 33, fol. 83, 12 June 1648; R.C. Anderson, 'The Royalists at sea in 1648', *The Mariner's Mirror*, 9:2 (1923), 38–9.
[114] Anderson, 'Royalists at sea in 1648', pp. 38, 41. The executive Committee of Both Kingdoms/Derby House Committee sat 1644–49, replaced by the Council of State.
[115] Coad, *The royal dockyards*, pp. 2 and 13.

Table 7.2 Chatham dockyard officer and artificer numbers, 1666 and 1667

Year quarter	1666				1667			
	1st	2nd	3rd	4th	1st	2nd	3rd	4th
Ships	4	2	2	23	27	19	18	21
Officers	16	16	16	16	16	16	16	16
Shipkeepers	36	28–26	33–31	290–276	373–233	256–174	190–120	199–179
Upnor, gunners	8	8	8	8	0	0	0	0
Total pay (£)	n.a.	292	319	342	439	341	259	260

Source: BNA, ADM 42/1, Officers and artificers Chatham Yard ordinary paybook, 1660–80. Officers include ship warrant officers and dockyard officers such as Clerk of the Cheque and Master Attendant who were in the ordinary. The lower (minimum) shipkeeper figures represent the number at the end of the quarter after men were discharged or run. Quarters were as follows: 1st Lady Quarter: 1 January to 31 March; 2nd Midsummer Quarter: 1 April to 30 June; 3rd Michaelmas Quarter: 1 July to 30 September; 4th Christmas Quarter: 1 October to 31 December.

proper place it is for the purpose'.[116] From November all cleaning, minor repairs and refits were ordered to Sheerness and the workforce was appointed October–December 1666. More workers entered in January and April 1667, the extensive increase visible in Table 7.2.[117]

In May 1667 the English had warning that the Dutch fleet was leaving, but commissioner Pett failed to implement 1648 lessons and the plan to protect the twenty ships moored at Chatham. Furthermore, de Ruyter's fleet included unemployed or alienated English seamen familiar with the Medway's eleven miles of twisting channels.[118] Before 1667, Medway fortifications comprised Henry VIII's Sheerness blockhouse, Elizabeth I's Upnor Castle, the unfinished Swaleness fort, the largely destroyed Queenborough Castle and four batteries downstream of Upnor Castle.[119] In May 1666 royal engineer De Gomme planned a 26-gun battery at Ness Point and walls enclosing the dockyard. A demi-bastion and moat would guard land access. He enclosed Henry VIII's square blockhouse and 'staked out' the yard. Charles and James approved De Gomme's plans in March 1667 and he signed contracts for groundworks, but then moved elsewhere.[120] On 21 March 1667 Sir William Penn, as master

[116] *The Diary of Samuel Pepys*, 18 August 1665.
[117] BNA, ADM 42/143 part 1, 1666–67; Coad, *The royal dockyards*, pp. 15–16; *idem*, *Support for the fleet*, p. 2.
[118] Rogers, *The Dutch in the Medway*, pp. 66–70; William Page (ed.), *Victoria County History* Kent (London, 1926), vol. 2, p. 368; Coad, *Support for the fleet*, p. 2. Coad, *The royal dockyards*, p. 13; *The Diary of Samuel Pepys*, 14 June 1667.
[119] Saunders, *Fortress builder*, p. 170.
[120] *The Diary of Samuel Pepys*, p. 126, 24 March 1666/67; Saunders, *Fortress builder*, pp. 170, 174–6 and 190–1; BL, Additional Ms. 16370, fols. 56–7.

of Trinity House responsible for the Thames defences, confirmed a platform for twelve culverins at Sheerness Point, the chain, two guardships and two fireships. Vice-Admiral Sir Edward Spragge commanded this squadron securing the Medway and Sheerness.[121]

But correspondence revealed unreadiness. Pett reported on 1 May that fireships would be ready by the end of the week, 'but all wante men' and the 'Chayne is almost finished & will suddenly be placed'. On 18 May the chain at Gillingham was 'almost fixed' and pinnaces 'all built'.[122] He regretted 'there is soe little hopes of money for the satisfying poore people whose cryes are very great'; on 8 May, Treasurer Carteret did 'not have money to meet all debts of the Navy'.[123] Table 7.2 reveals that there were no gunners at Upnor Castle during 1667.

Figure 7.14 Marcus Doornick, Representation de la maniere avec laquelle A' de Ruyter la ruine les navires anglois dans la riviere de Chattam. River of London the Haven of Chatham, Sheppey & ca. 9–13/19–23 June 1667, MPF 1/231.
Source: British National Archives (Kew).

[121] NMM, WYN/15/1, 21 March 1666/7. Spragge commanded the squadron to secure the Medway and Sheerness. J.D. Davies, 'Sir Edward Spragge (c.1629–1673)', *ODNB*, 2008; C.S. Knighton, 'Penn, Sir William (*bap.* 1621, *d.* 1670)', *ODNB*, 2008. Penn was also Navy Commissioner, Controller of Victualling Accounts. Collinge, *Navy Board officials*, pp. 23 and 129.
[122] BNA, SP 46/136, fol. 462, 1 May 1666; fol. 474, 18 May 1667.
[123] BNA, SP 46/136, fol. 462, 1 May 1666; fol. 470, Whitehall, 8 May 1667.

Sir William Coventry reported the Dutch approach on 3 June, proposing 'commanders of ships in the Hope and fireships to repair on board'. Two days later he requested oars for boats at Chatham and on the 9th asked commissioners 'to enquire after fireships to send against the Dutch in the Channel'. On 10 June, Coventry urged 'speed with fireships', while Pett announced 'Dutch ships approaching Thames' and 'expects stress to be at the Chain', confirming 'Sheerness taken by Dutch' and '2 small fireships to be sunk in Long Reach'.[124] Naval command was divided between fleet admirals Prince Rupert and the Duke of Albemarle. Albemarle was ordered to Chatham on 10 June to command and Prince Rupert to Woolwich on 13 June to arrange defences.[125]

Figure 7.15 Marcus Doornick, Dutch conquest of Sheerness Fort, Island of Sheppey 10/20 June 1667, 't Veroveren van 't Eylandt Schepeij op den 20 Junij Anno 1667. Illustrations, with descriptions, showing incidents during the Dutch War, 1665–67, MPF 1/232 F. Source: British National Archives (Kew).

[124] BNA, SP 46/136, fol. 481, 3 June 1667; fol. 482, 5 June 1667; fol. 485, 9 June 1667; fol. 487, 10 June 1667; fols. 488 and 489, 10 June 1667; fols. 491, 493 and 494, 11 June 1667. For Coventry see Collinge, *Navy Board officials*, pp. 22 and 94; J.C. Sainty, *Admiralty officials 1660–1870* (London, 1975), pp. 35–6 and 118.
[125] Rogers, *The Dutch in the Medway*, p. 76; *The Diary of Samuel Pepys*, 10 June 1667; 11 June 1667.

Lieutenant-Admiral Van Ghent captured Sheerness on 10 June, plundering buildings and stores on the 11th. Pett had removed his ship models and plans, but Chatham dockyard and the great ships were threatened. Pepys was shocked that 'we were in no readines to receive ye orders. y^t ye ships should want men and amunition, & be left wthout a sufficient defense to secure them'.[126] Navy commissioner William Brounker and comptroller Sir John Mennes went to Chatham.[127] Through the night of the 11th Pepys hired fireships, an Order-in-Council enabling him to requisition ships.[128] On the 12th he was hiring more fireships, and reassured by Albemarle's letter 'that all is safe as to the great ships under any assault – the boom and Chaine being so fortified' by two sunken ships, two batteries, and *Unity* stationed there.[129] His confidence was undone later that day, when he discovered that 'the Dutch have broke the Chain and burned our ships'.[130]

Pett and Brounker, who reached Chatham on the afternoon of Monday 10th, wrote to the Navy Board on Friday 14th that:

> It was the opinion of all sortes of persons here, that the whole Navy, Docke, and Stores would have been burnd upp on Wednesday, and for the prevencōn of the Enemies being possesd of the Shipps the Generall [Albemarle] gave express Orders that all the Shipps should be sunke where they ridd, but at length t'was resolvd that there Cables should be cutt at the Haulfe, and they turnd on shoare, and then sunke, which although it might prove the lesser evill of the two it hath put the ships to a very great hazard; some of them, especially the Victory Wee feare will scarce be gott offt, and this afternoon the Henry & Vantguard gott loose from the place where they were on shoare and drove up farther into the River where they lye dangerously enough.[131]

Brounker reported that on Monday night (10th):

> … more Shipps were brought to the Chayne and some sunke, besides it was also strenghtened wth Stages before and Cables between the Shipps suncke, the Marmaduke lay neare the Guardships in the middle, the *Monmouth* a

---

[126] *The Diary of Samuel Pepys*, 13 June 1667; 17 June 1667; BNA, SP 29/205 fol. 75, 13–16 June 1667.

[127] *The Diary of Samuel Pepys*, 11 June 1667. William Brounker, formerly Extra Navy Commissioner: Controller of Treasurer's Accounts since January 1667. Sir John Mennes had been Comptroller since 1661. Collinge, *Navy Board officials*, pp. 2, 21 and 122.

[128] *The Diary of Samuel Pepys*, 11 June 1667.

[129] *The Diary of Samuel Pepys*, 12 June 1667. George Monck, Duke of Albemarle, a royalist, then parliamentary commander, instrumental in restoring Charles II, in 1667 captain-general of the army and joint admiral of the fleet in 1667. Ronald Hutton, 'Monck, George, first duke of Albemarle (1608–1670)', *ODNB*, 2004.

[130] BNA, SP 29/205, fol. 91, 13–16 June 1667; *The Diary of Samuel Pepys*, 12 June 1667.

[131] BNA, SP 46/136, fol. 498, 14 June 1667.

Figure 7.16 Marcus Doornick, Dutch Burning the Ships on the River Medway 13/23 June 1667. 't Verbranden van de Schepen by Rochester op den 22 en 23 Junij Anno 1667. Illustrations, with descriptions, showing incidents during the Dutch War, 1665–67, MPF 1/232 G. Source: British National Archives (Kew).

little higher and the Roy.[ll] Charles something above her, all w[ch] notwith-standing they forced theire passage wth the help of ffireshipps about High water [midday] the next day [Wednesday 12th], and soe tooke the Roy.[ll] Charles, but y[e] Monmouth sayled away and is now above the yard. the next night Wee made a battery on the North side of the Yard for eight peices of Ordnance and since they have though not without oosition both from Upnorth Castle and us at the docke &a ... ffyred the Roy.[ll] James, Roy.[ll] Oake and Loy.[ll] London, and this morning they made off; and now ride below the Chayne.[132]

Fifteen vessels were lost. The Dutch towed away *Royal Charles* (which had transported the restored Charles II in 1660) on the 14th, flying the English flag upside down. They also recovered *Unity* (ex-*Eendracht*, captured in 1665).[133] The effectiveness of the navy was compromised, but it would have been more serious if the Dutch had advanced another half-mile, as Chatham ordinary

[132] BNA, SP 46/136, fol. 499, 14 June 1667.
[133] Rogers, *The Dutch in the Medway*, pp. 72–115 and 154–9.

held twenty crucial ships-of-the-line in June 1667: two first-rates (*Royal Charles* and *Royal James*), eleven second-rates, two third-rates, one fourth-rate and one fifth-rate, plus three captured ships. Six dated from the 1650s and five from the 1660s, some brand-new. The combined natural defence provided by the narrowness of the Medway at that point, the fierceness of English defence at Upnor Castle on 12 June, and the number of ships sunk above Upnor would have threatened their retreat. The Dutch halted.[134]

The House of Commons investigated in October and November 1667. Pepys perceived 'the whole world is at work in blaming one another'.[135] Rupert and Albemarle blamed Pett, Albemarle asserting that he had ordered Pett to move *Charles* in good time, 'and he neglected it'. Belatedly, Pett had ordered *Royal Charles* to be moved upriver on 11 June, but Albemarle's orders to sink eight fire and other ships in Gillingham Reach and set up batteries monopolised men and boats assigned by Pett.[136] Pepys regretted that at Woolwich and Chatham 'the ships that we have sunk have many, and the first of them, been ships completely fitted for fireships at great charge'.[137]

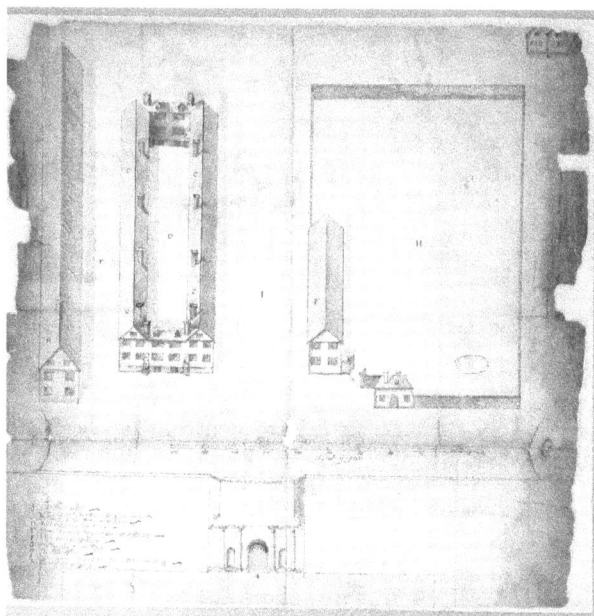

Figure 7.17 Bernard de Gomme, Scheme of the Buildings to be made at Sheerness 1677, MPI 1/155. Source: British National Archives (Kew).

[134] BNA, ADM 42/1 Chatham yard ordinary paybook, 1660–80; Rogers, *The Dutch in the Medway*, pp. 103 and 107.
[135] *The Diary of Samuel Pepys*, 23 October 1667.
[136] Rogers, *The Dutch in the Medway*, pp. 85–6.
[137] *The Diary of Samuel Pepys*, 14 June 1667.

A rough draft of part of this river with my opinion how it should be fortified against the Attaques or attempts by a fforreigne Enemy

1. Chatham Yard
2. St Mary Creek
3. The platform at Gillingham
4. The platform at the lower end of Cookram Wood
5. Cookram Wood
6. The Birds Nest in which are 18 Guns
7. The platform next the Castle wherein are 12 Guns
8. The wharf wherein are 3 Crabs for heaving taut the Boome or Chaine
9. Upnor Castle
10. One of His Majesty's Ships
11. Another Ship
12.)Two ships moared with their broadsides towards the Chain
13.) to rake any ships that shall come up the Reach fore & aft
14. The Boom or Chain
15. Two cables which I would have seased together
16. and a chain at each end, as at 18 and 19
17. Pieces of Mast or Great Balks to be seased to the upper part of the cable with small chains

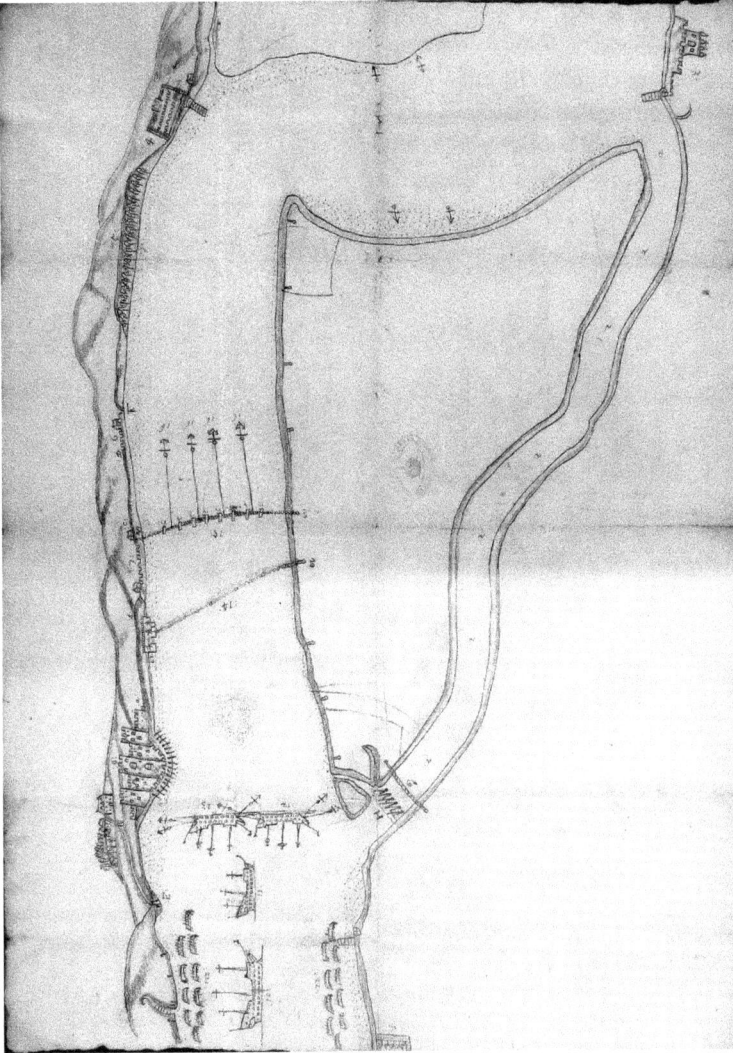

Figure 7.18 Chatham Dockyard Commissioner Sir Richard Beach's map of his Proposal re. Cables, 1 November 1678, ADM 106/330, fols 495-497. Source: British National Archives (Kew).

The Chatham raid shaped new defences. De Gomme upgraded Medway fortifications from 1667 to 1685, completing Sheerness Fort, two new batteries at Chatham dockyard and two at Gillingham and Cockham Wood to cover the approach to Upnor Castle.[138] In January 1668 the chain weighed 14 tons 6 cwt.[139]

The memory of the Dutch raid was still fresh in the Chatham commissioner's mind ten years later. In November 1678, Sir Richard Beach 'mustered all the workmen and warned them of the necessity to be ready to bear arms when the bell rings more promptly than previously when many of them did not appear when the Dutch came up the river'.[140] He proposed a Gillingham platform, Upnor Castle cables, Cockham Wood fort, a sentinel at Faversham, a platform at Queenborough Castle, a fourth-rate in Queenborough creek and fireships at Sheerness.[141] In May 1679, Chatham master attendant Captain Vittels 'secured the chain with anchors' and requested two ships at the '3rd and 4th moorings from the bridge'.[142]

Figure 7.19 Upnor Castle, 2016. Source: Ann Coats.

[138] Saunders, *Fortress builder*, pp. 171–91.
[139] BNA, SP 46/136/470, 14 January 1667/8. It listed sixteen shackles, eighteen rings, six forelocks, one fidd and bolt, a hook and buckle and a hook and great staple.
[140] BNA, ADM 106/330, fol. 426.
[141] BNA, ADM 106/330, fols. 495–7, Chatham dockyard commissioner Sir Richard Beach's map of his Proposal re. Cables, 1 November 1678.
[142] BNA, ADM 106/342, fol. 417.

Figure 7.20 Cockham Woods Fort, 2017. Source: Ann Coats.

Conclusions

In the decade leading up to the Second Anglo-Dutch War, the Dutch Republic created a standing fleet as a response to English aggression, complete with shore facilities, a domestic gunfounding industry and a marine regiment. However, this was to have unforeseen consequences. Fleet measures reflected the desire for economic security and political power, both essential to safeguard the hard-fought and only recently acknowledged Dutch freedom. Their character was therefore permanent. The military means to safeguard independence were financed with the profits from trade and, it was felt, should naturally be applied to protect that trade. Yet the tactical shift and consequent militarisation of naval defence were having far-reaching social effects, little perceived at the time, whereby commercial shipping and naval defence were irrevocably floating apart, as described above. The gap would grow wider still in the 1670s with the Third Anglo-Dutch War and the Franco-Dutch war of 1672–78. Naval strategy was now supplemented by territorial defence, against enemy attempts to overrun the country.

The years from 1666 to 1674 saw the heyday of the Dutch navy. The fleet would reach its peak strength in size and armament during William III's wars against Louis XIV from 1689 to 1713, when it was moulded to coalition performance with the Royal Navy, two steps away from mere trade protection as in the 1650s and 1660s. No longer well represented in the admiralty boards, Dutch merchants increasingly had to beg for convoy protection. At the same time, William III subjected the Dutch fleet to English command, which meant the end of Dutch naval supremacy. Meanwhile the Republic had acquired a naval infrastructure that would last for a century.

In 1688 William had inherited a model of English shipbuilding honed by four decades of strategic, financial and political exigency in harnessing state resources and technology.[143] English coastal defences depended on how effectively dockyards could mobilise their workforce and materials. During the First Anglo-Dutch War the state had invested one-off funds to build new ships but struggled to find day-to-day funding.[144] The problem remained unresolved at the restoration of Charles II. By 1667, the navy and the most vulnerable dockyards, Chatham and Sheerness, lacked crucial materials, workers and fortifications, due to national decisions to cut funding and ships at sea. This allowed the Dutch to make exceptional inroads into the Medway. Lack of funds also determined commitment. Seamen and dockyard workers were so alienated by pay arrears that they rejected appeals to loyalty and fled the Medway.[145] Dockyard effectiveness was thus constrained by national leadership and economic and manpower issues. The events of 1648 and 1667 showed how dissonance between national expectations and local preparedness threatened national security.

The short-term cause of English defensive failure in the Second Anglo-Dutch War thus lay in inadequate execution of local plans, but the long-term cause was a lack of central funding for personnel and materials at Chatham and the completion of fortifications at Sheerness. As in 1648, administrative failure opened the way for a seaborne invasion. As Pepys understood very well, the king was inclined to prioritise his own pleasures over the business of government.[146] However, after the 1670 Treaty of Dover, royal income increased, and by the time of the Third Anglo-Dutch War, naval spending amounted to one-third of total government expenditure.[147] The fiscal reforms of Charles II's reign, which by 1685 had centralised and improved the kingdom's tax collection, and from 1694 the loan-raising capacity of the Bank of England, ensured that loans raised to fund the navy were reliably repaid from taxes.[148]

---

[143] Fox, *Four Days' Battle*, p. 50; Davies, *Pepys's Navy*, p. 52; J. Glete, *Navies and nations*, I, 11–12, 19 and 216.

[144] *CSPD, Interregnum, 1651–52*, p. 540.

[145] *The Diary of Samuel Pepys*, 10 June 1667; 14 June 1667.

[146] *The Diary of Samuel Pepys*, 17 February 1666/67; 24 June 1667; 17 July 1667.

[147] Coleman, 'Naval dockyards under the later Stuarts', pp. 135–7.

[148] J. Brewer, *The sinews of power. War, money and the English state, 1688–1783* (New York, 1989), p. 144; Chandaman, *The English public revenue*, pp. 275–6; P.G M. Dickson, *The financial revolution in England* (London, 1967), pp. 42–4.

III

Conflict in the Atlantic World and Asia

View of Elmina Castle, one of the slaving stations in modern-day Ghana, as seen from the river. Produced by Johannes Vingboons. Source: wikimedia.org

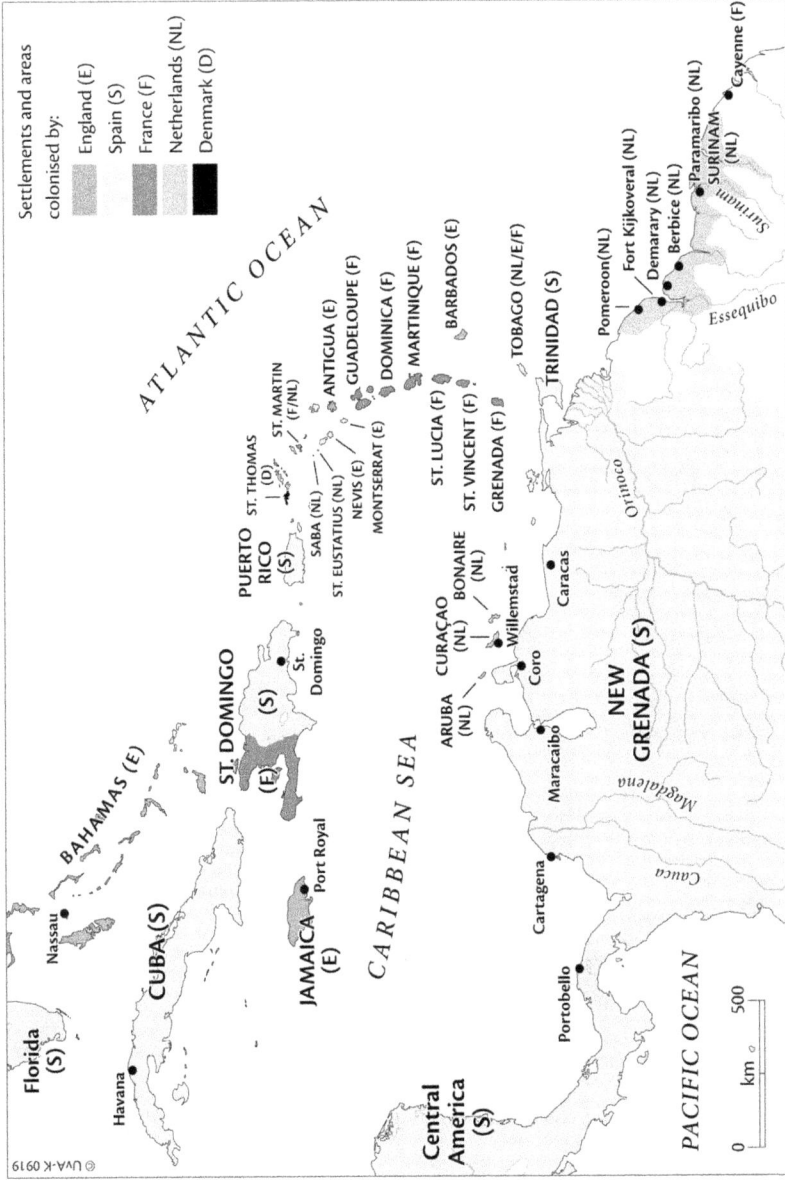

1. Europeans in the Caribbean and the Guyanas in the late seventeenth century. Cartography: UVA Kaartenmakers.

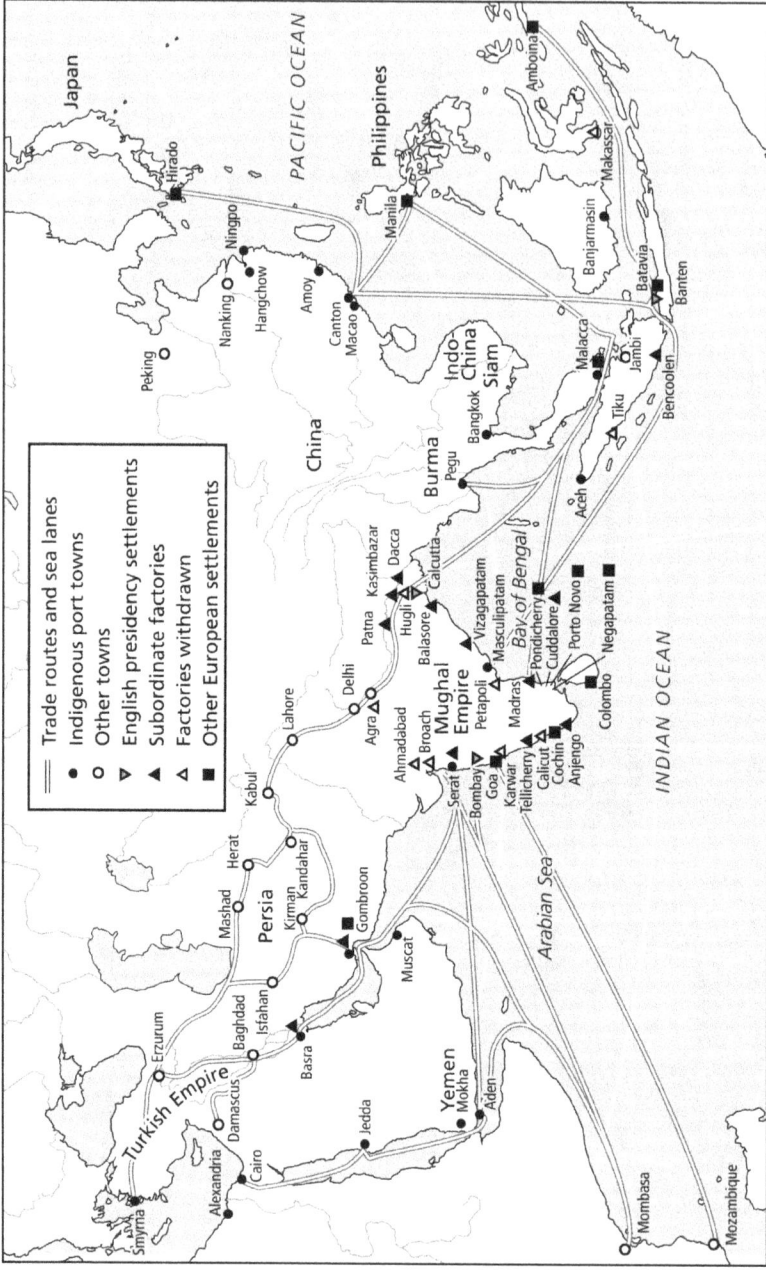

2. European trade routes and factories in Asia, c. 1700. Source: J. Tracy, 'Dutch and English trade to the East: The Indian Ocean and the Levant, to about 1700' in J. Bentley, S. Subrahmanyam, & M. Wiesner-Hanks (eds.), *The Cambridge World History* (Cambridge, 2015), vol. 6, pp. 240–62. Reproduced by permission of the Licensor through PLS clear.

3. The Banda Islands (shaded grey) to the south of Ceram, the largest of the Spice Islands. Pulo Run is the most westerly of the group; Amboyna and Ambon Island lie to the south-west of Ceram. Source: Malachy Postlethwayt, *The Universal Dictionary of Trade and Commerce*, 4th edition, 1774, vol. 1, maps of Asia, plate VIII.

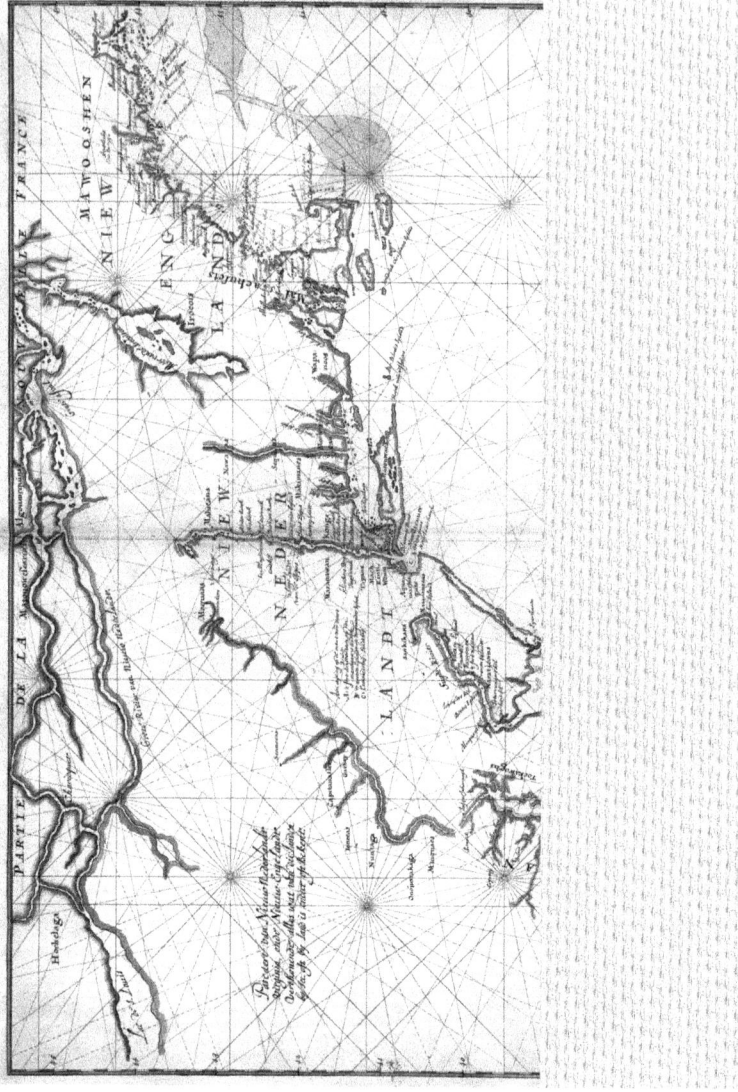

4. Virginia, New Netherland and New England, c. 1639, by the Amsterdam cartographer Johannes Vingeboons. Source: Library of Congress, Geography and Map Division (Washington DC).

8

The Second Anglo-Dutch War in the Caribbean

Nuala Zahedieh

The period between 1652 and 1674 spanned three Anglo-Dutch wars and was a defining moment in the histories of both the British and Dutch Atlantics. Commercial and territorial ambitions combined to attract members of both nations to America but, in the seventeenth century, the former prevailed. Most north Europeans ventured to America as merchants rather than as empire builders and, as competition for control of markets intensified, especially in the Caribbean, the two nations were drawn into more than twenty years of conflict. By 1674, when England extricated itself from the Third Anglo-Dutch War, leaving France to batter its Dutch rival, Atlantic history was on a new trajectory. The Dutch abandoned the grand territorial ambitions which some had nursed in the early days of the West India Company (WIC), especially after the conquest of northern Brazil. Instead they settled into their key role as ubiquitous middlemen trading across imperial boundaries. On the other hand, despite the far more improvisational style in which the English had embarked on colonial expansion, that nation was now clearly set on a path towards a grand territorial empire.[1]

Anglo-Dutch commercial rivalry in the Caribbean

Commercial rivalry between the English and Dutch in the Caribbean developed on three overlapping fronts. First, and foremost, was competition for access to Spanish American markets. This was the glittering prize which initially drew north Europeans to the New World and fuelled their interest in the Caribbean which was a convenient entry route. From the first discoveries, Spanish America was seen as a source of almost limitless treasure – an El Dorado – and, even though the fabled wealth of the Peruvian and Mexican silver mines was seen to falter in the early seventeenth century, it soon recovered.

---

[1] Wim Klooster, *The Dutch moment. War, trade, and settlement in the seventeenth century Atlantic world* (Ithaca, NY, 2016); Nuala Zahedieh, *The capital and the colonies. London and the Atlantic economy, 1660–1700* (Cambridge, 2010).

Between 1660 and 1700, annual bullion production was worth an estimated £2.5 million and far exceeded the value of any other New World commodity, including sugar.[2] A strong economy, and large towns, created a buoyant market for enslaved labour, provisions, and manufactured goods which were exchanged for, not only bullion, but also cochineal, cocoa, dye-woods, hides, indigo, precious stones, and other valuable commodities.[3]

The Spanish crown took steps to limit access to its American markets and maximize rents. With some exceptions, such as slave traders, foreign nationals were prohibited from entering Spanish American ports, or settling in Spanish American territories, and all commerce was regulated by the *Casa de Contratacion* in Seville. Trade was organized in two supposedly annual fleets: the *galeones*, which exchanged food, wine, and manufactured goods for Peruvian silver and other American commodities at Portobello, and the *flota* which collected New Spain's riches at Vera Cruz.[4] Although the law excluded foreigners, they had little difficulty in penetrating the system and, by the early seventeenth century, they dominated the trade.[5] However, mounting delays and costs in doing business with the fleets encouraged foreigners to turn increasing attention to the more opportunistic, and risky, direct smuggling trade.[6] There were new attempts to put it on a more solid footing with permanent bases, or factories, in the Caribbean, emulating those in Asia, which could be used to warehouse goods and coordinate business activities. The Dutch provided a model for development at Curaçao, an island off the north coast of Venezuela, seized by the WIC in 1634, and used to forge regular commercial links with the Spanish Main.[7]

---

[2] J.S. Stein and B.H. Stein, *Silver, trade and war. Spain and America in the making of early-modern Europe* (Baltimore, 2000), p. 24.

[3] *Ibid.*, pp. 97–9.

[4] C.H. Haring, *Trade and navigation between Spain and the Indies in the time of the Habsburgs* (London, 1947). The key book for understanding the operation of Spanish commerce was Joseph de Veita Linage, *Norte de la Contratacion de las Indias Occidentales* (1672). It was translated into English as *The Spanish rule of trade in the West Indies* (1702).

[5] Jean O. McLachlan, *Trade and peace with old Spain, 1667–1750. A study of the influence of commerce on Anglo-Spanish diplomacy in the first half of the eighteenth century* (Cambridge, 1940).

[6] Nuala Zahedieh, 'The merchants of Port Royal and Spanish American trade, 1655–89', *William and Mary Quarterly*, 43 (1986), 570–93; Wim Klooster, *Illicit riches. Dutch trade in the Caribbean, 1648–1795* (Leiden, 1998); Christian J. Koot, *Empire at the periphery. British colonists, Anglo-Dutch trade, and the development of the British Atlantic, 1621–1713* (New York, 2011).

[7] 'Description of the island of Curacao and convenience for trade with Spain', 1665, British National Archive [hereafter: BNA] CO 1/19, no. 25; Cornelius H. Goslinga, *The Dutch in the Caribbean and on the Wild Coast, 1580–1680* (Gainesville, Fla., 1971), pp. 263–73 and 275–81; Klooster, *Illicit riches*; Linda Rupert, *Creolization and contraband. Curacao in the early modern Atlantic world* (Athens, Ga., 2012).

England's second commercial concern was to protect its own developing markets in the Atlantic, above all, in the Caribbean where, after the introduction of sugar in the 1640s, commercial agriculture offered the best rewards. By the mid-seventeenth century, first tobacco, and then sugar, had demonstrated the potential profits and fiscal opportunities provided by colonial commodity production. England's political classes were determined that any benefits to shipping, trade, and entrepot activity should be reserved for their nation which, they argued, had provided the men and money needed to support territorial expansion, and had an ongoing commitment to colonial defence. It was a 'matter of exact justice' that England should be able to stand 'like the sun in the midst of its plantations' and it needed to devise strict laws to prevent foreigners, above all the Dutch, syphoning off profits.[8] The Republic's success in using investment in trade and shipping to obtain wealth, independence from Spain, and even to open a second front in the Atlantic, had shown how a small territory could achieve power. Success provoked, not only envy and emulation, but also fear.[9] Dutch designs 'to lay a foundation to themselves for engrossing the universal trade, not only of Christendom, but indeed of the greater part of the known world' became a central theme of English commercial discourse. The Dutch were seen to be 'the masters in the field of trade' and it was generally believed that, unless they were excluded from England's Atlantic trading system, they would 'carry away the greatest advantage by the plantations of all the princes in Christendom leaving us and others only the trouble of breeding men and sending them abroad to cultivate their industry'.[10]

A third area of Anglo-Dutch commercial rivalry was the African slave trade, which was inextricably linked to the other two. The human traffic not only supplied the labour which was increasingly seen as vital to expand commercial agriculture in the north Europeans' own plantations, but also provided access to Spanish American ports. On account of the Treaty of Tordessillas of 1494, which divided the globe between Spain and Portugal, Spain was excluded from Africa and it was the one trade which was not controlled by the *Casa* and was in the hands of independent crown licensees.[11] The enslaved Africans not only fetched high prices in Spanish American markets but, also, provided cover for a still more lucrative contraband trade. The perceived value of this chink in Spanish imperial walls does much to explain the very high esteem in which the slave *asiento* was held.[12]

---

[8] John Cary, *An essay on the state of England in relation to its trade* (Bristol, 1695), p. 70.

[9] Charles H. Wilson, *Profit and power. A study of England and the Dutch wars* (London, 1957), pp. 21–4.

[10] Josiah Child, *A new discourse of trade* (London, 1692), p. 94.

[11] Georges Scelle, 'The slave trade in the Spanish colonies of America: the Asiento', *The American Journal of International Law*, 4 (1910), 612–61.

[12] Nuala Zahedieh, 'Commerce and conflict. Jamaica and the War of the Spanish Succession', in *The Caribbean and the Atlantic world economy. Circuits of trade, money*

The Dutch became heavily involved in the African slave trade during their long war with Spain and Portugal which were in union until 1640. The Dutch capture of Pernambuco, in northern Brazil, in 1630, drew them into enthusiastic expansion of sugar production with its massive demand for labour and opened an attractive monopoly market for the WIC. The trade in human beings raised moral issues and, according to Goslinga, a commission was appointed to reconcile the commerce with the doctrines of Calvinism, but the triumph of profit over conscience was tragically swift.[13] The Company used war to built up considerable strength on both the Gold Coast, where they seized the main fort at Elmina in 1637, and, more briefly, in Angola, where they held Luanda from 1642 until 1648. After Portugal's cession from Spain in 1640, it reached a truce with the Dutch in 1641 which recognized their right to keep possession of the former Portuguese sphere in Guinea.[14] Thereafter, the Dutch asserted that the 'treasure and blood' expended in the conquest of the Gold Coast gave them the monopoly rights there which had been formerly claimed by Portugal by dint of first discovery.[15] Used in the Atlantic, it was hoped this monopoly would allow them to replicate the success of the Dutch East India Company (VOC) in Asia. Unsurprisingly, other north Europeans did not share their interpretation of international law. However, the English Guinea Company, first chartered in 1618, and again in 1632, was weakened by political problems during the Civil War, and afterwards, in 1652, by Royalist depredations in Africa, led by Prince Rupert. It made slow headway before the Restoration but, nonetheless, the English were anxious to prevent the Netherlanders from monopolizing slave sales in either English territories, where demand for labour rose steeply with the turn to sugar in the 1640s, or rich Iberian markets.[16]

All three sets of commercial rivalries played a role in the First Anglo-Dutch War, and gathered strength during the 1650s as Atlantic commitments grew and appreciation of the potential prizes increased. The English state had shown limited interest in colonial expansion in the early seventeenth century and was, of course, distracted by civil war in the 1640s. However, as the conflict ended it was becoming increasingly clear that the Atlantic world

and knowledge, 1650–1914, eds Adrian Leonard and David Pretel (London, 2015), pp. 68–86.

[13] Goslinga, *The Dutch in the Caribbean*, p. 146.

[14] Johannes Postma, *The Dutch in the Atlantic slave trade, 1600–1815* (Cambridge, 1990); Klooster, *Dutch moment*, pp. 63–73.

[15] Klooster, *Dutch moment*, p. 100.

[16] P.E.H. Hair and Robin Law, 'The English in Western Africa to 1700', in *The origins of empire. The Oxford history of the British empire*, ed. Nicholas Canny (Oxford, 1998), pp. 241–63; John J. McCusker and Russell R. Menard, 'The sugar industry in the seventeenth century. A new perspective on the Barbadian "sugar revolution"', in *Tropical Babylons. Sugar and the making of the Atlantic world, 1450–1680*, ed. Stuart B. Schwartz (Cambridge, 2004), pp. 289–330.

offered enticing possibilities for securing profits, and power. As Cromwell established himself in government, he embarked on the 'attentive, aggressive approach to commercial policy' which has been widely seen as the most characteristic feature of his rule.[17] The Navigation Act of 1651 attempted to exclude Dutch shipping from all English foreign trade and to seal England's expanding Atlantic empire. Such 'staggeringly ambitious' legislation would have proved impossible to enforce even had it not provoked the First Anglo-Dutch War, and been largely suspended.[18] Nonetheless, Cromwell's Act did pave the way for more enforceable regulation after the Restoration.

Even more audacious than the Navigation Act, was Cromwell's attempt to conquer Spanish America in 1655, the Western Design, which began with a humiliating military failure at Hispaniola but ended with the seizure of Jamaica.[19] The neglected outpost of the Spanish empire was, at first, seen as a poor consolation prize but the captors quickly recognized its geographic advantages. Early English settlements in the Caribbean were located on the eastern periphery where, owing to the prevailing winds, they had poor communications with the major Spanish ports. In contrast, Jamaica was located in the heart of the Spanish Indies, an invaluable base 'within the Spaniard's bowels', straddling the richest trade routes, and within easy sailing distance of the key staging posts.[20] Jamaica was an ideal launching pad for plunder, and trade, and more than a match for Dutch Curaçao.[21]

Restoration expansionism

At the Restoration, Charles, with enthusiastic support from his brother, James, Duke of York, built on Cromwell's Atlantic legacy and maintained his assertive commercial policy.[22] Parliament voted the customs to Charles for life and this revenue accounted for between 30 and 40 per cent of his income and, owing to heavy impositions on sugar and tobacco, colonial commodities

[17] Robert Brenner, *Merchants and revolution. Commercial change, political conflict and London's overseas traders, 1550–1653* (Cambridge, 1993), p. 542.

[18] Lawrence A. Harper, *The English navigation laws. A seventeenth century experiment in social engineering* (New York, 1939); Wilson, *Profit and power*, p. 87; David Ormrod, *The rise of commercial empires. England and the Netherlands in the age of mercantilism, 1650–1770* (Cambridge, 2003), p. 32.

[19] Carla Pestana, *The English conquest of Jamaica. Oliver Cromwell's bid for empire* (Cambridge, Mass., 2017).

[20] Edward Hickeringill, *Jamaica view'd* (London, 1661), p. 46.

[21] Nuala Zahedieh, 'Trade, plunder and economic development in early English Jamaica', *Economic History Review*, 39 (1986), pp. 205–22; A.P. Thornton, *West India policy under the Restoration* (Oxford, 1956), pp. 4–10 and 16–18.

[22] John Callow, *The making of James II. The formative years of a fallen king* (Stroud, 2000). Abigail Swingen, *Competing visions of empire. Labour, slavery and the origins of the British Atlantic empire* (New Haven, Conn., 2015).

contributed more than their proportional share of trade.[23] Beyond tariffs, the new lands in America held the promise of other gains to compensate the Stuarts for the substantial loss of crown estates in England and the uncomfortable dependence on Parliament. After years of exile, and uncertainty, Charles and his followers (including Prince Rupert, Edward Hyde, Lord Clarendon and others) shared an opportunism and a spirit of adventure which attracted them to the imperial project. Pragmatism prevailed and they willingly joined with like-minded survivors of the interregnum (including Ashley Cooper, Lord Shaftsbury, George Monk, Duke of Albemarle, and the merchants Martin Noell and Thomas Povey) in support of expansion. Jamaica was retained, Carolina was chartered, Willoughby's claim to Surinam was confirmed in partnership with Clarendon's son, Edward, and steps were taken to promote new projects elsewhere. The king, the Duke of York, who was appointed Lord High Admiral, courtiers, and mercantile allies also invested in privateering, the slave trade, and colonial joint-stock companies. In all cases, they attempted to use the political levers of power to extract a profit and promoted policies which put them on a collision course with the Dutch.[24]

At the Restoration, it was well known that, despite the Navigation Act, the Dutch continued to play a major role in shipping English plantation goods to market and supplying the colonies with enslaved labour and other necessities. In 1655, the Western Design's forces captured seven Dutch ships engaged in illegal trade at Barbados and the situation deteriorated during the ensuing war with Spain which weakened English shipping. As soon as Charles recovered his crown, he joined with Parliament to introduce a new, improved, version of the Commonwealth legislation which echoed its aspirations but made them more enforceable.[25] The Act of 1660 required that all goods taken to and from England's colonies should be carried in English, or colonial, ships; masters and three-quarters of the crew were to be English, or colonial subjects. A list of the most valuable Caribbean commodities including cotton, dye-woods, ginger, indigo, sugar, and one North American product, tobacco, were 'enumerated' and were to be exported to no place other than England, or an English possession. On paper, the Act eliminated the Dutch, and other foreigners (including the Irish and Scots), from England's colonial trade and promoted its entrepot function. The Staple Act of 1663 took this further and required that all European goods intended for sale in English colonies were to be unloaded, and reloaded, in England and Wales before being carried

---

[23] C.D. Chandaman, *The English public revenue, 1660–1688* (Oxford, 1975), pp. 9–36.

[24] Nuala Zahedieh, 'Regulation, rent-seeking and the Glorious Revolution in the English Atlantic economy', *Economic History Review*, 63:4 (2010), 865–90; Thornton, *West India policy*, pp. 4–10 and 16–18.

[25] The Act was formally approved by the Privy Council on 9 September 1660, *Lords Journals*, XI, 350.

directly to the colonies (with some exceptions such as servants and salt). The legislation was supported by fiscal policy which gave the English colonies preferential treatment in the home market and also allowed English traders to draw-back duties on re-exports to foster the development of England as a trading emporium to rival the Dutch Republic.[26]

It was understood that regulations on the statute book could not, alone, force change upon either the Dutch or their English colonial customers who generally welcomed the interlopers in their ports. Strategically placed warehouse colonies such as St Eustatius, a small rocky island with easy access to the English and the French Leeward Islands, or New Amsterdam which provided a similar back-door into England's mainland colonies, caused increasing concern which encouraged moves to back words with aggressive action. In December 1663, the Council for Plantations reported complaints from the customs farmers about 'the great abuses practiced by the planters of and traders to Virginia, New England, Maryland, Long Island, etc. in carrying great quantities of tobacco to the Dutch plantations contiguous, the customs of which would amount to £10,000', and Caribbean commodities were also passing through the North American back-door.[27] The Committee instructed the relevant governors to take measures to reform these abuses while, in March, the king took the more audacious step of granting his brother a patent for a massive tract of land stretching from Maine to the Delaware River and including areas settled by the Dutch.[28] Tempers rose and in June 1664, under orders from the Duke of York, Richard Nicolls set out with a small fleet of four frigates and launched a successful assault on New Amsterdam on 6 September.[29]

The Dutch governor, Stuyvesant, was taken by surprise and unable to mount a strong defence. Powder and lead were in short supply and, furthermore, despite the area being specialized in food production, provisions were scarce as a fleet laden with victuals had recently sailed for Curaçao. The situation felt hopeless and the local minister lamented that as 'no relief or assistance could be expected ... our authorities found themselves compelled to come to terms for the sake of avoiding bloodshed and pillage'.[30] As the

---

[26] Harper, *Navigation laws*; Ralph Davis, *The rise of the English shipping industry in the seventeenth and eighteenth centuries* (London, 1962), pp. 306–10.

[27] Minutes of the Council for Foreign Plantations, 7 December 1663, BNA CO 1/14, no. 59.

[28] W. Noel Sainsbury (ed.), *Calendar of state papers. Colonial, America and the West Indies, 1661–8* (London, 1880), nos. 683, 684 and 685.

[29] Megan Lindsay Cherry, 'The imperial and political motivations behind the English conquest of New Netherland', *Dutch Crossing*, 34 (2010), 77–94; L.H. Roper, 'The fall of New Netherland and seventeenth century Anglo-American imperial formation, 1654–1676', *New England Quarterly*, 87 (2014), 666–708.

[30] Quoted in Klooster, *Dutch moment*, p. 99; copies of the letters which passed between Nicolls and Stuyvesant, 29 August to 8 September 1664, *Calendar of state papers. Colonial, America and the West Indies, 1661–8*, no. 788.

English forces went on to take other parts of New Netherland, they displayed considerable brutality, as in Swandael, a Utopian community founded in 1663. In September 1664, Colonel Richard Carr ordered its total destruction and the settlers fled in every direction spreading reports that many were killed and others were sold as slaves in Virginia.[31] Dutch diplomatic protests at this unprovoked aggression fell on deaf ears. Charles insisted that the area had been English before Dutch encroachments and that, although individual Netherlanders had been permitted to settle there, the WIC had no authority.[32] The Dutch were reduced to silence but, at home, a group of seventy men with strong mercantile interests petitioned the States General to take steps to recover the territory. They argued that, in due course, New Netherland could replace the Baltic as a source of grain, timber, and naval stores.[33]

In parallel to measures taken to seal the walls of his own empire, Charles took steps to expand England's share of Spanish American markets at Dutch expense. Despite wide expectations to the contrary, the king made the decision to retain Jamaica, seized by Cromwell's men in 1655, largely because it provided a superb location for trade with the Spanish empire. The Dutch example at Curaçao, and local advice, indicated that the slave trade offered the best way to open Spanish doors to trade and the royal family took a leading role in strengthening England's position in the African trade. The king, with strong support from his family and court, chartered the Company of Royal Adventurers into Africa, with a monopoly of trade between Cape Blanco and the Cape of Good Hope, in December 1660 and, in the same month, provided the organization with five naval ships which departed for Africa under the command of Robert Holmes who had been involved in Prince Rupert's expedition to Africa in 1652. Holmes seized Dutch trading posts and ships and made it clear that the English were intent on challenging the Netherlanders' ambitions to monopolize the African trade. The Dutch complained about this aggression but, although Charles distanced himself from Holmes's exploits, the captain went unpunished on his return to England. The Dutch responded to the English insolencies in kind. They took strong action to obstruct English efforts to strengthen their presence, and the Royal Adventurers complained that they were able to make only limited headway.[34]

While the African Company faced difficulties, the attractions of the slave trade were rising, especially in Spanish markets. In March 1662, Thomas Modyford, a planter in Barbados, who became agent for the African

[31] Klooster, *Dutch moment*, p. 99.
[32] Ambassador Van Gogh to Secretary of the States General, 7 November 1664, *Calendar of state papers. Colonial, America and the West Indies, 1661–8*, no. 840.
[33] Klooster, *Dutch moment*, p. 100.
[34] George F. Zook, *The Company of Royal Adventurers trading into Africa* (Lancaster, Pa., 1919), pp. 8–18 and 28–41; K.G. Davies, *The Royal African Company* (London, 1957), 41–3.

Company, reported that Spanish merchants had been at the island in search of enslaved workers for Peruvian markets and had promised access to dizzying profits. He claimed that the king could expect to earn £100,000 a year (at a time when the customs revenue was valued at £315,000 a year).[35] Such figures were nonsensical. Spanish merchants did often pay more than twice as much as local planters but, even so, the trade would not have had a total turnover much in excess of £100,000 a year let alone such a share for the king. Nonetheless, in court circles, such stories fuelled appetites for expanding the slave trade and enabling the Company to line its pockets with Spanish silver.[36]

In summer 1662, the Spanish crown revived the slave *asiento* which had been terminated in 1640 after the outbreak of war with Portugal. Two Genoese merchants, Dominico Grillo and Ambrosio Lomelin, secured a contract to supply the Spanish colonies with 24,500 slaves over a period of seven years. The *asientistas* had no plans to engage directly in the African trade and obtained permission to purchase slaves in the Caribbean from merchants of any nation in amity with Spain. The Dutch were well-placed to take advantage of the new opportunity with their strong position on the Gold Coast, with six forts and nine lodges, and a well-established trading base at Curaçao, and the WIC sealed an agreement with the Genoese within ten weeks of the *asiento* being signed.[37] By contrast, the English found themselves hindered in striking a similar bargain both by their relative weakness on the Gold Coast, where they had only two forts and a handful of trading posts, and also by widely circulated reports that Jamaica continued to sponsor depredations on Spanish ships and territory, despite the peace of 1660. The news of Christopher Myngs's use of Jamaica as a base to raid, and plunder, Cuba in September 1662 excited outrage in Madrid. English claims that there was 'no peace beyond the line' had no purchase and the *asientistas* were informed that England could not be regarded as 'in amity' with Spain and was not eligible for a slave contract.[38]

Charles and James responded to their Company's lagging position by taking firm action. First, the African Company was reorganized with a new, extended, monopoly charter in January 1663 with a view to strengthening its funding and management to improve its competitiveness.[39] Secondly, colonial governors were commanded to create an environment which would

---

[35] Chandaman, *Public revenue*, p. 14.

[36] Extracts of letters from Thomas Modyford to his brother, 30 March, 30 April, 3 and 13 September 1662, BNA CO 1/17, nos. 7, 8, 9.

[37] The Dutch agreed to deliver between 1,400 and 2,000 *piezas* a year at a price of 107.5 pesos a head which was 25 per cent over the prevailing price in the Caribbean. Postma, *Dutch in the Atlantic slave trade*, p. 33.

[38] Nuala Zahedieh, '"A frugal, prudential and hopeful trade." Privateering in Jamaica, 1655–89', *Journal of Imperial and Commonwealth History*, 18 (1990), 145–68.

[39] Royal optimism was reflected in increased subscriptions made by the royal family. *Calendar of state papers. Colonial, America and the West Indies, 1661–8*, no. 508; Zook, *Royal Adventurers*, pp. 16–21.

encourage the Spanish trade. They were to waive the Navigation Acts in its favour, refrain from imposing any export taxes or other obstructions as planters had been prone to do in the past, and, above all, they were to give strict instructions to end all depredations on the Spaniards such as the attack on Cuba.[40] Thomas Modyford, the Company's agent in Barbados, and an experienced Spanish slave trader, was appointed to take over the government of Jamaica with orders to bring in the privateers and establish good relations with the island's Spanish neighbours.[41]

Residents of Jamaica, such as Thomas Lynch, warned that the strategy was wholly unrealistic, and had no chance of success, without strong naval support both to discipline the privateers, who would never voluntarily abandon their trade, and also to take active steps to deal with Dutch competition from 'the cursed barren island of Curacao'. Lynch also advised on the importance of taking strong steps to drive the Dutch out of Africa and cut off their slave supplies in the Caribbean.[42] Urgency increased as competition mounted in Africa and the Dutch aggressively defended their claim to have inherited Portugal's monopoly and the right to exclude other nations from the Gold Coast.[43] The Dutch drove the Swedes from Cape Coast Castle, denied access to foreign vessels, and seized cargoes despatched by the Royal Company. Such 'insolencies' aroused loud indignation in England and the king made an official protest in Amsterdam with a demand for reparations.[44] The Dutch government was unmoved and, in late 1663, Charles retaliated by sending Holmes on a third trip back to Africa with a fleet of eleven ships and instructions to protect the English Company's interests. In January and February 1664, Holmes captured two Dutch forts at Gorée and a trading post on the Grain Coast before sailing on to the Gold Coast, where in league with the Danish African Company, and various indigenous groups, he successfully captured Cape Coast Castle in May. The admiral then went on to seize two more Dutch lodges and one fort. Only Elmina proved to be impregnable.[45]

---

[40] King to Governor of Barbados, February 1663, BNA CO 1/17, no. 5; King to Governor of Jamaica, 13 March 1663, *ibid.*, no. 13. On planter obstructions in 1662, see: Thomas Modyford to brother, 3 March, 30 April, 3 and 13 September 1662, BNA CO 1/17, nos. 7, 8 and 9; King to Deputy Governor of Jamaica, April 1663, BNA CO 1/17, nos. 21, 22 and 23; Sir Henry Bennett to Lyttelton, 29 April 1663, *ibid.*, no. 26.

[41] *Calendar of state papers. Colonial, America and the West Indies, 1661–8*, nos. 407 and 408. 'Sir Thomas Modyford', *Oxford dictionary of national biography*.

[42] Thomas Lynch to Sir Henry Bennet, 25 May 1664, BNA CO 1/18, no. 68.

[43] Protest of John Valckenburgh against John Stoakes, 2 September 1663, BNA CO 1/17, no. 77; protest of John Valckenburgh against Francis Selwyn, 1 June 1663, *ibid.*, no. 74.

[44] Extracts of letters from Cormantin and other places in Africa, 1663, BNA CO 1/16, no. 111; order of King in Council, 26 August, *Calendar of state papers. Colonial, America and the West Indies, 1661–8*, no. 545.

[45] Zook, *Royal Adventurers*, pp. 42–8. Examination of Robert Holmes, 3 March 1665, *Calendar of state papers. Colonial, America and the West Indies, 1661–8*, no. 954;

In a dramatic fell swoop, the English became the dominant power on the Gold Coast and hopes of profit soared. In summer 1664, the African Company had eight ships with a lading valued at £50,000 ready to sail to the coast and a vision of being able to monopolize the slave trade in the Caribbean, including the *asiento*.[46] Despite continued qualms in Madrid about trading with the 'piratical' English, there is evidence that deals were struck under cover of Spanish merchants to supply slaves which were expected to yield above £86,000 a year for the Company.[47] However, the news of Holmes's exploits caused outrage in the Dutch Republic and delegates of Zeeland and Groningen insisted on a rapid response.[48] Great care was taken to ensure secrecy and, rather than organizing a conspicuous expedition in home ports, the States General assigned the operation to a squadron, fitted out to protect Dutch interests in the western Mediterranean, under the auspices of the Admiralties of Amsterdam, Maze and the Noorderkwartier. After receiving letters with secret instructions, the commander, Michiel de Ruyter, sailed from Cadiz on 5 October with a fleet of 12 sail and 2,272 men and set about reversing Holmes's actions in Africa.[49]

De Ruyter moved along the African coast, forced down the English flag in a string of places, recovered the island of Gorée (without firing a shot), and emptied the English lodge in Sierra Leone. At Tacovary, on the Gold Coast, he burned the village which housed 400–500 allies of the English, and then followed orders to seize further English factories and goods, which were

---

Resolution of Council of War on board HMS *Jersey*, 9 April 1665, BNA CO 1/18, no. 42.

[46] Petition of the Royal African Company to the King, 15 June 1664, *Calendar of state papers. Colonial, America and the West Indies, 1661–8*, no. 756.

[47] 'A brief narrative of the trade and present condition of the Royal African Company', January 1665, BNA CO 1/19, no. 5. In May 1667, John Allen reported to Lord Arlington that 'about three years past Domingo Grillo and Ambrosio Lamolini, residents in Madrid contracted with the Royal Company for blacks to be delivered at the plantations, Barbadoes or Jamaica, and Alex Bence and John Reid hired them two ships in England, at whose request the writer entered with them into the engagement; but in respect it was dangerous for the Grillos that the Court of Spain should know the ship's contracts were made with English, the freight was to be paid to a Spaniard, who instantly assigns it to George Wallis of Cadiz, for the use of the contractors in England. The Grillos are bound to pay the freight money every four months; the ships are in their service full two and a half years, and nothing paid since their departure from Cadiz, though there is much due from them; they pretend it is paid in the Indies, but has sent them several late letters from their own agents in Barbadoes and Jamaica that they have paid nothing.' *Calendar of state papers. Colonial, America and the West Indies, 1661–8*, no. 1481.

[48] Roger Downing and Gijs Rommelse, *A fearful gentleman. Sir George Downing in The Hague, 1658–1672* (Hilversum, 2011), p. 131.

[49] Klooster, *Dutch moment*, pp. 102–3.

delivered to the WIC.[50] By Christmas, only Cape Coast Castle remained in English hands, and the Royal Company had lost any hope of getting a return on its recent investment. On 27 February 1665, after beating the English 'to dirt', the admiral set sail for America to take revenge for English aggression in New Netherland.[51] During his Atlantic crossing, England and the Dutch Republic, at last, declared formal war and Parliament was sufficiently outraged by Dutch 'insolencies' to vote an unprecedented grant of £2,477,500, followed by another £1,250,000, in support.[52]

A privateering war

De Ruyter's expedition in American waters proved less spectacular than his exploits in Africa. He attacked Barbados in April, with a fleet of fourteen ships, and inflicted major losses on the thirty ships in Carlisle Bay. However, the Dutch paid a high price, with heavy damage, and many casualties, and strong winds forced a retreat at the end of the day.[53] De Ruyter turned north, and seized another seventeen English ships in the Leewards, before leaving the Caribbean on 17 May. Short of food, the fleet bypassed New Netherland, and sailed for Newfoundland where the force captured a further seven vessels and loaded provisions for the return journey to reach its home port, Delfzijl, on 6 August 1665. De Ruyter was given a hero's welcome. According to George Downing, his 'arrival has huffed them up beyond the skies' and, as reward, the States General made him Commander-in-Chief of the Navy.[54] Summoned to the island of Texel to take charge of another fleet, he made his way by barge through the provinces of Groningen and Friesland accompanied by loud cheering along his route.

Although African and American issues were central causes of the war, the English concentrated their naval resources in European waters. After providing fleets for Holmes and Nicolls in early 1664, the Admiralty claimed that it could not spare ships for service in the Americas and hoped to rely on local forces, above all the large body of privateers based at Jamaica.[55]

[50] 'Particulars of our voyage (in Capt. Reynolds' ship) on the coast of Africa', April 1665, BNA CO 1/19, no. 55; Zook, *Royal Adventurers,* pp. 60–2.
[51] Samuel Pepys quoted in Zook, *Royal Adventurers,* p. 61.
[52] L.H. Roper, *Advancing empire. English interests and overseas expansion, 1613–1688* (Cambridge, 2017), pp. 201–3.
[53] 'A true relation of the fight at Barbadoes between the English and Dutch, under De Ruyter, on April 20th', BNA CO 1/19, no. 50; Wim Klooster, 'De Ruyter's attack on Barbados. The Dutch perspective', *Journal of the Barbados Museum and Historical Society,* 60 (2014), 45–53.
[54] Goslinga, *The Dutch in the Caribbean,* pp. 385–8. George Downing to the Earl of Arlington, 14 August 1665, quoted in Klooster, *Dutch moment,* p. 103.
[55] Arlington to Willoughby, 16 May 1665, BNA CO 1/19, no. 57.

Despite Modyford's initial instructions to promote peace with Spain, and end the island's support of plunder, the governor quickly decided that, as Lynch and other experienced settlers had warned, it would be almost impossible to implement the policy without strong naval support and he wanted to avoid alienating the unruly privateers.[56] In June 1664, within three weeks of arrival at the island, Modyford sought permission to 'do by degrees and moderation what he had resolved to execute suddenly and severely'.[57] In November, the governor secured limited approval when the home authorities ordered that, while he should remain resolute in forbidding any action against the Spaniards, he should handle the privateers gently so that they could be put to the state's service in clearing the Dutch from the West Indies and engrossing the Spanish trade at low cost.[58] Secretary Bennet agreed that this was the 'best design in those parts'.[59]

By February 1665, Modyford reported that the plan was working: the privateers were coming in to Jamaica, taking commissions against the Dutch, and plotting to take Curaçao.[60] In April, the deputy-governor, Lieutenant Colonel Edward Morgan (father-in-law of the famous Henry), set out with a fleet of 10 ships with 650 men. They were 'chiefly reformed privateers, scarce a planter among them, being resolute fellows and well armed with fusees and pistols ... at the old rate of no purchase no pay, and it will cost the king nothing considerable, (save) some powder and mortar pieces'.[61] The design was to fall upon the Dutch fleet trading at St Christopher, then capture St Eustatius, Saba, and Curaçao. 'God sending good success, the Dutch will have no considerable place left them in the West Indies and the late kindness and moderation toward these privateers [in Jamaica] will be thought well bestowed.'[62]

At first, the expedition went according to plan. Arriving in the Leewards shortly after De Ruyter's departure, 326 men took St Eustatius on 23 July and 69 men went on to reduce Saba to obedience. Unfortunately, Edward Morgan, a 'corpulent man', displayed such vigour in the attack on St Eustatius that he 'surfeited and suddenly died to almost the loss of the whole design'.

---

[56] King to Sir Thomas Modyford, 15 June 1664, BNA CO 1/18, no. 73; Thomas Lynch to Henry Bennet, 25 May 1664, *ibid.*, no. 68.

[57] Sir Thomas Modyford to Sir Henry Bennet, 30 June 1664, *ibid.*, no. 83.

[58] Proposition of Mr Kendall concerning calling in the privateers of Jamaica, November 1664, *ibid.*, no. 137; Report of the Committee of Affairs for Jamaica, 7 November 1664, *ibid.*, no. 133; Sir Thomas Modyford to the Privy Council, 21 August 1666, BNA CO/20, no. 136.

[59] 'Sir Thomas Modyford's proposition of a design for rooting the Dutch out of the West Indies and increasing the settlements of Jamaica', February 1665, BNA CO 1/19, no. 29

[60] Sir Thomas Modyford to Lord Arlington, 20 February 1665, *ibid.*, no. 27.

[61] Sir Thomas Modyford to Lord Arlington, 20 April 1665, *ibid.*, no. 69.

[62] *Ibid.*

Theodore Cary, who took over Morgan's role, was unable to command the same discipline and, after squabbling over the division of the booty, the expedition fell apart. Abandoning the original plan to attack Curaçao, Cary returned to Jamaica with coppers, stills, and some 500 slaves and could, at least, claim to have delivered a valuable economic boost to the infant colony.[63] A small garrison remained behind to secure Saba and Eustatia, while two of the privateers, Searle and Stedman, led eighty men south to capture Tobago in January 1666, destroying all eighteen sugar plantations, just before the arrival of a force from Barbados commanded by Governor Willoughby of Barbados who went on to capture the Dutch colonies of Pomeroon and Essequibo in Guiana.[64]

This small success with the Jamaican privateers buoyed English faith in their value. The king urged Modyford to persevere with the plans to capture Curaçao and so 'root the Dutch out of all places in the West Indies'.[65] Modyford did promote a new expedition against Curaçao under Mansfield, a seasoned privateer, who gathered a strong fleet and set sail from the South Cays of Cuba in January 1666.[66] However, the policy of reliance on this ill-disciplined force unravelled at speed. France's entry into the war on the side of the Dutch in the same month made it increasingly difficult to manage the independent-spirited privateers. Most had little allegiance to any one nation and, if thwarted, they had few qualms about moving to join the enemy. At nearby Tortuga, the French not only licensed plunder of Jamaica, and its trade, but also allowed ships to operate against Spain under cover of Portuguese commissions. In February, the Council of Jamaica resolved that, in view of this danger, it was necessary for the island to issue commissions against the Spaniards as this was the only way to keep the privateers on side.[67]

Meanwhile, Mansfield was losing men to Tortuga. The governor despatched William Beeston to rally the troops and confirm them in their loyalty but, although he was well received, by June, Modyford reported that 'the Curacao fleet has done nothing and are dispersed on several designs of their own heads, their own disorders not being subject to any commands being the cause given'. The governor admitted that the private soldiers aboard the *Admiral* had little interest in targeting Curaçao as 'there was more profit with less hazard to be gotten against the Spaniard'. In June, he reported that two

[63] Sir Thomas Modyford to Lord Arlington, 16 November 1665, *ibid.*, no. 127; Col. Theodore Cary to Duke of Albemarle, 23 August 1665, *ibid.*, no. 97.
[64] Lord Willoughby to Lord Arlington, 29 January 1666, BNA CO 1/20, no. 6; John Reid to Lord Arlington, January 1666, *ibid.*, no. 7.
[65] King to Sir Thomas Modyford, 16 November 1665, BNA CO 1/19, no. 126.
[66] Sir Thomas Modyford to Lord Arlington, 8 March 1666, BNA CO 1/20, no. 26.
[67] Minutes of the Council of Jamaica, 22 February 1666, *Calendar of state papers. Colonial, America and the West Indies, 1661–8*, no. 1138.

of the Curaçao fleet had deserted to Tortuga while four others (including Mansfield) had attacked and seized Santa Catalina, or Providence, which had been in English hands earlier in the century. Modyford did not reprimand Mansfield fearing it might cause the privateers to desert 'that allegiance which they make great profession of now'. Furthermore, he advised that Providence should be retained as it was esteemed for its proximity to the Spanish Main, and he pressed hard in support of further concessions to the privateers.[68] As hopes of making a profit from peaceful trade with the Spanish colonists had ebbed since De Ruyter's exploits in Africa, Charles had lost faith in the value of a conciliatory policy towards Spain. Although the king did not formally endorse Mansfield's actions, he gave tacit approval by appointing Modyford's brother James as lieutenant-governor to take command of Providence.[69] However, any feeling of triumph was short-lived. By the time Sir James arrived in Jamaica, Providence had been recaptured by Spain and hopes that the privateers would provide disciplined support to a weak, and distant, authority were proved to be futile.[70]

With France's entry into the war, and their despatch of a strong fleet to America, the tide had turned firmly against the English. In contrast to what Thornton described as a 'mannered performance' in Europe, the French fought a ferocious campaign in the West Indies in what can be seen as the opening stage of the long struggle with England for supremacy in the Atlantic.[71] The first target was St Christopher, which obtained valuable help from the handful of privateers left by the English at St Eustatius but, nonetheless, fell to the French in April.[72] In August, Willoughby, of Barbados, assembled a fleet of six ships to retake St Christopher but it was scattered in a hurricane and the governor was lost.[73] In November, the French joined with a small Dutch force in recapturing St Eustatius, then took Antigua in December, and Montserrat in early 1667.

Alongside French aggression, the Dutch also raised their home contribution to the American war theatre and, in December 1666, the province of Zeeland financed, and organized, a fleet of seven ships with 750 sailors and 250 soldiers. The commander, Abraham Crijnssen, was given bold instructions to capture English merchantmen at the Cape Verde islands; conquer

[68] Sir Thomas Modyford to Duke of Albemarle, 8 June 1666, BNA CO 1/20, no. 24; Sir Thomas Modyford to Lord Arlington, 16 June 1666, *ibid.*, no. 100.

[69] Commission appointing Sir James Modyford Lieutenant Governor of the island of Providence, 10 November 1666, *ibid.*, no. 166.

[70] Sir Thomas Modyford to Duke of Albemarle, 14 January 1667, BNA CO 1/21, no. 5.

[71] Thornton, *West India policy*, p. 94. According to Wilson, the Dutch received virtually no help from the French in Europe. Wilson, *Profit and power*, p. 138.

[72] 'Relation of the loss of St Christopher', April 1666, BNA CO 1/20, no. 51.

[73] Capt. W. Bridall to his father, 15 August 1666, *ibid.*, no. 130; D. Grosse to Williamson, 27 November 1666, *Calendar of state papers. Colonial, America and the West Indies, 1661–8*, no. 1330

Surinam; recapture Essequibo, Pomeroon, and Tobago; ravage other English possessions in the West Indies; attack English colonies in North America; and cripple the fisheries in Newfoundland.[74] The fleet passed by the Cape Verde islands but arrived in Surinam in February 1667 where there was an immediate surrender (the colony was taken back by the English in October but after the Peace of Breda it was preserved in Dutch hands).[75] The Dutch also retook Pomeroon, Essequibo, and Tobago and then engaged with an English fleet at Nevis. The final act was to capture an English merchant fleet off the coast of Virginia, which yielded 345,991 guilders on sale of the ships and booty back in Zeeland.[76] Dutch America had came 'close to extinction' in late 1665 but survived.[77]

Late in 1666, as the futility of reliance on the privateers had been revealed, the English did, at last, allocate state resources to stage a fight-back. The Duke of York set out a squadron for the West Indies which arrived at Barbados in February 1667. It went on to retake Antigua and Montserrat as well as successfully defeating a Franco-Dutch assault on Nevis in May.[78] Sir John Harman followed with a fleet in June 1667 which did considerable damage to twenty-three French ships at Martinique although he failed to recover St Christopher, but, by this time, none of the belligerents had the stomach for further war and peace negotiations were underway in Europe.[79] The Peace of Breda ended the Second Anglo-Dutch War on 21 July 1667 and, although the Treaty was agreed in haste, it proved lasting.

Resolution

The Treaty provided that each country should remain in possession of the territories held on 10 May. This left the situation on the African coast as it was after De Ruyter's departure and the English failed to recover Fort Cormantine, and although the English retained Cape Coast Castle, captured by Holmes, the Dutch remained in control of the slave trade and Spanish markets.[80] In the Leewards, after massive damage to property and relocation

[74] Klooster, *Dutch moment*, p. 106.
[75] 'Narrative of the taking of the English colony of Surinam by the Zeeland fleet, together with the articles of surrender', 24 February 1667, BNA CO 1/21, no. 21.
[76] Klooster, *Dutch moment*, pp. 105–6
[77] *Ibid.*, p. 4.
[78] William Lord Willoughby to Lord Arlington, 25 May 1667, BNA CO 1/21, no. 50.
[79] Sir John Harman to William Lord Willoughby, 30 June 1667, *ibid.*, no. 70.
[80] Grillo and Lomelin introduced 21,232 slaves into Spanish America between 1662 and 1673 of which 93 per cent were furnished by the Dutch. Alejandro Garcia-Monton, 'The rise of Portobelo and the transformation of the Spanish American slave trade, 1640s–1730s. Transimperial connections and intra-American shipping', *Hispanic American Historical Review*, 99 (2019), 399–429.

of populations, the islands returned to their pre-war owners. However, the Dutch retained Surinam (despite a successful English assault in October) in what is often seen as a symptom of a lingering ambition for a different sort of empire, supported by a second Brazil, but which was also well located to prey on rival trade with the Spanish Main and defend Curaçao's competitive position.[81] Meanwhile, the English also secured a new strategic advantage in retaining New Netherland, which sealed a gaping hole on the eastern seaboard of North America and took them closer to controlling the whole length of the coast. The arrangements remained intact after the Third Anglo-Dutch War and confirmed each country on its divergent Atlantic path.

After 1674, the Netherlanders entered a new chapter in their colonial history under the auspices of a new slimmer WIC. The English did not succeed in clearing the Dutch from the African coast, or American waters, and the Netherlanders did not disappear from the Atlantic. With strategic trading bases at Elmina, Curaçao, St Eustatius, and resident communities in New York, the Dutch remained universal middlemen. As free-riders, they played an especially important part in the large illegal market which linked competing empires, defying mercantilist boundaries imposed by the British, French, and Spanish authorities and maintaining a major role in the *asiento* until 1701.[82] Dutch Atlantic trade went far beyond the legal cargoes recorded in the customs ledgers and, according to recent estimates, matched the value of British and French Atlantic trade in per capita terms until the final decades of the eighteenth century.[83]

The English, by contrast, moved along a trajectory which eventually took them beyond their early parasitic activities to a grand territorial empire, acquired by settlement, rather than conquest. The 'brash self-confidence' noted by Thornton as characterizing the later Stuarts proved ill-founded.[84] After vast expense of men and money, the Second Anglo-Dutch War highlighted the difficulties, and expense, of organizing military action across oceans, and reliance on local resources such as colonial militias, or Jamaica's privateers, proved highly unsatisfactory. The English did not have the economic, or organizational, resources to eliminate rivals and impose monopolies on the African coast, or in Spanish markets, and continued to operate in competitive conditions. However, England's acquisition of New Netherland did encourage further territorial expansion in the Carolinas, and Pennsylvania,

---

[81] In June 1667, there was a report that a ship of the Guinea Company, Captain Yard, laden with slaves was taken by a Dutch ship out of Surinam which 'by its situation is like much to gall the Guinea trade'. TNA CO1/21, no. 66.
[82] Postma, *Dutch in the Atlantic slave trade*, pp. 36–55.
[83] Wim Klooster and Gert Oostindie, *Realm between empires. The second Dutch Atlantic 1680–1815* (Ithaca, NY, 2018); Gert Oostindie and Jessica Roitman, 'Repositioning the Dutch in the Atlantic, 1680–1800', *Itinerario*, 36 (2012), 129–60; idem (eds), *Dutch Atlantic connections, 1680–1800* (Leiden, 2014).
[84] Thornton, *West India policy*, p. 124.

to create a continuous line of settlement from Maine down the east coast of North America and a growing belief that the political classes stood to gain from building their own empire and protecting it behind their own mercantilist walls. Similar ambitions were forming across the Channel and, as presaged by the war in the Caribbean in the 1660s, the Dutch threat was receding while England was moving towards a second Hundred Years War with France.

9

Competing claims: international law, diplomacy and Anglo-Dutch rivalry in seventeenth-century North America

*Jaap Jacobs**

Like other neighbouring countries, England and the Netherlands produced a fair amount of vehement propaganda against each other. The obvious example for their confrontations in seventeenth-century North America comes in the shape of a 1653 pamphlet: *The Second Part of the Tragedy of Amboyna or, a True Relation of a Most Bloody, Treacherous and Cruel Design of the Dutch in America, for the Total Ruining and Murthering of the English Colonies in New England.* Based on events that took place thirty years earlier in Asia, transplanted to North America, and printed in London, it is a truly global example of vituperation. It asserts that 'Amboyna's treacherous Cruelty' has moved from the 'East to the West Indiaes ... running in its proper channel of Dutch blood'. The pamphlet relates how in March 1653, the Dutch authorities in New Amsterdam, the capital of the Dutch colony of New Netherland, had bribed four Native American sachems to attack the English colonists on a Sunday, when all families attended church. In order to execute 'this Diabolical Plot', the Natives had been furnished with arms and munitions, which arrived on a ship sent for that purpose from Holland, 'the Fountain of Treacheries'. However, the omnipotent God had, in his infinite goodness, notified the English through a Native messenger and they were now preparing to withstand the onslaught. The obvious intention of *The Second Part of the Tragedy of Amboyna*, published during the Second Anglo-Dutch War, was to

* This essay was in earlier incarnations presented at 'The Dutch in the Medway, 1667: Anglo-Dutch rivalry in its global context', University of Kent, Royal Dockyard Church, Historic Dockyard Chatham, 30 June and 1 July 2017, and at 'Terres lointaines: companies, commerce, colonies (17th–18th centuries)', Université de Poitiers (France), 10–12 October 2018. The author wishes to thank Dr Martine van Ittersum (University of Dundee) and Dr L.H. Roper (State University of New York – New Paltz) for their support and advice.

gain authorization and military support from the English government for an all-out attack on New Netherland.[1]

In its venomous rhetoric, *The Second Part of the Tragedy of Amboyna* constitutes the pinnacle of acrimony in Anglo-Dutch rivalry in North America. Many of the other exchanges were of a more subdued if not less biased nature. Over the course of more than sixty years, the Dutch and English employed five legal principles to corroborate their competing claims: first discovery, governmental charters, legitimate purchase from rightful owners, actual occupation, and conquest in a just war.[2] Before exploring the use of these legal principles in the context of Anglo-Dutch rivalry in North America, two historiographical points need to be made. First, Adam Clulow, building upon the work of Lauren Benton, has pointed out that in early modern Asia, claims-making was a relational process. The tendency was 'to amass as many separate justifications as possible in order to counter potential rivals'.[3] Indeed, at first glance, there does not appear to be an established international consensus as to the priority amongst these legal principles. Within the context of seventeenth-century Anglo-Dutch rivalry in North America too, the choice of legal principles to be employed depended on what was considered most opportune at that specific moment and what would provide the readiest pretext. The main difference between the Atlantic and Asian theatres in this respect was a greater variety of diplomatic, political, and hierarchical contexts. It mattered on which side of the Atlantic the discussions between the English and Dutch took place, what the immediate issue at stake was, and whether the two countries happened to be at war at the time. This difference may have been the result of the greater distance of the Asian theatre from Europe, leading to a less rigid hierarchy and more opportunities for local Company officials to act semi-independently. In addition, over the course of the seventeenth century, the repertoire of legal arguments employed in the Atlantic theatre slowly contracted, leaving only two of the initial five principles intact. Whether this trajectory was mirrored in the Asian theatre remains to be seen.

---

[1] *The Second Part of the Tragedy of Amboyna or, a True Relation of a Most Bloody, Treacherous and Cruel Design of the Dutch in America, for the Total Ruining and Murthering of the English Colonies in New England* (London, 1653). For the original Amboyna incident, see W.Ph. Coolhaas, 'Notes and comments on the so-called Amboyna Massacre', in *Dutch authors on Asian history*, eds M.A.P. Meilink-Roelofsz, M.E. van Opstall and G.J. Schutte (Dordrecht, 1988), pp. 198–240; Karen Chancey, 'The Amboyna Massacre in English politics, 1624–1632', *Albion*, 30 (1998), 583–98; Adam Clulow, 'Unjust, cruel and barbarous proceedings. Japanese mercenaries and the Amboyna Incident of 1624', *Itinerario*, 31:1 (2007), 15–34.
[2] James Muldoon, 'Discovery, grant, charter, conquest, or purchase. John Adams on the legal basis for English possession of North America', in *The many legalities of early America*, eds Christopher L. Tomlins and Bruce H. Mann (Chapel Hill, 2001), pp. 31–9.
[3] Adam Clulow, 'The art of claiming. Possession and resistance in early modern Asia', *American Historical Review*, 121 (2016), 17–38.

The second historiographical point concerns the role some of the legal principles outlined above played in the corroboration of European claims on Native lands in the Atlantic theatre, particularly in North America, where it eventually led to large-scale appropriations and the rise of settler colonialism in the nineteenth century. Yet the process of acquisition of land for the purpose of actual settlement should be distinguished from that of acquisition for the purpose of thwarting other European nations. Mark Meuwese has argued that the cooperation of indigenous peoples was essential for the establishment of the Dutch Atlantic World. In a similar vein, Saliha Belmessous maintains that treaties operated as instruments of empire, enabling colonizers to establish a dominant position. Both Meuwese and Belmessous have however analysed treaties and other arguments between indigenous peoples and European colonizers in an exclusively bipolar model. This essay proposes a corrective to the model of Meuwese and Belmessous by adding the exigencies of inter-European rivalry to the mix of formative factors that shaped form and content of treaties and agreements.[4]

Legal principles

First then, the principle of first discovery. As Adriaen van der Donck put it in the 1650s:

> This region was for the first time found and discovered in the year of our Lord Jesus Christ 1609, when the ship *Halve Maen* was dispatched at the expense of the chartered East India Company to seek a westerly passage to the Kingdom of China. The captain and merchant of this ship was one Henry Hudson, who, although English by birth, had long been associated with the Dutch and was now in the service of the East India Company earning monthly wages.[5]

Van der Donck's emphasis on Hudson's employ was aimed to neuter the English stress on Hudson's country of birth and points to a vexing

---

[4] Mark Meuwese, *Brothers in arms, partners in trade. Dutch-indigenous alliances in the Atlantic world, 1595–1674* (Leiden, 2012); Saliha Belmessous, *Native claims. Indigenous law against empire, 1500–1920* (New York, 2012); idem (ed.), *Empire by treaty. Negotiating European expansion, 1600–1900* (New York, 2014).

[5] 'Dit lantschap is eerstmael gevonden en ontdeckt in den jare onses heeren Jesu Christi 1609, als wanneer ten koste van de Geoctroyeerde Oost-Indische Compagnie afgevaerdight is het schip de Halve Maen, om bij westen eenen doorgangh naer het Coningrijck van China te soecken; op dit schip was schipper en coopman eenen Hendrick Hudson, wel een Engelsman geboortig, maer lang onder de Nederlanders verkeert hebbende, ende nu in dienst en maentgelt van de Oost-Indische Compagnie.' Adriaen van der Donck, *Beschryvinge van Nieuw-Nederlant (gelijck het tegenwoordigh in staet is)* (Aemsteldam, 1655, 2nd edn 1656), pp. 1–2; Adriaen van der Donck, *A description of New Netherland*. ed. Ch.T. Gehring and W.A. Starna, trans. D.W. Goedhuys (Lincoln, 2008), pp. 1–2.

conundrum: whose discovery was it anyway? This question surfaced several times in Anglo-Dutch diplomatic exchanges in the seventeenth century, but was never definitively settled. By the nineteenth century, the issue had taken on a different role. When tracking the so-called 'doctrine of discovery' in 1823, the United States Supreme Court referred to Hudson's voyage and acknowledged the difference between Dutch and English opinions as to who could pursue a claim based on this legal principle. Yet, in the opinion of the Supreme Court, this difference did not diminish 'the universal recognition' of European claims based on first discovery, thus brushing aside any Native claims.[6]

The second legal principle employed in Anglo-Dutch exchanges centred on governmental charters. English colonists usually referred to the charter of James I of 1606 to the Virginia Company and the London Company. This allowed them to set up colonies in

> that part of America, commonly called Virginia, and other parts and territories in America, either appertaining unto us, or which are not now actually possessed by any christian prince or people, situate, lying, and being all along the sea coasts, between four and thirty degrees of northerly latitude from the equinoctial Line, and five and forty degrees of the same latitude.

The charter included the desire to spread the Christian religion among 'such people, as yet live in darkness and miserable ignorance of the true knowledge and worship of God', in the expectation of future 'civilization'. The charter did not, however, include an explicit reference to Native sovereignty, nor did it assign any land to the two companies, who only received authority to colonize. Later charters rectified this omission, but with the caveat that they covered only those areas 'which wee by oure lettres patents maie or cann graunte'. This was a reference to international rivalry, as is evident from the mentioned latitudes. The specification avoided conflict with the Spanish presence in Florida and the French colonization in Canada. However, as the 1606 charter did not allow the two English companies to begin settlements within a hundred miles, the area in between, i.e. between the 38th and 41st parallels, unintentionally remained open to colonists from other countries. As they were not subjects of the English king, the stipulation in the English

---

[6] Blake A. Watson, 'John Marshall and Indian land rights. A historical rejoinder to the claim of "universal recognition" of the doctrine of discovery', *Seton Hall Law Review*, 36 (2006), 481–549; Johnson & Graham's Lessee v. McIntosh, 21 U.S. 543 (1823), supreme.justia.com/cases/federal/us/21/543/ (accessed 22 October 2018). For a general perspective, not confined to seventeenth-century North America, see: Mamadou Hébié, 'The acquisition of derivative titles of territorial sovereignty in the law and practice of European colonial expansion', in *Research handbook on territorial disputes in international law*, eds Marcel G. Kohen and Mamadou Hébié (s.l., 2018), pp. 87–144.

charter that 'no other of our subjects shall be permitted' to found colonies technically did not prohibit other Europeans from settling within the area specified in the charters. In practice, however, such nuances did little to stop English claims based on royal charters acquiring an assumed exclusivity well beyond its original phrasing. Nor did it prevent the Swedes and Dutch establishing footholds.[7]

The Dutch legitimated their presence in North America with reference to governmental charters too. After Hudson's 1609 voyage, several merchant companies made seasonal trading voyages. Increased competition led to the promulgation of a first ordinance by the Dutch States General, which awarded a four-year monopoly on trade and shipping between the 40th and 45th parallels to the New Netherland Company. The States General did not grant exclusive rights to territories or colonization, but only offered the New Netherland Company legal protection against Dutch competitors. A second charter issued by the States General far exceeded the first in scope, duration, and importance. The end of the Twelve Years' Truce in 1621 sparked the creation of the Dutch West India Company, which was granted extensive powers by the States General. This included a monopoly on shipping and trade, similar to that of the New Netherland Company, but established an extended reach through the inclusion of the right to make treaties with indigenous peoples, the right to exercise jurisdiction over conquered territories (subject to the overlordship of the States General), and the right to appoint governors. The 1621 charter did not explicitly dispossess Native Americans, who were naively regarded by the Dutch as potential allies against Spain, nor did it erect formal obstacles against shipping and trade by other Europeans, although, like the English charters, it did establish an informal claim against them.[8]

---

[7] William Waller Hening (ed.), *The Statutes at large. Being a collection of all the laws of Virginia, from the first session of the legislature in the year 1619* (New York, 1823), vol. 1, pp. 57–66. See also John Thomas Juricek, 'English claims in North America to 1660. A study in legal and constitutional history' (unpublished PhD thesis, University of Chicago, 1970), pp. 463–577 (quotation p. 477); Lauren Benton and Benjamin Straumann, 'Acquiring empire by law. From Roman doctrine to early modern European practice', *Law and History Review*, 28 (2010), 1–38; Lauren Benton, *Law and colonial cultures. Legal regimes in world history* (New York, 2002); idem, *A search for sovereignty. Law and geography in European empires, 1400–1900* (New York, 2010); Anthony Pagden, *Lords of all the world. Ideologies of empire in Spain, Britain, and France, 1492–1830* (New Haven, 1998); idem, *European encounters with the New World. From Renaissance to Romanticism* (New Haven and London, 1993, 2nd edn 1994).

[8] Jaap Jacobs, *The colony of New Netherland. A Dutch settlement in seventeenth century America* (Ithaca, 2009), pp. 20–9; idem, 'Early Dutch explorations in North America', *Journal of Early American History*, 3 (2013), 59–81; Charles T. Gehring, 'New Netherland. The formative years, 1609–1632', in *Four centuries of Dutch-American relations*, supervisory eds Cornelis A. van Minnen, Hans Krabbendam and Giles Scott-Smith (Amsterdam, 2009), pp. 74–84; Benjamin Schmidt, *Innocence abroad. The Dutch imagination and the new world, 1570–1670* (Cambridge, 2001).

In issuing such charters, England and the Dutch Republic eschewed making explicit claims to sovereignty similar to those made in the papal bull *Inter Caetera* of 1493 and the subsequent Treaty of Tordesillas. Instead, territorial sovereignty could be acquired through legitimate purchase from rightful owners, the third legal principle to be discussed here. Land purchases operated in two ways. First, they created an understanding between the European and indigenous groups involved in the transaction. Often, this understanding was incomplete, as the Native perspective on ownership of land and other natural resources differed from that of the Europeans. Native groups usually considered these transactions not in terms of a transfer of ownership or sovereignty in European terms but as temporary and non-exclusive agreements relating to usufruct, becoming void when land was abandoned. In the case of Staten Island, the Dutch had to repurchase the island twice after withdrawing its settlers from it. Second, the written record of such land transactions was used as evidence in inter-European diplomatic exchanges. European authorities therefore instructed their colonial officers to take good care in producing documents that adhered to European practices, so as to avoid them being declared invalid. When drafting 'Indian deeds', colonial officials ensured that references to ownership of the local Indian community and the sachems acting on their behalf were included. The extent to which such legalese was conveyed to negotiating partners and, if so, whether the legal framework of which the stipulations were part was fully understood, can be doubted.[9]

Buying indigenous land was a first step, but in order to ensure perfection of a claim, actual occupation, the fourth legal principle to be used in Anglo-Dutch rivalry, was required. Actual occupation marked the transition from a theoretical claim, based on documents, to physical ownership. The main means of actual occupation were cultivating the land, i.e. clearing the ground and making it suitable for agriculture, and erecting a defensive structure, such as a blockhouse or a fort. Physical ownership served different purposes. First, it provided a clear marker of ownership for both indigenous peoples and European competitors. Second, land use served as a deterrent against hostile encroachments which would quickly be spotted if colonists working

---

[9] See for instance: New York State Archives [hereafter NYSA], New Netherland Council Dutch colonial patents and deeds, vol. GG (A1880-78_VGG), docs. 1–20, digitally available through digitalcollections.archives.nysed.gov/, like all references in this essay to NYSA documents; Charles T. Gehring, *Land papers. Volumes GG, HH & II: New York historical manuscripts: Dutch* (Baltimore, 1980), pp. 1–7; William A. Starna, *From homeland to new land. A history of the Mahican Indians, 1600–1830* (Lincoln, 2013), pp. 106–18; Meuwese, *Brothers in arms, partners in trade*, pp. 228–85; Martine van Ittersum, 'Empire by treaty? The role of written documents in European overseas expansion, 1500–1800', in *The Dutch and English East India Companies. Diplomacy, trade and violence in early modern Asia*, eds Adam Clulow and Tristan Mostert (Amsterdam, 2018), pp. 153–77.

the land were present. And third, a fort, with all its connotations within European culture, served not just as a symbol of authority, but also as a means of defence.[10]

Yet even a fort would not automatically deter an enemy when a state of war existed. The fifth legal principle used to corroborate claims in Anglo-Dutch rivalry in North America was conquest in a just war, a concept with a long and extensive history in the European tradition. The three Anglo-Dutch wars of the second half of the seventeenth century may have originated in Europe, but they exerted an obvious influence on affairs in North America, as will be highlighted below. Discussions in which the argument of just war was employed also occurred in the colonies. The disagreement between Massachusetts and the other New England colonies in 1652–54 has already been alluded to. The argument was also used to corroborate conquest of indigenous land. For instance, in contemplating retaliation for the Native American attack on colonists in and around New Amsterdam of September 1655, Director General and Council included in their deliberations the question of whether it constituted a sufficient cause for a just war.[11]

The remainder of this essay will analyse the use of the five legal principles outlined above over the course of the seventeenth century, set within their diplomatic, political, and hierarchical context. It is important to keep in mind that, as a battleground between England and the Dutch Republic, North America was relatively unimportant. The focus of the English and Dutch authorities at the highest level was firmly fixed on the European theatre and colonial affairs were at best a sideshow, albeit of significant interest to particular stakeholders. Only by the end of the seventeenth century did this situation begin to change, leading to an increased importance of the colonies in domestic political considerations. Within the seventeenth-century Dutch Atlantic World, New Netherland and its capital New Amsterdam played second fiddle to New Holland, the Dutch conquest in Portuguese Brazil, which remained the crown jewel during the first half of the century. The demise and fall of Dutch Brazil coincided with the end of the Eighty Years' War, after which Dutch rivalry with the Iberian powers receded and competition with England came to the fore. From the English perspective, the New England colonies were far less important than the Caribbean islands, which drew many more colonists to them. For England too, economic and political

---

[10] For an overview of forts in New Netherland, see Jaap Jacobs, *Dutch colonial fortifications in North America 1614–1676* (e-Book, Amsterdam, 2015), digitally available through www.newhollandfoundation.nl/wp-content/uploads/2015/11/PDF-Dutch-Colonial-Fortifications-in-North-America.pdf; and Paul Huey, 'Dutch colonial forts in New Netherland', in *First forts. Essays on the archaeology of proto-colonial fortifications*, ed. Eric Klingelhofer (Leiden and Boston, 2010), pp. 141–68.

[11] NYSA, New Netherland Council Dutch colonial council minutes, vol. 6 (A1809-78_V06), pp. 149–50; Charles T. Gehring (ed. and trans.), *Council minutes 1655–1656* (New Netherland document series, vol. 6) (Syracuse, 1995), pp. 130–2.

considerations within the European theatre remained paramount. Still, the Dutch and English colonies were essential to a number of stakeholders. Foremost of these were the colonists themselves. Their livelihood depended to a large extent on obtaining arable land and participating in the rich fur trade. On both counts, New Netherland was much better situated than the New England colonies. In several cases, colonization efforts were organized and funded by wealthy proprietors in Europe, such as members of the nobility or, in New Netherland, so-called patroons. A third group of stakeholders consisted of the merchants and ship captains conducting the transatlantic shipping and trade. The interests of these groups of stakeholders played a larger role than national *raison d'état* as the driving force behind colonization. Their political influence, or lack thereof, was an important element in the mix that shaped Anglo-Dutch rivalry.[12]

First claims

Although news of Henry Hudson's 1609 voyage quickly reached Europe, the discoverer never returned to the Dutch Republic to report in person. He may have been hesitant to do so as his attempt to discover the Northwest Passage was in direct contravention of his instruction, which had ordered him to explore the Northeast Passage instead. When Hudson stopped off at Dartmouth, the English authorities arrested his ship and disallowed him to continue his service to the Dutch East India Company. Although details are unavailable, it is generally presumed that his transgression of the 1606 charter to the Virginia Company was one of the reasons for detaining Hudson.[13]

During the following years, the activities of Dutch merchants on the river that Hudson had discovered appear to have gone largely unnoticed. By the end of the decade, the continuing efforts of the Leiden group of English Separatists, later called the Pilgrim Fathers, to find passage to America created a minor problem in Anglo-Dutch relations. In 1619, the Pilgrims contacted representatives of the Virginia Company in London, which was too much in turmoil to take up the project. Subsequently, they turned to one of the Amsterdam merchant companies involved in the New Netherland trade,

---

[12] L.H. Roper, *Advancing empire. English interests and overseas expansion, 1613–1688* (Cambridge, 2017); L.H. Roper and B. Van Ruymbeke (eds), *Constructing early modern empires. Proprietary ventures in the Atlantic world, 1500–1750* (Leiden, 2007); Jaap Jacobs, '"Act with the cunning of a fox". The political dimensions of the struggle for hegemony over New Netherland, 1647–1653', *Journal of Early American History*, 8 (2018), 122–52.

[13] Jacobs, *The colony of New Netherland*, p. 22; Donald S. Johnson, *Charting the sea of darkness. The four voyages of Henry Hudson* (New York, 1995), p. 128; Emanuel van Meteren, *Belgische ofte Nederlantsche oorlogen ende gheschiedenissen* (s.l., 1622), fols. 346–7.

where they encountered a receptive audience. In requesting permission and protection from the States General, the merchant company argued that using the Pilgrims as colonists would serve 'the preservation of this country's rights' against English claims. After much delay and consultation with the stadtholder, Prince Maurits, the States General turned the request down. Various arguments, such as the fear of antagonizing England, the danger of using Englishmen, instead of Dutchmen, as colonists to counter English claims, as well as the ongoing plans for the foundation of the Dutch West India Company, may have played a role in the decision. Eventually, the Pilgrims, destined for Jamestown in Virginia, ended up well north of New Netherland, in Plymouth Colony. When the English ambassador at The Hague, Sir Dudley Carleton, with reference to the *ius primae occupationis*, complained about Dutch activities in 1622, the States General could truthfully reply that there was no plantation or settlement there to impeach the English rights.[14]

A few years later, matters had changed. After one of its ships bound for North America had been held up at Plymouth by the English authorities in 1624, the West India Company felt obliged to counter claims based on a royal charter. In reply, the directors asserted that the presence of fifty colonists constituted a sufficient claim to an area with a circumference of thirty miles. This was, of course, a self-serving definition, as the Company was in the process of implementing just such a policy in New Netherland. A group of Walloons, mainly refugees from the southern Netherlands, some of them living in Leiden, had first approached Carleton to offer themselves as colonists of the English crown. When the plan fell through, they turned to the West India Company, which used them for their colonizing ventures in Guyana and in New Netherland. The colonists sent to the part of North America to be claimed by the Dutch were distributed over the three major river systems in the area: the Delaware River, where they settled on Burlington Island, the Connecticut River, where a settlement was erected at Saybrook Point, and the Hudson River, which boasted two settlements, Governors Island at the mouth and Fort Orange upstream. Distributing the settlers over several sites was aimed at laying claim to a large area of land. Yet the danger of small settlements falling prey to hostile Native Americans led to a concentration of settlers on the southern tip of Manhattan before long. The West India Company began to build Fort Amsterdam, and, adding

---

[14] Jeremy Dupertuis Bangs, *Strangers and pilgrims, travellers and sojourners. Leiden and the foundations of Plymouth Plantation* (Plymouth, 2009), pp. 580–91; H.J. Trap, 'Een reis die niet doorging', *Leids Jaarboekje*, 90 (1998), 54–7; British National Archives (London) [hereafter: BNA], Colonial Papers [hereafter: CO], 1/1/35; BNA, CO, 1/2/1; BNA, State Papers Foreign, Holland [hereafter: SP 84], 104/74; BNA, SP 84, 105/211; Dutch National Archives (The Hague) [hereafter: DNA], States General [hereafter: SG], inv. nr. 3181, fols. 91 and 150; E.B. O'Callaghan and B. Fernow (trans. and ed.), *Documents relative to the colonial history of the state of New York* (15 vols, Albany, 1853–83) [hereafter: DRCHNY], I, 27–8.

an additional argument to that of actual occupation, purchased the island of Manhattan from its indigenous owners in 1626.[15]

The claim made by the West India Company in 1624 was connected to negotiations between the Dutch Republic and England with the aim of forming an alliance against Spain by agreeing the Treaty of Southampton of 1625. This allowed West India Company ships 'free ingresse, egress, and regresse into and out of all his Ma[ties] ports, havens, roads, and creekes'. In 1627, this freedom was specifically extended to ships of the West India Company. Despite such measures, peaceful relations between the Dutch and English colonies were by no means guaranteed. News of threats made by New Plymouth caused the colonial government of New Netherland to request assistance from the West India Company in the form of a detachment of soldiers. It is doubtful these reinforcements were actually dispatched. As the two colonies, both sparsely populated, were located far apart and the area in between had not been colonized, the chances of armed conflict were remote, for the time being.[16]

The founding of the Massachusetts Bay Colony and the subsequent Great Migration in the 1630s changed the balance of power in North America. From the start, colonists in cold and stony New England cast an envious eye over the fertile land to their southwest. As Emmanuel Downing wrote to his brother-in-law John Winthrop senior in 1630: 'you may [there] enioye greater Comfort in respect of milder winters and fruitfuller and earlyer harvestes. [...] if yt be trew that mr. Allerton reportes of Hudsons river, there is noe place Comparable to yt for a plantacion and t'will quitt Cost for you to remove thither.'[17]

The reference to Isaac Allerton, one of the Pilgrims, indicates that regular contact between Plymouth Plantation and New Netherland was now well established. News of the growth of the Dutch colony had reached London as well. In 1632 John Coke, Secretary of State, received information from captain John Mason about the Dutch presence. Mason called the Dutch 'interlopers', referred to the royal charter of 1606, asserted that Englishmen had discovered the area before the Dutch did, contested the 'pretended authority from y[e] West India Company of Holland', and accused the Dutch colonists of giving

[15] Bangs, *Strangers and pilgrims*, pp. 590–1; BNA, CO, 1/1, no. 35; BNA, SP 84, 105/128–32, 211; DNA, SG, inv. nr. 5751A, doc. 11, art. 4; Bertrand Van Ruymbeke, 'The Walloon and Huguenot elements in New Netherland and seventeenth-century New York. Identity, history, and memory', in *Revisiting New Netherland. Perspectives on early Dutch America*, ed. Joyce D. Goodfriend (Leiden, 2005), pp. 41–56; Gehring, 'New Netherland. The formative years'; Jacobs, *The colony of New Netherland*, pp. 28–31.

[16] *DRCNHY*, III, 12; DNA, SG, inv. no. 12564.49, littra H, inv. no. 5751A; *DRCHNY*, I, 38.

[17] Allyn B. Forbes and Malcolm Freiberg (eds), *Winthrop papers, 1498–1649* (6 vols, Boston, 1947–92), vol. 2, 324–5.

'proude and contumacious answers' when challenged. For good measure, he ended with the detail that the Dutch had procured no less than 15,000 beaver skins, thus underlining the commercial importance of ousting the Dutch. Mason was also involved in the arrest at Plymouth of the Dutch ship *Eendracht*, returning from New Netherland to Amsterdam, an action endorsed and perhaps instigated by Sir Ferdinando Gorges, who was heavily involved in colonizing efforts. When the arrest of the *Eendracht* became known in Amsterdam, the West India Company alerted the States General which in turn contacted their ambassadors in London. Their efforts to obtain the release of the ship became entangled with their struggle to contain the fallout of a recent publication on the Amboyna affair, which they suspected was the work of a still dissatisfied English East India Company. The ambassadors, doubtlessly informed by the West India Company, argued that Manhattan had been legally purchased from the Native Americans. In an English memorandum, this argument was declared void:

> mais premierement on nie que les sauvages sussent possessores bone fidei de ces pays Là, en forte qu'ils en puissent disposer soit par vente ou par donation, Leurs demeures estant mouuantes et incertaines, et ne se saisain qu'en comun. Et en second Lieu on ne scauroit prouuer de facto que tous les naturels desd^ts pays ayent contracté avec ceux de cette vente pretendue.[18]

The memorandum went on to claim the area for England on the basis of first discovery as well as royal letters patent, declaring that Dutch settlers had not received such authority from their superiors. While the English claim was thus upheld, the Dutch ambassadors did obtain a promise from Secretary Coke to give orders for the release of the *Eendracht*, of course without prejudice to His Majesty's right. The *Eendracht* incident underlines three important points. First, the denial of Native sovereign rights in the diplomatic exchanges appears to have been used as an ad hoc argument, a sign that thinking on the issue was still in flux. Second, the role of the parties who sought to protect their interests in colonization is significant. On the English side, John Mason and Sir Ferdinando Gorges jolted governmental authorities into action. It is a reminder that the English crown took a reactive rather than an initiating role in furthering colonial ventures for most of the seventeenth century. On the Dutch side, the Amsterdam directors initiated the process that led the ambassadors in London to plead on their behalf. Third, the incident highlights the importance of the political context. Coke's decision to order the release of the *Eendracht* may have been influenced by a desire not to put further strain on Anglo-Dutch relations at this point in time, rather than by an assessment of the legal merits of the claims put to him.[19]

[18] DNA, SG, inv. no. 5892 (answer of the English government to remonstrances, April 1632).
[19] *DRCHNY*, III, 15–18; *DRCHNY*, I, 45–60.

Clashes north and south

It is likely that, as in the 1620s, developments in the European theatre precipitated actions in the American theatre. The concentration of settlers on Manhattan had resulted in the Dutch and English colonies being so far apart that direct confrontations were unlikely. But, as indicated before, the 1630s brought change. The first flash in the pan occurred on the Connecticut River. In early 1633, the new director of New Netherland, Wouter van Twiller, dispatched an expeditionary force under the command of Jacob van Curler. They purchased land from the local Native Americans, initiated trading relations with them, constructed a small fortification, called the House of Good Hope, and began cultivating the land. In a letter to John Winthrop senior, Van Twiller defended the validity of the Dutch claim, using familiar arguments:

> I have in the name of the Lords the States Generall and the authorized West India Company taken possession of the forementioned River, and for testimony thereof have sett upp an howse on the North side of the said River, with intent to plant &c. Itt's not the intent of the States to take the land from the poore Natives, as the Kinge of Spaine hath done by the Pope's donation, but rather to take itt from the said Natives att some reasonable and convenient price, wch God be praysed wee have done hitherto. In this parte of the world are divers heathen lands that are emptye of inhabitants, soe that of a litle part or portion thereof there needes not any question.[20]

Van Twiller's arguments notwithstanding, a group of English colonists from New Plymouth, led by William Holmes, sailed up the Connecticut River in September 1633 to start a settlement. The Dutch and English outposts were separated only by a small creek. Dutch protests were to no avail. Numerous minor incidents ensued in subsequent years, with the English gaining the upper hand due to the arrival of more colonists. Yet neither side was willing to oust the other by force, either because of military inability, on the Dutch side, or fear of repercussions in Europe, on the English side.[21]

On the southern edge of New Netherland a similar development took place. The Dutch presence on the Delaware River had been limited to seasonal trading voyages, for which Fort Nassau, most likely constructed in 1627, acted as a basis. Manned by a small number of soldiers, the fort was only occupied during the summer months. This made the Dutch claim tenuous at best, while English colonists from Virginia coveted the fertile soil along the river, as well as the possibilities for fur trade with the Native Americans. In 1635, a small

---

[20] BNA, CO, 1/6/83; *DRCHNY*, III, 18–19.
[21] DNA, SG, inv. no. 12564.49 (littra B); *DRCHNY*, II, 140); Jacobs, *Dutch colonial fortifications*, pp. 67–8; *idem*, 'A troubled man. Director Wouter van Twiller and the affairs of New Netherland in 1635', *New York History*, 85 (2004), 213–32.

English trading expedition under George Holmes arrived and took possession of the fort. In this case Wouter van Twiller immediately took counter-measures, sending out a small force to retake the fort and reinforce the garrison. The English intruders were escorted back to Virginia. If an exchange of written protests in corroboration of the respective claims took place, it left no trace in the few extant records. That was also the case in subsequent instances of English intrusion in the 1640s. Attempts by the English colonies New Haven, Virginia and Massachusetts to establish settlements on the Delaware River were thwarted in 1641, 1643, and 1644. In one instance, the Dutch collaborated with the Swedes, who had been successful in establishing a foothold, to keep out the English. However, instead of challenging the English right of access to the river, the Swedish and Dutch authorities, in a rare joint international tribunal, put the English on trial for the offence of smuggling, i.e. not paying duties, thus avoiding the larger issue. In eloquent Latin protests, John Winthrop senior employed royal charters as his main argument, only to be met with Swedish references to charters from their monarch. Another English attempt at settlement occurred in 1640, when a small group of colonists were led from Lynn, Massachusetts, to western Long Island by James Farrett, an agent of the Earl of Stirling. They removed the coat of arms of the States General, which had been affixed to a tree, and replaced it with a fool's head. The director of New Netherland sent twenty-five soldiers to apprehend them. After a short interrogation, the English colonists were sent back to New England. The proceedings show that the Dutch considered that punishing English insolence, committed by removing the material signs of Dutch overlordship, was much more important that entering into a debate on the legal principles for their claim. The quick succession of incidents in the early 1640s resulted in reverberations in London. Dutch ambassador Albert Joachimi received such vehement protests from a Puritan colonist, recently returned from New England, that he advised the States General to take measures to avoid an English attack on New Netherland. These protests were supported by William Fiennes, Lord Say and Sele, who, like Gorges, was heavily involved in colonization projects.[22]

The repeated references to governmental charters in the 1640s are an indication that this legal principle gained weight, even though it had by no

---

[22] Jacobs, 'A troubled man'; *idem, Dutch colonial fortifications*, pp. 29–30; NYSA, New Netherland Council Dutch colonial council minutes, vol. 4 (A1809-78_V04), p. 134; Arnold J.F. van Laer (trans. and ed.), *Council minutes, 1638–1649. New York historical manuscripts: Dutch* (4 vols, Baltimore, 1974), vol. 4, pp. 157 and 164; Richard S. Dunn, James Savage and Laetitia Yeandle (eds), *The journal of John Winthrop, 1630–1649* (Cambridge, Mass., 1996), pp. 471 and 79–80; Edward C. Carter II and Clifford Lewis III, 'Sir Edmund Plowden and the New Albion Charter, 1632–1785', *The Pennsylvania Magazine of History and Biography*, 83 (1959), 150–79; Amandus Johnson, *The instruction for Johan Printz, governor of New Sweden* (Philadelphia, 1930), pp. 209–20 and 29–47; BNA, CO 1/6/29, 44 and 60–2; DNA, SG, inv. no. 5892 I, 31–4; *DRCHNY*, I, 47, 128–9 and 134–5.

means blotted out the others. Of course, for colonial officials a reference to a governmental charter was essentially an argument of hierarchy and authority: in employing it, the colonial officials underlined their inferior position as well as their loyalty to their superiors, while at the same time refusing to deal with the fundamental issue at stake. The logical corollary was that the tension between conflicting charters could only be resolved through agreement between the entities which had issued them, i.e. the English crown and the Dutch States General. On the Dutch side, there certainly was willingness to achieve an agreement as to 'limietscheijdinghe' [settlement of the limits], even though there was no full congruity of interests between the West India Company and the various factions in the States General. In England the situation was much more complicated. The relation between the Puritan colonies in New England and the English king had been problematic at best in the 1630s. When open warfare broke out between the Long Parliament and supporters of the monarchy in 1642, the issue of boundaries in insignificant overseas areas was not very high on the agenda. This metropolitan neglect allowed New Haven and Connecticut, both operating without a royal charter, to adopt an aggressive and at times belligerent tone in their letters to the New Netherland authorities from 1643 onwards.[23]

A provisional settlement

In this light it is hardly surprising that the instructions for Petrus Stuyvesant, who was appointed as Director General of New Netherland in 1645 and took office in 1647, stipulated that he had to seek an agreement with the New England colonies. At the same time, Stuyvesant was ordered to prevent any further incursions by the English. English colonists who had already settled on land claimed by the Dutch were allowed to stay, provided they took an oath of allegiance to the States General and the West India Company. Upon his arrival, Stuyvesant quickly struck up a correspondence with John Winthrop senior and other colonial leaders in New England. Professing his desire for a 'neighbourlie correspondencie', he suggested a meeting with the Commissioners of the United Colonies, composed of representatives of Massachusetts Bay, Plymouth, Connecticut, and New Haven. In the same breath, Stuyvesant asserted the West India Company's 'indubitable right [...] to all that land betwixt the riuer called Connecticut, & that by the English

---

[23] Simon Groenveld, *Verlopend getij. De Nederlandse Republiek en de Engelse Burgeroorlog, 1640–1646* (Dieren, 1984); Dunn, Savage and Yeandle, *The journal of John Winthrop*, pp. 468–9, 79–80 and 499–500; Nathaniel B. Shurtleff and David Pulsifer (eds), *Records of the colony of New Plymouth in New England* (12 vols, Boston 1855–61), IX, 13; Ebenezer Hazard, *Historical collections, consisting of state papers and other authentic documents* (2 vols, Philadelphia, 1792–94), II, 55.

named Deleware'. In later letters, Stuyvesant even extended the claim 'to all the lands, rivers, streames, etc: from Cape Hinlope[n to Cape Cod]'. Stuyvesant backed up these claims in two ways. The first one concerned the Dutch ship *Beninjo* which broke bulk at New Haven without proper authorization from the West India Company. In an audacious operation, Stuyvesant sent troops that managed to capture the ship, lying at anchor in the Connecticut River at Hartford, and sail it back to New Amsterdam, where it was duly confiscated. The second one was to thwart another English attempt to claim Long Island. Andrew Forrester, using a commission of the Earl of Stirling, tried to persuade the colonists to submit to his authority as governor of Long Island. He was quickly arrested and put on a ship back to Europe.[24]

These actions produced a verbal counter-attack from Theophilius Eaton, the governor of New Haven. In 1646, Eaton had indicated his firm intention to prevent the Dutch becoming 'Lords of the countrye' in his correspondence with Winthrop senior and he turned out to be the most vocal opponent of the Dutch colonial presence. Eaton protested vehemently against the Dutch actions, which in his view amounted to 'disturbing the peace betwixt the Engl: & Dutch in these ptes'. Eaton corroborated his stance by reference to three of the well-known legal principles: he cited the charter of James I, claimed that the land at Hartford had been obtained through 'due purchase from the Indians, who were the true proprietours of the land (for we fownd it not a vacuum)', and pointed out that the English colonists had built houses and cultivated the land, i.e. actual possession. In his defence of the capture of the *Beninjo*, Stuyvesant referred to the precedent of Dutch attacks on Spanish ships in English waters, i.e. the victory of Maerten Harpertsz Tromp at the Battle of the Downs in 1639, which was authorized by the States General by reference to the Treaty of Southampton. This was a rather weak argument, as it implied a tacit recognition of the English ownership of Hartford. Unsurprisingly, Eaton found it unacceptable: 'this reacheth not the question'. Despite these exchanges, Eaton expressed the hope that the differences could be resolved to mutual satisfaction.[25]

[24] DNA, SG, inv. no. 12272, fols. 197–9v; DRCHNY, I, 160–2; NYSA, New Netherland Council Dutch colonial administrative correspondence, vol. 11 (A1810-78_V11), docs. 2b–11f; Charles T. Gehring (trans. and ed.), *Correspondence 1647–1653. New Netherland documents series, vol. XI* (Syracuse, 2000), pp. 7–53 (quotations on pp. 7 and 40); NYSA, New Netherland Council Dutch colonial council minutes, vol. 4 (A1809-78_V04), pp. 298–9, 330–3, 343–7; Van Laer, *Council minutes, 1638–1649*, vol. 4, 383–6, 432–8 and 453–60; Isabel M. Calder, 'The Earl of Stirling and the colonization of Long Island', in *Essays on colonial history presented to Charles M. Andrews by his students* (New Haven, 1931), pp. 74–95.
[25] Forbes and Freiberg, *Winthrop papers*, V, 95–6; NYSA, New Netherland Council Dutch colonial administrative correspondence, vol. 11 (A1810-78_V11), docs. 2b–11f;. Gehring, *Correspondence 1647–1653*, pp. 7–53.

Over the next few years, Stuyvesant continued to correspond with the English governors. In a letter to Stephen Goodyear, deputy governor of New Haven, Stuyvesant explained 'that claimes to pretended rights are noe iniuries & giues me noe lawfull pprietie to what I claime, vnlesse lawfullie adiudged, (in which neither hee nor I can be competent judges) and I suppose yow and he [i.e. Eaton] well knowes, that many protests and passages in this nature are only pro formâ'.[26]

The implicit referral to higher authority and the pro forma nature of protests emphasizes the hierarchical context of the diplomatic exchanges. Claims were being made in order to show superiors that their rights were being defended and should not be interpreted as an indication of belligerent intentions. Stuyvesant's eagerness to meet with the Commissioners of the United Colonies was another indication. However, practical considerations led to delays and postponements. In the meantime, Stuyvesant kept his superiors informed and they did likewise. In 1648 the West India Company considered asking the States General for another charter, one that would specifically include the areas claimed by other European countries. A little naively perhaps, they presumed that such a charter would deter further claims or actual occupation by competitors. In order to make such a request, the directors asked Stuyvesant for exact information as to the area of land claimed as belonging to New Netherland. Stuyvesant indicated that while he had initially claimed all the land up to Cape Cod, a diplomatic agreement with the English could draw the line at the Connecticut River. Stuyvesant also informed his superiors that his English counterparts in America supported the idea of a provisional settlement. When an attempt to enter into negotiations with representatives of the English Parliament failed, the Amsterdam directors authorized Stuyvesant to give it a try.[27]

Stuyvesant's meeting with the Commissioners of the United Colonies took place in 1650, on the banks of the Connecticut River. The actual negotiations were preceded by formalities and diplomatic rituals. Technically, the two negotiating parties each stayed in their own territory, the English in Hartford, the Dutch at the House of Good Hope, with only a small creek separating the two. The first exchanges took place in writing, to avoid passing into territory claimed by the opponent. In his first letter, Stuyvesant underlined his formal position, by signing it 'New Netherland'. The Commissioners reciprocated by signing their reply with 'Hartford in New England'. Such datelines made it impossible for the other party to discuss the content of the letters, as that

[26] NYSA, New Netherland Council Dutch colonial administrative correspondence, vol. 11 (A1810-78_V11), doc. 6b; Gehring, *Correspondence 1647–1653*, p. 25.
[27] NYSA, New Netherland Council Dutch colonial administrative correspondence, vol. 11 (A1810-78_V11), doc. 12, p. 5, doc. 14, pp. 13–15, doc. 20, pp. 5–6; Gehring, *Correspondence 1647–1653*, pp. 58, 68–9 and 89–90; DNA, SG, inv. no. 12564.36; *DRCHNY*, I, 447.

would constitute a recognition of the implied claim. So a solution had to be found. Stuyvesant indicated his willingness to compromise by signing his subsequent letter just with 'Conecticott' and the Commissioners reciprocated. Such pro forma manoeuvres, often neglected or misinterpreted by twentieth-century scholars, were required to safeguard the officials involved against charges that they had not defended the rights of their superiors.[28]

Once this stumbling block was out of the way, the parties could engage in actual negotiations. Two delegates from each side were appointed to hammer out the 'articles of agreement', later called the 'Hartford Treaty'. Some of the issues raised resulted from the already mentioned competing claims on the Delaware River. The incidents that had taken place there had occurred under Stuyvesant's predecessors, and Stuyvesant therefore referred the claims to the authorities in Europe. The validity of the legal principles underpinning the claims was not discussed either, but the parties did agree upon a settlement of the boundaries between New Netherland and the New England colonies. Under the terms of the treaty, the Dutch relinquished their claim to eastern Long Island. Although the agreement was provisional, as ratification in Europe was required, it still constituted a considerable diplomatic victory for Stuyvesant. By obtaining official recognition by the English colonies of New Netherland's northeastern boundary he had achieved the maximum that was achievable under difficult circumstances. With a settlement in place, the threat of an outright attack on New Netherland was considerable reduced, for the time being.[29]

In September 1650, no one could foresee that mutual ratification of the Hartford Treaty in Europe would never take place and it is doubtful whether the New England colonies ever bothered to advocate it. Indeed, the Dutch Republic and England would be at war within two years. Growing Anglo-Dutch rivalry may have played a role in the failure of a Dutch embassy to London in 1651, which, among many other things, had been tasked to initiate the process for ratifying the provisional boundary. The English Council of State, however, considered this quite unnecessary and replied:

---

[28] David Pulsifer (ed.), *Acts of the Commissioners of the United Colonies* (2 vols, Boston, 1859), I, 174; Ronald D. Cohen, 'The Hartford Treaty of 1650. Anglo-Dutch cooperation in the seventeenth century', *New-York Historical Society Quarterly*, 52 (1969), 311–32; John Joseph Chiodo, 'The foreign policy of Peter Stuyvesant. Dutch diplomacy in North America, 1647–1664' (unpublished PhD thesis, University of Iowa, 1974), pp. 80–1; Max Savelle, *The origins of American diplomacy. The international history of Anglo-America, 1492–1763* (New York, 1968), pp. 159–64; Harry M. Ward, *The United Colonies of New England, 1643–90* (New York, 1961), pp. 165–6; Dixon Ryan Fox, *Yankees and Yorkers* (New York, 1940), p. 82; Henry M. Kessler and Eugene Rachlis, *Peter Stuyvesant and his New York. A biography of a man and a city* (New York, 1959), p. 120.

[29] Pulsifer, *Acts of the Commissioners of the United Colonies*, II, 21.

The English were the first Planters of the Northerne firme land of America, and have plantations there from the Southermost part of Virginia, in thirtie seven degrees of north Latitude to Newfoundland in fiftie two degrees. And not knowing of any plantation of the Netherlanders there, save a small number up in Hudsons River, Wee thinke it is not necessary at present to settle the limits which may be done hereafter in convenient tyme.[30]

The Council of State here amalgamates first discovery and actual possession into 'first Planters', while denying a significant Dutch presence in the same breath. It is likely that the words 'save a small number' reflect the influence of Edward Winslow, agent of the United Colonies in London. The Council of State may have relied on information obtained from him and others within his network in order to brush off this demand of the Dutch ambassadors.[31]

Amboyna in America

The outbreak of the First Anglo-Dutch War in 1652 provided Winslow and Edward Hopkins, who had represented Connecticut at meetings of the Commissioners of the United Colonies, with an opportunity to propose aggressive plans to the Council of State. They suggested sending a ship to New England, carrying not just the news of the outbreak of war, but also a considerable amount of arms and ammunition, plus the required authorization to attack New Netherland. While they obtained permission, there is no indication that their plan was actually implemented.[32] The news of the outbreak of war did not reach North America until February 1653 and led to frenzied activity in New Amsterdam, including the construction of a stockade at the location later called Wall Street. In New England, fear of a Dutch attack was rife, especially as rumours were flying that the Dutch authorities were supplying arms to the Native Americans in order to incite them to attack the English. A hastily arranged meeting of the Commissioners of the United Colonies received extensive information from the delegates of New Haven concerning their suspicions. It included a full narrative of injustices and insolences committed by the Dutch, who had settled within the bounds of an 'ancient pattent to bee graunted by the Kings of Engeland to their Subiects to settle and plant vpon'. It ended with a venomous rumour showing the depth

---

[30] DNA, SG, inv. no. 8460, num. 21, art. 12; *DRCHNY*, II, 486–7; Frances Gardiner Davenport, *European treaties bearing on the history of the United States and its dependencies* (2 vols, Washington, 1929), II, 9.

[31] Jeremy Dupertuis Bangs, *Pilgrim Edward Winslow. New England's first international diplomat. A documentary biography* (Boston, 2004), pp. 261–95.

[32] W. Noël Sainsbury (ed.), *Calendar of state papers, colonial series, 1574–1660, preserved in the State Paper Department of her Majesty's Public Record Office* (London, 1860), pp. 386–7; Bangs, *Pilgrim Edward Winslow*, pp. 297–8.

of English distrust: 'And wee heare that some of the Duch att or about the Monhatoes tell the English they shall shortly have an East India breakfast; In which it is conceived they Refer that horrid Treacherus and crewill plott and execution att Amboina.'[33]

New Haven, supported by Connecticut, used such rumours to argue in favour of a pre-emptive attack. Massachusetts, the largest of the New England colonies and also the one furthest removed from New Netherland, was however not convinced and was supported by New Plymouth. At the very least, their delegates considered it necessary to allow Stuyvesant the opportunity to reply to the allegations. To that purpose an embassy was sent to New Netherland, arriving in New Amsterdam in late May 1653. Due to a lack of sufficient preparation on the English side, Stuyvesant was able to outwit the delegates, who returned to New England dissatisfied. Stuyvesant quickly followed up with a letter to the Commissioners of the United Colonies, denying all allegations and offering to submit to the judgment of independent arbitrators or of the respective superiors in Europe. The Massachusetts delegates remained unconvinced that the available evidence was sufficient to warrant a just war against the Dutch colony, especially as the Dutch had not initiated any hostilities as yet. Their stance frustrated the bellicose delegates of New Haven and Connecticut and strained relations between the United Colonies to breaking point. Yet without the support of Massachusetts, which would supply the lion's share of the required manpower, the success of a military expedition was by no means assured. One of the ambassadors to New Amsterdam, John Leverett, therefore decided to seek military support in London instead. It is possible that he was also involved in the publication of *The Second Part of the Tragedy of Amboyna* in London in August 1653. Six months later, in February 1654, John Leverett and his father-in-law Robert Sedgwick received permission from John Thurloe, secretary of the Council of State, to proceed with the expedition. The Admiralty advanced a substantial sum of money that allowed them to hire ships and men. In May 1654, they arrived back in Boston, where they used their commission from Cromwell to circumvent the reluctance of Massachusetts. Just as the expedition was about to set off for New Amsterdam, news of the Peace of Westminster arrived, and the whole thing was grudgingly called off. The French settlements in Acadia were attacked instead.[34]

---

[33] Pulsifer, *Acts of the Commissioners of the United Colonies*, II, 3–23 (quotation on p. 23); Julia A. Fisher and David J. Silverman, *Ninigret, sachem of the Niantics and Narragansetts. Diplomacy, war, and the balance of power in seventeenth-century New England and Indian country* (Ithaca, 2014), pp. 46, 73–6 and 163; Forbes and Freiberg, *Winthrop papers*, VI, 275–6.

[34] Pulsifer, *Acts of the Commissioners of the United Colonies*, II, 26–65 and 71–112; Nathaniel B. Shurtleff (ed.), *Records of the governor and company of Massachusetts Bay in New England* (6 vols, Boston, 1853–54), III, 311; Charles Jeremy Hoadley (ed.), *Records of the colony and plantation of New Haven* (2 vols, Hartford, 1857), II, 4–15;

The episode of rising tension during the First Anglo-Dutch War is significant for two reasons. First, it marks the first occurrence of the legal principle of just war being employed relative to claims on New Netherland. Even if its use was confined to consultations between the English colonies – and not, of course, in diplomatic exchanges between the English and Dutch in North America or Europe – its occurrence indicates that this was the principle that could supersede all others, given the right circumstances. Second, the rising tension between New Netherland and New England was a direct result of the outbreak of war in Europe, presumably a just war, from the English perspective. Still, the Massachusetts colony saw fit to make up its own mind, based solely on colonial evidence. Thus Massachusetts implicitly asserted a degree of autonomy that is remarkable. Even when Leverett and Sedgwick returned with a commission from the government in England, Massachusetts refused to cooperate wholeheartedly, condoning but not supporting the recruitment of troops within its jurisdiction. In order for a takeover of New Netherland to happen, the desire for territorial expansion by New England colonies at the expense of the Dutch needed to coincide with metropolitan interests in order to obtain the required authorization and military force from Europe. By the time that peace returned, the only casualty of war was the House of Good Hope on the Connecticut River, captured in June 1653.[35]

First claims

Despite efforts of the West India Company, which had submitted a large number of documents to the States General to support its claim to New Netherland, the text of the Peace of Westminster contained no explicit reference to North America. It did stipulate a provision to sort out any remaining Anglo-Dutch differences, although that proved to be ineffectual. Subsequent negotiations did not yield a positive result for New Netherland, even after the States General ratified the Treaty of Hartford in early 1656. This left the authorities in New Netherland in a delicate position. As intrusions and encroachments by colonists from New England continued, either authorized or unauthorized by the English authorities, Director General and Council of New Netherland had to decide how to prevent the continued erosion of their

---

Ward, *The United Colonies*, pp. 178–200; instructions of Cromwell to Sedgwick and Leverett, Massachusetts Historical Society, Saltonstall Family Papers; John Thurloe, *A collection of state papers of John Thurloe* … (7 vols, London, 1742), I, 721–2; BNA, SP18/79/133 and SP18/80/193.

[35] Pulsifer, *Acts of the Commissioners of the United Colonies*, II, 52; John Underhill to John Winthrop junior, 23 March 1665, Massachusetts Historical Society, Winthrop Collection, reel 8; J. Hammond Trumbull and Charles J. Hoadly (eds), *The public records of the colony of Connecticut* (15 vols, Hartford, 1850–90), I, 244, 54 and 75.

territory without, however, employing forceful means that could provoke English repercussions. They did so by complaining to the English colonies in writing and attempting to buy land from the local Native Americans when they became aware of English plans to encroach within the New Netherland boundaries. Settling disputed lands with Dutch colonists proved difficult as population growth in the English colonies far outpaced that in New Netherland. In some cases, Director General and Council had no option but to remove English colonists when detected at an early stage of settlement. As a last resort, they sometimes acquiesced to English settlement under nominal Dutch sovereignty, with the requirement of taking an oath of allegiance. This was a dangerous policy. It created a fifth column of untrustworthy subjects, who could be called upon to change sides. Several encroachments took place between 1654 and 1660, including the establishment of English villages on Long Island and in Westchester. In their protests, the Dutch authorities predominantly used the argument of legitimate purchase from legitimate Native American owners. In their replies, English colonists on Long Island sometimes asserted that their place of settlement was east of the line agreed upon in the Hartford Treaty, which ran from Oyster Bay on the shore of Long Island south to the Atlantic coast. It quickly transpired that the English and Dutch had different locations in mind when using the name 'Oyster Bay', with the English Oyster Bay being considerable further to the west than the Dutch one. The Amsterdam directors ordered the establishment of a small fort or redoubt at the Dutch Oyster Bay to indicate the extent of the Dutch. This is a clear example of the use of forts to signify actual possession. However, Director General and Council in New Amsterdam procrastinated for years. They were aware that such an action would amount to the *de facto* annexation of the English village of Huntington, which would undoubtedly provoke an English reaction. In the end, nothing was done. By 1660, the main aim of the Dutch colonial authorities was to defend their crumbling position as best as they could, avoiding incidents, placating English colonists, waiting for a final settlement of the boundaries to be approved in Europe and hoping that no new war in Europe would worsen their relations with the New England colonies.[36]

---

[36] *Articulen van vrede, unie, ende eeuwich verbondt, besloten tusschen Syne Doorluchtighste Hoogheyt, den Heere Olivier, Heere Protector vande Republijcque van Engelandt, Schotlandt ende Yrlandt, etc. ter eenre: ende de Hooge ende Mogende Heeren Staten Generael der Vereenighde Nederlandtsche Provintien, ter andere zyde. Over-gheset uyt de Latijnsche tale* (Den Haag, 1654); DNA, SG, inv. no. 12564.38; *DRCHNY*, I, 539–49; Davenport, *European treaties*, II, 7–21; Roper, *Advancing empire*, pp. 152–3; Jaap Jacobs, 'The Hartford Treaty. A European perspective on a new world conflict', *de Halve Maen*, 68 (1995), 74–9; NYSA, New Netherland Council Dutch colonial council minutes, vol. 5 (A1809-78_V05), pp. 394–9 and 421–2; Charles T. Gehring (trans. and ed.), *Council minutes, 1652–1654. New York historical manuscripts: Dutch* (Baltimore, 1983), pp. 193–4, 201; Nat. Arch, SG, inv. no. 12564.49, littra G; *DRCHNY*, II, 160–2;

On the Delaware River, the Dutch position had come under increased pressure in the second half of the 1650s too. After a number of incidents, Johan Risingh, the newly arrived Swedish governor, had in 1654, during the First Anglo-Dutch War, captured the Dutch outpost, Fort Casimir. The Amsterdam directors of the West India Company were outraged and, without even bothering to inform the States General, enlisted the aid of the city government of Amsterdam to assemble a force that conquered New Sweden in its entirety in 1655. In order to strengthen the southern flank of New Netherland, the West India Company then proceeded to grant the city of Amsterdam a colony of its own under Company overlordship, the city-colony New Amstel. Amsterdam dispatched a number of colonists, but their number dwindled through famine and disease, while the threat of an invasion from Maryland or Virginia induced others to desert.[37]

In 1659, the antagonism over the Delaware River came to a head when Colonel Nathaniel Utie arrived to claim the entire area in the name of Lord Baltimore, the proprietor of Maryland. Utie confined himself to asserting claims without, from a Dutch perspective, offering anything in the form of corroboration, thus blurring the line between civil diplomatic exchanges and unveiled threats. Initially, the Dutch defence was based on the legal principles of a governmental charter to the West India Company and legitimate purchase, to which a reference to article sixteen of the Treaty of Westminster, containing an order to refrain from hostilities, was added. But the subsequent embassy sent from New Netherland to Maryland delivered a document that amounted to an extensive exposé. Written by Director General Petrus Stuyvesant and delivered by two ambassadors, it provides an overview of European claims, going back to the first discovery of America by Spain and to the subsequent explorations of Verrazano and others. Stuyvesant ingeniously argued that the Spanish claim had partly devolved unto the Dutch Republic. The Dutch had been Spanish subjects at the time of discovery and the king of Spain had subsequently renounced and ceded his right and title to the New World to the Dutch Republic when peace was concluded. Although Stuyvesant did not elaborate, this was a reference to articles five and six of the Peace of Munster of 1648. He then pointed out that the English charter of James I stipulated that the settlements of New England and Virginia should stay well apart, contending cleverly but not entirely truthfully that this was done in order to allow the Dutch to settle in between. He reiterated that the first settlement of the Delaware River was undertaken by the Dutch, based on their lawful and legal purchase from the Native proprietors, and went on to denounce the illegal claim and hostile conduct of Utie, based on undated,

Jacobs, *Dutch colonial fortifications*, pp. 20–2; NYSA, New Netherland Council Dutch colonial administrative correspondence, vol. 13 (A1810-78_V13), doc. 17, p. 8; *DRCHNY*, XIV, 440.
[37] Jacobs, *The colony of New Netherland*, pp. 74–5.

unsigned, and thus unauthorized documents. Stuyvesant asserted that this was not just against the law of nations but also a contravention of at least seven separate articles of the Treaty of Westminster. Lord Baltimore should have addressed himself before 18 May 1652 to the arbitrators tasked with resolving any remaining grievances between the Dutch and English. Yet, Stuyvesant showed himself willing to submit to arbitration in America, with all remaining points to be decided in Europe. Despite a few inaccuracies and suppositions, this was the kind of riposte that his superiors were undoubtedly proud of. It is not surprising that a copy of the document eventually made its way via Amsterdam to the States General for use in diplomatic exchanges.[38]

Royal power

Yet the time when finely tuned legal niceties held water was coming to an end. Maryland's governor did not bother to argue against the points put forward by Stuyvesant. He just showed the Dutch ambassadors a copy of Charles I's grant of 1632 to Lord Baltimore with geographical specifica- tions that included the Delaware River. Whether it was the king's to grant was not up for discussion. After the Restoration of the English monarchy in 1660, English efforts to settle in New Netherland from New England in the northeast and Virginia and Maryland in the south intensified. References to charters now became the English argument of choice and were boosted by the return of royal authority. In Europe, the Restoration incited the West India Company to ask the States General to push the Dutch claim in London, employing the familiar arguments. Similarly, interested parties in England sprang into action and attempted to curry favour with Charles II in order to obtain royal approval for their own claims. The Earl of Stirling, renewing his claim on Long Island, was one of them, although he eventually decided to sell his claim to the Duke of York instead. In the American colonies, the Restoration had a similar effect. Some of the New England colonies had never acquired appropriate charters and had survived in a legal limbo. And even if they had been granted charters, the delineation of their boundaries was often unclear, resulting in several conflicts among them. In order to gain the upper hand, they now entered into a scramble for royal favour. The governor

---

[38] NYSA, New Netherland Council Dutch Delaware River settlement administrative records, vol. 18 (A1878_78_V18), doc. 62; Charles T. Gehring (ed. and trans.), *Delaware papers (Dutch period). A collection of documents pertaining to the regulation of affairs on the South River of New Netherland, 1648–1664. New York historical manuscripts: Dutch*, vols XVIII–XIX (Baltimore, 1981), pp. 150–2; 'Declaratie ende manifestatie', Amsterdam City Archives, *toegangsnummer* 5028, inv. no. 541; DNA, SG, inv. no. 12564.49, littra H; DRCHNY, II, 80–4; S. Groenveld, *Unie – Bestand – Vrede. Drie fundamentele wetten van de Republiek der Verenigde Nederlanden* (Hilversum, 2009), pp. 162–3.

of Connecticut, John Winthrop junior, embarked on a trip to London in 1661 with this purpose in mind. As a result, Connecticut obtained a charter in 1662 that subsumed the rival colony of New Haven. Meanwhile, New Netherland was left to fend for itself. Without much support from the Dutch Republic in the form of military reinforcements or sufficient numbers of new colonists, the Dutch authorities in New Netherland were still able to ward off English encroachments until John Scott arrived from England. He claimed part of Long Island, showing several papers to that effect. Although his claims were at best far-fetched, the English villages under Dutch rule elected him as their leader. While this severely eroded Dutch authority, it also posed a threat to Connecticut's desire to annex Long Island. John Winthrop junior therefore had Scott arrested and put on trial in Hartford.[39]

The real danger for New Netherland did not come from chancers like Scott, annoying though he was. It emanated from the convergence of the expansionist drive of local, colonial stakeholders, such as Winthrop junior, with the rise of anti-Dutch sentiments and royal vigour in London, bringing together motive, means, and opportunity. In New Netherland, Stuyvesant knew what was coming and impressed upon his superiors that Connecticut in particular was implacable in denying the legitimacy of the Dutch presence: 'they know of no New Netherland, nor government of New Netherland, but they do know of the Dutch plantations on Manhattan Island'. In March 1664, King Charles II granted his brother, James, Duke of York, a large swathe of North America. The charter specifically included the Hudson River, but the presence of New Netherland was not mentioned. Nor did the charter contain a reference to earlier royal charters or any corroboration of the monarch's right to make this grant. Preparations for an expedition started straightaway, with commissions for Richard Nicolls as governor and precise instructions for him and others as to how to settle boundaries in New England being drawn up. When Nicolls arrived in North America with his flotilla of frigates and force of soldiers, the militias of New England were ready to support him.[40]

---

[39] 'Extract out off yr patente off my lort Cecilius Calvert and Barron Balthamoor etc', Amsterdam City Archives, *toegangsnummer* 5028, inv. no. 541; *DRCHNY*, II, 84–8; III, 42–3; L.H. Roper, 'The fall of New Netherland and seventeenth-century Anglo-American imperial formation, 1654–1676', *The New England Quarterly*, 87 (2014), 666–708; Lilian T. Mowrer, *The indomitable John Scott, citizen of Long Island, 1632–1704* (New York, 1960).

[40] Roper, 'The fall of New Netherland'; 'datse geen N: Nederlandse noch gouvernement van N: Nederlant en kennen maer wel vande duytse plantagien opt Manhatans Eylant'; Stuyvesant to the Amsterdam directors, 10 November 1663, DNA, SG, inv. no. 12564.57; *DRCHNY*, II, 484; Peter R. Christoph and Florence A. Christoph (eds), *Book of general entries of the colony of New York, 1664–1673. Orders, warrants, letters, commissions, passes and licenses issued by governors Richard Nicolls and Francis Lovelace. New York historical manuscripts: English* (Baltimore, 1982), pp. 1–5.

In the subjugation of New Amsterdam all the usual formalities were observed. When the English ships arrived, Dutch emissaries asked for their intentions. Nicolls informed them that he had come to reduce the place to His Majesty's obedience. He failed, however, to sign the first letter demanding surrender, which allowed Stuyvesant to play for time and return the letter. An invitation to discuss the relative merits of the Dutch and English claims was rebuffed by Nicolls, who indicated that he would follow his orders to take over the city, using violent means if necessary. Both the population of New Amsterdam and the Dutch colonial authorities were aware of the weakness of the fortifications and knew that armed resistance would provide the English force with legitimate pretext for bombardment and plunder. They also anticipated that the English action would in all likelihood result in a full-scale war in Europe. This meant that the arrival of a Dutch fleet to take back New Netherland was a realistic option in the not too distant future. Within a few days, therefore, articles of capitulation were agreed upon, and New Amsterdam surrendered, quickly followed by the rest of New Netherland.[41]

As it turned out, the colonists lived in hope and governor Richard Nicolls in fear of the arrival of Michiel de Ruyter and his fleet in 1665. However, a lack of supplies and the weakening condition of his ships forced De Ruyter to return to Europe. His later actions on the Medway were one of the factors that brought an end to the Second Anglo-Dutch War. The peace treaty of Breda employed the principle of *uti possidetis*: both parties retained the territories in their possession at the time of the signing of the peace treaty. The *status quo post bellum* was, in this case, preferred over the *status quo ante bellum*. The treaty did not, as is sometimes suggested, constitute a simple exchange of New Netherland for Surinam. Obviously, the news that New Netherland was to remain in English hands was greeted with disappointment by the Dutch colonists. One grumbled: 'It has pleased the Lord to ordain that we must learn English', but 'one has no liking for it'. In March 1667, with negotiations ongoing, the Amsterdam chamber of the West India Company had tried to persuade the States General to demand the return of Dutch rule over New Netherland. A petition of seventy Amsterdam merchants with New Netherland trading interests provided additional support. The request fell upon deaf ears. It seems unlikely that it was fully supported by the Amsterdam representatives in the States of Holland and the States General.[42]

---

[41] Roper, 'The fall of New Netherland'. For documents relating to the surrender of New Netherland, see: NYSA, New Netherland Council Dutch colonial council minutes, vol. 10-3 (A1809-78_V10_pt3), New Netherland Council Dutch colonial administrative correspondence, vol. 15 (A1810-78_V15), and DNA, SG, inv. no. 12564.57.

[42] Jeremias van Rensselaer to Anna van Rensselaer, 10/20 June 1668: 'neu schijnt dat het Godt de heer belieft heeft dat wy Engels moeten leeren, slimst van als is dat wy al by de vier jaer der onder gestaen hebben en dat noch soo wijnigh geleerdt heb, is dat men daer geen lust in heeft'. New York State Library, Van Rensselaer Manor

Nevertheless, the Dutch colonists were correct in anticipating the arrival of a Dutch fleet. During the Third Anglo-Dutch War, a combined Zeeland-Amsterdam force, under the command of Jacob Benckes and Cornelis Evertsen de Jonge, arrived at New York. The English delegates enquiring after the Dutch commission received an answer that brooked no delay: 'that it was stuck in the mouth of the canon, as they would soon become aware if they did not surrender the fort'. As the English fort did not capitulate in a sufficiently speedy manner, the Dutch ships opened fire. Six hundred Dutch marines under captain Anthony Colve conducted an amphibious landing under enemy fire to take New York. A year later the city was returned to the English, as the Peace of Westminster restored the *status quo ante bellum*. This Dutch concession reflects the relatively minor importance of North America for the economy of the Dutch Republic. As in 1667, the Dutch stakeholders in the New Amsterdam trade, mainly second-rank Amsterdam merchants, simply did not have sufficient political clout to put pressure on the Amsterdam city council, and, in turn, on the States General.[43]

Conclusion

The claim of the Dutch Republic to a large swathe of the North American mainland effectively became defunct in 1674, even though many of the colonists stayed. Their descendants upheld vestiges of their ethnic culture, including the Dutch language and reformed religion, for many years to come. Out of the five legal principles put forward in defence of English and Dutch claims over sixty years, two became paramount: claims based on a government charter and the just war. The English takeover of 1664 was corroborated by a new charter, tailor-made for the occasion. The Dutch reconquest of 1673 was an extension of the just war fought by the Dutch against the English attack of 1672. The diplomatic exchanges that took place on the

Papers (SC7079_1), box 5, folder 35–36, digitally available through digitalcollections.archives.nysed.gov; A.J.F. van Laer (trans. and ed.), *Correspondence of Jeremias van Rensselaer 1651–1674* (Albany, 1932), p. 403; Jaap Jacobs, '"It has pleased the Lord that we must learn English". Dutch New York after 1664', in *Dutch New York between east and west. The world of Margrieta van Varick*, eds Deborah L. Krohn and Peter Miller (New York, 2009), pp. 55–66; DNA, SG, inv. no. 5768; *DRCHNY*, II, 510–15.

[43] Jacobs, *The colony of New Netherland*, pp. 103–5; Artyom Anikin, 'The lost soldier of Orange. A brief biography of governor Anthony Colve 1644–1693', *New York History*, 96 (2015), 336–53; C. de Waard (ed.), *De Zeeuwsche expeditie naar de West onder Cornelis Evertsen den Jonge 1672–1674. Nieuw Nederland een jaar onder Nederlandsch bestuur* (Werken Linschoten-Vereeniging vol. 30, The Hague, 1928); Jan de Vries, *Verzwegen zeeheld. Jacob Benckes (1637–1677) en zijn wereld* (Zutphen, 2018); DNA, SG, inv. no. 5769, inv. no. 4577, fols. 42 and 66, inv. no. 11147, fol. 212; *DRCHNY*, II, 531–4 and 541–2.

American as well as the European side of the Atlantic highlight the importance of diplomatic customs: formalities relating to honour often trumped the arguments of *raison d'état* that seem important to the modern mind. Also of importance is the extent to which the exchanges in the colonies were shaped to conform to the requirements of the superiors in Europe. In the minds of the colonial authorities, the superiors in the fatherland were constantly looking over their shoulder. Hence also the desire of the colonial authorities to avoid the use of violence, which could give rise to vehement protests and prolonged diplomatic wrangling in Europe. But there was another aspect too: the role of seapower. Neither the Dutch nor the English colonies were able to wage war without military support from Europe. In the end, the arrival of a fleet from Europe, whether anticipated or not, always proved to be decisive.

10

Merchant companies at war: the Anglo-Dutch wars in Asia

Erik Odegard

… we clashed with the English ships in question around the hook of Masulipatnam, three of which were captured by us and we greeted the rest so well that, so we believe, they were glad to escape from us by night, we being so hampered by our prizes and our own damaged ships that we had enough on our hands simply to keep the fleet together …[1]

The battle between a fleet of thirteen Dutch East India Company (VOC) warships and ten vessels of the English East India Company (EIC) that took place on 29 August 1673 near Petapoli (Nizampatnam) is a rare example of a fully-fledged naval battle between the two powers fought in Asia during the three Anglo-Dutch wars of the seventeenth century. In penning these words, the Dutch commander, Cornelis van Quaelbergen (also: Quaelberg), was not just reporting a victorious battle to his superiors in Batavia.[2] Implicitly, he was also defending his conduct and explaining why he had failed to capture the seven other English ships. Ironically, the battle was very much a sideshow to a more important event taking place further south: the siege of French-held São Tomé de Meliapor (Mylapore) by the combined forces of the VOC and the Qutb Shahi of Golconda. The fleet under Van Quaelbergen had been dispatched north to pick up accumulated goods from the VOC's important Masulipatnam factory and, if possible, to track down and destroy the English ships that had been spotted in the area. Ironically, after the fall of São Tomé in September 1674, the EIC's Madras council would vociferously support the destruction of the town and its important defences. Even though England and France were still allies, England not dropping out of the war until February 1674, the Madras council felt a French return to an important fortified city on its doorstep would strain relations between the two powers. The Madras council might have agreed with Johan de Witt's famous maxim

---

[1] Dutch National Archives (The Hague) [hereafter: DNA], 1.04.02/1295, fol. 258 ro. Van Quaelbergen to Batavia.

[2] The English having lost not only three ships but also an estimated 360 casualties and prisoners. W.H. Strous, 'Int schip Rhenen', *Oud Rhenen*, 13:1 (1994), 25.

'Gallicus Amicus, non vicinus' (freely translated as 'France is a good friend, but not a good neighbour').[3] The complex relations between the three rival companies, the VOC, EIC and *Compagnie des Indes* heavily supported by the French state, illustrate that warfare between Europeans in Asia was never as straightforward as it might seem. This raises the question of the importance of the Asian theatre of the Anglo-Dutch wars, to the larger war effort of the countries involved, to the trajectory of their respective chartered companies, and finally to the local polities which were either caught up in the rivalry between the Europeans or which could enforce their neutrality in these conflicts.

These issues form the heart of this chapter. It will not only shed light on the actual combat operations of the chartered companies, but also argue that the war aims of the companies did not always accord well with those of their respective governments. By the Third Anglo-Dutch War (1672–74), the VOC was so successful as a polity *in Asia* that it could quickly muster the ships and manpower required for its Asian war effort from its local resources. It was this resource base and the concomitant logistical support of shipyards, supply depots and a refined diplomatic network that allowed the VOC to stave off the combined Anglo-French-Portuguese threat. But war was both costly and inconclusive. It is noteworthy that the most severe blows against the EIC's operations were not attacks on that company's shipping or possessions, but the conquest and occupation of Makassar in 1663–69 and Bantam in 1682. The chapter will argue that the wars, though inconclusive, offered the Dutch company opportunities to disrupt rival trading networks by blockading ports, capturing ships and, ultimately, capturing territorial possessions, such as the island of Pulau Run in the 1660s and São Tomé (Mylapore) in the 1670s. The long Anglo-Dutch peace that followed 1674 was more problematic for the VOC, as the need to maintain good diplomatic relations with England after 1674, and especially after 1688, meant that it could no longer use its military advantage to cull the growing commercial power of its main rival.

This chapter will proceed by first describing the connections between the English and Dutch companies in Asia before the outbreak of the First Anglo-Dutch War in 1652. This will help identify the aims of the companies in the wars. It will briefly elaborate causes of tensions, from the inability to make the anti-Portuguese alliance of the 1610s and 1620s work, to the infamous 'Amboyna massacre' of 1623 and English fears of the Dutch conquest of Portuguese possessions on Ceylon and in India in the 1650s and 1660s. We then turn to the three wars themselves, focusing on the third war, as this presented perhaps the best opportunity for France and England working in concert to break the power of the VOC. The final section will examine the

---

[3] H.H. Rowen, 'John de Witt and the Triple Alliance', *The Journal of Modern History*, 26:1 (1954), 3.

evolution of the relation between the companies into the early eighteenth century, arguing that the most important changes took place in the period of Anglo-Dutch peace and alliance after 1674.

Rivalry before warfare: Anglo-Dutch relations in Asia, 1600–50

In 1595 a small fleet of four vessels left Amsterdam bound for Asia. The ships of the so-called *Compagnie van Verre* ('Company of far-away lands') would attempt to break the Portuguese monopoly of European navigation to Asia. The voyage faced numerous obstacles related to a lack of information. Not only did they need to solve navigational problems, but the ships under the command of Cornelis de Houtman also faced numerous commercial obstacles. What products could one actually sell in Asia, and what were considered reasonable prices? The directors prepared themselves by amassing relevant information, including *roteiros* (illustrated navigational guides) and lists of prices of products in various ports in Asia.[4] The voyage was nevertheless a commercial fiasco, but as a feat of navigation it was a tremendous success. In the subsequent decade, the number of Dutch ships sailing to Asia actually surpassed the number of vessels on the *Carreira da India*. Unlike the first voyage, later voyages were commercially successful, prompting ever more investment in Asian trades.

It was this success that initiated the reaction of English merchants. Afraid the Republic would usurp Portugal and dominate trade with Asia, and faced with the failure of English ventures like James Lancaster's voyage of 1591, a group of merchants engaged with or interested in the trade with Asia petitioned Queen Elizabeth and received a royal charter in December 1600.[5] In the Netherlands, in the meantime, more companies were being founded in more cities, and competition amongst Dutch traders in Asia was driving up prices of spices in Asia, and down in Europe. To remedy this, and to form an organization that could not only trade but also defend their trade without the need of the involvement of the Republic's admiralties, the so-called *voorcompagnieën* (precursor-companies) were disbanded and mostly amalgamated in a single 'united' company in 1602, hence the name of the new Dutch East India company: the United East India Company.

Despite the fact that both organizations were dubbed a 'company' and both had acquired state-issued charters, their internal composition was remarkably different. In terms of capitalization, governance, the rights of shareholders, the relations to government (at central, regional, and local level) and in their policy on the use of force, the companies differed markedly. The

---

[4] National Maritime Museum of the Netherlands, Amsterdam, A.4592.
[5] P. Lawson, *The East India Company. A history* (London and New York, 1987), pp. 13–17.

EIC's invested capital of £70,000, though sizeable, was barely one-eighth of the VOC's starting capital of a little over six million guilders.[6] This difference helps explain the disparity of activity and ambitions that the companies were to display in the first decades of their existence. But besides the difference in scale, there were also differences in organization. The VOC was a federal company, with six separate chambers established in six separate cities. General management was entrusted to the *Heren XVII* (the 'seventeen gentlemen', referred to as the XVII for brevity's sake), but it would take until the end of the first twenty-year charter period for the XVII to attain a firm position of directors over the chambers, in a position to give orders.[7] The chambers built their own ships, recruited their own personnel and organized their own auctions. The XVII guarded the balance between the activities of the separate chambers and set general policy. The major difficulty in the creation of the VOC had been getting merchants from Holland and Zeeland to cooperate. In fact, the majority of the clauses in the VOC's charter dealt with the organization of the company in the Netherlands and the relations between the chambers.[8] The EIC's European organization, by comparison, was much more efficiently organized, operating only from London, and after an initial period of operating its own shipyard at Blackwall, the EIC opted to lease ships from private owners.[9]

The relation of the companies to their respective national governments differed markedly as well. The EIC, having received its charter from the crown, remained vulnerable to the crown's vacillating policy regarding Asian trade until 1688 at least.[10] In 1634, for example, Charles I granted a group of merchants led by William Courteen the privilege of trading with Asia in locations where the EIC was not established.[11] This was prompted by the attempts of Charles to wrest more revenues for the crown. The VOC had received its charter from the States General, but the more dispersed nature

---

[6] The comparison is made in H. Dunlop, *Bronnen tot de geschiedenis der Oostindische Compagnie in Perzië, eerste deel* (The Hague, 1930), p. XI.

[7] R. Schalk, O. Gelderblom and J. Jonker, 'Schipperen op de Aziatische vaart. De financiering van de VOC kamer Enkhuizen, 1602–1622', *BMGN – Low Countries Historical Review*, 127:4 (2012), 3–27.

[8] F. Gaastra, *De geschiedenis van de VOC* (7th rev. edn, Zutphen, 2002), pp. 16–22.

[9] The EIC sold its yard in 1655 to Henry Johnson for £4,350. 'Blackwall Yard: development, to c.1819', in *Survey of London: Volumes 43 and 44, Poplar, Blackwall and Isle of Dogs*, ed. H. Hobhouse (London, 1994), pp. 553–65. Digitally available at: http://www.british-history.ac.uk/survey-london/vols43-4/pp553-565 (accessed 19 July 2018).

[10] Michael Fischer has argued that only with the merger into the United East India Company in 1709 did relations between the crown and the company become more stable and predictable. M.H. Fischer, 'Diplomacy in India', in *Britain's oceanic empire. Atlantic and Indian ocean worlds, c. 1550–1850*, ed. H.V. Bowen, E. Mancke and J.G. Reid (Cambridge, 2012), p. 253.

[11] Lawson, *The East India Company*, p. 34.

of its organization meant that there was a natural support in the States of Holland and Zeeland for the continuation of the company's operations.[12] Opposition could occasionally cause trouble, as in the 1640s, but on the whole the continuation of the company's privileges was more secure in the case of the VOC, supporting share prices. The transferability of shares was indeed another important difference in the early years of the companies.[13]

In their charter areas, the companies displayed a markedly different approach to the maintenance and utility of armed forces. Jan Pieterszoon Coen, in his famous argument to the company directors in the Netherlands, argued the following:

> You gentlemen ought to know from experience that trade in Asia should be conducted and maintained under the protection and with the aid of your own weapons, and that those weapons must be wielded with the profits gained by trade. So trade cannot be maintained without war, nor war without trade.[14]

Recent scholarship has argued that to understand the VOC in Asia, it is crucial to frame it not as a shipping firm or a trader, but as a colonial state or a company-state.[15] The EIC was more ambiguous in its stance over the use of force. Though it did occasionally order naval reprisals, such as in the 1620s at Surat,[16] EIC officials also argued that trade and warfare were incompatible and that the VOC was making the same mistake as the Portuguese had.[17] By the 1650s the VOC was being referred to as a 'sea-monarchy'.[18]

---

[12] Since the appointment of directors was entrusted to the city governments of the chambers, the position of company director became part of the oligarchic city elite's competition for prestigious jobs: see J. Adams, 'The familial state. Elite family practices and state-making in the early modern Netherlands', *Theory and Society*, 23:4 (1994), 518.

[13] The EIC only really became a joint-stock enterprise in 1657. Lawson, *The East India Company*, p. 21.

[14] J.P. Coen to the XVII, 1614, as quoted in the English translation in G. Parker, *The military revolution. Military innovation and the rise of the West, 1500–1800* (Cambridge, 1988), p. 132.

[15] G. Knaap, *De 'core business' van de VOC; Markt, macht en mentaliteit vanuit overzees perspectief* (Utrecht, 2014). Philip Stern, *The company-state. Corporate sovereignty and the early modern foundations of the British empire in India* (Oxford, 2011), pp. 3–15; Arthur Weststeijn, 'The VOC as a company-state. Debating seventeenth-century Dutch colonial expansion', *Itinerario*, 38:1 (2014), 13–34; Erik Odegard, 'A company of state. The Dutch East India Company and debates on the company-state in Asia, 1660s–1690s', in *Mechanisms of global empire building*, eds C. Antunes and A. Polonia (Porto, 2017), pp. 127–44.

[16] K.N. Chaudhuri, *The trading world of Asia and the English East India Company, 1660–1760* (Cambridge, 1978), pp. 110–11.

[17] *Ibid.*, p. 110.

[18] J.R. Jones, *The Anglo-Dutch wars of the seventeenth century* (London and New York, 1996), p. 32.

Throughout the 1620s, the EIC was wracked by internal disputes over the strategy that should be followed. The growing strength of the VOC in the archipelago put the presence of EIC factories in the area, operating in the shadow of the Dutch company, increasingly in doubt.[19] Though England and the Republic were allied against the Habsburg kings of Spain and Portugal until 1604 and again in 1625–30, alliance in Europe did not translate into alliance in Asia. In the Indonesian archipelago, VOC commanders, most notably Jan Pieterszoon Coen, resented the fact that the VOC's military efforts had defeated the Portuguese threat, but that English merchants who had contributed little to this effort would now also benefit from this security.[20] The presence of English merchants in the Moluccas undercut the VOC's attempt to control the supply of fine spices through exclusive contracts with local rulers. These contracts were of course one-sided and backed up with military force, which the VOC was not hesitant to use, either against the local population or against its European rivals. This came to a head in the early 1620s in two separate but related massacres. In 1621, the VOC conquered the island of Banda as a reprisal for what it saw as illegal sales of nutmeg to rivals. The conquest was a bloody affair and the majority of the inhabitants were either killed or enslaved and forced off the island. Two years later, the VOC's governor of Ambon, an important island in the Moluccas, arrested the ten EIC employees on the island and, after having them tortured, executed them on the charge of conspiring to seize the VOC's fort. Both these massacres, though widely different in scope, had the purpose of underpinning the VOC's control of the supply of fine spices.

The murder of EIC officials at Ambon would haunt the relations between the companies and indeed between the Dutch Republic and England for the remainder of the century. The whole affair was deeply embarrassing to both governments and when James I finally authorized the navy to intercept the homeward-bound VOC fleet, this was only intended as a show of support for the EIC, as the VOC fleet was allowed to safely traverse the channel.[21] 'Amboyna' would remain both a concrete ill that needed to be put right, and more general proof of the untrustworthiness of the Dutch. It was to become a staple of anti-Dutch propaganda during the later wars.

A year prior to the events on Ambon, the EIC had taken part in the conquest of the Portuguese fort at Hormuz: by offering vessels to block the fort, the siege became effective and Hormuz fell to the Persians. Ironically, it was the VOC that would profit more from the opening up of the Persian trades, as

---

[19] K.N. Chaudhuri, *The English East India Company. The study of an early joint-stock company 1600–1640* (London, 1965), pp. 66–8.

[20] The early tensions and conflicts between the companies are very well described in J. van Goor, *Jan Pieterszoon Coen (1587–1629). Koopman-koning in Azië* (Amsterdam, 2015), pp. 251–84 and 418–20.

[21] Chaudhuri, *The English East India Company*, p. 65.

it had both the commodities to sell and the capital to buy, making it a more attractive trading partner. In India, too, the companies clashed repeatedly. The VOC had been present on the Coromandel Coast at Masulipatnam and Pulicat since the 1610s. The company tried to prevent the establishment of English factories for fear of competition, but this proved ineffective.[22] During the 1630s, the EIC tried to interfere with the supplies of Pulicat. But until the 1660s, the affairs of the EIC on the coast were always hampered by a lack of funds. All together, there were thus long-running tensions between the two companies, despite that fact that they had for considerable periods of time been allies against a common foe.

The wars in Asia: combat operations and failed schemes

When war broke out between the Dutch and English republics in 1652, the companies would inexorably be brought into the conflict by virtue of the ships at their disposal or in their possession. Both the English and the Dutch would press armed Indiamen into service with the battle fleet in Europe in this and the next war. But the service of the Indiamen was relatively more important to the Dutch, as the Dutch navy was essentially a cruising navy, not a battle fleet. Maerten Harpertszoon Tromp had proposed a fleet plan in the late 1640s, arguing that the admiralties should focus on small and medium-sized warships. To form a battle fleet, should that be necessary, the large ships of the East and West India Companies could be inducted into naval service.[23] The VOC readily offered its cruisers, intended to escort homeward-bound ships in European waters, to the navy, but the Indiamen were another matter. Ultimately forced to yield, the VOC would lose a number of ships in the battles in European waters. The war in Asian waters presented a different picture, however.

Though war was officially declared in Europe in July 1652, it was not until January of 1653 that the Dutch factory in Surat received the news. This prompted preparation to seize English ships before the outbreak of hostilities in Europe became known to them.[24] That same month, a small EIC flotilla led by the *Welcome* (32) was able to fight its way into Gamron (Bandar Abbas) and departed again with 400,000 guilders' worth of bullion as well as a load of silk. The VOC's director and the three ships at his disposal were unable to stop the four English vessels. But the small flotilla was intercepted by five VOC

---

[22] T. Raychaudhuri, *Jan Company in Coromandel, 1605–1690. A study in the interrelations of European commerce and traditional economies* (The Hague, 1962), p. 102.

[23] J.E. Elias, *De vlootbouw in Nederland 1596–1655* (Amsterdam, 1933), pp. 72–4.

[24] W. Ph. Coolhaas, *Generale missiven van Gouverneurs-Generaal en Raden aan Heren XVII der Verenigde Oostindische Compagnie: deel II, 1639–1655* (The Hague, 1964), p. 731.

warships near Sindi (Thatta), and one ship was sunk and another captured.[25] In February 1654, the High Government of the Indies reported that in Persia cargoes worth a little over 251,000 guilders had been taken from the English and the Portuguese, and the *Dove* (*d'Engelsche Duyff*), captured near Bantam, yielding nearly 30,000 guilders. That same year, the High Government did not report any ships as lost due to enemy action. The first war, in Asia, was thus a one-sided affair. But compared to the more dramatic events in Europe, it also seems a muted conflict. The trade of the EIC in many regions came to a standstill as a lack of funds precluded any activity. Only the siege and capture of one of the bases of the EIC would have fundamentally changed the relations between the companies. But although president Aaron Baker was reported to have augmented the defences of Madras in preparation for a siege, Batavia judged this as 'premature'.[26] Upon the conclusion of peace, the VOC was forced to agree to hand Pulau Run back to the EIC. Yet an agreement made in Europe proved difficult to enforce in Asia.[27] Run would only be handed back in April 1665, and would be retaken by the VOC the next year.[28] Yet a lack of success in Asia itself could be compensated for by winning the war in home waters. The conditions of the Peace of Westminster stipulated that the VOC would need to pay to the EIC an indemnity of £88,615, of which £3,615 was intended for the heirs of the EIC employees killed at Ambon more than thirty years earlier.

The first half of the 1650s was actually a period of incessant warfare for the VOC, but its main foe was not the English company, but rather the Portuguese *Estado da India*. The collapse of Dutch control in Brazil in the face of a rebellion of Luso-Brazilian planters and mill-owners had prompted the resumption of hostilities between the Dutch Republic and Portugal. In Asia, this conflict was fought out primarily on Ceylon (Sri Lanka) and the Coromandel and Malabar Coasts of India. Between 1656 and 1663, the VOC would capture the cities and forts of Colombo, Mannar, Jaffna, Negapatnam, Cranganore, Cochin and Cannanore, along with a host of smaller forts. Though England and Portugal had concluded a peace treaty in 1642 and the Viceroy in Goa had supported the EIC's settlement at Madras, both countries proved unable to come to a workable alliance in Asia.[29] The inability of Cromwell's regime to conclude an alliance with Catholic Portugal would seriously hamper the ability of England to compete in Asia during the First Anglo-Dutch War.

[25] *Ibid.*, p. 768.

[26] *Ibid.*, pp. 715–16.

[27] For a more elaborate discussion on the issue of Pulau Run, see the contribution by Martine van Ittersum in this volume.

[28] F.W. Stapel, *Pieter van Dam's Beschryvinge van de Oostindische Compagnie, eerste boek, deel II* (The Hague, 1929), p. 547.

[29] G.D. Winius and M.P. Vink, *The merchant-warrior pacified. The VOC (the Dutch East India Company) and its changing political economy in India* (Oxford, 1995), pp. 57–61, talks of an 'Anglo-Portuguese entente cordiale'.

Erik Odegard

Yet the VOC remained fearful of an Anglo-Portuguese alliance. These fears seemed justified in 1661, with the conclusion of the Anglo-Portuguese treaty which, among other things, would see the transfer of Bombay to the English crown. Secret clauses stipulated that both countries would ally against the VOC, but mutual bickering over the transfer of Bombay again scuttled the prospects for an effective alliance.[30]

Naval operations during the Second Anglo-Dutch War extended far beyond the North Sea, stretching into the Atlantic, as English raids on Dutch islands in the Caribbean helped set up the ailing sugar industry on Jamaica.[31] In the Americas New Netherland would pass into English orbit, but an attempt to take the WIC's west African forts was thwarted by the intervention of the Mediterranean squadron under De Ruyter. For the VOC, the outbreak of the war again meant an increased risk for its in- and out-going Indiamen and, as in the first war, the company would deliver ships to fight with the States' fleet. Unlike in the previous conflict, relations between the company and the Generality were more amiable and, even before war was formally declared, the VOC had reached an agreement which stipulated that it would deliver twenty ships for the fleet and pay a lump sum as a contribution to the war effort in exchange for an extension of its charter until the end of the year 1700.[32] The previous charter renewal process during the 1640s had been highly contentious, with both the WIC and the States of Friesland arguing against a renewal of the VOC's charter.[33] War or the threat of war could be used to bolster the company's position *vis-à-vis* the Generality.

The VOC's contribution to the fleet has often been criticized as not being composed of 'real warships', but this is fallacious. Of the twenty ships there were at least four which had been designed and built as warships. *Nagelboom* and *Beurs van Amsterdam* had been bought by the VOC during the 1650s from the commercial shipyards which had built them, likely as speculative investments during the first war. The other two vessels had been built in Dutch yards for foreign navies. The *Huys te Zwieten* had been ordered by the Genoese admiralty before the first war, had been taken into service with the Amsterdam admiralty during the war and was sold to the VOC during

[30] G.J. Ames, 'The role of religion in the transfer and rise of Bombay, c. 1661–1687', *The Historical Journal*, 46:2 (2003), 321–3.
[31] W. Klooster, *The Dutch moment. War, trade, and settlement in the seventeenth-century Atlantic world* (Ithaca, 2016), pp. 103–5.
[32] For the negotiations between the Generality and the VOC, see E. Odegard, 'The sixth admiralty. The Dutch East India Company and the military revolution at sea, c. 1639–1667', *International Journal of Maritime History*, 26:4 (2014), 675–7.
[33] The conflict with the WIC is better known and described in H.J. den Heijer, 'Plannen voor samenvoeging van VOC en WIC', *Tijdschrift voor Zeegeschiedenis*, 13:2 (1994), 115–30. For the conflict between the VOC and the States of Friesland, see H. Deelstra, 'Van octrooi tot fooi. De Friese strijd voor medezeggenschap in de VOC' (unpublished MA thesis, Leiden University, 2017).

the 1650s. It was lost in September 1665 during the return of the fleet from Norway and served in the English navy as the *House of Sweeds*. Ironically, it was expended as a blockship at Chatham during the Dutch raid on the dockyard in 1667.[34] *Delffland* was built in Amsterdam as *Nuestra Senora de Rosario* for the Spanish navy when it was sold to the company by its builder because of unpaid bills.[35] The company had in fact amassed a respectable fleet of large warships itself. The fact that it was both able and willing to place these ships at the disposal of the fleet in Europe attests both to the financial power of the VOC by this time, as well as to the low estimation of the EIC's power in Asia. Even the companies would fight the war mainly in European waters and the greatest losses to the VOC – the destruction of the 78-gun *Maarsseveen* in the battle of Lowestoft and the loss of the homeward-bound *Phoenix* and *Slot van Honingen* in the aftermath of the battle of Bergen – occurred in European, not Asian waters.[36] In terms of territorial losses or gains, the war changed little. Pulau Run was quickly overrun by the VOC at the start of the war. For the remainder of the war in Asia, the EIC would lay up its ships in its own or friendly neutral ports rather than risk their loss to the VOC. Rumours of a large English force prompted the VOC to equip twelve ships to cruise in the Sunda Straits early in the war, but as it became apparent that no EIC fleet was coming, this squadron was disbanded.[37] The peace would be concluded on the basis of *uti possidetis*, with each side keeping what was conquered. This meant in practice that New Netherland would be lost to the Dutch and the WIC, but that Surinam and Pulau Run would be retained. The occupation of Run, now also formally agreed to by England, would save the VOC the headache of an EIC island in the middle of its most important possession. Run was to be used to raise cattle, as it lacked water and a safe anchorage.

Throughout the 1640s and 1650s, the VOC was actually less concerned about the English and French companies. We should be careful not to project backwards the concerns of a later age, while ignoring the concerns that most animated contemporaries. In the entire period that covers the Anglo-Dutch wars, the VOC was most concerned with its conflict with the Portuguese *Estado da India* and was most vexed by the possibility of an anti-VOC grand alliance between Portugal, England, and possibly France. Any European foe would seek to ally itself to the local kingdoms of Calicut and Kandy

---

[34] Frank Fox, *Great ships. The battlefleet of King Charles II* (Greenwich, 1980), pp. 179–80.
[35] See the file in DNA, 3.01.09/540.
[36] The *Golden Phoenix* was also used as a blockship at Chatham. The *Slot Honingen* (renamed *Sancta Maria*) sunk while being towed to bring it in position to cover the chain at Gillingham. Ironically, defence of the chain was entrusted to *Charles V* (ex-*Carolus Quintus*) and *Geldersche Ruyter*, both of which had been equipped by the VOC in 1665 as part of its twenty-ship programme.
[37] DNA, 1.01.02/5739, unfoliated, scan 278.

which had their own reasons for disliking the VOC.[38] The problematic truce between the *Estado* and the VOC between 1644 and 1650 meant there were no overt hostilities in this period, but with the Dutch position in Brazil steadily worsening during the 1640s, hostilities resumed in 1650. Batavia was appraised of this fact in June 1652.[39] Over the next decade, the VOC would wage war on the *Estado da India*, conquering Colombo, Mannar and Jaffna on Ceylon, Negapatnam on the Coromandel Coast, and finally in the last campaigns of the war, Cranganore, Cochin and Cannanore on the Coromandel Coast, 1662–63. By then, VOC officials were aware of the marriage treaty between Portugal and England and were apprehensive of the possibility of a combined Luso-English counteroffensive. The marriage pact had in fact been concluded during the VOC's offensive in Malabar and one of the stipulations was English support for the beleaguered *Estado* further south. But when Antonio Mello de Castro, the new Viceroy tasked with the transfer of Bombay to the English crown, requested English support to lift the siege of Cochin, he was refused. In retaliation, he refused to hand over Bombay.[40] The diplomatic repercussions of this refusal effectively doomed a Luso-English alliance for the foreseeable future.[41] By late 1664 the royal garrison intended for Bombay had withered away to 130 men, while the EIC in Surat had only thirty employees.[42] Even the outbreak of war between the Dutch Republic and England did not help drive the erstwhile allies together. Portugal had concluded a peace treaty with the Dutch Republic in 1662 and could not be brought to support its ally. But in the VOC's ranks, the possibility of a renewed and more successful Luso-English alliance remained an option that was seriously taken into account when the question of the refortification of the newly-conquered Malabar fortresses came up.[43] The war that broke out in 1672 seemed much more threatening to the VOC, as it potentially brought together all three of the VOC's main allies in Asia. Unlike the first two wars, the VOC war effort during the Third Anglo-Dutch War (coinciding of course with the 'Guerre de Hollande') was primarily in Asia.

The third Anglo-Dutch naval war offered better opportunities for the EIC to use force to improve its position *vis-à-vis* the VOC. The alliance with France and the royal connection to Portugal held out the hope of constructing

---

[38] G.J. Ames, 'Colbert's Indian Ocean strategy of 1664–1674. A reappraisal', *French Historical Studies*, 16:3 (1990), 541 and 544–8.

[39] D. Alden, *The making of an enterprise. The Society of Jesus in Portugal, its empire and beyond, 1540–1750* (Stanford, 1996), p. 188.

[40] Ames, 'Role of religion', 320–1.

[41] *Ibid.*, 326–9.

[42] *Ibid.*, 329.

[43] The plans for the refortification of Cannanore from the early 1670s make frequent mention that the fort is in a position to block any advance by a European foe southwards, leaving open the question whether this would be an English or Portuguese foe. DNA, 1.04.02/1295, fol. 269vo.

a grand anti-VOC alliance in Asia. The EIC's behaviour would indeed be quite different than during the last war. Instead of ordering its vessels home or laying them up in friendly harbours, the EIC's ships would come out and fight the VOC. Ships were used to support the defence of EIC possessions, such as at Bombay in 1673, but would also face VOC ships in open waters. But to little avail: the largest open-water confrontation between the two companies was the battle of Masulipatnam in August 1673, between ten EIC ships and thirteen VOC vessels commanded by Cornelis van Quaelbergen.

When news of renewed hostilities became known in Batavia in October 1672, the High Government quickly mobilized vessels for wartime duty. On 19 October, the ships *Het Wapen van Middelburg, 'T Sticht Utrecht, Nuijschenburg, Pau, Cabeliau, Egmont* and the *Chialoup* (sloop) *Ackersloot*, under the command of Lucas van der Dussen, were dispatched to cruise in the vicinity of Pulau Simaon and the Malacca Strait to intercept and escort the Batavia-bound ships coming from Japan.[44] Since it was known that the English factory at Bantam was expecting one or more EIC ships, the *Amerongen, De Swarte Leeuw, Bock* and *Fortuijn* were dispatched to cruise in the Bangka Strait on 8 November. Four days later, the *Eendracht* and *Stompneus* captured the EIC's *Hannibal* on the 'inner' or east coast of Sumatra. This was reported as being a new vessel of 200 last, armed with 26 pieces and with 70 men on board, loaded with pepper from Jambi.[45] The capture was heralded as 'a good start, so we hope, of further victories'.[46] The blockade of Bantam was further strengthened later that month by the *Burg van Leijden, Hollants Thuijn, Makassar, Vrye Zee, Jonge Prins, Beurs van Amsterdam* (which had served with the fleet during the second war), *Nieuwpoort, Barm* and *Rotgans,* accompanied by two smaller sloops. These vessels blockaded the bay of Bantam itself and patrolled the Sunda Straits.[47] By December 1672, therefore, with sizeable squadrons patrolling the vicinities of the Malacca and Sunda Straits, Southeast and East Asia were inaccessible to either the EIC or the French. The main conflict would be fought out further west, where the situation was much less promising for the VOC.

In 1671, even before the outbreak of hostilities, the French navy had placed a powerful squadron under the command of Admiral de la Haye at the disposal of the *Compagnie des Indes*. In full knowledge that war with the Republic would be declared next year, it was deemed opportune to send a powerful fleet to Asia to be in a position to strike when news was received that hostilities had commenced. The High Government reported to the XVII in January 1672 that the French fleet had anchored at Surat and was repairing its ships. Batavia was most afraid of a French-Portuguese alliance, illustrating

---

[44] DNA, 1.04.02/1285, fol. 36 vo.
[45] *Ibid.,* fol. 37 ro. Batavia to the Heren XVII, 11-12-1672.
[46] *Ibid.,* fol. 37 ro.
[47] *Ibid.,* fol. 37 ro.

the lingering fears of a revanchist Portugal.[48] The French fleet, composed of the vessels *Breton, Flamen, Phénix, Europe, Triomphe, Jule, Diligente, Sultane* and two smaller vessels, descended down India's west coast in the winter of 1672, alarming Dutch commanders as it proceeded.[49] Hendrik Adriaan van Reede tot Drakenstein, commander of the Malabar Coast at Cochin, hastily brought the defences of Cochin, the command's main fortress, into a state of defence. In Malabar as well as Ceylon, the VOC's defensive preparations were hampered by the fact that it was in the middle of a large-scale programme of refortifying the places it had captured from the Portuguese, a process that would last until the end of the century.[50]

La Haye would ultimately descend on Trincomalee, the crucial strategic bay on Ceylon's east coast, in March 1672. This posed an acute problem to the VOC's commander in the area, Rijckloff Volckertsz. van Goens, formerly governor of Ceylon and now reinstated in his old position of superintendent and commander-in-chief in the West. Trincomalee had been taken by the VOC on the pretext of securing it for the king of Kandy against a rebellion only in 1667. La Haye now entered the bay arguing he had permission of the king, the rightful sovereign of the area, to do so. The VOC pulled back its outlying forces into the main fort at Trincomalee and the French proceeded to entrench themselves on the island of Dwars-in-de-weg. Since neither side had yet received news of the commencement of hostilities in Europe, both sides were loath to start fighting. By May 1672, Van Goens and his council had had enough of negotiations and ordered the concentration of available warships in the West at Trincomalee. The *Tulbenburgh, Brederode, Rijsende Son* and *Papenburgh* were already available at Trincomalee; they were to be joined by the *Damiaten, Noortwijck, Durgerdam, T Wapen van Batavia, Rammekens* and *Ysselsteijn*, which were patrolling the coast, *Clavenskercke* from Colombo, and *Osdorp* expected from Tuticorin. All ships were to be brought under Van Goens's command in one fleet 'to maintain our lawful possession against the French'.[51] Disagreements within the French command between Admiral de la Haye and François Caron, formerly of the VOC, meant that the French were loath to commence hostilities.[52] Van Goens, for his part, was satisfied to effect a blockade of the French ships in the bay. He knew of the difficulty

[48] W. Ph. Coolhaas, *Generale missiven van Gouverneurs-Generaal en Raden aan Heren XVII der Verenigde Oostindische Compagnie: deel III, 1655–1674* (The Hague, 1968), pp. 789–90.

[49] For the list of ships: H.D. Love, *Vestiges of Old Madras, 1600–1800, traced from the East India Company's records preserved at Fort St. George and the India Office and from other sources*, vol. I (New York, 1968), p. 313.

[50] Van Goens would remark that it was a stroke of luck that the French had attacked Sao Tomé instead of Negapatnam, since that city was indefensible. DNA, 1.04.02/1288, fols. 365–6 missive Van Goens, Galle, 28-10-1672.

[51] DNA, 1.04.02/1288, fols. 309 vo–310 ro.

[52] Ames, 'Colbert's Indian Ocean strategy', pp. 551–2.

of supplying garrisons on the east coast as supply problems and disease had spelled the end of an earlier attempt to garrison Trincomalee in 1660.[53] The large force that La Haye had brought to the bay could not be supplied locally, and the VOC would stop any supply ships from reaching the French. By July, La Haye was forced to leave for the Coromandel Coast in search of supplies, leaving a small garrison behind at Trincomalee. It was only here that La Haye learnt of the war with the Netherlands. But in Paris, the strategy had already shifted. It had proved impossible both to entice the Portuguese to join the anti-Dutch alliance and to persuade Charles II to send men-of-war to Asia. Charles demurred to send ships to Asia, arguing it was impossible to attack the VOC effectively, given its power on land and sea.[54]

La Haye had been ordered to seek a firm foothold in Asia to fortify and defend, sending all but two of his ships home. It was with this object in mind that the French took São Tomé on 23 July 1672. The city, though well-fortified, was taken by storm and the French quickly set about fortifying their new possession. But taking São Tomé was a mistake. It had formerly been a Portuguese town and the *Estado* still hoped to see it returned to them. Situated close to Madras, the French capture of the town angered their English 'allies' since it placed a powerful commercial rival right on the doorstep of what was still the most important EIC settlement in India. Finally, by conquering the city, the French gained the enmity of the Qutb Shahi sultan of Golconda, the sovereign of the city. Golconda raised an army and set about to besiege the town from the summer of 1672 onwards. This first siege was in fact broken by the French, but by June 1673, the VOC, having secured its position in Southeast Asia and having reduced the French garrison left behind in Trincomalee, joined forces with the Qutb Shahi and the town was besieged again, on land by the forces of Golconda, and on the sea side by the fleet of the VOC under Van Goens. It was this fleet that was sent north to Masulipatnam to defeat the EIC's fleet.

The siege of São Tomé would last until late August 1674, when the French garrison capitulated to Van Goens.[55] The capitulation of the French garrison was due to its lack of supplies of food and gunpowder. As the VOC had agreed with Golconda that the town would be handed over to the Qutb Shahi and demolished, the Dutch would not retain the port. EIC officials in Madras were actually very eager to see the destruction of this neighbouring town, going so far as to write to the Qutb Shahi urging him to demolish it quickly. If the Dutch were to keep it, they might have to hand it over to France in the case of a European siege, and if the town was retained by Golconda, what

---

[53] E. Odegard, 'Colonial careers. Johan Maurits van Nassau-Siegen, Rijckloff Volckertsz. and career-making in the seventeenth century Dutch empire' (unpublished PhD thesis, Leiden University, 2018), p. 136.

[54] Ames, 'Colbert's Indian Ocean strategy', p. 554.

[55] Love, *Vestiges of Old Madras*, p. 316.

was to stop the French from returning?[56] The town was therefore demolished, to the great benefit of nearby Madras. Peace between England and the Netherlands was, it turned out, more profitable for the EIC than war.

Allies and rivals: Anglo-Dutch rivalry in Asia after the wars

Warfare with the VOC had been a most unsatisfactory affair for the EIC. In three conflicts, the EIC had been unable to seriously undermine the VOC's strong position in both the intercontinental route and in intra-Asian trades. Peace would prove to offer far more profitable ways to undermine its rival, however. EIC offices in Bantam would continue operations until the VOC's conquest of that kingdom in the 1682. Though the VOC had not intervened in Bantam's succession war with the intent of closing off the port to rivals, it did not miss the opportunity to do so when it presented itself.[57] But the EIC would not consent to it being locked out of the pepper trade entirely. Though negotiations with Achin failed, the company was granted permission to establish a fort in Priaman on West Sumatra. When Ralph Ord, the EIC official entrusted to found the new settlement, arrived off Priaman in 1685, he found three VOC vessels in the bay. Instead, a new EIC factory was founded at Benkulen, to the south and closer to the supply of pepper.[58] New offices in Malabar would also disrupt the VOC's attempt to achieve a pepper monopoly there, and the Dutch company's attempt to control intra-Asian trades through a system of passes was undermined by selling English papers to local merchants. Since the events of 1672, the Republic was careful not to drive England into French arms and the VOC could not stop this practice. The Dutch company could occasionally still present impressive shows of force. In the summer of 1693, the VOC besieged Pondicherry for three months with a force of 1,600 men and seventeen ships. The town fell, but was restored to the French *Compagnie des Indes* during the peace negotiations, indicating the limited usefulness of force for company directors already disenchanted with the high costs of warfare.[59]

Throughout the period of the Anglo-Dutch wars and beyond, both companies studied one another and tried to adopt those traits they identified as advantageous. Ironically, this meant that the companies were moving in opposite directions. Throughout the 1670s, EIC directors and governors sought

---

[56] Love, *Vestiges of Old Madras*, p. 316.
[57] Gaastra, *Bewind en beleid bij de VOC. De financiële en commerciële politiek van de bewindhebbers, 1672–1702* (Zutphen, 1989), pp. 141–3.
[58] J. Bastin, *The British in West Sumatra (1685–1825). A selection of documents, mainly from the East India Company records preserved in the India Office Library, Commonwealth Relations Office, London* (Kuala Lumpur, 1965), pp. xi–xvi.
[59] J. Israel, *Dutch primacy in world trade, 1585–1740* (Oxford, 1990), p. 331.

to replicate what they saw as strong points of the VOC: sovereign control over important ports and their settler population, and strong garrisons, fleets and the willingness to use them to back up the company's trade.[60] At the same time, VOC directors in (mainly) Amsterdam were arguing that the company was in need of a 'general redress'. The expenses of the campaigns fought since 1650 had been too high, they argued. These expenses had been compounded by the need to fortify the new possessions. Directors in Amsterdam critically wondered whether territorial possessions were really necessary for a trading firm. Both companies thus sought to become more like the other, and by the 1740s the willingness to intervene militarily in local politics in India was indeed much stronger in the EIC than in the VOC.

Conclusion and broader relevance

The Anglo-Dutch wars were global conflicts and in Asia, as elsewhere, warfare was only the logical culmination of a rivalry that went back to the very first North European voyages at the end of the sixteenth century. Since the VOC had succeeded in all but expelling its rival from the spice islands themselves, any conflict would be fought out not there, but further west, in the approaches to Bantam or, given the latter's proximity to Batavia, in India. It was in India and the Persian Gulf that the companies would most directly clash, and it was here that such naval battles as there were, were fought. Older historiography of the companies focuses on the VOC's role in Indonesia and the EIC's role in India, with the first concentrating mainly on spices and the latter on textiles and, later, tea. Chris Nierstrasz has recently argued that this was in fact a simplified view of the strategies adopted by the two companies.[61] In fact, in South Asia, the VOC remained far larger than either the EIC or the *Compagnie des Indes* in India in terms of its territorial possessions, military presence and commercial activities. It would remain so well into the 1740s, but this position became ever more tenuous throughout this period.[62]

What, then, was the importance of the Anglo-Dutch wars for the chartered companies themselves? The Anglo-Dutch wars saw the final expulsion of the EIC from the spice islands which had initially grabbed the imagination of Northern Europeans at the end of the sixteenth century. But the remaining

---

[60] Stern, *The company-state*, pp. 63, 71–2 and 80.

[61] C. Nierstrasz, *Rivalry for tea and textiles. The English and Dutch East India Companies, 1700–1800* (Basingstoke, 2015), pp. 124–50 and 190–7.

[62] Winius and Vink named the period 'the competitive phase', following on a 'monopolistic phase'. Winius and Vink, *The merchant-warrior pacified*, pp. 47–84. Om Prakash calls the same period 1680–1740 one of 'growing competition by the English and the French': Om Prakash, *European commercial enterprise in pre-colonial India. The new Cambridge history of India*, II.5 (Cambridge, 1998), pp. 239–52.

presence of English traders in Makassar until the VOC's conquest in the second half of the 1660s and in Bantam until the 1680s meant that the VOC's control of fine spices remained leaky and a monopoly of pepper would never be achieved. It is noteworthy that the reduction of Makassar and Bantam to VOC protectorates and the expulsion of rival traders took place in periods of European peace. A weakness in the EIC's presence in present-day Indonesia was therefore a lack of sovereign bases, the conquest of which would have sparked European war. A base like this, Pulau Run, had been lost in the wars and would not be replaced. The EIC's position in India was quite different. Here the English company was present in Madras, Calcutta and Bombay (after its transfer by the crown) in forts that either operated under protection of the Mughal empire or which were sovereign territory. In retrospect, the VOC's inability to conquer any of these three positions was to cause much trouble later on.

But even a conquest of one of the three towns that were to become the presidency capitals is unlikely to have fundamentally changed the relations between the companies. Upon the conclusion of a European peace, the English could simply set up operations somewhere else with the permission of one of the local states. The VOC could not conquer all of India, nor in fact did it want to. Indeed, throughout the period of the Anglo-Dutch wars and beyond, the Dutch company's directors were bemoaning the high expenses on military matters, seeking to be more like the EIC, while the EIC sought to become more like the VOC. After the conclusion of what would prove to be a long-lasting Anglo-Dutch peace in 1674, the EIC could cleverly use the peace to start operations close to VOC positions in Malabar, thereby undercutting its attempt to control the pepper trade. Only during the VOC's war with the Zamorin in 1715–19 would the VOC succeed in dislodging the EIC from Chettuvay, but this was mainly due to the fact that the fledgling EIC factory there was not fortified or garrisoned. Tellicherry (Thalaserry) was inviolate and here the EIC could undermine the VOC's attempt to control the pepper trade. Similarly, the EIC's issuing of papers to local merchants undermined the VOC's attempt to regulate and control its local rivals through the selling of passes. On the Coromandel Coast, the EIC was finally able to provide enough capital to its merchants from the late 1670s onwards. This rapidly changed the relative positions of the two companies in this important area, with the EIC now being the commercially more important of the two companies.[63] From the 1680s onwards, it would be VOC commanders complaining of the 'arrogant' behaviour of EIC personnel, indicating a perception of shifting dominance.[64] The Anglo-Dutch wars thus did not initiate Anglo-Dutch rivalry in Asia, nor did their conclusion stem this rivalry. Since Asia was a secondary

[63] Raychaudhuri, *Jan Company in Coromandel*, pp. 110–12.
[64] C.R. Boxer, *Jan Compagnie in war and peace 1602–1799. A short history of the Dutch East-India Company* (Hong Kong, 1979), p. 54.

theatre for the parties concerned in terms of men and resources committed and in terms of war aims to be achieved, the peace treaties did not resolve the underlying rivalries.

What was the importance of the wars for the Asian polities with whom the companies traded and with whom they occasionally fought? The most important conflict is perhaps again the third war. It was during the Third Anglo-Dutch War that the VOC at all its levels – the Netherlands, Batavia and the Coromandel government – decided that it was preferable to ignore the neutrality of local polities in wars with European rivals. This pertained specifically to the position of the port of Masulipatnam. While during the first and second wars, the threat of retaliation by Golconda of the neutrality of the port and its anchorage had deterred an attack on ships at anchor, the fleet under Van Quaelbergen ignored such niceties and attacked its English opponents. It showed that the restrictions Golconda placed on hostilities in coastal waters could safely be ignored and hints at the growing discrepancy between the military power of the European companies and the ability of states like Golconda to constrain the Europeans if war should break out amongst them.[65] The VOC's seizure of Pondicherry in 1693 and the subsequent blockade of the French ports in Bengal drove home this point.[66] But the southwards expansion of the Mughal empire meant that these lessons could not be applied in the subsequent war of Spanish Succession. It was not until the collapse of imperial government and the eruption of a new Anglo-French war in the 1740s that these lessons would be brought to their logical conclusion. The Third Anglo-Dutch War is also the most interesting from another perspective. This was the only conflict in which a combination of forces, European and Asian, could have put serious pressure on the VOC in a period when sending reinforcements from Europe was difficult. If France, Portugal, England and local powers such as the Zamorin of Calicut and Raja Singha of Kandy had cooperated, the VOC might have been seriously damaged. But since even the nominal allies France and England could not and would not coordinate their actions, the VOC could pick off its enemies one by one. It could do so because it had become, in Philip Stern's phrase, a 'company-state', something that the EIC would now strive to become as well.

[65] Raychaudhuri, *Jan Company in Coromandel*, pp. 109–10.
[66] K.N. Chaudhuri and J.I. Israel, 'The English and Dutch East India Companies and the Glorious Revolution of 1688–1689', in *The Anglo-Dutch moment. Essays on the Glorious Revolution and its world impact*, ed. J.I. Israel (Cambridge, 1991), p. 424.

11

Arguing over empire: international law and Anglo-Dutch rivalry in the Banda Islands, 1616–67

Martine van Ittersum

As legal scholars are well aware, modern international law is still informed by the claims-making of former European colonial states, including the chartered companies of the early modern period. The international legal order attaches great significance to written treaties and contracts, frequently at the expense of other forms of negotiation and agreement. Historians have now entered the debate about the role of written texts in European expansion abroad. Particularly important are two recent edited volumes from Saliha Belmessous which examine whether treaties between Europeans and indigenous populations can be read as alternatives to conquest and war, providing a means by which native peoples sought to turn the tide of Western imperialism and colonialism – the case made by Belmessous, Andrew Fitzmaurice and Craig Yirush. Another contributor, Tamar Herzog, sounds a critical note. In her view, Spanish and Portuguese treaties with native peoples were little more than 'instruments of containment', aimed at realizing 'the subjection of all things indigenous'.[1]

What was the role of treaties in Dutch expansion overseas? Mark Meuwese convincingly argues that Dutch expansion overseas could not have occurred without native cooperation in one form or another. Yet Meuwese also realizes that alliances with indigenous populations were marriages of convenience, quickly dissolved if and when it suited the Dutch. Adam Clulow discusses native legal resistance against the VOC, showing that the inhabitants of the Banda Islands used treaty texts and indigenous ceremonies to manipulate the representatives of the English East India Company (EIC) into supporting them

---

[1] Saliha Belmessous (ed.), *Native claims. Indigenous law against empire, 1500–1920* (Oxford, 2012), pp. 3–18 and 85–151; *idem* (ed.), *Empire by treaty. Negotiating European expansion, 1600–1900* (Oxford, 2015), pp. 11, 15 and 78–9 (quotations); see also: Antony Anghie, *Imperialism, sovereignty and the making of international law* (Cambridge, 2005); Lauren Benton and Adam Clulow, 'Legal encounters and the origins of global law', in *The Cambridge world history*, ed. Jerry H. Bentley (Cambridge, 2015), pp. 80–100; Martti Koskenniemi, *The gentle civilizer of nations. The rise and fall of international law, 1870–1960* (Cambridge, 2001).

against the Dutch East India Company (VOC). Clulow recognizes, however, that both chartered companies put their own spin on treaty texts and indigenous ceremonies, which they routinely over-interpreted to serve their own interests.[2]

A slightly different approach is taken in this essay. My focus is on the written documents that connected the negotiating tables in London and The Hague with the furthest reaches of empire. Such far-flung European communication networks played a far more important role in Anglo-Dutch imperial rivalry than any indigenous ceremony ever could. The peace negotiations that ended the Anglo-Dutch naval wars of the seventeenth century included extensive discussions about the parties' claims to various parts of the globe. As I have shown elsewhere,[3] Europeans lacked a clear and unambiguous formula for deciding these kinds of questions. A constantly changing legal suite extended to first discovery, freedom of trade and navigation, contracts and alliances with native peoples, just war, conquest, actual possession, and the (perceived) surrender of native ownership or sovereignty. Peace negotiations were an opportunity to weigh the written evidence for claims-making generated by European colonial officials, and to assess the relative importance of various legal principles invoked by the claimants. Written accounts of the negotiations were then made available to European colonial officials, in a continuous feedback loop. Many of the legal principles that underpin international law today were harnessed to European overseas empire in this constant flow of documents.

Anglo-Dutch rivalry in the Banda Islands in the period 1616–67 is examined here as a case study, marked by the EIC's attempts to reverse the Dutch conquest. How did claims-making overseas relate to diplomatic negotiations back home? A recognizable pattern quickly established itself. Since the disorganized and poorly capitalized EIC could not hope to triumph militarily in the East Indies, it had to obtain concessions through bilateral negotiations between the Dutch and English governments. The Dutch Republic was at a disadvantage in such negotiations. It did not become independent until 1648 – not officially, at least. It was also a junior partner of the English and French monarchs, who offered military and naval support during the Eighty Years' War against the king of Spain and Portugal. By trading on this power imbalance in Europe, the EIC sought to serve its own interests in Asia. The collapse of the English monarchy in the 1640s almost put paid to this strategy. Yet a merger with the Assada Adventurers in 1650 once again gave the EIC sufficient political heft to hit back hard at the VOC.

---

[2] Mark Meuwese, *Brothers in arms, partners in trade. Dutch-indigenous alliances in the Atlantic world, 1595–1674* (Leiden, 2012); Adam Clulow, 'The art of claiming. Possession and resistance in early modern Asia', *American Historical Review*, 121:1 (2016), 17–38.

[3] Martine J. van Ittersum, 'Debating natural law in the Banda Islands. A case study in Anglo-Dutch imperial competition in the East Indies, 1609–1621', *History of European Ideas*, 42:4 (2016), 459–501.

Following the Peace of Westminster (1654), a joint commission of Dutch and English arbiters awarded the tiny island of Pulau Run to the EIC. This was easier said than done, since VOC officials in Asia refused to hand over Pulau Run to Englishmen who could not display proper commissions. The VOC officials were not just being obstructive or playing for time – the allegations invariably made in EIC documents. The question who counted as a *bona fide* EIC servant or what constituted a commission by a valid government was a very real one in the aftermath of the English civil wars and interregnum.

Finally, it is important to analyse the EIC's failure to establish a viable colony on Pulau Run in the aftermath of the Treaty of Friendship (1662) signed by the Dutch States General and Charles II of England and Scotland. The treaty mandated the island's return to the EIC. For a variety of reasons, the company left it too late to occupy the island. The EIC officials who arrived on Pulau Run in April 1665 had to surrender to a superior VOC force eight months later, when news of the Second Anglo-Dutch War reached the Banda Islands. Pulau Run remained a VOC possession under the terms of the Treaty of Breda of July 1667. Yet it was the fall of Makassar (modern-day Sulawesi) four months later that really determined the island's fate. The so-called Treaty of Bongaya (1667) reduced Makassar to the status of a VOC vassal and banned all other Europeans from its territories, thus ending what had once been a lively English smuggling trade with the Spice Islands.

Anglo-Dutch rivalry in the Banda Islands in the first half of the seventeenth century

The VOC's aim to gain complete control of the trade in nutmeg, mace and cloves may not have been realized until the 1660s, but it had been on the cards right from the start. In 1608, the VOC directors authorized Admiral Pieter Willemszoon Verhoef (1573–1609) to sign contracts with 'all the villages in the Moluccas and Banda' and to build fortresses in strategic places. Verhoef was brutally murdered by the Bandanese when he tried to impose the VOC's protection/tribute exchange. Still, the directors saw no reason to change their policy. Other VOC commanders gradually expanded Dutch influence and sovereignty in the Banda Islands, mainly through a combination of treaty-making and brute force. Dutch fortresses were established on Nera in 1609, on Pulau Way in 1616 and on Great Banda (also known as Lonthor) in 1621 (see map 4). Yet unsurprisingly the indigenous inhabitants had no intention of surrendering without a fight, and took up arms against the VOC.[4]

[4] The directors' instructions for VOC commanders and officers in the East Indies, 10/11 April 1608, Dutch National Archives (The Hague) [hereafter: DNA], 1.04.02/478 fol. 1v, 2v; Van Ittersum, 'Debating natural law in the Banda Islands', pp. 464–5, 469–70

In order to increase their leverage over the company, the Bandanese sought to play it off against its main European competitor. A succession of EIC representatives visited the Banda Islands in the 1610s, eager to secure their own trading interests. Nathaniel Courthope (d. 1620) did not just establish a stronghold on Pulau Run, but also persuaded the islanders to sign a treaty with him in December 1616. They promised to sell the EIC all their spices in perpetuity and surrendered their country to James I of England, putting themselves under the latter's protection as his subjects. It was all to no avail. The inhabitants of Pulau Run were crucially dependent for their survival on food and water reaching them from Great Banda. In spring 1621, Governor-General Jan Pieterzoon Coen (1587–1629) led a successful assault on Great Banda with sixteen warships and nearly a thousand soldiers. Confronted with this formidable force, there was nothing the EIC representatives on Pulau Run could do. The Dutch troops that landed on the island summarily expelled the English and compelled the inhabitants to recognize the VOC's authority. A new, highly detailed treaty stipulated that the Bandanese did not acknowledge any other 'princes or potentates as Sovereign'.[5]

It was hardly the end of the story. Imperial competition overseas could not be disentangled from diplomatic relations back home. The Dutch and English governments sought to ease tensions between the VOC and EIC, sponsoring negotiations in 1613, 1615 and 1619, for example. The two governments feared – as well they might – that a continuing standoff between the companies in Asia would endanger the Anglo-Dutch alliance in Europe. With an eye to the expiration of the Twelve Years' Truce (1609–21), they put pressure on the company directors to agree to a Treaty of Defence in June 1619. According to the treaty terms, the VOC and EIC were to give each other mutual assistance in Asia, open up the trade with China, reduce the purchase price of pepper in Java, and restrain excessive duties imposed by local rulers. In the Spice Islands, one-third of the trade would be reserved for the EIC, the other two-thirds for the VOC. An Anglo-Dutch Council of Defence would administer a fleet of twenty warships, ten of each company, and decide on its disposition, on the garrisoning of forts and on the payment and maintenance of the companies' armed forces.[6]

---

and 487–8; *idem, Profit and principle: Hugo Grotius, natural rights theories and the rise of Dutch power in the East Indies, 1595–1615* (Leiden, 2006), pp. 266–79.

5 J.E. Heeres and F.W. Stapel (eds), *Corpus diplomaticum Neerlando-Indicum* (6 vols, The Hague, 1907–55), I, 162–3 (quotation); Vincent C. Loth, 'Armed incidents and unpaid bills. Anglo-Dutch rivalry in the Banda Islands in the seventeenth century', *Modern Asian Studies*, 29:4 (1995), 705–40; Jur van Goor, *Jan Pieterszoon Coen (1587–1629). Koopman-koning in Azië* (Amsterdam, 2015), pp. 433–66; Clulow, 'The art of claiming', p. 34; Van Ittersum, 'Debating natural law in the Banda Islands', pp. 470–5, 478–84 and 487–90.

6 Van Ittersum, *Profit and principle*, pp. 359–483; J.C. Grayson, 'From protectorate to partnership. Anglo-Dutch relations, 1598–1625' (unpublished DPhil thesis, University of London, 1978), pp. 251–68.

The Treaty of Defence was meant to last twenty years. It did indeed inaugurate a brief era of Anglo-Dutch collaboration in the East Indies (see map 3). A joint fleet of twenty ships imposed a maritime blockade on the Spanish port of Manila in the first six months of 1621 and 1622, in an attempt to bring its trade to a complete standstill. In October 1621, a joint squadron set sail for the port of Goa, again with the aim of blockading the Portuguese headquarters in Asia and disrupting its trade. Much the weaker party, the EIC had great difficulty meeting its commitments, however. It explains why the Fleet of Defence was disbanded in June 1622. Another factor was Coen's continued distrust of EIC servants. The Governor-General performed the Treaty of Defence according to the letter, not the spirit. He insisted that, in return for a third of the trade, the impecunious EIC pay a third of the costs of the VOC forts and garrisons in the Spice Islands. This was an important factor in the treaty's unravelling in Asia.[7]

The Treaty of Defence did not address all outstanding disputes between the VOC and EIC, nor was it meant to. In summer 1621, three Dutch envoys travelled to London to negotiate a final settlement. Pulau Run was mentioned explicitly in the agreement reached with the English Privy Council two years later. In August 1622, the EIC had lodged an official complaint with the Privy Council regarding the VOC's seizure of Pulau Run. Under pressure from the Privy Council, the Dutch envoys offered to return the island and its fortifications to the EIC 'in the same condition as these were at the time that the Treaty of Defence was concluded'. The 1623 treaty, then, gave some sort of recognition to the English claim to Pulau Run, and would still be cited by the EIC forty years later.[8]

Asian realities were very different, however. The undercapitalized EIC had few means to take back Pulau Run. Thanks to a lively smuggling trade, English merchants managed to obtain nutmeg, mace and cloves in Makassar instead (see map 3). Makassar had been a gateway to the Spice Islands for centuries. Indeed, this formidable indigenous state was a crucial element in any EIC plans to resettle Pulau Run. VOC troops occupied Pulau Run for a short time in 1625. Shortly afterwards, it was depopulated and left to grow wild. EIC captain Randoll Jesson paid a surprise visit in 1636. Cornelis Acoleij, Governor of the Banda Islands, politely received him and offered to transfer Pulau Run in accordance with the 1623 treaty. Yet Jesson replied that

---

[7] Loth, 'Armed incidents and unpaid bills', pp. 722–5; Van Goor, *Jan Pieterszoon Coen*, pp. 405–20.

[8] *Acts of the Privy Council of England*, ed. J.V. Lyle (New Series, London, 1932), vol. 38 (1621–23), 301–25 and 399–400 (quotation on p. 304); 'Rapport van de heeren van Sommelsdyck, Bas, ende Stavenisse, over hunne Engelsche legatie ende besoigne gevallen t'sedert den 5 Decembris 1621 totten 12en February 1623', DNA, 1.01.02/8343, fol. 291r–v; *Calendar of state papers colonial series: East Indies, China and Japan*, ed. W.N. Sainsbury (8 vols, London, 1862–92), IV (1622–23), no. 232.

he had come for an inspection only, and sailed off to Makassar eight days later. Captain John Hunter, the head of the English trading post at Makassar, crossed over to the Banda Islands in 1638, bringing along a small party of twenty settlers. Yet he had reckoned without Governor-General Antonio van Diemen (1593–1645), who visited the Banda Islands on his way to Ceram, one of Ambon's dependencies. Van Diemen's priority was to put down the indigenous revolts that threatened the VOC's tenuous control of Ambon (see map 3). He did not need any Englishman to fish in these troubled waters. He refused point-blank to hand over Pulau Run without express orders from the English crown, the Dutch States General, and the VOC and EIC directors. As he explained to Hunter, there had been a great shift in Anglo-Dutch relations, most notably on account of a 1630 peace treaty between Charles I of England and Scotland and Philip IV of Spain and Portugal. He abhorred the idea of a Portuguese or Spanish ship anchoring in the roadstead of Pulau Run by virtue of that treaty. What he did not mention – but what must have been at the forefront of his mind – was the near-certainty that an EIC base in the Banda Islands would increase the smuggling trade via Makassar. While lavishly entertained by the Governor-General, Hunter left empty-handed.[9]

Dutch and English claims to Pulau Run in the aftermath of the Peace of Westminster (1654)

The peace treaty that ended the First Anglo-Dutch War brought Pulau Run back into play. It authorized the establishment of a joint commission of Dutch and English arbiters (four each), which could pass binding judgments with respect to damages sustained by either party anywhere in the world since 1611. Why should Pulau Run have figured in these arbitration proceedings? Part of the answer lies in the VOC's success in tightening its monopoly of trade in the Spice Islands. The ruler of Makassar was under constant pressure from the VOC, which alternated maritime blockades and armed attacks with superior buying power in the Makassar market. The EIC's smuggling

---

[9] *Dagh-register gehouden int Casteel Batavia vant passerende daer ter plaetse als over geheel Nederlandts-India* (30 vols, The Hague, 1887–1931), *Anno 1636*, pp. 131–3; Rupali Mishra, *A business of state. Commerce, politics, and the birth of the East India Company* (Cambridge, Mass., 2018), pp. 272–301; Loth, 'Armed incidents and unpaid bills', pp. 727–8; Gerrit Knaap, 'Crisis and failure. War and revolt in the Ambon Islands, 1636–1637', *Cakalele*, 3 (1992), 1–26; Menno Witteveen, *Antonio van Diemen. De opkomst van de VOC in Azië* (Amsterdam, 2011), pp. 217–21; William Foster, *The English factories in India, 1634–1636* (Oxford, 1911), pp. vii–x and 88; A.R. Ingram, *The gateway to India. The story of Methwold and Bombay* (London, 1938), pp. 52–61; D.K. Bassett, 'English trade in Celebes, 1613–1667', *Journal of the Malayan Branch of the Royal Asiatic Society*, 31 (1958), 1–39; John Villiers, 'One of the especiallest flowers in our garden. The English factory at Makassar, 1613–1667', *Archipel*, 39 (1990), 159–78.

trade in cloves peaked in the early 1640s, but was reduced to a trickle a decade later. Nutmeg and mace, which commanded the highest prices in Europe, had become even harder to obtain in Makassar.[10] Another factor that contributed to Pulau Run's prominence in the proceedings was the rise of the Assada Adventurers, led by the London merchant and Commonwealth supporter Maurice Thompson (1604–76). Already in autumn 1649 the Assada Adventurers had asked the English Council of State to settle 'all former differences with the Dutch in India'. They had developed plans to colonize the island of Assada (Nosy Be), off the northern coast of Madagascar. Their aim was 'to get mace and nutmeg of our own growing and a free trade in the South'.[11] Sufficiently impressed, the Council of State had ordered a merger with the EIC in 1650. Protests against the VOC could now be articulated more forcefully than before. In January 1652, the EIC asked the Council of State to pursue the recovery of itemized damages totalling an eye-watering £1,681,996 15s. The damages that the joint commission of Dutch and English arbiters awarded the EIC came nowhere near this figure, however. The VOC paid out £85,000 in cash, promptly pocketed by the Council of State as, supposedly, a loan to the Commonwealth regime. The arbiters also determined that Pulau Run had to be returned to the English company.[12]

The EIC directors wrote to the VOC's Governor-General in early June 1656, informing him of their plans to take possession of Pulau Run and requesting 'all appropriate assistance and favour'. A similar letter was addressed to the Governor of the Banda Islands. Both missives reached the VOC headquarters in Asia, the port of Batavia (now Jakarta), seven months later. They did not travel any further. The Peace of Westminster was an inconvenient truth for Governor-General Joan Maetsuycker (1606–78). A jurist by training, he had no intention to entertain the directors' request or to cooperate with Frederick Skinner, the English agent in the port of Bantam, located just west of Batavia (see map 3). Skinner's predilection for selling arms and gunpowder to the indigenous rulers of Bantam and Makassar

---

[10] Frances G. Davenport *et al.* (eds), *European treaties bearing on the history of the United States and its dependencies* (4 vols, Washington, DC, 1917–37), II, 15 and 18–19; Bassett, 'English trade in Celebes'; Villiers, 'One of the especiallest flowers in our garden'; Leonard Y. Andaya, *The heritage of Arung Palakka. A history of South Sulawesi (Celebes) in the seventeenth century* (The Hague, 1981), pp. 45–72; Tristan Mostert, 'Scramble for the spices. Makassar's role in European and Asian competition in the Eastern archipelago up to 1616', in *The Dutch and English East India Companies. Diplomacy, trade and violence in early modern Asia*, eds Adam Clulow and Tristan Mostert (Amsterdam, 2018), pp. 25–54.

[11] As cited by L.H. Roper, *Advancing empire. English interests and overseas expansion, 1613–1688* (Cambridge, 2017), pp. 148–9; 'Thomson [Thompson], Maurice (1604–1676), merchant', *Oxford dictionary of national biography*, www.oxforddnb.com (accessed 15 March 2018).

[12] Roper, *Advancing empire*, pp. 151 and 161–2; British Library (London) [hereafter: BL], India Office, IOR/G/21/2C, pp. 370–2, 390–2 and 405–7.

was a point of concern to Maetsuycker. For example, a substantial quantity of gunpowder had been discovered in the *Marigold*, an EIC frigate destined for Bantam, in December 1656. When Skinner visited Batavia the following month in order to negotiate the frigate's release, he was told in no uncertain terms that all Bantam residents, 'including the English', were considered the VOC's 'public enemies'.[13]

As Skinner's response to Maetsuycker shows, the reverberations of the First Anglo-Dutch War continued to be felt in Asia. VOC and EIC officials were well aware that their employers would use their reports (including copies of the protests exchanged) to put pressure on the Dutch and English governments, which could then decide to renegotiate various clauses of the Peace of Westminster or pursue additional trade deals. Consequently, the company officials couched their written exchanges in the language of European diplomacy. Skinner denounced the VOC's maritime blockade of Bantam as 'a private war', of no concern to either the Dutch or the English state. Yet he considered the seizure of EIC ships and cargoes a flagrant violation of the law of nations (*jus gentium*) 'observed by all Christian rulers and indeed by all heathen ones'. Skinner also accused VOC servants in Taiwan of having publicly displayed a rather unflattering portrait of Oliver Cromwell. Allegedly, the Protector had been depicted with 'a long tail', pulled at by 'lions, tigers, bears, dogs, cats etcetera' (see Figure 1.2). If true, the Dutch Republic had succeeded in producing anti-English war propaganda on a truly global scale. It will come as no surprise that Maetsuycker and Skinner failed to arrive at an agreement, whether about the *Marigold*, Pulau Run or anything else. It fell to George Downing (1623–84), the Commonwealth's ambassador in The Hague, to press the EIC's case. In February 1659, the VOC consented to pay a substantial sum in compensation for three EIC ships captured off Bantam.[14]

Meanwhile, the English company had not given up on its aim to take back Pulau Run. In December 1657, the EIC directors received a report on the

---

[13] *Dagh-register Anno 1656–57*, pp. 74–85 (quotations on p. 83); Minutes of the meetings of the 'Committee for Polaroon', 31 May/10 June 1654 to 21 February 1655/3 March 1656, BL, India Office, IOR/G/21/2C, pp. 425–39; Villiers, 'One of the especiallest flowers in our garden', pp. 169–70; Bassett, 'English trade in Celebes', pp. 23–6; Ruth Paley, 'Skinner, Thomas (c. 1616–1695), merchant', *Oxford dictionary of national biography*, www.oxforddnb.com (accessed 15 March 2018).

[14] *Dagh-register Anno 1656–57*, pp. 74–85 (quotations on pp. 76 and 81); EIC to George Downing, 16 August 1661 OS, in *Calendar of the court minutes of the East India Company, 1660–1663*, eds E.B. Sainsbury and W. Foster (Oxford, 1922), pp. 123–4; Simon Schama, *The embarrassment of riches. An interpretation of Dutch culture in the Golden Age* (New York, 1987), pp. 235–8; Helmer Helmers, *The Royalist republic. Literature, politics and religion in the Anglo-Dutch public sphere, 1639–1660* (Cambridge, 2015), pp. 43–5; Roger Downing and Gijs Rommelse, *A fearful gentleman. Sir George Downing in The Hague, 1658–1672* (Hilversum, 2011), p. 43.

Banda Islands from Captain John Dutton, an Englishman who had served the VOC for many years. Impressed by his plan for the colonization of Pulau Run, the directors appointed him Governor of the island in October 1658. Yet they first dispatched him to St Helena in order to further their interests in the Guinea trade. Three years later, Dutton finally set sail to Bantam in the ship *Africa*.[15]

The English captain made quite a splash on his arrival in early August 1661. The ruler of Bantam was keen to encourage greater EIC activity as a counterweight to growing Dutch power. According to the VOC factor in Bantam, the *Africa* had a crew of 150, including 'many carpenters, brick-layers, blacksmiths, and other craftsmen', evidently hired with an eye to the colonization of Pulau Run. Dutton was said to have brought 20,000 rixdollars with him, and to expect the arrival of two more EIC ships. The Sultan of Bantam and his courtiers received muskets, textiles and other lavish gifts from the English captain. They gave him various handsome presents in return, including a sloop captured from the VOC. The Sultan then visited the Dutch trading post at Bantam to ask a couple of pointed questions. He clearly sought to determine whether Dutton's arrival would tip the balance of power between the two chartered companies. How many ships had arrived at Batavia from the Dutch Republic that year and how many were still expected? Could any VOC ships be spared in order to institute a maritime blockade of Goa? And, crucially, would the VOC give Dutton permission to sail to the Spice Islands and establish a fortress on Pulau Run? The answers of the VOC factor in Bantam must have been suitably vague and non-committal.[16]

Dutton realized, of course, that the VOC's cooperation was crucial to his success. In late September 1661, his wife and private secretary paid a courtesy visit to Maetsuycker in Batavia. EIC representatives returned in early November, carrying Dutton's request for the transfer of Pulau Run and two letters of the VOC directors of October 1660, addressed to the Governor-General and the Governor of the Banda Islands, respectively. The directors' instructions were to hand over Pulau Run to any English national who could present adequate authorization from both the VOC and Charles II of England and Scotland. Therein lay the rub, however.[17]

Maetsuycker took his time to respond to Dutton. New orders had arrived from the VOC directors, issued in March 1661 in direct response to ongoing

[15] Court Minutes, 22 December 1657, 10 September 1658, 11 October 1658 OS, BL, India Office, IOR/B/26, pp. 31, 131 and 139–40; Roper, *Advancing empire*, pp. 171–3 (including footnote 24 on p. 171).

[16] *Dagh-register Anno 1661*, pp. 256, 261, 262, 346, 353 and 364 (entries of 12, 18, 20 August 1661, 26 October 1661, 5 and 18 November 1661).

[17] *Ibid.*, pp. 287, 311, 346, 351–2 (entries of 24 September 1661, 16 and 26 October 1661, and 3 November 1661).

negotiations between Charles II and the Dutch States General.[18] Predictably, Pulau Run was one of the flashpoints of the negotiations. The directors' orders made it very clear that no agreement had been reached yet with regard to the island's transfer. Indeed, one of the enclosures suggested that the English company had used the talks in London to issue 'several threats against our state'.[19] In early February, the EIC directors rejected the Dutch demand that, in return for Pulau Run, they relinquish their claims to damages worth 'three hundred thousand pounds or thereabouts'. Indeed, they threatened their Dutch counterparts with 'such other expedients as the justice of God and our King shall make us masters of'. Upon receipt of this unwelcome news, the VOC directors wrote to Maetsuycker immediately. It was essential to hold on to Pulau Run as long as the talks continued in London.[20]

The small, isolated island was now a pawn in a complicated diplomatic game back in Europe. In February 1661, the Dutch envoys complained to Charles II about the stinging language of the EIC reply. They also explained that the Dutch States General considered the king's commission, authorizing the EIC to take possession of Pulau Run, to be insufficient. It lacked a clause to the effect that the island's transfer would put an end to all differences and disputes between the two companies. Only two years previously the VOC had reached an agreement with Sir George Downing, now Charles II's envoy in The Hague, to pay compensation for the capture of three English ships. Surely the king disapproved of his subjects renewing claims resolved by recent treaties?[21]

The EIC begged to differ in its own petition to the king of March 1661. The island's restitution was mandated by the 1622–23 agreement between the two companies. The VOC had promised 'the late Usurper' [Cromwell] to return it, but got away with doing precisely nothing – allegedly thanks to judicious bribery. Charles II's restoration had induced the petitioners to resume their plans for the island's settlement. However, they had met with obfuscation and delay when they requested the cooperation of the VOC directors and the Dutch envoys in London. They also demanded compensation for losses suffered since 1654. They could not afford to relinquish these claims in

---

[18] Treaty of Friendship between Great Britain and the United Netherlands, concluded at Whitehall, September 4/14, 1662. Ratification by Charles II, December 24, 1662/January 3, 1663, in *European treaties*, eds Davenport *et al.*, II, 73–85.

[19] *Dagh-register Anno 1661*, p. 352 (entry of 4 November 1661).

[20] Quotations taken from 'The Company's Answer to the Memorial of the Dutch Ambassadors, 1 February 1661', in *Calendar of the court minutes of the East India Company, 1660–1663*, p. 86; N. Japikse, *De verwikkelingen tusschen de Republiek en Engeland van 1660–1665* (Leiden, 1900), pp. 86–92; Gijs Rommelse, *The Second Anglo-Dutch War (1665–1667). Raison d'état, mercantilism and maritime strife* (Hilversum, 2006), pp. 87–9.

[21] 'The Dutch Ambassadors to the King', February 1661, in *Calendar of the court minutes of the East India Company, 1660–1663*, pp. 95–9.

exchange for an island denuded of nutmeg trees, requiring at least £30,000 of investment to make it a viable plantation.[22]

Alarmed by these acrimonious exchanges in London, the VOC directors dispatched a fast-sailing yacht to Batavia, which arrived in the Sunda Straits in early November 1661. A few days later, the Governor-General returned a non-committal answer to Dutton, claiming that he was waiting for more news from the Dutch Republic. Later that month, he sent armed reinforcements to the Banda Islands and appointed Joan van Dam (1617–77) as the new Governor. When the latter reached his destination in December, he found most VOC strongholds in poor condition and immediately authorized major repairs. He was determined to obstruct Captain Dutton's plans for the colonization of Pulau Run.[23]

Maetsuycker could not have selected a better man for the job. Van Dam had gained a reputation as a reliable fixer and troubleshooter ever since his arrival in Batavia in 1655. A lawyer by training, he had served as Vice-President of the Council of Justice and commanded the garrison of Batavia Castle. In spring 1660, Maetsuycker had dispatched him to Makassar with a fleet of thirty-one vessels and 2,600 soldiers in order to teach its troublesome ruler a lesson. As soon as Van Dam captured the fortress of Panakoekang, Sultan Hassan Udin had sued for peace. The treaties concluded in August and December 1660 were meant to eradicate Makassar's smuggling trade in spices and thus give the VOC greater control of Ambon and the Banda Islands. Neither Maetsuycker nor Van Dam intended to surrender these gains when confronted with new EIC efforts to recover Pulau Run.[24]

---

[22] Quotations taken from 'Petition of the Company to the King touching Pulau Run' of 15/25 March 1661, BL, India Office, IOR/I/2/6, fols. 103r–v – I thank the British Library for making the digital scans available; quotations taken from the Court Minutes, 31 December 1660 OS and 6/16 March 1660/1661, BL, IOR/B/26, pp. 330 and 349; *Calendar of the court minutes of the East India Company, 1660–1663*, pp. 99–102; Pieter van Dam, *Beschryvinge van de Oostindische Compagnie*, eds F.W. Stapel and C.W.Th. van Boetzelaer van Asperen en Dubbeldam (The Hague, 1927–54), I-1, 217; Japikse, *De verwikkelingen tusschen de Republiek en Engeland*, p. 87.

[23] *Dagh-register Anno 1661*, pp. 352, 355 and 365 (entries of 4, 8, 19 November 1661); Joan Maetsuycker to the Gentlemen XVII, 26 December 1662, in *Generale missiven van gouverneurs-generaal en raden aan heren XVII der Verenigde Oostindische Compagnie* (13 vols, The Hague, 1960–2007), vol. 3 (1656–74), p. 406; W.E. van Dam van Isselt, 'Mr. Johan van Dam en zijne tuchtiging van Makassar in 1660', *Bijdragen tot de Taal-, Land- en Volkenkunde (Journal of the Humanities and Social Sciences of Southeast Asia)*, 1 (1908), 1–44, particularly pp. 32–3.

[24] Van Dam, *Beschryvinge*, II-1, 224–31; *De Oost-Indische voyagie van Wouter Schouten*, ed. Michael Breet (Zutphen, 2003), pp. 87–109; *Nieuw Nederlandsch Biografisch Woordenboek* (NNBW) I, columns 677–8; Van Dam van Isselt, 'Mr. Johan van Dam en Zijne Tuchtiging van Makassar in 1660', pp. 10–30; Bassett, 'English trade in Celebes', pp. 29–32; *Corpus Diplomaticum Neerlando-Indicum*, II, 168–79 (VOC treaties with Makassar of 19 August and 2 December 1660).

We can reconstruct Dutton's voyage to the Banda Islands from his written report to the EIC directors and from the *Daghregisters* ('Daily Registers') of Batavia Castle and Maetsuycker's letters to the VOC directors. Dutton left Bantam on the yacht *Discovery* in the middle of January 1662, accompanied by the *London*, which carried building materials for a stronghold on Pulau Run. His next stop was Japara, a port on Java's northern coast, where he was warmly welcomed by the indigenous authorities. Yet he suspected that the two Dutch vessels in the roadstead were there 'to attend and observe our actions'. Makassar was reached by the middle of February. Dutton and his wife spent six days at the EIC trading post, 'worthily entertained' by William Turner, who informed him about the VOC's recent war with Sultan Hassan Udin. Apparently, Dutton tried to persuade the locals to come with him to Pulau Run, but without success. Did the VOC's political and military ascendancy in the region deter any potential recruits for the EIC's proposed colonization of Pulau Run?[25]

The *London* and *Discovery* set sail for the Banda Islands in late February 1662 and arrived at Pulau Run three weeks later (see map 4). Six soldiers, commanded by a corporal, manned a small VOC redoubt on the western side of the island. The corporal politely refused Dutton's request to take possession of the island and directed him to Van Dam instead. The Governor of the Banda Islands sent an 'impertinent answer' by return of post. Undeterred, Dutton wrote again, requesting 'the quiet and peaceable delivery of Poularoone into our possession'. However, he continued to receive similar replies from Van Dam, who 'slighted our gracious sovereign's commission' and then dispatched eleven more soldiers to Pulau Run to reinforce the message.[26] Maetsuycker was slightly more diplomatic in his letter to the VOC directors of December 1662. Allegedly, Van Dam and his council had deferred the handover until they received new orders from the VOC directors regarding the 'difficulties raised again by the English side regarding the island's transfer' – a clear reference to the negotiations in London in winter and spring 1661. Maetsuycker noted that Dutton had used the exchange of written protests to calculate the estimated EIC losses, which, allegedly, came to nearly £125,000. Van Dam had given the English captain permission to move his two ships to the roadstead of Castle Nassau (on the island of Banda Nera) in order to wait there for the turning of the monsoon. Strange to say, Dutton had made

[25] *Dagh-register Anno 1661*, pp. 370, 469, 526 (entries of 23 November, 11 December and 31 December 1661); BL, Lansdowne Mss. 213, fols. 436–7; 'Narrative of abuses, indignities, and affronts offered by the Dutch Company to the English, July 1663', in *Calendar of the court minutes of the East India Company, 1660–1663*, pp. 325–7; Bassett, 'English trade in Celebes', pp. 29–32; Joan Maetsuycker to the Gentlemen XVII, 26 December 1662, in *Generale missiven*, vol. 3, p. 408. I thank Prof. Lou Roper for making his detailed notes on 'A Brief Relation of a Voyage from St Helena to the Coast of Africa to Bantam', contained in Lansdowne Mss. 213, available to me.

[26] BL, Lansdowne Mss. 213, fols. 436–7; Roper, *Advancing empire*, pp. 173–4.

no attempt to go ashore – as if, so the Governor-General mused, he had come with no other purpose in mind than to return to Bantam in the confidence that his written protests would more than cover the costs of his voyage. In Maetsuycker's view, blackmailing the VOC had been the EIC's preferred way of doing business for many years.[27]

Dutton saw it differently, of course. He reported to the EIC directors that, while lying at anchor in the roadstead of Castle Nassau, one of the *London's* boats had been stolen and an African slave had been taken from the *Discovery*. The captain left the Banda Islands at the end of April 1662, shadowed by VOC vessels. When he arrived in Makassar, he unloaded the building materials for the projected EIC stronghold at Pulau Run. He stayed at the port for over a month, largely due to illness among his crew. It was no undivided pleasure: 'the insolent Hollanders' jeered at the English in the streets of Makassar, 'saying these are the men that would have the Poula Roone but are returned like fools'. In early July, Dutton was back in Bantam. There he fired off more written protests, to which Maetsuycker responded in much the same way as Van Dam had done. The captain left for England in October.[28]

The imperial endgame in Batavia, the Banda Islands and Makassar

When Dutton arrived back in London in May 1663, he was well received by the EIC directors. They blamed the VOC for Dutton's failures and saw no reason to change their plans for the colonization of Pulau Run. A Treaty of Friendship had been concluded between Charles II and the Dutch States General eight months earlier. Article fifteen arranged for the island to be transferred to Charles II or anybody appointed by him carrying 'a commission under the Great Seal of England'. It also stipulated that Pulau Run's restitution would *ipso facto* extinguish and annul 'all offenses, injuries, and losses ... which one party has suffered, and can in any way pretend to have suffered from the other in the East Indies'. The *terminus ad quem* was 20 January 1659, a date taken straight from Downing's agreement with the VOC three and a half years earlier. This was something the VOC directors and Dutch envoys had insisted on all along.[29]

Initially, it seemed as if the Treaty of Friendship might succeed in allaying Anglo-Dutch rivalry in the Banda Islands. In response to a friendly reminder

[27] *Generale missiven*, vol. 3, pp. 406–8; Roper, *Advancing empire*, pp. 173–4.

[28] BL, Lansdowne Mss. 213, fols. 436–41; *Generale missiven*, vol. 3, pp. 406–8; Van Dam van Isselt, 'Mr. Johan van Dam en zijne tuchtiging van Makassar in 1660', p. 33; *Calendar of the court minutes of the East India Company, 1660–1663*, pp. 311 and 324 (entries of 15 May and 15 July 1663 OS); Roper, *Advancing empire*, pp. 173–4.

[29] Davenport *et al.*, *European treaties*, II, 73–85 (quotation on p. 84); Downing and Rommelse, *A fearful gentleman*, pp. 89–110.

from Charles II, the Dutch ambassador in London supplied the EIC directors with letters from the Dutch States General and the VOC directors, authorizing the company officials in Asia to return the island to such person(s) as could exhibit a royal commission, passed under the Great Seal of England. There were two packages: one for the Governor-General, the other for the Governor of the Banda Islands. The packages also contained copies of article fifteen of the Treaty of Friendship. The delivery took place in Batavia in early October 1663, courtesy of John Hunter, now EIC agent in Bantam. Maetsuycker immediately replied that he would be happy to authorize the restitution of Pulau Run as soon as he had seen Charles II's commission. Yet when three EIC representatives returned to Batavia a fortnight later, they could not convince Maetsuycker and his Councillors of the Indies that they were in possession of a royal commission passed under the Great Seal of England.[30]

Was it another example of VOC officials reverting to their time-tested practice of stalling and obfuscation, just like they had done on previous occasions? The EIC directors certainly came to this conclusion. Yet it is possible to adopt a different perspective, one that recognizes the entangled histories of Anglo-Dutch relations in Asia and Europe. Long paper trails connected the negotiating tables in London and The Hague with even the most remote outposts of empire. When Dutch and English diplomats, the VOC and EIC directors and the latter's servants in the East communicated with each other, they tended to act as if they found themselves in a court of law, adopting the *habitus* of a plaintiff or defendant. They conceptualized the interconnections between political developments at home and abroad through the shared language of Roman law. Written documents, executed in an appropriate fashion, were key to their exchanges. Since medieval times, European authorities had bestowed property, offices and titles by means of highly stylized texts on parchment, with proper seals attached. European expansion abroad increased the importance of such materials. Without a physical copy of a charter, a title deed or an appointment letter, how could a colonial official on the other side of the globe establish the validity of a claim made by another European? This is the context in which Maetsuycker and his Councillors of the Indies raised their objections against Hunter's commission.[31]

The Governor-General took the precaution of having verbatim copies of the English materials inserted in the *Daghregister*, including descriptions

---

[30] Japikse, *De Verwikkelingen tusschen de Republiek en Engeland*, pp. 263–4; *Dagh-register Anno 1663*, pp. 466–509.

[31] Downing and Rommelse, *A fearful gentleman*, p. 107; Japikse, *De verwikkelingen tusschen de Republiek en Engeland*, pp. 368–9; Lauren Benton, *Law and colonial cultures. Legal regimes in world history, 1400–1900* (Cambridge, 2009); Lauren Benton and Benjamin Straumann, 'Acquiring empire by law. From Roman doctrine to early modern European practice', *Law and History Review*, 28 (2010), 1–38; *The Roman foundations of the law of nations. Alberico Gentili and the justice of empire*, eds Benedict Kingsbury and Benjamin Straumann (Oxford, 2010).

of the parchments and seals, along with drawings of the latter. He and his Councillors of the Indies subjected the documents to sophisticated primary source criticism. They noted that the supposed royal commission had not been signed by Charles II, but by a person called 'Barker', without any indication of the latter's rank or standing in society. The document failed to mention the Treaty of Friendship and the VOC. The date and signature at the bottom of the parchment were written in a different hand, and probably of recent vintage. The parchment looked grimy and soiled. The seal was not wrapped in the customary tin box, but in creased and filthy paper, which looked as if 'it had been used by children for reading practice for several years, or left in a chimney'. The seal had been made of 'soft wax', which made the flattened image difficult to distinguish – as if 'it had been lying in sand somewhere'. Nor could they detect the 'arms of England'. They concluded that, at best, they were dealing with the king's Privy Seal. Yet article fifteen of the Treaty of Friendship stipulated that the royal commission for the delivery of Pulau Run had to be passed under the Great Seal of England. These were no trivialities. Whose representative was Hunter, really? Could somebody else show up at a later point in time, carrying a commission passed under the Great Seal of England that would entitle him to take possession of Pulau Run? The EIC's monopoly of English trade with Asia had been under attack throughout most of the 1630s, 1640s and 1650s. Who could guarantee that Charles II would stand by the company?[32]

For the next six weeks, Hunter and Maetsuycker engaged in written exchanges about the Treaty of Friendship and its stipulations for the island's transfer to the EIC. In the end, the Governor-General and his Councillors of the Indies accepted the agent's assurances regarding the authenticity of his commission. They issued orders to Van Dam to deliver Pulau Run to the EIC representatives nominated by Hunter. Of course, the English would have to fend for themselves once they arrived on Pulau Run, and should not be allowed to visit any of the other Banda Islands, with the exception of Fort Nassau, the VOC headquarters at Nera. In accordance with the law of nations, Dutch colonists would be permitted to bring fresh water to Pulau Run. The Governor-General and Councillors of the Indies made it very clear, however, that they expected the VOC forces in the Banda Islands to forestall any kind of surreptitious deliveries of nutmeg and mace to the English.[33]

---

[32] *Dagh-register Anno 1663*, pp. 509–20 (entries of 18, 21, 23, 24, 26, 29 and 30 October 1663 – all quotations taken from p. 514); Davenport *et al.*, *European treaties*, II, 84; Roper, *Advancing empire*, pp. 148–9; Mishra, *A business of state*, pp. 272–301.

[33] *Dagh-register Anno 1663*, pp. 509–31, 541–2, 556–9, 584, 662–3 (entries of 18, 21, 23, 24, 26, 29 and 30 October, 5, 6, 9, 14, 17 and 28 November and 9 December 1663); *Dagh-register Anno 1664*, p. 232 (entry of 8 June 1664); Joan Maetsuycker and the Councillors of the Indies to the Gentlemen XVII, 30 January 1666, in *Generale missiven*, vol. 3, p. 484.

The island's actual transfer would not occur until April 1665. Apparently, Pulau Run was not sufficiently high on the EIC's list of priorities. Van Dam wrote to Maetsuycker in May 1664 that no Englishmen had shown up at Fort Nassau yet. Why did the EIC representatives in Bantam and Makassar fail to use the western monsoon to sail to the Banda Islands that spring? The *Malacca*'s arrival in Batavia in the middle of October provided the answer. The VOC ship carried detailed reports written by Van Dam, a rich cargo of nutmeg and mace, and three EIC servants: Robert Rawlings, an unnamed mestizo, and Vincent Vette, born in the Dutch Republic, but employed by the EIC.[34]

Anglo-Dutch imperial rivalry in Southeast Asia focused on the Barat Daya Islands, northeast of Timor, in spring and summer 1664. There was a connection with the Banda Islands, of course. Van Dam took a broad view of his remit to maintain the VOC's monopoly of the spice trade. In early February 1664, he sent two vessels to the islands of Serua and Damar to destroy any nutmeg trees found there and thus 'forestall the English'. He drew on a well-established legal toolbox to justify this drastic course of action. He arranged for the creation of both written documents and 'facts on the ground' that would prove 'actual possession' – the most potent claim to overseas lands that Europeans could muster in the early modern period. Predictably, he presented his plans as a renewal of 'the old alliance of subjection', the protection/tribute exchange that had been key to the VOC's ascendancy in Southeast Asia for over six decades. Treaties were duly signed with orang kayas (local leaders) on the islands on 6 and 30 March and 3 July 1664, respectively. Van Dam arranged for physical markers of possession to be erected as well, such as bamboo huts designated as Dutch trading posts and flags of 'the Prince of Orange', which stood on stone flag-pole bases displaying 'the Company's shield and initials'. In early June 1664, Van Dam dispatched three more vessels to the Barat Daya Islands, carrying forty soldiers. The commander, Jan van der Linden, was in for a nasty surprise.[35]

On arrival, he discovered that EIC representatives had established a trading post on the island of Damar, flying the flag of St George. Naturally, he demanded to see the commission of his EIC counterpart, Vincent Vette, only to discover that it lacked a royal signature and seal. Vette claimed regardless that Damar was now in the possession of the king of England. Armed conflict had broken out between pro-EIC and pro-VOC indigenous groups on the island. Van der Linden

---

[34] *Dagh-register Anno 1664*, pp. 231–2 (entry of 8 June 1664), 399 (entry of 12 October 1664), 445–6 (entries of 15 and 19 October 1664), 462–6 (entries of 22–25 October 1664); Christopher Joby, *The Dutch language in Britain (1550–1772). A social history of the use of Dutch in early modern Britain* (Leiden, 2015).

[35] *Dagh-register Anno 1664*, pp. 231–2 (entry of 8 June 1664 – all quotations from these two pages), 303–4 (entry of 2 August 1664); Van Dam, *Beschryvinge*, II-1, 173, 180; VOC treaties concluded with the inhabitants of Serua, Damar and Nila, on 6 and 30 March and 3 July 1664, respectively, in *Corpus Diplomaticum Neerlando-Indicum*, II, 272–7; Benton and Straumann, 'Acquiring empire by law'.

turned for help to orang kaya Kery, who was still loyal to the VOC. The latter provided him with a copy of the declaration issued by the EIC representatives in late April 1664. It was a perfect example of the protection/tribute exchange that undergirded so much of European empire building in Southeast Asia. The EIC undertook to 'protect' and 'defend' the Damarese, who, in return, 'freely and voluntarily' gifted their island to 'our king of England from henceforth forever'. Any interference with 'our English coulors or flagg' or other physical markers of 'actual possession' would be considered an offence against 'our kings Majestie', punishable by 'the lawes of England'. When Van der Linden confronted Vette with the text of the declaration, the result was a shouting-match about the legitimacy of Dutch and English claims-making in Southeast Asia.[36]

The Dutch commander decided against the use of force at Damar, at least for the time being. Together with Kery, he crossed over to the island of Nila. In early July 1664, he signed a treaty with six orang kayas there, allegedly 'in the presence of most of the inhabitants'.[37] The Nilese became VOC subjects. They could not welcome anybody to their country apart from the Dutch. In addition, they were required to sell their spices to the VOC and, more importantly, to reveal the location of nutmeg trees – to be destroyed for 'an agreed price per tree'. In return, the VOC promised to protect the Nilese against the latter's enemies and to 'show them all friendship, as a good ruler ought to treat his subjects'. The islanders accepted a Prince's flag, and immediately set to work building a bamboo hut for the new sovereign.[38]

Meanwhile, the situation at Damar had spun out of control completely, due to heavy fighting between pro-EIC and pro-VOC indigenous groups. The EIC representatives, who feared for their lives, begged Van der Linden to take them to the Banda Islands, which he did. When Van Dam learnt of the deteriorating situation at Damar in early August 1664, he immediately sent Van der Linden back to the island with two vessels and a force of eighty soldiers. Van der Linden was not entirely successful in executing his superior's orders to punish the 'rebels' and remove 'all English markers of possession'. A month later, Van Dam dispatched another yacht with thirty soldiers to finish the job.[39]

The turmoil at Damar was a perfect excuse for the Governor of the Banda Islands not to cooperate with the EIC representatives. He had no intention whatsoever to let Vette and his companions anywhere near Pulau Run. He insisted that the VOC be reimbursed first for the damages suffered at Damar,

[36] *Dagh-register Anno 1664*, pp. 303–6 (entry of 2 August 1664 – quotations on pp. 304–5), 402 (entry of 12 October 1664); *Corpus Diplomaticum Neerlando-Indicum*, II, 272–7; Martine J. van Ittersum, 'Empire by treaty? The role of written documents in European overseas expansion, 1500–1800', in *The Dutch and English East India Companies*, eds Clulow and Mostert, pp. 153–78.

[37] *Dagh-register Anno 1664*, p. 402 (entry of 12 October 1664).

[38] VOC treaty concluded with the inhabitants of Nila, 3 July 1664, in *Corpus Diplomaticum Neerlando-Indicum*, II, 276–7.

[39] *Dagh-register Anno 1664*, p. 402 (entry of 12 October 1664).

and for the soaring costs of Damar's pacification. According to his calculations, the two expeditions of August and September 1664 had cost over 5,000 Dutch guilders already. Another reason to send the EIC representatives packing was Vette's increasingly erratic behaviour. Vette was in a state of constant intoxication during his stay on Banda Nera, and tried to murder Robert Rawlings at one point.[40]

When the EIC representatives arrived in Batavia in October 1664, Maetsuycker immediately released Rawlings and the mestizo, but detained Vette. As he explained to Hunter, the Dutch States General prohibited 'born subjects of the Dutch state' from being employed by the EIC. The English agent in Bantam did not seem unduly troubled by Vette's confinement. True to form, he sought to be reimbursed for the losses that, he claimed, the EIC had incurred on the Dutchman's account. Meanwhile, Vette issued one written protest after another. Among other things, he accused Van Dam of having 'up to 3,000 nutmeg trees' cut down on Pulau Run. The Governor-General did not reply to the detainee. He had the young man locked up in Batavia's insane asylum, in order that 'he might come to his senses'. Vette travelled back to the Dutch Republic on board the VOC fleet that left Batavia in late December 1664.[41]

In response to Van Dam's letters, the Governor-General and his Councillors of the Indies took a raft of measures to strengthen the VOC's position in the Spice Islands. At the same time, they sought to honour the terms of the Treaty of Friendship. They authorized Van Dam to station four VOC soldiers on each of the Barat Daya Islands as proof of 'actual possession'. They took his point that, by fomenting rebellion on Damar, the EIC had caused 5,000 Dutch guilders' worth of damages, but did not consider it a valid reason to hold on to Pulau Run. The VOC was bound to perform treaties in good faith, particularly agreements between the Dutch Republic and its European neighbours and allies. Yet deliveries of fresh water could not be countenanced once the EIC had taken possession of Pulau Run. Any EIC representatives who, like Vette and his companions, wished to return to Batavia could do so on board VOC ships. Meanwhile, the garrison in the Banda Islands would be reinforced with another 180 soldiers. Van Dam was promoted to the position of Governor of Ambon, where he was expected to deal decisively with a series of indigenous uprisings. His replacement in the Banda Islands, Jacob Cops, left Batavia in early December 1664.[42]

---

[40] *Ibid.*, pp. 402–6 (entry of 12 October 1664), 465–6 (entry of 25 October 1664).

[41] *Ibid.*, pp. 406–9 (entries of 12 and 14 October 1664 – quotations on pp. 407 and 409), 445–6 (entries of 15 and 19 October 1664), 462–4 (entries of 22–24 October 1664); *Dagh-register Anno 1665*, p. 19 (entry of 31 January 1665).

[42] *Dagh-register Anno 1664*, pp. 483 and 541 (entries of 11 November and 3 December 1664); Van Dam van Isselt, 'Mr. Johan van Dam en zijne tuchtiging van Makassar in 1660', p. 35; Joan Maetsuycker to the Gentlemen XVII, 23 December 1664, in *Generale*

Pulau Run's belated transfer to the EIC proved an anti-climax. Three vessels dispatched by Hunter reached the Banda Islands in late March 1665. The EIC representatives carried a copy of Maetsuycker's orders of the previous November, authorizing Pulau Run's surrender. Much to their surprise, they received a positive reply from Cops. The next day, VOC merchant Joan van Aelmonde handed over the island to François Wibbe, former commander of the English garrison at Dunkirk.[43] It was hardly an auspicious moment to take possession of Pulau Run. The turning of the monsoon made it difficult to unload foodstuffs and building materials, for example. In late April, EIC representatives went to Castle Nassau for urgent supplies of fresh water and vegetables. While granting it on this occasion, Cops explained that he would not be so forthcoming in the future.

The news of the Second Anglo-Dutch War reached Bantam and Batavia in August 1665. Apparently, William Turner – now EIC agent in Bantam – was confident of a quick English victory over the Dutch Republic. This message was spread in Makassar as well. EIC representatives seem to have goaded Sultan Hassan Udin into a new rupture with the VOC, dropping vague hints of English naval assistance from Europe. It turned out very differently. No English navy ships entered Asian waters during the armed conflict in Europe. Instead, it was the VOC that could bring overwhelming force to bear on Pulau Run and Makassar.[44]

The Governor of the Banda Islands received Maetsuycker's instructions to recapture Pulau Run in early December 1665. An EIC sloop arriving from Makassar and filled with provisions was captured first. Following a successful landing of VOC troops on Pulau Run, the EIC commander Thomas Harington surrendered without a fight. Yet he managed to negotiate generous terms. Nearly thirty EIC prisoners were taken to Castle Nassau and thence to Batavia. They were released there and joined their countrymen in Bantam.[45]

In October 1666, the Governor-General and his Councillors of the Indies declared war on Sultan Hassan Udin. They responded to a string of Makassarese victories over the Sultan of Ternate, a key VOC ally in the

---

missiven, vol. 3, p. 468; Gerrit Knaap, 'Headhunting, carnage, and armed peace in Amboina, 1500–1700', *Journal of the Economic and Social History of the Orient*, 46:2 (2003), 165–92.

[43] *Dagh-register Anno 1665*, pp. 7, 11, 16, 18, 34, 122–3, 128 (entries of 14, 17, 21 and 29 January, 23 February, 31 May and 5 June 1665); Joan Maetsuycker to the Gentlemen XVII, 30 January 1666 and 25 January 1667, in *Generale missiven*, vol. 3, pp. 484 and 528; Villiers, 'One of the especiallest flowers in our garden', p. 166.

[44] *Dagh-register Anno 1665*, p. 128 (entry of 28 August 1665); Bassett, 'English trade in Celebes', p. 35; F.W. Stapel, *Het Bongaais Verdrag* (Groningen and Leiden, 1922), p. 86.

[45] Joan Maetsuycker to the Gentlemen XVII, 25 January 1667, in *De opkomst van het Nederlandsch gezag in Oost-Indië*, ed. J.K.J. de Jonge (13 vols, The Hague, 1862–88), vol. 6, pp. 102–3.

Moluccas, whose sphere of influence extended as far as Ceram and Sulawesi. Van Dam, now a Councillor of the Indies, was asked to take command of the military expedition. When he declined, Cornelis Janszoon Speelman (1628–84) stepped up to the plate. Only a year earlier, he had been found guilty of private trade and suspended from his position as Governor of the Coromandel Coast. The expedition against Makassar would prove to be a turning point in the career of this future Governor-General.[46]

Speelman made his first appearance before Makassar in December 1666, largely to intimidate, rather than engage the enemy. He quickly sailed east, in order to dislodge Makassarese troops from Buton, an island claimed by the ruler of Ternate. He then made his way to the Moluccas, where he reconciled the Sultan of Ternate with his next-door neighbour, the Sultan of Tidore. In late March 1667, both rulers sat down with the VOC commander for a lavish dinner, celebrating the company's victory at Buton as well as English defeat in the Four Days' Battle. Having collected reinforcements in the Spice Islands, Speelman reappeared before Makassar in late July 1667. Dutch and indigenous forces captured the strategically located castle of Barrombom three months later. The next target was the royal residence of Samboepo. Following a crushing defeat of the troops of Sultan Hassan Udin, the Treaty of Bongaya was signed on 18 November 1667, reducing Makassar to a vassal state. When news of this 'superb victory' reached Batavia in the middle of March 1668, Maetsuycker and his Councillors of the Indies immediately declared a day of celebration and thanksgiving. They took their wives for an all-night stroll around the European quarter of Batavia, where they visited lower-ranking VOC servants and Dutch burghers to toast 'the welfare of the sweet fatherland and the United Dutch East India Company'.[47]

Arguably, it was the Treaty of Bongaya that made the VOC the dominant power in Southeast Asia. As such, it was far more important than the Peace of Breda of July 1667. The VOC imposed a protection/tribute exchange on Makassar similar to the way it did business in the Spice Islands. Sultan Hassan Udin was required to raze all his fortresses to the ground, except for the royal residence of Samboepo. The stronghold of Jum Pandan was ceded to the VOC. As Fort Rotterdam, it would remain the focal point of Dutch power and authority in the region for centuries to come. Naturally, the ruler had to renounce his claims to a number of territories and pay substantial damages to

---

[46] Stapel, *Het Bongaais Verdrag*, pp. 89–190; Andaya, *The heritage of Arung Palakka*, pp. 68–99; Gerrit Knaap, 'De Ambonse eilanden tussen twee mogendheden. De VOC en Ternate, 1605–1656', in *Hof en handel. Aziatische vorsten en de VOC, 1620–1720*, eds Elsbeth Locher-Scholten and Peter Rietbergen (Leiden, 2004), pp. 35–58.

[47] *Dagh-register Anno 1668–69*, pp. 42–7 (quotations on pp. 45, 47); Van Dam, *Beschryvinge*, II-1, 237–46; Villiers, 'One of the especiallest flowers in our garden', p. 174; Bassett, 'English trade in Celebes', pp. 35–8; Stapel, *Het Bongaais Verdrag*, pp. 89–190; Andaya, *The heritage of Arung Palakka*, pp. 68–99.

the VOC and its allies, including the Sultan of Ternate. The company gained complete control of Makassar's import and export trade. Local merchants would be permitted to sail to a limited number of destinations only, provided they obtained a relevant pass from the commander of Fort Rotterdam. On no account could they sail to the Spice Islands or engage in trade there. All other European nations were banned from the port forever. Speelman arranged for the EIC personnel in Makassar to be taken to Batavia. The Peace of Breda was officially declared there in May 1668, but without any public celebrations.[48]

What were the implications of the Peace of Breda for the VOC? Charles II and the Dutch Republic had reached an agreement on the basis of *uti possidetis* (lit. 'as you possess'), meaning that territory and other property captured in war would remain with its possessor. There is little truth in the media stories circulating in summer 2017 that the Dutch traded Manhattan for Pulau Run. The Peace of Breda did not result in any exchanges of territory – that was the whole point of it. Of course, it would have been possible to go back to the *status quo ante*. But, crucially, the EIC would not have gained anything by that either. Its servants in Bantam and Makassar realized that Pulau Run could not become a viable colony unless they were able to route provisions and spices through Makassar. Yet this was no longer an option following the Treaty of Bongaya. Consequently, it was this treaty, not the Peace of Breda, which secured the VOC's monopoly of the spice trade and its hegemonic position in Southeast Asia.[49]

Conclusion

The VOC and EIC routinely contested each other's claims to trade and territory, both on the ground in the East Indies and at the negotiating tables in Europe. Dutch and English claims-making drew on a suite of well-rehearsed legal arguments, which extended to first discovery, freedom of trade and navigation, contracts and alliances with indigenous peoples, just war, conquest, actual possession, and the (perceived) surrender of native ownership or sovereignty. The chartered companies did not hesitate to involve the Dutch and English governments in their disputes. It worked both ways, of course: the Dutch and English governments exerted pressure on the companies if doing so suited their particular needs. State and trade could not be separated in the early modern period. The fate of Pulau Run depended

---

[48] *Dagh-register Anno 1668–69*, pp. 42–5 and 80; Treaty of Bongaya, 18 November 1667, in *Corpus diplomaticum Neerlando-Indicum*, II, 370–80; Villiers, 'One of the especiallest flowers in our garden', p. 174; Bassett, 'English trade in Celebes', pp. 37–8; Andaya, *The heritage of Arung Palakka*, pp. 100–16.

[49] Treaty of Bongaya, 18 November 1667, in *Corpus diplomaticum Neerlando-Indicum*, II, 370–80; Treaty of Breda, 31 July 1667, in *European treaties*, eds Davenport *et al.*, pp. 132–42.

on a complicated game of chess that lasted several decades and involved five major players at least, including Makassar. The voice of the indigenous population of the Banda Islands disappeared from the VOC and EIC records after Coen's military conquest of 1621. Yet the companies' archives attest to plenty of engagement with indigenous states and communities closely linked to the Banda Islands well into the 1660s.

Scribal communication connected the far-flung theatres of politics and war. Indigenous vassals and supporters of the VOC, such as orang kaya Kery, were well aware of the importance of written documents. Treaty texts tended to work to the advantage of the VOC and EIC, rather than Asian rulers and peoples. As Adam Clulow has shown, a notable exception to this rule was documents generated and/or archived by the complex state machineries of pre-modern China and Japan, which were more than a match for the European chartered companies. It reinforces the point that the VOC and EIC could become major Asian powers precisely because they functioned simultaneously as 'empires of paper'. Incidentally, the same was true of the Dutch and English navies – a thought that does not seem to have occurred to many maritime historians. Michiel de Ruyter may have started his working life in the ropeyard of the Lampsins family in Flushing, but he acquired the reading and writing skills necessary to climb to the top of the Dutch naval hierarchy. De Ruyter wrote elaborate journal entries during long tours of duty in the Mediterranean and Atlantic, for example. There was a similar need for VOC and EIC servants in Asia to justify their actions through scribal communication. The company directors and the government authorities back home responded with paper trails of their own. For example, the peace conferences that took place in Breda (1667) and London (1654 and 1674) generated both ample diplomatic correspondence and blow-by-blow accounts of the negotiations by one or more of the participants. Treaty texts appeared in print, including large compendia such as Rymer's *Foedera*. Handwritten accounts of the negotiations in Europe and copies of treaty texts circulated widely throughout the Dutch and English empires, facilitating continuous feedback loops. It is through the prism of such interconnected communication networks that Anglo-Dutch rivalry in the overseas world can best be analysed and understood.[50]

---

[50] Adam Clulow, *The company and the shogun. The Dutch encounter with Tokugawa Japan* (New York, 2014); *Michiel de Ruyter in eigen woorden*, ed. L. Koelmans (Franeker, 2007); *Foedera, conventiones, literae et cujuscunque generis acta publica, inter reges Angliae et alios quosvis imperatores, reges, pontifices, principes, vel communitates, ab ineunte saeculo duodecimo, viz ab anno 1101. ad nostra usque tempora habita aut tractate*, eds Thomas Rymer, Robert Sanderson, George Holmes, Adam Clarke and Fred Holbrooke (London, 1704–35).

IV

Public history

The Raid on the Medway and the capture of the *Royal Charles*, and four other allegedly significant events of the year 1667. Produced by Emrik and Binger, some time during the nineteenth century. Source: Rijksmuseum (Amsterdam), RP-P-OB-82.352

12

Michiel de Ruyter: a multi-purpose hero

Remmelt Daalder

During his lifetime seventeenth-century Dutch admiral Michiel de Ruyter was already a popular figure. His fame has lasted until the present day, although recently it has suffered considerably because of his involvement in the Dutch Atlantic slave trade. Much more than his expedition to West Africa and the Caribbean (1664–65), or the great naval battles against the British on the North Sea, it was the Medway Raid of June 1667 that formed De Ruyter's principal claim to fame and honour. This essay analyses how Michiel de Ruyter has been used for varying ideological purposes in the last four centuries. Pictorial sources (prints, paintings, posters and statues), film, music and song texts are among the sources underpinning the thesis that De Ruyter was a multi-purpose national hero, usable for any ideological purpose. In this respect his public image was considerably more flexible than the image of comparable heroes in neighbouring countries like Horatio Nelson.

Michiel de Ruyter is the prototype of a hero. The Dutch historians Jan and Annie Romein-Verschoor devoted a chapter to De Ruyter in *Erflaters van onze beschaving* (Testators of our civilisation), a collection of short biographies of men and women they regarded as key figures of Dutch history, originally published in 1938. They defined 'heroes' as 'persons who, by birth and social prestige, by an exceptional deed or function, by the sacrifice of their life – or a combination of all that – have become figures of collective imagination. In addition, each of their features or accomplishments became part of their extraordinary greatness.'[1] In De Ruyter's case, his violent death during a sea battle in 1676, his austerity and his friendly association with his men added greatly to his status as a hero. His god-fearing Christian lifestyle also contributed to his popularity and status, a virtue more appreciated in the past than nowadays.

De Ruyter was very popular among the crew of the fleet. Sailors called him *Bestevaer* (granddad), and on land he was equally known and loved.

---

[1] Jan and Annie Romein, *Erflaters van onze beschaving* (9th impression, Amsterdam, 1971), p. 257. This and other quotes below from Dutch and German sources have been translated by the author.

Figure 12.1 Portrait of Michiel de Ruyter, one of the six canvases painted
by Ferdinand Bol for the admiralties of the Dutch Republic, 1667.
Source: Rijksmuseum (Amsterdam).

Pamphlets, prints and illustrated broadsheets are proof of this. Another sign
of contemporary respect is the series of identical portraits of De Ruyter as
the commander of the navy.[2] They were painted by Ferdinand Bol after the
victorious Four Days' Battle (June 1666) during the Second Anglo-Dutch War,
to decorate all the offices of the five admiralties that made up the navy of the
Republic.[3] No other admiral had ever been honoured in this way before,
nor were any of his successors ever granted this sign of respect in later years.

---

[2] Bol painted six identical portraits for the admiralty offices in Holland, Zeeland
and Friesland. The National Maritime Museum in Greenwich, the Amsterdam
Rijksmuseum and the Mauritshuis in The Hague each have one of these portraits.
In addition Bol's studio produced several copies for private admirers of De Ruyter.
[3] Norbert Middelkoop (ed.), *Ferdinand Bol and Govert Flinck, Rembrandt's master pupils*
(Zwolle and Amsterdam, 2017), p. 162.

Two monuments

Michiel de Ruyter died on 29 April 1676 off the coast of Sicily, after being heavily wounded a week earlier, during a sea battle near Mount Etna. His squadron had been sent to the Mediterranean to support the Spanish fleet against the French. The embalmed body was sent back to Holland on the *Eendraght*, De Ruyter's flagship. When the ship passed the French coast it was greeted by a salute of honour, ordered by King Louis XIV, who, despite the state of war between the two countries, showed his respect for his enemy and former ally (during the Second Anglo-Dutch War).[4] Back in Holland, De Ruyter was immediately immortalised in two ways. He received the usual honour bestowed upon flag officers who had died in battle: a state funeral and a monumental tomb in a public church, usually in the city where the admiralty under which the hero had served was located. That tradition had started with Jacob van Heemskerck, who died in 1607 during the Battle of Gibraltar against the Spanish fleet. The commanding admiral was officially in the service of the Rotterdam admiralty, the oldest of the five admiralty colleges. This gave Rotterdam the right to equip the flagship of the fleet. In Hellevoetsluis, a naval base southwest of Rotterdam, where the *Eendraght* had anchored, the coffin with De Ruyter's body was transferred to a funeral yacht, to take it to Amsterdam. When the yacht passed through Rotterdam, the city council actually tried to keep De Ruyter's body there. De Ruyter, however, had lived in Amsterdam for over twenty years and both the States General and his relatives, especially his son Engel de Ruyter, insisted on a funeral in Amsterdam's *Nieuwe Kerk* on Dam Square. A monumental tomb was erected on the site of the high altar of this former Catholic church, a fitting place for a secular saint. It is to this day the largest and most impressive monument ever built for a Dutch admiral, or for any dignitary, including the members of the House of Orange.

In addition to the tomb there was another monument that contributed greatly to De Ruyter's everlasting fame: the biography written by Gerard Brandt (1626–85), an Amsterdam pastor and author. The relatives of the admiral commissioned him to write the book: *Het Leeven and Bedryf van den Heere Michiel de Ruiter* (Life and deeds of Mr Michiel de Ruiter), published in 1687. Brandt had access to De Ruyter's papers and he spoke with many eyewitnesses. The biography is the most important source for many details about De Ruyter's personal life and contains all kinds of anecdotes. A famous example is the story of young Michiel who turned the big wheel in Lampsins' ropeyard in his birthplace Flushing (Vlissingen), and suffered 'unbearable grief', as the children's song tells us.[5] Equally well known is his unexpected

---

[4] Ronald Prud'homme van Reine, *Rechterhand van Nederland. Biografie van Michiel Adriaenszoon de Ruyter* (Amsterdam, 1996), p. 329.

[5] The song *Een draaiersjongen* (A ropemaker's apprentice) was written by A.L. de Rop in 1873, and put to music by Richard Hol. The song describes De Ruyter's career in

Figure 12.2 Michiel de Ruyter on a pedestal: frontispiece of the first edition of the biography by Gerard Brandt, 1687. Source: Rijksmuseum (Amsterdam).

meeting in 1664 with Jan Kompanie, on the island of Gorée off the coast of Senegal, one of the Dutch settlements De Ruyter had recaptured during his transatlantic expedition. Brandt tells us that this Jan Kompanie was an African man who had lived in Flushing before and had sailed with De Ruyter in their younger years. His surname refers to the (Dutch) West India Company, which apparently had taken him to the Netherlands, probably as a slave.

Brandt's book, more than a thousand pages in folio size, forms an inexhaustible treasure trove, from which later admirers could glean whatever they needed. Despite his thorough research, the book is not a scholarly biography, it is more like a hagiography.[6] The whole text is meant to illustrate De Ruyter's greatness, even when Brandt emphasises De Ruyter's modesty and his austerity. The reader does not learn anything about the

---

three verses. It became immensely popular and was part of the standard repertoire in primary schools, well into the twentieth century.

[6] In this respect Brandt's book is comparable to biographies of British naval heroes in the nineteenth century: C.I. Hamilton, 'Naval hagiography and the Victorian hero', *The Historical Journal*, 23:2 (1980), 381–98.

Ontmoeting met Jan Company.

Figure 12.3 Michiel de Ruyter meets Jan Kompanie. Detail of a sheet with pictures of his life. Lithography, late nineteenth century. Source: Het Scheepvaartmuseum (Amsterdam).

weaknesses or mistakes of the man. In this paper monument Brandt created a De Ruyter in the shape of a classical hero, as an example to posterity. He compares De Ruyter with Themistocles, the Athenian leader whose fleet crushed the Persians at Salamis (480 BC), and even with Alexander the Great. Brandt not only described the hero according to the wishes of the admiral's family, he also seems to have modelled him on his own views. Reverend Brandt belonged to the Remonstrant wing of Dutch Calvinism, which held less strict beliefs than the orthodox majority. He strongly stressed certain character traits in De Ruyter with which he must have felt affinity: his gentleness, his mildness and his devoutness. Brandt had the habit of including all kinds of sources in his text: official documents, instructions, letters and lists of navy vessels. Consequently the size of his book increased to more than a thousand pages. Despite its prolixity the biography was reprinted nine times, even fifteen times if we include anthologies and adaptations. The first five editions, published between 1687 and 1745, still fit into a fairly normal pattern for a well-written bestseller on a popular subject. That the book was repeatedly re-edited subsequently indicates that

Dutch society wanted to be uplifted and inspired by this naval hero again and again.[7]

The Medway Raid: De Ruyter's claim to glory?

In 2004 a Dutch television channel organised the election of the 'Greatest Dutchman of All Time', based on the BBC programme *Great Britons*, two years earlier. Eventually the television audience chose the founding father of Dutch independence, William the Silent (1533–84), as the winner.[8] A more surprising outcome was the final ranking of Michiel de Ruyter, who finished in seventh place. Not a bad performance for a seventeenth-century admiral! He did even better than Horatio Nelson, who barely reached the top ten in the original British programme. One of De Ruyter's key achievements, the Medway Raid, only played a minor role in the information offered to the public. Each nominee had his own representative in the broadcast who explained to the viewers why his or her candidate was entitled to the title 'Greatest Dutchman of All Time'. Michiel de Ruyter's claim was defended by Rob de Wijk. According to this well-known military commentator, De Ruyter's greatest achievement by far was the Battle of the Texel (Kijkduin, 1673). De Ruyter prevented an invasion by defeating a combined English-French fleet off the coast of Holland in 1673, which made him the saviour of his country. De Wijk's argument is remarkable: until recently, it was not the victory at Kijkduin but the destruction of a part of the English fleet at Chatham which was seen as De Ruyter's most important heroic deed.

With that action, six years before Kijkduin, the Dutch had indeed shown exemplary bravery, but De Ruyter received more praise than he deserved. He did not play a major role in either the preparation or execution of the Medway Raid. The admiral was ill around that time – he suffered from 'fevers', possibly malaria – and had serious doubts about the plans which he considered too risky. The idea of launching 'something great' against the English had come from the De Witt brothers. Cornelis de Witt even joined the expedition as the representative of the States General. Although supreme commander of the fleet, De Ruyter had to follow De Witt's instructions. In contemporary

---

[7] Full editions appeared in 1687, 1691, 1701, 1732, 1746, 1794–97 (5 volumes), 1835–37 (5 volumes) and in 1971, 1988 and 2007. The complete text of the first edition is digitally available at: www.dbnl.org/tekst/bran002leve01_01/index.php. The latest abridged edition is: Gerard Brandt, *Het leven van Michiel de Ruyter*, selected, edited and translated into present-day Dutch by Vibeke Roeper and Remmelt Daalder (Amsterdam, 2007, reprinted 2015).

[8] In the last broadcast, Pim Fortuyn (1940–2002), the Dutch politician who had been murdered two years earlier, was declared the winner. The next day this was corrected, after counting of all the votes, and William the Silent eventually won. This, of course, gave rise to rumours about fraud and conspiracy.

Figure 12.4 *The Apotheosis of Cornelis de Witt.* He is represented as an admiral, his command staff in his right hand, an episode of the Medway Raid in the background. Copy after a painting by Jan de Baen, late seventeenth century. Source: Rijksmuseum (Amsterdam).

pictorial representations De Witt and the other commanders received the same honours as De Ruyter for their shared victory, but gradually Michiel de Ruyter started receiving all the credit. After 1672, De Ruyter's star completely outshone that of his contemporaries. In that year the Orangist party came to power again, installing the Prince of Orange, William III, as stadtholder. Cornelis de Witt was imprisoned in The Hague where he and his brother Johan were brutally murdered by an Orangist mob. De Ruyter, although sympathising with the De Witt brothers, managed to adjust to the new regime. The important role of Johan and Cornelis de Witt as the organisers of the Medway Raid was played down, whereas De Ruyter suddenly became the central hero of this bold action. The leading role of Cornelis de Witt was censored in an especially violent way. Shortly after the Medway Raid, the town hall of Dordrecht, the birthplace of the brothers, was decorated with a painting by Jan de Baen: *The Apotheosis of Cornelis de Witt*. It showed Cornelis as an admiral in armour, a command staff in his right hand, with scenes of the Medway Raid painted in the background. This large canvas was destroyed by Orangist supporters during the riots preceding the downfall of the De

Witt brothers in 1672. Fortunately, the picture is not completely lost: there is a second version of the painting, smaller in size, in the Rijksmuseum.[9]

Naval hero of the Enlightenment

Every period seems to have created its own version of De Ruyter, always with the help of Gerard Brandt. During the so-called 'Patriot period', the reform movement of the last decades of the eighteenth century, the latent interest in De Ruyter came to life again. This time he was no longer a contemporary hero, but a historical figure whose example should be followed. Many Dutchmen regretted the fact that their country was no longer a great European power, as it had been a century earlier, during the Dutch Golden Age. Now they lived in a land where corruption and nepotism had become usual features of public administration. The Fourth Anglo-Dutch War (1780–84) was a disaster for the Dutch and anti-British feelings increased sharply. As the Dutch fleet was hardly a match for the Royal Navy, there were many who longed for the glorious days of the Medway Raid and other victories. The Battle of Dogger Bank (1781) was the only encounter of any size during this war. The outcome can at best be described as a draw. Nevertheless it was celebrated as a huge victory. Rear-Admiral Arnold Zoutman led his squadron during the battle from a flagship called *Admiraal de Ruyter*, a telling detail about the worship of De Ruyter in those days.[10]

Characteristic of this period is a large print after a drawing by Dirk Langendijk (1748–1805). The Medway Raid is the subject, and the print was, not surprisingly, published in 1782 during the war with England. The artist based his image on the description by Gerard Brandt, who relates how, on 23 June 1667 (NS), Michiel de Ruyter arrived near Upnor Castle on the Medway. 'At that time, Admiral de Ruyter himself jumped into a sloop', writes Brandt, 'to be in the frontline.' When Cornelis de Witt asked him where he wanted to go, De Ruyter replied: 'I want to see how my men are doing there'.[11] De Witt then joined him. The print shows the two leaders standing in a sloop, in the midst of a savage man-to-man fight, the *Royal Charles* and several burning English ships in the background. Here is the hero in full: a leader who feels best in the midst of his men!

The naval hero was effortlessly integrated into the contemporary Enlightenment ideology, characterised by ideas about the freedom of the

[9] Rijksmuseum (Amsterdam), inv. no. SK-A-4648.
[10] This was the beginning of a long tradition of ship-naming in the navy. The last in that series is the current air-defence and command frigate HNLMS *De Ruyter*. In 1749 the Dutch East India Company had already launched a ship named *Admiraal de Ruyter*.
[11] Brandt, *Leven van De Ruyter*, p. 566.

Figure 12.5 The Dutch Raid on the Medway and the Capture of the Royal
Charles, 1667. The standing figures in the sloop are Michiel de Ruyter (l.) and
Cornelis de Witt. Print by Mathias de Sallieth, after Dirk Langendijk, 1782.
Source: Rijksmuseum (Amsterdam).

individual, about democracy and human rights. De Ruyter was especially
popular in circles that strove for political reform, the *Patriotten*. Engelbert M.
Engelberts (1731–1807), a pastor from Hoorn, wrote the introduction to the
1794–97 edition of Brandt's biography. Engelberts, a man with strong Patriot
views, saw the time of De Ruyter as a period of prosperity, freedom and
tolerance. 'It is generally acknowledged', he wrote, 'that the Divine blessing
favoured the decency of our God-fearing ancestors in an extraordinary way,
and destined this Land to be a refuge for the oppressed.'[12] According to
Engelberts, De Ruyter was a fine example of such tolerance: 'no one was
ever more careful not to cause someone grief: no one more friendly and more
modest than this great admiral'.[13]

---

[12] 'Het is algemeen erkend dat de Goddelyke zegen de braafheid onzer godsdien-
stige voorouderen, op eene buitengemeene wyze begunstigde en dit Land tot eene
vryplaats voor alle verdrukten bestemde.' Gerard Brandt, *Het Leeven en Bedryf
van den Heere Michiel de Ruiter ... op nieuw uitgegeeven door E.M. Engelberts* (Hoorn,
1794–97), unpaginated introduction.
[13] 'niemand was minder, dan hy, genegen om iemand verdriet aan te doen: niemand
minzaamer en bescheidener dan deez groote Admiraal'.

A similar form of contemporary projection may be found in the drama *Michiel Adriaansz de Ruiter* (1780) by Jan Nomsz (1780–1803), a prolific playwright.[14] Nomsz had served as a naval officer for some time, but despite this resemblance to his subject, the whole play is situated on land, albeit in a country overseas. The gist of the story is as follows: in Fort Elmina on the Gold Coast a Dutch army officer is accused of manslaughter in a duel. As duelling is forbidden by law, he is sentenced to death. He is about to be hanged, but fortunately for him De Ruyter's fleet arrives in the roadstead, which elicits the following reaction from one of the players:

> De Ruyter is highly praised: people say
> His heart leans more to mercy than to punishment.[15]

At once, the admiral is consulted in this criminal case. In Nomsz's play De Ruyter is portrayed as an enlightened King Solomon. He speaks extensively about justice and about 'reason itself ... that forbids the duel'. Of course the officer is eventually pardoned. Jan Nomsz frames Michiel de Ruyter as the champion of humanity and reason. The story is not entirely fictitious: De Ruyter had indeed been to West Africa, and Gerard Brandt even relates how he pardoned a sailor suspected of manslaughter after the man survived his hanging from the gallows.

Within a century of his death, it seems, De Ruyter came to occupy a special place in the nation's history, recognised as a naval hero of the Enlightenment.. For the Patriots, he personified the greatness of the fatherland in the Golden Age and the importance of reasonable and unbiased authority, while in naval circles he became an example of impeccable courage and virtue.

Great hero, small kingdom

In spite of the possession of a vast colonial empire, the kingdom of the Netherlands, founded by the Congress of Vienna in 1815, had to play second fiddle in international affairs, and even more so after Belgian independence. The support of the United Kingdom for the Belgians after their Revolt of 1830 fanned anti-English feelings in the remaining northern part of the kingdom. The result was a wave of nostalgia, similar to that during the Fourth Anglo-Dutch War.

The nineteenth century was the heyday of heroism and hero-worship, not only in Holland but in the rest of Europe as well. The Dutch, however, did not look for 'strong, masculine heroes', as in Thomas Carlyle's lectures on *Heroes, Hero-Worship and the Heroic in History* (1841). What the Dutch needed

---

[14] Th.M.M. Mattheij, *Waardering en kritiek. Johannes Nomsz en de Amsterdamse schouwburg 1764–1810* (Amsterdam, 1980), pp. 93–4.

[15] Johannes Nomsz, *Michiel Adriaansz. de Ruyter, treurspel* (Amsterdam, 1780), p. 14.

was a quiet, honest hero to serve as an example. Inspiring contemporary figures like Nelson in England and Napoleon in France were not available. A seemingly good candidate for the role of national hero was Jan van Speyk (1802–31). This young naval officer commanded a gunboat on the Scheldt before Antwerp in 1831, during the Belgian Revolution. When Belgian insurgents were about to capture his vessel, he blew up his ship, including himself and twenty-seven members of the crew, in order to prevent the flag from falling into the hands of the Belgians. This heroic deed earned him a state funeral and the highest military decoration, granted posthumously. Van Speyk's suicide action resulted in a huge flow of occasional poetry, relics and memorials. De Ruyter seems to have been Van Speyk's source of inspiration. As a boy growing up in the Amsterdam city orphanage Van Speyk was said to have spent many hours by the tomb of his great example, just around the corner from the orphanage. In a painting by Dominicus Dubois (1800–40), depicting Van Speyk at the moment he fired a bullet into the gunpowder, we even see a copy of Brandt's *Life of De Ruyter*.[16] Although Van Speyk managed to save the flag, he did not prevent the loss of half his country to the insurgent Belgians. This might be one of the reasons why, in the long run, De Ruyter would turn out to be a more satisfactory hero for the nation: not an overconfident, unstable young man who had already alluded in advance to a heroic act in the service of the fatherland, but a virtuous, balanced man, who had convincingly beaten the enemy and 'saved the nation'.[17]

In this time of emerging Dutch nationalism a new cult around Michiel de Ruyter was born. In the associated rhetoric the veneration of great men from the past, including naval heroes, played a major role. It is no coincidence that in 1831 the play by Jan Nomsz, discussed above, was reprinted and performed in many theatres.[18] The erection of statues was another fitting expression of the need for inspiration by great men from the past. Before the nineteenth century, the Netherlands had no tradition of statues of important figures on streets and squares.[19] Now monuments were erected all over the country, not only of important cultural figures like Rembrandt and the seventeenth-century poet Joost van den Vondel, but also of naval heroes like Piet

---

[16] *J.C.J. van Speyk fires in the powder on board HMS Gunboat No. 2, lying before Antwerp on 5 February 1831*, oil on canvas by Dominicus Dubois. Het Scheepvaartmuseum (Amsterdam), inv. A.0112(01). According to other sources, it was not a bullet, but a cigar that detonated the gunpowder.

[17] The hysteria surrounding Van Speyk's heroic death went so far that King Willem I gave order that the Royal Netherlands Navy should always contain a vessel named *Van Speyk*. Nowadays this is the multi-purpose frigate called HNLMS *Van Speyk*.

[18] Apart from the first edition of 1780, the Amsterdam University Library holds editions of this play from 1781, 1793 and 1831.

[19] For a long time, the bronze statue of Erasmus in Rotterdam (1622) was the only statue on a public road.

Figure 12.6 Jan van Speyk fires into the gunpowder on HMS Gunboat Nr. 2, as Belgian insurgents storm his ship on 5 February 1831. The book on the table is Brandt's *Life of De Ruiter*. Painting by Dominicus Dubois, 1832. Source: Het Scheepvaartmuseum (Amsterdam).

Heyn. De Ruyter's cast-iron statue erected in 1841 in his birthplace Flushing was the first for a naval hero.[20]

Since the nineteenth century Dutch children have been encouraged to follow Michiel de Ruyter's example. Until well into the twentieth century, large coloured pictures of his deeds decorated the walls of primary schools: the Medway Raid, of course, but also the glorious Four Days' Battle. In school books and children's books De Ruyter's deeds, but mostly his virtues, received ample attention. The maritime youth novel even became a separate genre. Such books propagated all sorts of positive values of which De Ruyter had plenty: patriotism and bravery, but also perseverance. Moreover, he was an excellent example of social mobility. After all, De Ruyter had managed to climb up from cabin boy to admiral.[21]

[20] As public subscription for a bronze statue faltered, it was decided to use cast iron.
[21] A well-known writer of maritime youth novels was Johan H. Been (1859–1930), who wrote bestsellers like *De drie matrozen van Michiel de Ruijter* (1907) (The three sailors

Figure 12.7 Cast-iron statue of Michiel de Ruyter in Flushing (Vlissingen), by Louis Royer, 1841. Anonymous contemporary print. Source: Rijksmuseum (Amsterdam).

The nationalistic worship of Michiel de Ruyter reached its highest peak in 1907, when his 300th birthday was celebrated. There were exhibitions, costumed parades, theatre performances and dozens of publications. In addition, the Post Office issued a series of stamps with the admiral's portrait, the first time the Dutch king or queen did not adorn a stamp with their portrait.

Foreign admiration

One of the most striking forms of 'De Ruyter worship' may be found in an unexpected place, in the Hungarian city of Debrecen where a monument for

---

of Michiel de Ruyter) and *Paddeltje, de scheepsjongen van Michiel de Ruijter* (1908) (Paddeltje, Michiel de Ruyter's ship's boy).

Michiel de Ruyter was erected in 1895. During a visit to Naples, a few months before he was killed, De Ruyter managed to free twenty-six Hungarian Protestant pastors. They had ended up there as galley slaves, a result of religious persecution by the Catholic Habsburg regime in their homeland. Since that day Hungarians have honoured De Ruyter as a champion of religious freedom and Hungarian independence. Even today, the Hungarian ambassador in the Netherlands regularly visits De Ruyter's tomb in Amsterdam.

This unexpected appreciation for De Ruyter in a landlocked country is remarkable, but nobody would take offence. For some time, however, there was foreign interest in De Ruyter of a more dubious nature. Between 1940 and 1945, during the German occupation of the Netherlands, the Nazis used the historic Dutch admiral for their own ends. In 1943 De Ruyter was one of ten heroes on a new series of stamps showing naval heroes. That seems fairly innocent, but the issue had a political motive. The series replaced the old stamps depicting Queen Wilhelmina, who had fled to England in 1940. De Ruyter appeared on the 7½ cent stamp for domestic letters, the one most commonly used. In more ideological terms, he was an ideal ally for the German Reich: a fearless hero, who had fought against the English most of his life. This suited the German Reich perfectly, as the English were also their major enemy. An additional asset was the fact that he belonged to the same Teutonic tribe. The Nazi viewpoint about De Ruyter can be illustrated with a remarkable German book by a certain Wilhelm Wolfslast, with the title *Admiral Michael de Ruyter*, published in Leipzig in 1943. The book opens with a conversation between Adriaan Michielszoon (De Ruyter's father) and his then eight-year-old son Michiel: 'Daddy, why are the English here? ... Oh, you know that, my dear Michiel.'[22] Then the father explains to his son why their hometown Flushing is occupied by English troops.[23] The main tenor of the book is immediately clear: the English are strangers who have no right to be in the Netherlands. Wolfslast concludes his book in a sad tone: 'What could De Ruyter have achieved as an admiral of the war fleet of the German Reich!'[24] This was, according to this author, De Ruyter's tragic fate: he gave his life for a tiny state, too small to play a permanent role of any importance in the world. Despite the great admiral's talents and efforts, his country was doomed to become a vassal of England.

During the war years a veritable De Ruyter hype arose, at least among the German occupiers and Dutchmen who sympathised with them. In 1944, 500 members of the *Nationale Jeugdstorm* (National Youth Storm, a Nazi organisation) praised their hero in a *De Ruyter cantata*. Two years earlier

---

[22] 'Vater, warum sind die Engländer hier? ... Das weisst du doch, Michielchen ...': Wilhelm Wolfslast, *Admiral Michael de Ruyter* (Leipzig, 1943), p. 7.

[23] Wolfslast refers to the English garrison in Flushing, one of the guarantees for the English support to the rebellious Dutch provinces agreed in the Treaty of Nonsuch, 1585.

[24] Wolfslast, *Admiral Michael de Ruyter*, p. 270.

Figure 12.8 Michiel de Ruyter urges his fellow countrymen to join the Waffen-SS and beat Soviet Bolshevism, c. 1943. Source: NIOD Institute for War, Holocaust and Genocide Studies (Amsterdam).

the Amsterdam Rijksmuseum had staged an exhibition about De Ruyter, organised by the propaganda bureau of the German administration, the Department of Public Information and Arts.[25] Originally the commemoration of De Ruyter's death was to be the subject of the exhibition, but after the Battle of the Java Sea and the subsequent capitulation of the Dutch armed forces in the Dutch East Indies (8 March 1942) the propaganda bureau opted for a less charged subject: the Medway Raid. At the official opening a representative of the department said: 'The Netherlands played an important role in the conflicts of the Germanic world of those days and fought as a champion of the Germanic mainland for the freedom of the sea, which was threatened by England in that time, too.' The exhibition lasted only two weeks. During this period some 5,000 people visited the museum, among them Arthur Seyss-Inquart, the *Reichskommisar* for the Occupied Netherlands Territories.[26]

[25] The 'Departement van Volksvoorlichting en Kunsten' was founded in 1940 after the model of Goebbels's 'Reichsministerium für Volksaufklärung und Propaganda'.
[26] Jet Baruch and Liesbeth van der Horst, *Het Rijksmuseum in oorlogstijd* (Amsterdam, 1985), pp. 40–2.

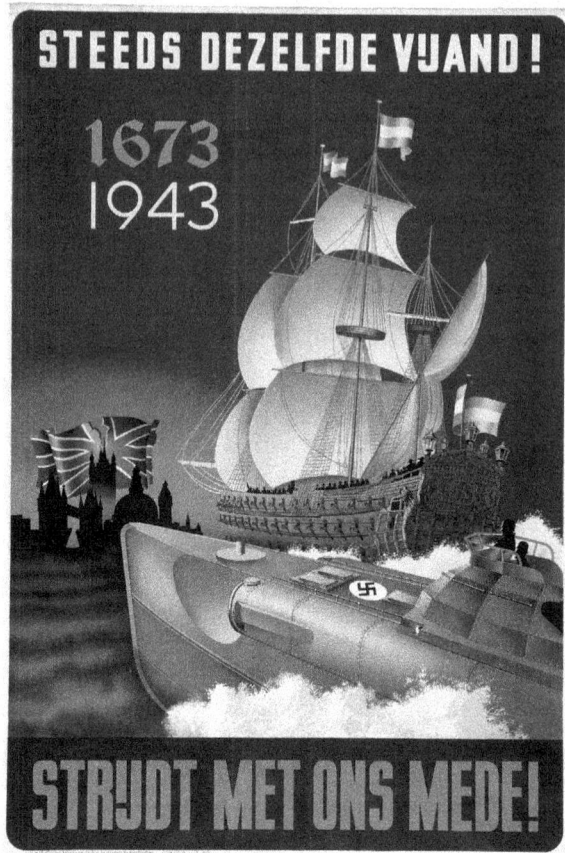

Figure 12.9 The Dutch text on this 1943 Nazi propaganda poster reads: 'Always the same enemy! Join us in our fight!' Source: Het Scheepvaartmuseum (Amsterdam).

The occupiers made good use of De Ruyter's reputation, depicting him on posters that called for service with the *Waffen SS*. From the poster the naval hero addressed his compatriots: 'Show that you are a true Dutchman' (and join the SS). The Medway Raid was still alive among the target group, as is visible on another propaganda poster showing a German U-boat and De Ruyter's flagship sailing full-speed, side-by-side towards England. In the picture the Union Jack over the skyline of London is already torn to pieces.

A hero of our time

Apparently Michiel de Ruyter's reputation did not suffer. After the war his short-lived flirtation with National Socialism seemed forgotten and he

Figure 12.10 Banknote of 100 guilders, with the portrait of Michiel de Ruyter. Design by R.D.E. Oxenaar, 1970. Source: Het Scheepvaartmuseum (Amsterdam).

promptly reappeared on the stage in his former role, the symbol of freedom and Dutch independence. The dates of his birth and death were commemorated again with the usual honours: stamps, exhibitions, conferences, reprints of Brandt's biography and other books.[27] In 1970 his portrait was even depicted on a banknote of 100 guilders. Yet his popularity seemed to decline in these years. In 1976 there was not much official enthusiasm for a commemoration of De Ruyter's death, 300 years earlier.[28] The left-wing government of Labour leader Joop den Uyl felt no need to actively participate in memorial ceremonies for a naval hero.[29] In those years, monuments for military heroes, such as General Van Heutsz (1851–1924), empire builder in the Dutch East Indies, were the target of daubing rather than wreath-laying.[30]

But miraculously, at the beginning of the twenty-first century, Michiel de Ruyter made his comeback in the collective consciousness, once more in an entirely positive way. The result of the televised election of the 'Greatest Dutchman of All Time' discussed above confirms this. He got a 'window' of

---

[27] Photographic reprints of the first edition of Brandt's De Ruyter biography were published in 1971 and 1988.

[28] Prud'homme, *Rechterhand van Nederland*, p. 361.

[29] This attitude was not unusual among socialists. In 1948 Clement Attlee's Labour government, for example, put an end to the annual allowance of GBP 5,000 to Nelson's descendants. R.J.B. Knight, *The pursuit of victory. The life and achievement of Horatio Nelson* (London, 2005), p. 540.

[30] To reduce associations with colonial wars, the name of the enormous Van Heutsz Monument in Amsterdam (1935) was changed in 1999 to the more neutral 'Monument Indië-Nederland'.

his own in the semi-official Canon of Dutch History, a list of fifty topics that aims to provide a chronological summary of the history of the Netherlands. The introduction of De Ruyter's 'window' sounds remarkably martial: 'He led one of the most brutal military actions ever: the journey to Chatham via the Thames in 1667 to destroy the shipyards and ships of the English, in the lion's den. The plan worked. Sailors had great respect for De Ruyter's fleet worldwide.' In 2008 the government agreed to include the Canon in the school curriculum.[31]

At the national commemoration of 2007, 400 years after his birth in Flushing, the emphasis would no longer be put on De Ruyter's qualities as a naval officer, at least according to the coordinating committee, the *Stichting 400 Jaar Michiel de Ruyter*. Their aim was to 'promote mutual solidarity and unity between and among broad layers of the Dutch multicultural population, based on the values and norms of which De Ruyter gave us an example during his lifetime'.[32] This way, De Ruyter even became a factor of influence in the debate about national identity and the discussion about norms and values of those days.

In more recent years Michiel de Ruyter's star has risen ever higher, thanks to the feature film *Michiel de Ruyter*, released in 2015.[33] This film, remarkably enough the first entirely devoted to this naval hero, breathes the atmosphere of our time, albeit in a slightly different way than the commemoration in 2007. The storyline covers the period of the Anglo-Dutch wars, a period when the homeland is threatened from all sides, both by foreign enemies and by internal party struggles. In the film De Ruyter is someone who distances himself from intrigues in The Hague, the seat of government. As a loyal and capable servant of the fatherland he simply and faithfully does his duty. Again we discern a contemporary narrative: The Hague, then and now the centre of government, is a hotbed of intrigue, a place which honest men like De Ruyter want nothing to do with. The film is in line with populist distrust of established power, but it offers the present-day Dutchman also something positive to hold onto, in a time of uncertainty about national identity in a globalising world.

De Ruyter and other heroes

Michiel de Ruyter appears to be a national celebrity who can be used for almost every social or ideological purpose. This observation raises several questions. For example: how unique is Michiel de Ruyter, not only in his

---

[31] www.entoen.nu/nl/michielderuyter. On the Canon see also: www.wikiwand.com/en/Canon_of_Dutch_History (consulted 14 June 2018).

[32] Remmelt Daalder, 'Held voor alle gezindten', *Marineblad*, 127:4 (June 2017), 27.

[33] The director was Roel Reiné, Frank Lammers played the title role.

own country, but also abroad? And is his applicability guaranteed for the future? Popularity polls such as those of the 'greatest man or woman ever' are obviously strongly distorted by contemporary sentiments and the influence of lobby groups. Nevertheless the list of nominees contains more people with the same characteristics of heroes as described above by Jan and Annie Romein. William the Silent, for example, performed 'exceptional deeds', brought the 'sacrifice of death' (he was murdered in 1584) and gained a place in the 'collective imagination' of posterity. People know and respect him as the founding father of the independent Dutch state. But he was never used for such a large number of different political purposes and ideals as De Ruyter. Neither do any of the other nominees meet all the criteria to be qualified as a 'multi-purpose hero'. Like William the Silent, Erasmus, Rembrandt, Aletta Jacobs and Anne Frank owe their fame primarily to one single quality, as a Christian humanist, as an artist, as a protagonist of feminism or as the writer of a poignant war diary. Michiel de Ruyter may not have been a pioneer in his field, and even less heroic than other great men or women, but his almost universal usability distinguishes him from the vast majority of historical heroes. None of them, either in the Netherlands or elsewhere, have such a large palette of usable qualities. Horatio Nelson, for example, was an admiral with an even greater service record than De Ruyter, but he has almost exclusively been praised for his military prowess. As such he was extremely useful in propagating British imperial ambitions. Besides, in a moral sense he was certainly not as flawless as his Dutch colleague, bearing in mind his extramarital relationship with Emma Hamilton, an affair that was glossed over or ignored by Nelson's first biographers.[34] At the commemoration of the Battle of Trafalgar in 2005, a commentator in the *Times* rightfully called him the 'first modern super-celebrity', but he added: 'just as his body, his character was full of holes'.[35] Nevertheless, Roger Knight, Nelson's most recent biographer, notes that only Churchill 'has a more powerful claim than Nelson as an historical focus for the defence of British national identity'.[36]

The supposed unique nature of De Ruyter's hero status has never been the subject of extensive comparative research, but there seem to be few heroes who, in practical terms, come close to him. A national hero, or rather a heroine, who is similar to De Ruyter in a number of ways, is Jeanne d'Arc.[37] Like her Dutch counterpart she was seen as the saviour of the fatherland, driving back the English armies, and – this proves to be an indispensable condition for immortality – sacrificing her life, in her case by dying at the stake in 1431. Over the years various groups in France have claimed the Virgin of Orleans

---

[34] Knight, *The pursuit of victory*, p. 542.
[35] Ben MacIntyre, 'Nelson: enough blind hero worship', *The Times*, 25 June 2005.
[36] Knight, *The pursuit of victory*, p. 546.
[37] Jeanne d'Arc was number 31 in the French election of 2005, far behind winner Charles de Gaulle.

for their own purposes. Nineteenth-century historian Jules Michelet saw this innocent, brave girl as the personification of the French nation, socialists emphasised her humble origins, Catholics her divine inspiration.[38] Feminists, as well as far-right movements like the *Front National*, saw in Jeanne a kindred spirit – *bien étonnés de se trouver ensemble*.

On a global scale Michiel de Ruyter is probably less unique than it seems, but so far his fame in his own country has stood the test of time. He offers a firm anchor to his admirers in times of uncertainty about our national identity. But will this national figure still be useful in the future? Nowadays many inhabitants of the Netherlands have roots in other countries of the world. They are not able and possibly not willing to identify with such a very white hero, who fought wars that do not matter to them, or even harmed their ancestors. And until now De Ruyter's impeccability was an important point in his favour, but cracks are starting to show in the façade. Descendants of enslaved people from former Dutch colonies realise that De Ruyter also played a role in the slave trade, not as an active trader, but by facilitating that trade, when in 1664 his squadron recaptured a number of Dutch trading forts on the Atlantic coast of Africa that had been seized by the English.[39] When the film *Michiel de Ruyter* was released in 2015, several critical reviewers noticed that this episode from his life was completely lacking in the chronological story.[40] So, perhaps completely different role models will be needed in the future, but it is doubtful whether there will ever be such a universal national hero again.

Since the seventeenth century every era has constructed its own Michiel de Ruyter, focusing on different aspects of his personality and his deeds. In 2026 De Ruyter will have been dead for 350 years. Will that again be a reason for a national memorial, comparable to the large-scale commemoration of his birthday in 2007? Or will only a handful of maritime historians dwell on that fact, with perhaps a symposium or a volume of essays? There are plenty of reasons to doubt that the veneration of De Ruyter will continue in the same way and on the same scale as in past centuries, at least in the Netherlands. Maybe only the Hungarians will still be grateful for the liberation of their twenty-six (white) pastors from slavery in 1676.

---

[38] Jules Michelet, *Jeanne d'Arc* (Paris, 1853). The different forms that the Virgin of Orleans assumed over the centuries are described in Gerd Krumeich, *Jeanne d'Arc in der Geschichte: Historiographie – Politik – Kultur* (Sigmaringen, 1989).

[39] On this expedition see: H.J. den Heijer, 'Michiel de Ruyter's expedition to West Africa and America, 1664–1665', in *De Ruyter. Dutch admiral*, eds J.R. Bruijn, R.B. Prud'homme van Reine and R. Hovell tot Westervlier (Rotterdam, 2011), pp. 162–81; N.A.M. Rodger, *The command of the ocean. A naval history of Britain, 1649 –1815* (London, 2005), pp. 67–8.

[40] See, for example, the film review by Gijs Rommelse in *Holland – Historisch Tijdschrift*, 2 February 2015, tijdschriftholland.nl/recensie-michiel-ruyter/.

13

Anglo-Dutch historical commemorations and the public, 1973–2017

David Ormrod

Interest in historical commemoration is closely bound up with the Durkheimian paradigm of collective memory and national identity. In nineteenth-century Europe, state-making invariably gave rise to narratives of national history, which entered cultural life through many channels including the visual and performing arts, literature, school curricula, and the invention of historic anniversaries. The pace quickened during the decades immediately preceding the Great War, by which time the 'cult of the centenary' had become well established across the Western world.[1] The centennial celebration served as 'a barometer of contemporary esteem and reflected popular and elite attitudes to both the past and the present'.[2] Pierre Nora, reacting to the contradictions produced by the bicentennial of the French Revolution, commented that by the late twentieth century, 'commemorative bulimia has all but consumed our efforts to control it'.[3] But it was from the domain of Anglo-Dutch history in the seventeenth century that the first centennial events in Britain emerged: the 1788 celebration of the 'Glorious Revolution'.

The stuff of 'round' anniversaries of political events is frequently found in national victories or defeats, with heroes and villains cast in leading roles: Drake and the Spanish Armada, Nelson and Trafalgar, the Medway Raid and De Ruyter. The Revolution of 1688 forms an unusual case in which both parties, the Dutch and the English, could be portrayed as winners. In what was to become the classic Whig paradigm, 1688 brought deliverance from Catholic absolutism, provided a temporary halt to French expansionism, and prevented the outbreak of another civil war. But William's invasion also

---

[1] Eric Hobsbawm, 'Mass-producing traditions: Europe, 1870–1914', in *The invention of tradition*, eds E. Hobsbawm and T. Ranger (Cambridge, 1983), p. 281; R. Quinault, 'The cult of the centenary, c.1784–1914', *Historical Research*, 71:176 (1998), 303–23; H. Hoock (ed.), *History, commemoration, and national preoccupation. Trafalgar, 1805–2005* (Oxford, 2007), p. 1.

[2] Quinault, 'Cult of the centenary', p. 303.

[3] P. Nora, *Realms of memory. The construction of the French past*, vol. III, *Symbols* (New York, 1992), p. 609.

marked the conclusion of a longer Anglo-Dutch moment from c. 1648 to 1689, which saw three Anglo-Dutch wars followed by the consolidation of Orangist leadership. The 1648 Peace of Westphalia brought Spanish recognition of Dutch independence, and ended the Thirty Years' War, leaving the Protestant maritime powers to settle their differences, and confront the rise of French military and naval strength. The context of Anglo-Dutch relations during this period was clearly one of profound transformation, in a Europe which was itself undergoing a shift towards decentralised sovereign states, Catholic and Protestant, of varying size and influence. Commemoration of these events therefore involved much more than bilateral victory celebrations to encompass a wider review of European politics, religion, and cultural exchange.

Anglo-Dutch commemorative events, 1973–2017

The essays in this volume originated in two conferences in Amsterdam and Chatham in June 2017, arranged to reconsider the Second Anglo-Dutch War and its denouement in the Medway Raid of 1667, 350 years after the event itself. The 2017 anniversary, however, formed part of a twentieth-century sequence of Anglo-Dutch commemorative events beginning, significantly, with the 1973 celebration of British entry to the European Economic Community (EEC). The author was closely involved as historical consultant and exhibition curator.

Anglo-Dutch public and commemorative events

1973   Fanfare for Europe, including *The Dutch in London, 1550–1800* exhibition

1982   State visit of Queen Beatrix and Prince Claus

1988–89 Tercentenary of the Glorious Revolution of 1688–89

2017   Commemoration of the Dutch Raid on the Medway, after 350 years

When the 1667 commemorative idea began to take shape in 2015, we assumed that Britain would choose to remain in the European Union after the 2016 referendum. Historical debate and civic events would mark the shift from naval conflict to Anglo-Dutch friendship, understood as a significant step towards today's united Europe. In the event, our expectations proved unfounded, although the so-called 'Brexit' proposal remains unsettled three years later, and is unlikely to succeed in the form originally envisaged.[4] Nevertheless, our assumption followed that of the organisers of the earlier commemorations of 1973 and 1988–89, based on an almost Whiggish sense of historical progress and the conviction that the forging of increasingly close economic and cultural links with our European partners was something worth celebrating.

This was the explicit rationale underlying the 'Fanfare for Europe' of 1973, a national festival of the arts arranged to celebrate Britain's entry into the EEC. It was Prime Minister Edward Heath's single-minded commitment to European unity that secured British membership, and the festival programme reflected his personal tastes in music and the visual arts.[5] It opened, literally, with a specially-commissioned *fanfare* by the Royal Military School's trumpeters at Covent Garden. (The theme was derived from the notes: E-E-C.) Benjamin Britten and Colin Davis conducted the chorus and orchestra in the presence of the Queen and the royal family.[6] In the weeks that followed, a number of exhibitions were staged to illustrate British relations with each of the European member nations. The art historian John Hayes, then Director of the London Museum, proposed an exhibition on *The Dutch in London, 1550–1800*, a particularly appropriate choice since the museum was then housed in Kensington Palace, bought and enlarged by William and Mary in the 1690s as their London home.[7]

The Dutch in London was one of thirty exhibitions staged alongside 150 other major events.[8] Like the later events of 1988, it celebrated four centuries of Anglo-Dutch friendship and cooperation, and specifically, the contribution of successive waves of mainly Protestant migrants. The light and dark sides of the equation involved, respectively, the benefits of immigration and the question of religious toleration, which had resurfaced in Northern Ireland with renewed bitterness from the late 1960s. Orangist banners became a familiar sight on television screens across the UK, commemorating a distorted

---

[4] See the Introduction by Ormrod and Rommelse in this volume.

[5] S. Wall, *The official history of Britain and the European Community*, vol. II: *From rejection to referendum, 1963–1975* (London and New York, 2013), chapter X, emphasises the continuity of purpose from Harold Wilson to Edward Heath, whilst acknowledging the success of Heath's high-level diplomacy; E. Heath, *The course of my life. My autobiography* (London, 1998), chapter 13, 'Fanfare for Europe', pp. 354–95.

[6] The then Minister of State for Education and Science, Margaret Thatcher, answered questions in the Commons about the programme, coordinated by Lords Goodman and Mancroft, at an estimated cost of £350,000; see Hansard, Commons Debates, 846, 23 November 1972, cc. 1507–8.

[7] David Ormrod, *The Dutch in London. The influence of an immigrant community, 1550–1800* (London, 1973), preface and p. 3.

[8] British Tourist Authority, *Fanfare for Europe. Programme of events* [1972], listed pp. 3–31.

view of the Protestant ascendancy secured in 1690 by William's victory over James II at the Battle of the Boyne.

The early 1970s saw an explosion of political violence in Northern Ireland. The greatest loss of life during the entire conflict occurred in 1972, and the imposition of direct rule from London followed. Edward Heath survived two IRA attempts on his life.[9] A temporary respite came in 1973 with the Sunningdale agreement, which raised hopes for an early power-sharing agreement (not realised until 1998). And so Heath's Fanfare for Europe provided a welcome distraction from the Irish Troubles. At Kensington Palace, the history of the Protestant diaspora provided special opportunities for an information-rich exhibition with enormous visual appeal. It was aimed, perhaps unconsciously, at a public which saw itself heading towards a stable European future: tolerant, inclusive, and aiming to free itself from sectarian conflict. The exhibition scenario included sections on economic and financial innovations from the Netherlands, advances in experimental science, navigation, drainage, farming techniques, and above all, the fine and decorative arts. John Hayes curated the pictures, hung on one of the palace staircases and in the spacious exhibition foyer. Lenders included Her Majesty the Queen, the National Trust, the British Museum, the V&A, the Rijksmuseum and several other Dutch museums and record offices.[10]

The second intractable problem of these years was racism and discrimination against immigrant groups. Enoch Powell, MP for Birmingham, was delivering increasingly inflammatory speeches on the dangers of unrestricted immigration, as new legal structures for improved race relations were being put in place. An exhibition about the history of immigration could hardly avoid noting parallels and differences between past and present, and so the 1973 guidebook ended with two conclusions or suggestions: first, that immigrants were frequently and unjustly made to shoulder the blame for social problems brought by economic dislocation and population growth; and second, that the enormous long-term gains were not always of a kind which could be predicted beforehand. The writer included a quotation from one of Enoch Powell's speeches alongside two provocative broadsides of the 1570s and 1580s, intended as a warning. John Hayes thought it best to exclude these from an HMSO publication, to avoid any misunderstanding, and his better judgement prevailed. The museum's next special exhibition, the less controversial *Mary Quant's London*, must have been an easier ride.

---

[9] In December 1974 and November 1975. Heath, *Course of my life*, pp. 532 and 550–2.
[10] London Museum, *The Dutch in London. Guide to the exhibition*, 1973 (Handlist of exhibits in nine sections, including Dutch Communities in London, Anglo-Dutch Commerce and Finance, Science and Technology, Crafts and Applied Arts, Topographical Drawings, Architectural Influences, Sculpture and Woodwork, Ship models &c, and Pictures).

In November 1982, two years after her accession, Queen Beatrix and Prince Claus paid a state visit to Britain. Mrs Thatcher's Conservative party was then strongly pro-European, with similar ideas to the Dutch government on the controversial question of strategic nuclear deterrence. Ruud Lubbers, often described as her 'ideological heir' in the Netherlands, had just assumed leadership of the newly-elected coalition government.[11] Apart from two state banquets at Buckingham Palace and Hampton Court, Beatrix found time to visit Mrs Thatcher at Downing Street and attend a splendid reception and banquet at Guildhall. The guest list of 730 included several of those previously involved in the Fanfare for Europe celebrations, sitting among the liverymen, cabinet ministers, judges and journalists. The visit provided the perfect opportunity to formulate more detailed plans to commemorate the Tercentenary of the Glorious Revolution, proposed earlier in the year by the British Foreign Office's Anglo-Netherlands Cultural Committee.[12]

In the planning and staging of these commemorative events, we can see a remarkable collision of past, present, and future, involving the search for a 'usable past' reflected in the distorting mirror of time. As Ludmilla Jordanova reminds us, 'marking time is the business of historians', as they select for analysis from a vast stock of events and historical actors; but from the later nineteenth century, the nation state also played a major role in representing the past to the public through the funding of museums and archive repositories, alongside the initiative of private sponsors. It follows that public history invariably becomes entangled with politics through its representations of power relations.[13] Nowhere can this be followed more clearly than in changing representations of the 1688 Revolution across three centuries.

Changing representations of the 'Glorious Revolution' over three centuries

Within a few years of William's landing in 1688, the conservative and incomplete nature of the 'Glorious Revolution' had become apparent. It was in the 1720s, during Walpole's ministry, that the Whigs began to divide between

---

[11] His obituary in the *Guardian*, 19 February 2018. Both the Dutch and British governments favoured the siting of US cruise missiles on their territory, despite popular opposition. Queen Beatrix had endorsed this controversial policy in her Guildhall speech the previous evening to the surprise of many of those present; Mrs Thatcher was an enthusiastic supporter of the proposal which was finally accepted by Lubbers, but dropped in 1984 as a result of disarmament negotiations between the USSR and the USA.

[12] L.G. Schwoerer, 'Celebrating the Glorious Revolution, 1689–1989', *Albion*, 22:1 (1990), 14; Corporation of London, Guest list for a reception and banquet, Guildhall, 17 November 1982.

[13] L. Jordanova, 'Marking time', in *Trafalgar*, ed. Hoock, p. 7; and *idem*, *History in practice* (London, 2000), pp. 155–6.

serious reformers (opposition Whigs) and the untroubled majority who, like Walpole, felt that 1688 had delivered a permanent constitutional blueprint for newly-united Britain (establishment Whigs).[14] The legacy of 1688–89 continued to be debated in conditions of relative political stability, until the atmosphere began to change with the accession of George III. The question of American independence and growing opposition to slavery underlaid the turn towards political theory and a more radical politics, as an increasingly divided Whig party struggled to deal with royal intransigence. By the end of the American War in 1783, the party was in a state of disintegration and in need of strong leadership, which the king did his best to frustrate.[15]

The centenary celebrations of 1788 provided the trigger for wide-ranging public debate on all sides, and increased the prospect of resolving a range of pressing issues including parliamentary reform, Catholic emancipation, and the abolition of slavery. The legacy of the Glorious Revolution was claimed by radicals, Whig reformers and conservatives alike. 'Revolution clubs' and Constitutional Societies sprang into existence before the anniversary itself, and were patronised especially by Whigs and dissenters. Commemorative events took place in London and many of the larger provincial towns of England, accompanied by the ringing of bells. Church services, assemblies, balls and dinners were ubiquitous. In Birmingham, silver and copper commemorative medals were struck, and Orange ribbons were commonly worn.[16] Below the surface of these displays, of course, ran deep currents of unease, expressed in pamphlets, sermons and speeches. The Revolution clubs served to focus political rivalries, expose restrictions on civil liberties, and argue the case for widening the franchise. But in 1788, both reformers and radicals remained for the most part enmeshed in a constitutionalist culture.[17]

It could be said that the context for the 1788 centenary arose from the process of 'marking time', common to most if not all anniversaries. But within a matter of months, the situation was transformed by the outbreak of the French Revolution – hardly an exogenous moment insofar as its origins lay in the struggle for American independence and the unsustainable costs incurred by Britain and France in attempting to maintain their transatlantic empires.[18] This is not the place to review this historiography: suffice it to say that events in France served to further sharpen political debate and widen

---

[14] J.H. Plumb, *The growth of political stability in England, 1675–1725* (London, 1967), chapter 6, *passim*; S. Pincus, *1688. The first modern revolution* (New Haven and London, 2009), chapter 1, *passim*.

[15] L.G. Mitchell, *Charles James Fox and the disintegration of the Whig Party, 1782–1794* (Oxford, 1971), chapters 2 and 3, *passim*; G. Ditchfield, *George III. An essay in monarchy* (Basingstoke, 2002), pp. 71–4.

[16] Schwoerer, 'Celebrating the Glorious Revolution', pp. 3–5.

[17] E.P. Thompson, *The making of the English working class* (New York, 1963), p. 88.

[18] S. Schama, *Citizens. A chronicle of the French Revolution* (New York, 1989), pp. 24, 288 and 680–1.

party differences. In some circles, it was supposed that the French intended to copy the English constitution, but news of the Terror produced an abrupt change, and attitudes to reform quickly hardened. Edmund Burke famously revised his initial feelings of support in his *Reflections on the Revolution in France*, as a rebuttal of Dr Richard Price's assertion of the sovereign's accountability to the people; and he did so, it should be noted, in the earlier, quieter years of the revolution, well before the Terror, when 'constitution-making' was in progress. The circulation of reformist and radical literature by the Constitutional Societies continued, however, and as Burke reminded his readers, some was exported to France.[19]

Unsurprisingly, it was the moderate, conservative interpretation of 1688 which prevailed after war broke out with France in 1793. Radicals began to part company with the legacy of 1688, for whom reason, rationality and the *Rights of Man* became the basis of political discourse. Although social polarisation intensified during the long French wars, serious class conflict was held in check by patriotism reinforced by paternalism.[20] It remained for T.B. Macaulay to capture and transmit to future generations the conservative Whig view of 1688 in his multi-volume *History of England* of 1848–59, as *the* Whig view of history. It was avidly read by the Victorians and the Edwardians – a lavish illustrated six-volume edition appeared in 1913 – though later generations regarded it as partisan and frequently inaccurate. J.H. Plumb dated the demise of Macaulay's *History* from Butterfield's 1931 critical essay *The Whig Interpretation of History* and its attack on the idea of historical progress, adding that grand narratives of this kind 'no longer [filled] the social needs of an oligarchy of declining power'.[21]

By the later 1880s, the Glorious Revolution had lost its political edge for mainstream English politics, but continued to provide an accessible narrative which served to bolster a certain sense of national identity and exceptionalism. Although anti-Catholicism persisted during the decades following the 1829 Emancipation Act, it is reasonable to suggest, as Louise Schwoerer does, that the 1880s were 'too constitutionally settled and religiously tolerant, too concerned with social questions … to bother celebrating the overthrow

---

[19] Edmund Burke, *Reflections on the revolution in France* [1790], ed. C.C. O'Brien (London, 1968), pp. 86–7.

[20] See Harold Perkin, *The origins of modern English society, 1780–1880* (Toronto, 1969), pp. 208–17, where the argument for the 'delayed birth' of class society is developed; the emphasis on paternalism was rejected by Edward Thompson, *Customs in common* (London, 1991), pp. 22–4; and G. Eley, 'Edward Thompson, social history and political culture. The making of a working-class public, 1780–1850', in *E.P. Thompson. Critical perspectives*, eds H. Kaye and K. McClelland (Philadelphia, 1990), pp. 12–49.

[21] C.H. Firth (ed.), *The history of England from the accession of James the second, by Lord Macaulay*, 1913 (6 vols, London, 1913–15); J.H. Plumb, *The death of the past* (London, 1969), pp. 41–2.

of a Catholic king'.[22] It was amongst relatively narrow religious groups that interest in the Revolution of 1688 was strongest, arising from Anglo-Irish politics. Gladstone's Irish Home Rule Bill was narrowly defeated in 1886, splitting the Liberal party in the process. The breakaway Liberal Unionists and the Ulster Protestants were quick to appropriate the history of the Williamite Revolution along lines set out by Macaulay, but the divisiveness of post-1886 Anglo-Irish politics encouraged the state to downplay the legacy of 1688. There were no national state-backed celebrations, but as Edmund Rogers has shown, public meetings and sermons were widespread in those communities for whom 1688 retained some meaning. English Congregationalists were particularly active in drawing on the older opposition Whig understanding of 1688 in their campaigns against denominational education.[23]

In the years leading up to the Tercentenary of 1688, there was once again a powerful case for avoiding memories of Protestant triumphalism, as conflict in Ireland worsened. But this was outweighed by an upsurge of public interest in Britain's relationship with the European Community, involving a mixture of scepticism and enthusiasm, dividing roughly along party lines.[24] In fact the Thatcher government remained pro-European for most of its life, in spite of efforts to revise Britain's budget contribution.[25] The Anglo-Dutch relationship could play an important part in strengthening Britain's role in Europe, as governments and business in both countries realised. After committing themselves to the Tercentenary idea following the state visit of 1982, preparations were made for joint celebrations involving both royal houses with coordinated governmental support.[26] Planning and organisation were devolved to two distinct bodies, the William and Mary Tercentenary

---

[22] Schwoerer, 'Celebrating the Glorious Revolution', p. 11; E. Rogers, '1688 and 1888. Victorian society and the bicentenary of the Glorious Revolution', *Journal of British Studies*, 50:4 (2011), 893. On attitudes to Catholicism after emancipation, see O. Chadwick, *The Victorian church, part I, 1829–1859* (London, 1966), pp. 7–24, 202–11 and 271–309. K.S. Inglis concluded that 'At the upper levels of English society, Catholicism was regarded more acquiescently in 1900 than it had been at the restoration of the hierarchy fifty years earlier.' *Churches and the working classes in Victorian England* (London, 1963), p. 141.

[23] Rogers, '1688 and 1888', pp. 894–6.

[24] Wall, *Official history*, chapter 10. In 1975, Labour Prime Minister Harold Wilson agreed to a referendum on continued EEC membership which produced a two-thirds majority in favour. On Wilson's shifting position, see 'The new Roman empire', chapter 3 in Tony Benn, *Dare to be a Daniel. Then and now* (London, 2005). In October 1980, however, the Labour Party conference committed a future Labour government to withdrawal from Europe, producing a split in the party and a 1983 election defeat. The governments of Margaret Thatcher and Ruud Lubbers shared a common interest in developing the European single market, but diverged on the question of the Euro.

[25] S. Wall, *A stranger in Europe. Britain in the EU from Thatcher to Blair* (Oxford, 2008), chapter 3, *passim*.

[26] See above, p. 297.

Trust, with Prince Charles as its patron, and the William and Mary Organising Committee with Princess Margriet as patron. On the British side, the Trust's fifty-five-strong Committee of Honour included several of those whose families had taken part in the events of 1688, the Dukes of Portland and Devonshire, Viscount De L'Isle, and the Countess of Albemarle, together with diplomats, distinguished historians and museum directors; a smaller but equally distinguished management committee did the work.[27] It was then left to historians in both countries to explain to politicians, business leaders and the general public what actually happened three hundred years or so earlier. In the British case at least, this was far from straightforward.

It was Professors Charles Wilson in Cambridge and Fred Bachrach of Leiden who provided the historical backbone. In June 1985, the former recruited a core group of colleagues to advise, which expanded to include several Anglo-Dutch specialists.[28] A year later, the US Congress designated the College of William and Mary, Virginia, as official US representative to the Tercentenary celebrations in a document signed off by Ronald Reagan.[29] It was the national and international scale of the Tercentenary which distinguished 1988 from the two earlier centenaries, neither of which attracted official state interest. Beyond this, the direct involvement of two royal heads of state, both descended from William the Silent, imparted a deeper level of meaning to the significance of 1688. To those who saw a foreign invasion, albeit a Protestant Dutch invasion, the dynastic connections between Orange and Stuart emphasised the elements of legitimacy and continuity in the shift to constitutional monarchy. At a time when some feared a loss of national identity as Britain moved ever closer to Europe, the Tercentenary provided reassurance; and the Dutch, federal from the start, were undoubtedly the best and most agreeable of European friends.

For sponsors and business people especially, the attraction of royal participation in a number of events was irresistible, set out in the 100-page British programme. The splendid dinners and receptions provided opportunities to rub shoulders with those who mattered, and to promote business interests

---

[27] M. Butler, B. Price and S. Brand (eds), *William and Mary. The revolution that shaped our world* (London, 1988), p. 1.

[28] Personal correspondence, Charles Wilson (Cambridge) to David Ormrod, 11 June 1985, suggesting the formation of a History Advisory Committee, which first met at the British Council, 20 November 1985 (C.R. Boxer, K.H.D. Haley, Wilson and Ormrod). A.G.H. Bachrach of Leiden University led the Dutch Tercentenary Committee, having curated a major exhibition at the Victoria & Albert Museum, *The orange and the rose. Holland and Britain in the age of observation, 1600–1750* (London, 1964). On Bachrach's role as the 'father' of the Tercentenary, see the report by Laura Raun, *Financial Times*, 23 November 1987.

[29] College of William and Mary in Virginia, Papers relating to the 'World of William and Mary' Celebration: 99th Congress of the USA, Second Session, Joint Resolution approved 23 August 1986.

in what some hoped would be a new 'Europe without frontiers'. H.F. van den Hoven, Bachrach's successor as Chairman of the Dutch Organising Committee, stressed the appropriateness of celebrations taking place 'at a time when the United Kingdom and the Netherlands are actively shaping the future of Europe based on a *single unified market*'. William and Mary, he went on to say, had pretty much the same idea when they were 'thinking not only in political terms but also of maintaining free trade'.[30] The History Committee knew all about the massive tariff increases approved in the 1690s to finance William's war against French trade, and something was evidently lost in translation. Unfortunately, our advice was not always welcome: earnest historiographical talk at the Royal Netherlands Embassy in London in the early days soon gave way to discussions about funding and the kind of projects most likely to attract it. History was pushed into second place, and Macaulay's version of events often crept in by default.

From the start, the Dutch celebrations received substantial and predictable public funding compared with the British, who were forced to make repeated requests to the Foreign Office in order to keep going. In 1984, the William and Mary Trust was allocated a miserly £22,000 to serve the needs of the growing number of subcommittees required to run an enormous programme, the costs of which finally reached £500,000.[31] This was consistent with the Thatcherite embrace of 'enterprise culture' and aversion to state support for the arts, in which Margaret Thatcher herself had no interest whatever. During the summer of 1986, the William and Mary Trust was facing bankruptcy, and its secretary reluctantly resigned. Charles Wilson reported (privately) from Australia, where he was organising the Sydney bicentennial celebrations, 'Geoffrey Howe is being difficult about funds. What bloody cheek when it was the Foreign Office who started it all off & got us all involved!! ... The FCO needs its corporate ass booted.'[32] Other resignations followed, until Geoffrey Howe finally produced a £20,000 cheque. Valuable time was lost, and on the British side, we were pushed into increased dependence on private sector funding.[33] The Chairman of the Trust's management committee (nominated by Howe) was Charles Tidbury, Chairman of Whitbread and Head of Margaret Thatcher's 'Centre for Policy Studies'. After much cajoling, the funding gaps were gradually filled: the two great Anglo-Dutch multinationals

---

[30] H.F. van den Hoven, 'Foreword', in *William and Mary*, eds Butler, Price and Brand, p. 3 (author's italics).

[31] Schwoerer, 'Celebrating the Glorious Revolution', pp. 14–16.

[32] Personal correspondence, Charles Wilson (Sydney) to David Ormrod, 18 June 1986.

[33] William and Mary Tercentenary Trust, History Advisory Committee Minutes, 17 November 1986, at which the new Secretary reported that sponsorship had been secured from more than twenty firms, following a sponsorship launch at St James's Palace, with 'first round' projects selected by the Chairman, Charles Tidbury, Minutes, 5 November 1987, by which time £200,000 had been raised from firms for specific projects, along with fellowships from the Leverhulme Trust.

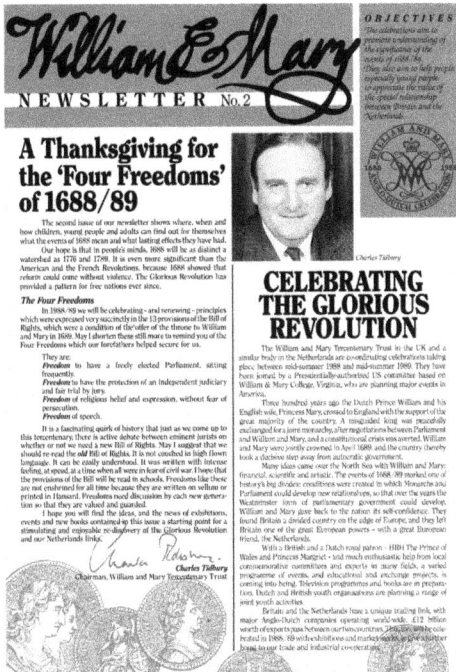

Figure 13.1 William and Mary Newsletter, no. 2
Source: Central Office of Information (London), HMSO 1987.

Unilever and Shell, BP, ICI, British-American Tobacco, several other giants in food, drink and retailing, and major banks, insurance companies and shipping firms stepped forward. Almost inevitably, the 1688 story would be translated into terms that would appeal to the City of London, the kinds of people who joined in the 1982 Guildhall welcome for Queen Beatrix.

So it was that a shift of emphasis took place, from the ambiguous language of Revolution, albeit quasi-rhetorical, to a simpler focus on the accession of William and Mary and the passage of the Bill of Rights. The Prince of Wales expressed it succinctly in his Tercentenary Message, which introduced the official programme and accompanying requests for sponsorship:

> The arrival of William and Mary resolved a constitutional crisis which could have wrecked this country's mercantile and industrial progress. Thanks to new ideas they brought with them from the continent, trade, commerce and government finance developed a practical working structure which remains to this day … King William was an Enabler, not a Conqueror.[34]

---

[34] Butler, Price and Brand (eds), *William and Mary*, p. 2.

This was a neat formulation of what the entire Tercentenary came to represent: a story which supported the renewal of a stable framework for doing business in Europe. An extensive programme of trade fairs was rolled out from May 1988 onwards, with publicity emphasising that 'about half of each country's private direct investment in the European Community is located in the other'.[35]

It was fairly straightforward to communicate how London absorbed many of the commercial influences of Amsterdam during the 1690s, but the Bill of Rights was a more difficult story. The solution was to celebrate the famous 'four freedoms' which the emerging Protestant capitalist international of the 1690s had embraced: freely elected parliaments, an independent judiciary, a measure of religious toleration, and freedom of speech. With difficulty, members of the History Committee argued for revisionist views of 1688, and tried to emphasise the very limited degree of toleration given to Roman Catholics in England along with the suppression of Irish autonomy after the Boyne – the work of the Irish Parliament rather than William.[36] But it was an uphill struggle, and our failure nearly ended in tragedy. Charles Tidbury was placed on an IRA hit-list, and narrowly escaped an assassination attempt at his home in September 1990. He was rewarded with a knighthood, but lived under constant police protection until his death in 2003.[37]

Sectarian tension and violence continued in Northern Ireland throughout the 1980s. Fuelled on the republican side by Mrs Thatcher's uncompromising treatment of the hunger strikers in the Maze prison, and on the Unionist side by the 1985 Anglo-Irish agreement, peace seemed elusive. When it came to devising a William and Mary programme for Kent, we also encountered problems involving accusations of anti-Catholic bias.[38] Our travelling exhibition, 'Kent and the Glorious Revolution', focused mainly on the cultural and economic contributions of immigrant communities in Kent, mainly Protestant refugees, in Sandwich, Dover, Canterbury and Maidstone. So a Protestant emphasis was unavoidable and appropriate, and the organisers tried to provide a balanced assessment of the Anglican compromise reached in the years immediately following 1689.[39]

[35] In a twelve-month programme of nearly eighty Dutch and British events from May 1988 to Spring 1989. DTI and Netherlands Foreign Trade Agency, *Programme of Anglo-Dutch commercial and technological activities* (London, 1988), p. 2.
[36] Memorandum from Charles Wilson to Sir Bernard Audley on the Dutch contribution to the City of London and English commercial and financial institutions, 20 January 1987; R. Cathcart, 'Ireland and "King Billy"', *History Today*, 38 (July 1988), 41–5; Charles Tidbury, 'A thanksgiving for the "Four Freedoms" of 1688/89', *William and Mary Newsletter*, No. 2 (1988).
[37] *The Telegraph*, Obituaries: Sir Charles Tidbury, 10 July 2003.
[38] *North Kent Weekly News*, Letters, 21 October, 28 October and 4 November 1987.
[39] Minutes of the inaugural meeting of the Kent William and Mary Tercentenary Committee, Chatham Dockyard, 3 October 1987, chaired by Viscount De L'Isle. The proposal for a single travelling exhibition harnessed the interest of several

It would be impossible to fully describe here the bewildering variety of cultural events which supported the underlying Tercentenary theme, which was unashamedly Anglocentric, with a regional bias towards London and the South.[40] There were 're-enactments and revels', performing arts events, exhibitions, conferences and lectures, youth programmes, yacht races, and an avalanche of souvenirs. The author Alison Payne recreated Celia Fiennes's *Journeys through England on a Sidesaddle in the Time of William and Mary*; daily re-enactments of William's landing at Brixham took place in late July; one hundred Dutch yachts followed William's voyage from Hellevoetsluis to Torbay in November; and the passage of the Bill of Rights was commemorated with a tableau of life-size 'speaking' figures in the Banqueting House, Whitehall.[41] Many of these events doubtless passed unnoticed by the general public, but the constitutional significance of 1689 was widely debated on radio, television and in the press, involving historians and politicians. It was in December 1988 that the *New Statesman* launched the influential centre-left movement, Charter 88, prompted by these debates and named after the Czech dissident movement founded by Vaclav Havel, Charter 77. Mounting discontent with the Thatcher government after the 1987 general election gave added momentum to Charter 88, which campaigned for a written constitution, proportional representation, devolved regional government, reform of the House of Lords, freedom of information, and other constitutional changes. Several were adopted in quick succession by the first Blair government of 1997–2001, including devolution of powers for Wales and Scotland, and the creation of the Northern Ireland Assembly in 1998, central to the Irish Peace Agreement.

The Medway Raid and the Anglo-Dutch wars

The 1667 Dutch attack on the Medway arguably constituted a significant step, albeit involving catastrophe for the English, which helped to determine the swing of English opinion towards an Anglo-Dutch alliance against France in

---

sponsors: Kent County Council Archives Department, the University of Kent and Canterbury's Heritage Museum, Chatham Historic Dockyard, Dover Castle and Lord De L'Isle at Penshurst Place. A full programme of local events, including concerts, day schools and lectures, ran in parallel with the exhibition. English Tourist Board, *Kent and the Glorious Revolution, 1688–1988. Events and exhibitions* (London, 1988).

[40] The programme, in magazine format, ran to 104 pages. Butler, Price and Brand (eds), *William and Mary*.

[41] On the British side, the Whitehall exhibition, *Parliament and the Glorious Revolution*, represented the central historical focus of the entire Tercentenary: constitutional legitimacy. It was opened by HM the Queen, immediately following a loyal address by the Lord Chancellor and the Speaker of the House of Commons in Westminster Hall, 20 July 1988.

1689.[42] But it formed no part of the story we told in 1989. This provides a reminder, if one were needed, of the highly selective character of collective memory, and the agency of historians in shaping it. We prefer to celebrate success rather than catastrophe, victory rather than defeat.

So why commemorate a defeat, an event which John Evelyn described in 1667 as 'a dreadful spectacle as ever any English men saw, and a dishonour never to be wiped off'? The question was asked many times during the planning of the 2017 commemorations, and especially by Dutch colleagues worried that overt celebration of De Ruyter's attack on the Medway would cause offence and concern in Britain. Journalists too often found it hard to understand why the British were commemorating defeat in a battle that 'no one has ever heard of' – a real difficulty in engaging with the story.[43]

Commemoration of the Medway Raid of 1667 was fundamentally very different from the earlier Anglo-Dutch commemorations of the 1970s and 1980s, in both its genesis and objectives. It was not a national or state-inspired commemoration, but one that developed through the efforts of individuals, museums, local authorities and organisations on both sides of the North Sea, with varied but often complementary objectives.[44] In Kent, the Chatham Historic Dockyard Trust identified the anniversary as a real opportunity to shine a light on what has become part of Medway's forgotten history, and perhaps one of the most significant historical events to have taken place there. The Trust secured funding from the Heritage Lottery Fund to support the mounting of a summer exhibition at the Historic Dockyard, entitled *Breaking the Chain*, together with a reinterpretation of the permanent displays at Upnor Castle, undertaken by Medway Council's heritage services team. A working partnership was developed between the Historic Dockyard, Medway Council (a relatively new unitary authority for the Medway towns), and Visit Kent, the county's main tourism management agency.[45]

The driving force for the commemoration thus came from local interests keen to stimulate Kent's tourism industry, drawing on the county's maritime heritage. Although similar considerations applied on the 300th anniversary of the raid, celebrations were relatively modest in 1967 when a 'River Medway Dutch Week' was held 'to help publicise the excellent port facilities in the Medway', as one local councillor admitted.[46] Fifty years later, the bulk of the trade of the Medway Estuary had moved to Sheerness, while Chatham

---

[42] C.H. Wilson, '1688 and the historians', *History Today*, 38 (July 1988), 4.
[43] Richard Holdsworth, Director of Education at the Historic Dockyard, presentation to the Medway Symposium, 1 July 2017.
[44] E. Edwards, 'The Dutch in the Medway 1667. Commemoration and reflection', *Archaeologia Cantiana*, 139 (2018), 155 and 160.
[45] Discussed by Richard Holdsworth, n. 43 above.
[46] For a brief summary of the 1967 commemorative events, see the 'Postscript' to P.G. Rodgers, *The Dutch in the Medway* (Oxford, 1970), pp. 173–5.

Dockyard, closed as a working dockyard in 1984, had become one of the most successful heritage attractions in the southeast. The eighty-acre site constitutes 'the most complete dockyard of the age of sail in the world', and additionally provides a second home to three universities (Kent, Greenwich and Canterbury Christ Church) alongside local businesses and housing.[47] It contains over sixty scheduled ancient monuments and 150 listed buildings dating mainly from the eighteenth and nineteenth centuries. With its working ropery, covered slipways, sail and colour loft, and Brunel's former steam-powered sawmills, the core of the dockyard constitutes both a 'living museum' and a site museum. For local residents, the historic dockyard provides a permanent reminder of the working lives of their forebears, spanning more than four centuries; and for visitors, the historic environment and special exhibitions counterbalance the country houses, gardens and cathedrals of Kent as an alternative type of tourist attraction.

As a 'living museum', and one of a wave of projects aiming to regenerate former industrial, maritime and defensive sites in Britain, the future of the Historic Dockyard depends on its success in maintaining a flow of visitors and income.[48] Outside the sphere of great national museums and galleries, with their blockbuster exhibitions and accompanying sponsorship, local heritage attractions rely on persuading local people to make repeat visits as well as encouraging visitors from further afield. The Medway Raid of 1667 provided an outstanding opportunity to do these things by commemorating and reconstructing history on the ground, 'history *where* it happened', after a significant, 350-year, lapse of time. Of course De Ruyter's expeditionary force failed to reach the dockyard itself, and the main actions took place at Sheerness and Upnor Reach, where the defensive boom chain was suspended across the Medway. The exhibition's title 'Breaking the Chain' highlighted both the challenges facing the raiders and the difficulties involved in reconstructing what actually happened at the time. Although links from the original chain have not survived, a seventeenth-century wrought-iron link from Portsmouth harbour's boom chain, over a metre in length and weighing 61 kg, served as a central referent for the entire sequence of events. As a museum object, its form (size, evident weight, and near-indestructability) was highly suggestive; and in terms of representativity, it stood as a fragment of something much larger, impossible to display, but which nevertheless carried a high information load. It remains uncertain whether the chain was in fact broken, released by marines, or forced under water by the weight and force of the ships.[49] But the object served to remind visitors that the chain and its

[47] Chatham Historic Dockyard Trust, *Corporate plan, 2016–2021*, n.d. [2016], p. 2.
[48] R. Ormond, 'The maritime heritage', in *National Maritime Museum guide to maritime Britain*, ed. K. Wheatley (London, 1990), pp. 7–8.
[49] B.H.St.J. O'Neil and S. Evans, 'Upnor Castle, Kent', *Archaeologia Cantiana*, 65 (1952), 6; J. Coad, *Upnor Castle*, English Heritage, n.d., pp. 24–8. It was Van Brakel,

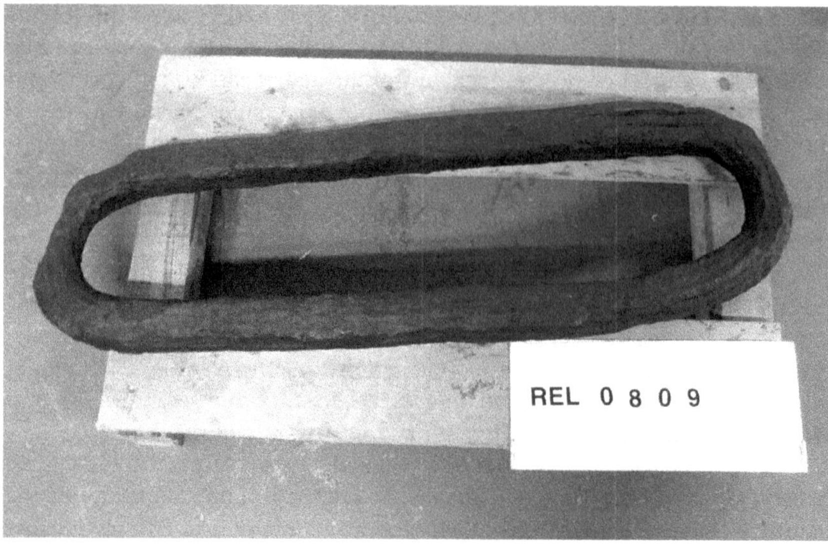

Figure 13.2 Wrought-iron link from the Portsmouth harbour chain boom, seventeenth century, weighing 61 kg; 110 x 33 x 6.5 cm. Source: National Maritime Museum (London), REL 0809.

supports, protected by guardships and gun batteries, provided a formidable obstacle to the Dutch which delayed and frustrated their planned assault on the dockyard itself. Johan de Witt made his disappointment on this score plain when he wrote to his brother days after the raid, it must not be said 'he knows how to win a victory, but not how to exploit it'.[50]

The seizure of the flagship *Royal Charles* in these circumstances constituted a grand piece of bravado, with no strategic significance but carrying enormous propaganda value. Like the objects on display in the Chatham exhibition centuries later, the flagship became a tourist attraction once it arrived at its temporary home in Hellevoetsluis, only to be dismantled after being auctioned for scrap in 1673. The surviving sternpiece became a popular museum exhibit when it entered the Rijksmuseum in the late nineteenth century. Once again, a fragment became a key referent in a larger historical narrative. It now occupies a position of enhanced importance in the redesigned historical galleries in the new Rijksmuseum.

It is of course rarely the case that museum objects 'speak for themselves', and museum specialists continue to debate the circumstances in which

---

commander of the *Vrede*, who claimed that he had broken the chain on his return to Holland.
[50] Rogers, *The Dutch in the Medway*, p. 171.

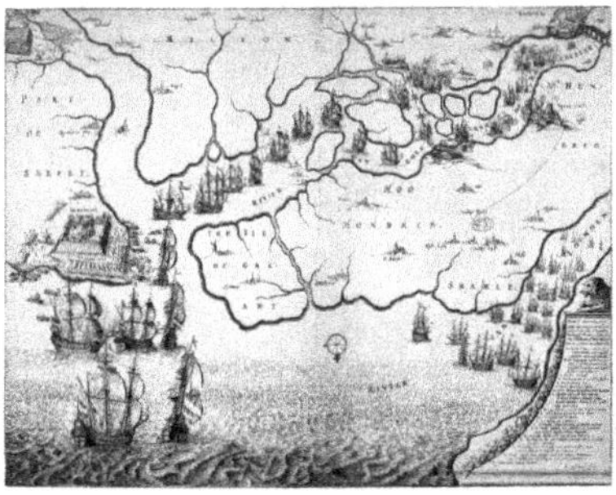

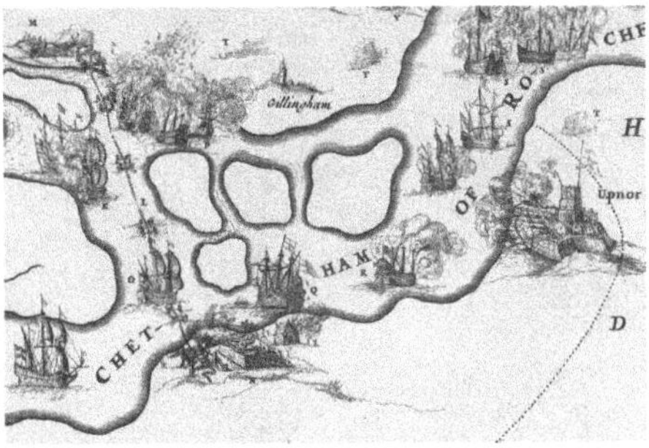

Figure 13.3a Map of the Medway Estuary showing fortifications, batteries and the defensive chain, by Michiel Comans (II), 1667; 418 x 553 mm. Source: Rijksmuseum (Amsterdam), RP-P-1935-1499. [This is incorrectly described as the Thames estuary, 'Kaart van monding van de Theems met de Tocht naar Chatham'.] The chain was positioned between Hoo Ness and Gillingham.

Figure 13.3b Detail of 13.3a, showing the defensive chain and supporting pontoons, with batteries installed on 11 June 1667 by the Duke of Albemarle.

artefacts are perceived *'primarily* as things of themselves, rather than as things beyond themselves'.[51] If the role of objects in history curatorship is indeed problematic, the evidence provided by contemporary artists can prove even more ambiguous. A market for prints and paintings of the Medway Raid soon arose in the Netherlands, which Willem Schellinks amongst others was quick to exploit. At least seven versions of his well-known painting of the Dutch Raid exist, one of which took pride of place in the 2017 Chatham exhibition. But all derive from sketches made during the artist's earlier visits to the Medway towns in 1661, and attempt to compress the events of several days into a single image. The version exhibited at Chatham in 2017 seems to suggest that Albemarle's troops appeared too late to halt the raid, an interpretation currently accepted by the Rijksmuseum. In fact additional munitions arrived at Upnor on 11 June, along with a battery of fifty guns for the opposite bank, which slowed the Dutch advance before the chain was broken on the following day.[52] In time-honoured fashion, the image also foreshortens the

---

[51] P. Gathercole, 'The fetishism of artefacts', in *Museum studies in material culture*, ed. S.M. Pearce (Leicester, 1989), p. 73; G. Kavanagh, 'Objects as evidence', in *ibid.*, pp. 125–6; E. Taborsky, 'The discursive object', in *Objects of knowledge*, ed. S. Pearce (London, 1990), pp. 50–77.

[52] M. Exwood and H.L. Lehmann (eds), *The journal of William Schellinks' travels in England, 1661–1663* (London, 1993), pp. 5 and 24; Coad, *Upnor Castle*, pp. 24–5 and 27 (Schellinks panorama).
For Schellinks's stay in Kent, and his association with the immigrant Flemish merchant Sir Arnold Braems and his circle, see also K. Hearn, *Cornelius Johnson* (London, 2015), pp. 43–4.

Figure 13.4 William Schellinks, *The Raid on the Medway*, c. 1668; 111 x 168 cm.
Source: Rijksmuseum (Amsterdam), SK-A-1393.

topography of the Medway valley and estuary, just as Visscher had done for the Thames in his celebrated 1616 panoramic view of London.[53]

Historical accuracy is not necessarily the primary object of commemorative events, and the organisers of the 2017 celebrations were clear that theirs was to 'have fun with history while following in De Ruyter's footsteps'. As momentum built up, groups and organisations outside the region began to get involved, including the Netherlands Embassy in London, the British Embassy in The Hague, and the Dutch and British Royal Navies. The opening of two weeks of civic events in Medway was marked by the arrival of a flotilla of boats and yachts from the Netherlands, accompanied by Dutch and British warships.[54] The bands of the Dutch and British Royal Marines paraded in front of the dockyard buildings in the presence of HH Prince Maurits and the Lord Lieutenant of Kent, Lord de L'Isle, whose ancestor, Henry Sidney, had authored the invitation to William of Orange to invade in 1688. Sporting and

---

[53] R. Hyde, *Gilded scenes and shining prospects. Panoramic views of British towns, 1575–1900* (New Haven, 1985), pp. 14–15.

[54] Described in Medway Council's dedicated website and brochure, *Medway 2017, the 350th anniversary of the Battle of the Medway*, www.medway.gov.uk/BoM (consulted 7 February 2019).

musical events, yacht racing, fireworks and river-borne festivities enlivened the celebrations, and the finale – Medway in Flames – brought out local people in their thousands.[55] In spite of this high level of interest, however, the 1667 commemoration remained, at least on the British side, a civic rather than a national affair. There was no Royal Presence, signifying that the Medway Raid lay outside the reach of the national memory. There were no heroes corresponding to De Ruyter, and Peter Pett, the unfortunate Resident Dockyard Commissioner, made a relatively unconvincing villain.

Although the Dutch attack on the Medway has been described as a *national* humiliation for England, it would be more accurate to regard it as a humiliation for the king and his circle, especially the Earl of Clarendon. After the formation of a new administration, Charles was compelled to rebuild the fleet, which by the opening of the Third Anglo-Dutch War in 1672 was a comfortable match for that of the Republic. So it is worth returning to the question of the appropriateness of the language of victory and defeat, which arguably recedes in importance the further one moves from the events in question. To journalists writing in 2017, the Dutch media were predictably motivated by the story of Dutch audacity and success in carrying out the raid; but perhaps more surprisingly, the British media seemed equally taken by the tale of defeat and failure, judging by the attention which they gave to it. Compared with the Tercentenary celebration of the 1688 Revolution, however, the events of 1667 could only be portrayed as marginal to the course of British history, although capable of being understood in more clear-cut terms than those of 1688–89, with the latter's manifold complexities and continuing constitutional implications. For Dutch audiences, on the other hand, the Medway victory and the Treaty of Breda symbolised a highly significant national moment, one which marked the zenith of their maritime strength.

---

[55] The Historic Dockyard estimates were 34,500 visitors to the exhibition, and 35,000 attending the 'Medway in Flames' event (Minutes of the 8th General Meeting Commemorating the Battle of the Medway, 20 September 2018, Scheepvaartmuseum, Amsterdam, provided by Jeroen van der Vliet, Senior Curator, Scheepvaartmuseum).

Index

Index

www.ingramcontent.com/pod-product-compliance
Lightning Source LLC
Chambersburg PA
CBHW070410100426
42812CB00005B/1689